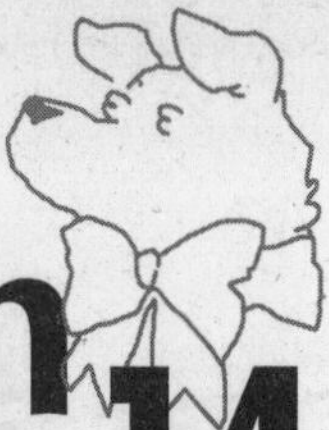

maison ikkoku 14

STORY AND ART BY RUMIKO TAKAHASHI

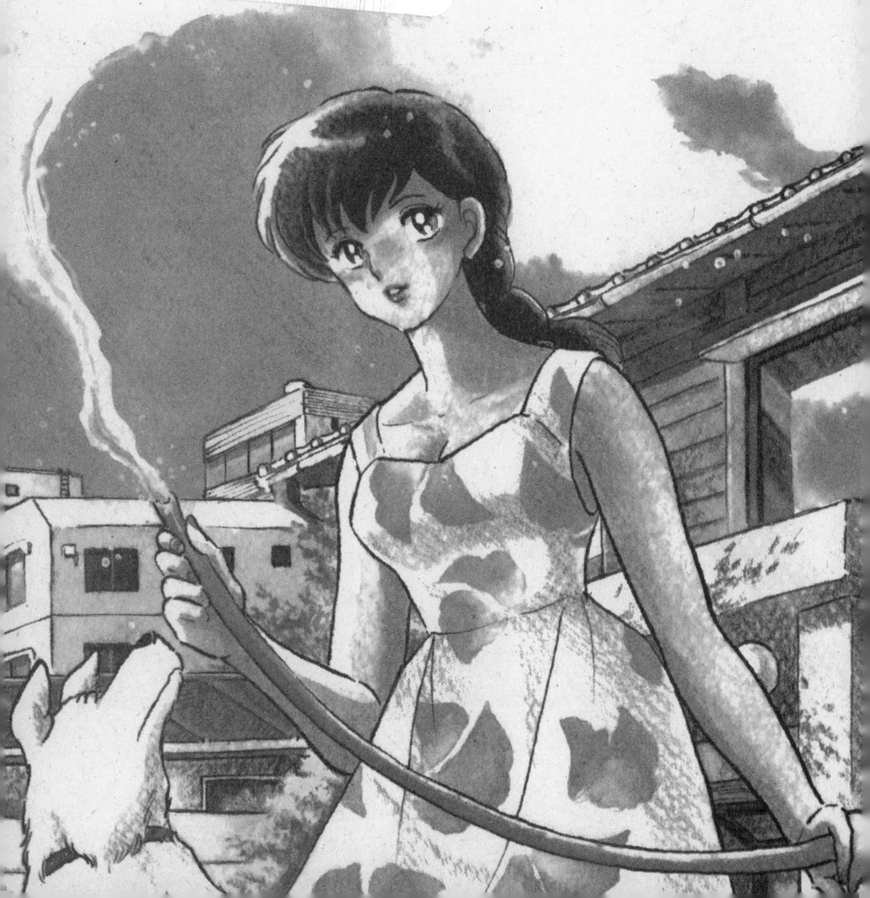

TABLE OF CONTENTS

PART ONE

THE HAPPINESS CURVE

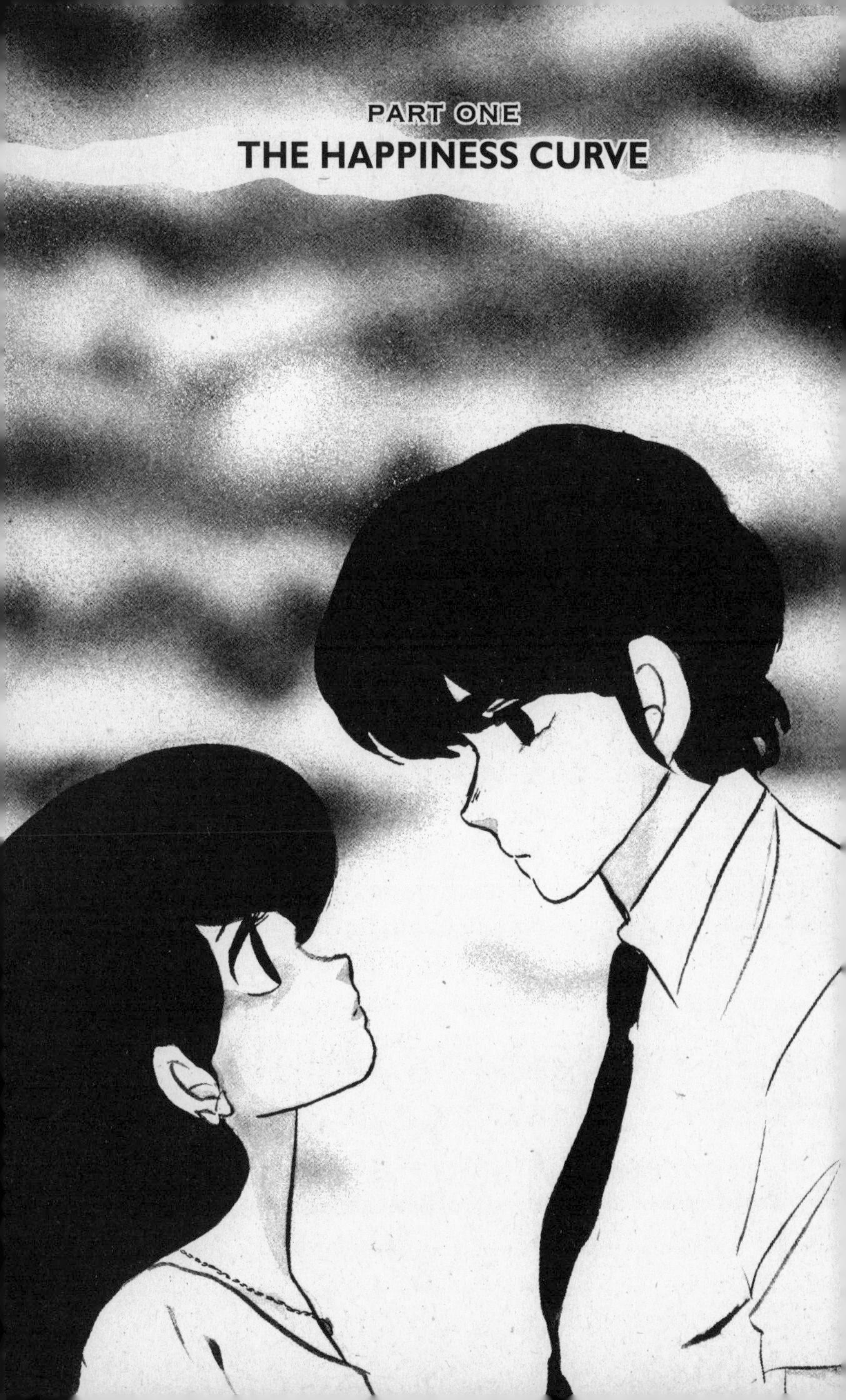

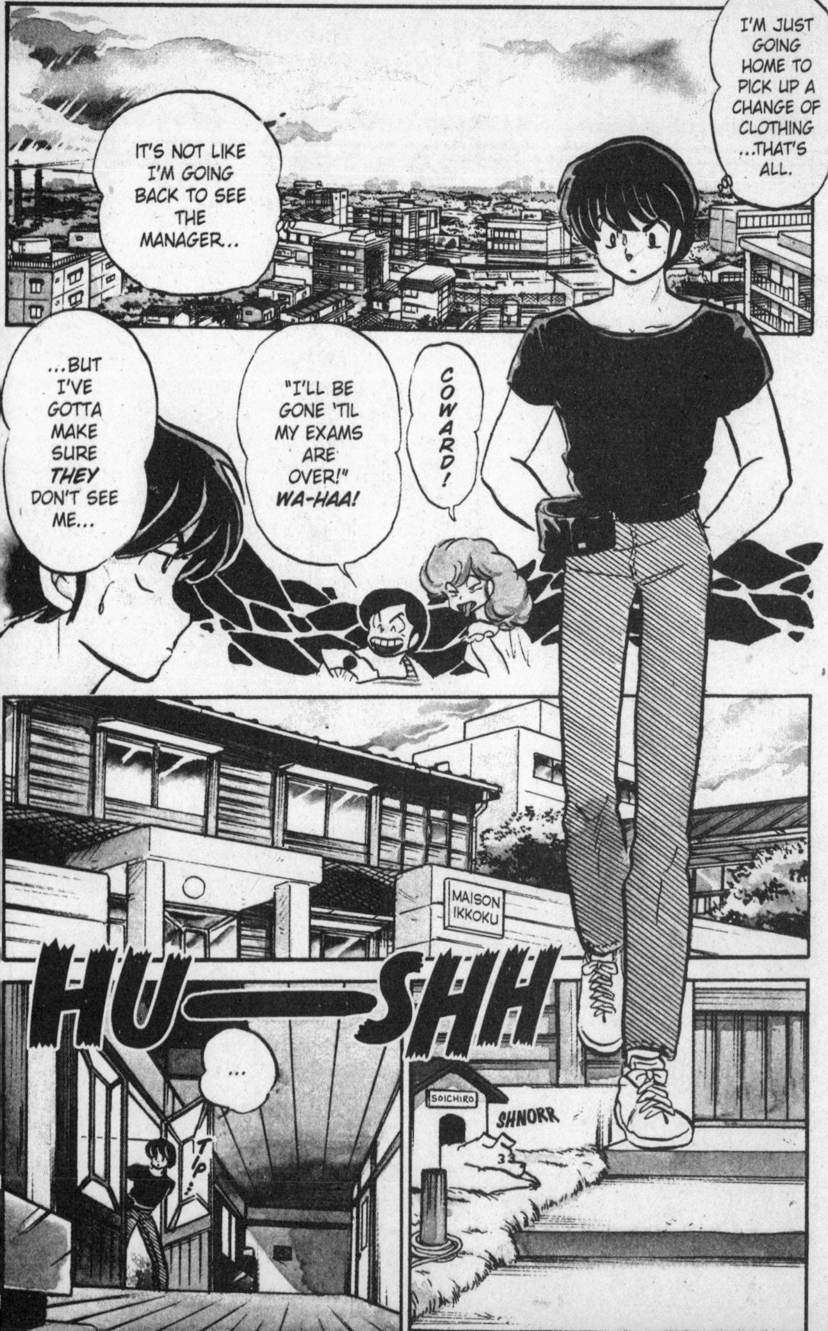
IT'S NOT LIKE I'M GOING BACK TO SEE THE MANAGER..
I'M JUST GOING HOME TO PICK UP A CHANGE OF CLOTHING ...THAT'S ALL.
...BUT I'VE GOTTA MAKE SURE THEY DON'T SEE ME...
"I'LL BE GONE 'TIL MY EXAMS ARE OVER!" WA-HAA!
COWARD!
MAISON IKKOKU
HU—SHH
...
TIP...
SOICHIRO
SHNORR

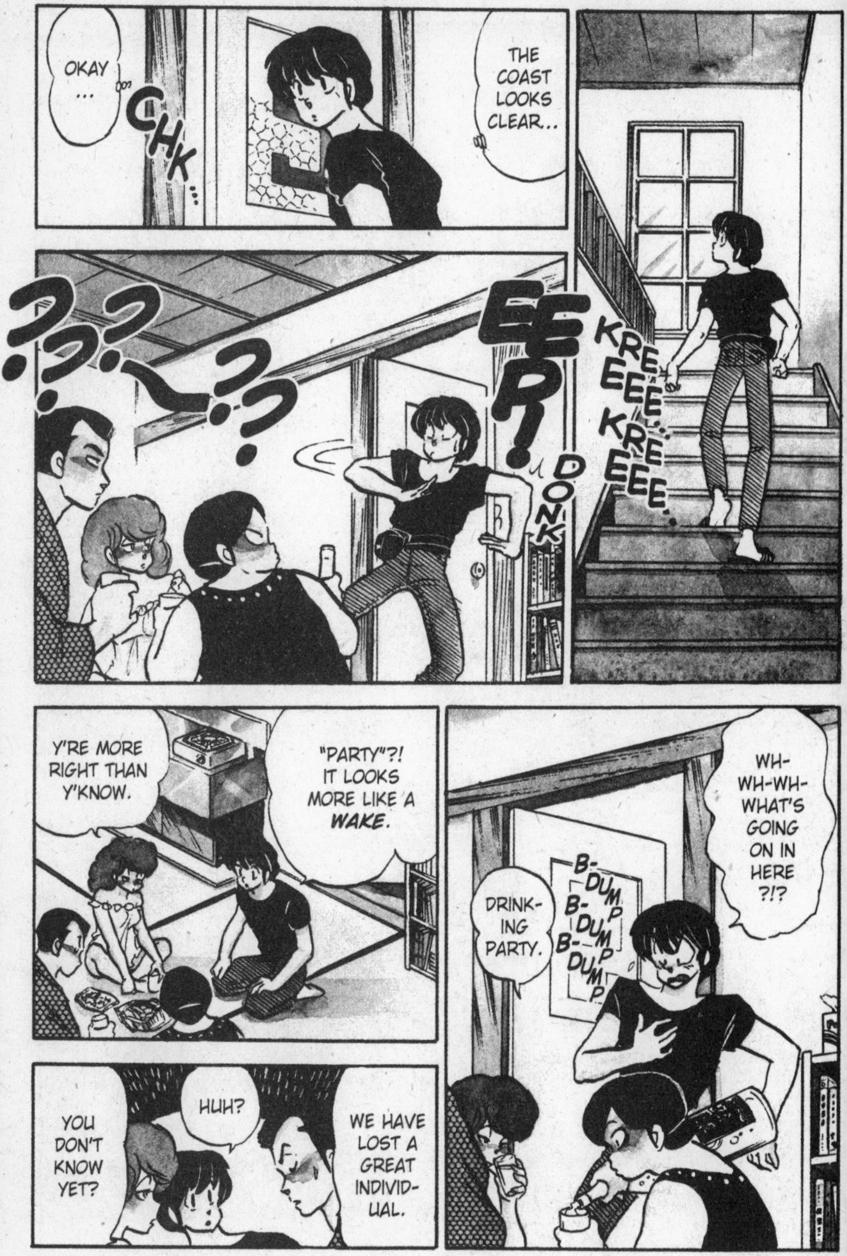
THE COAST LOOKS CLEAR...
OKAY ...
CHK...
KREEEEE... KREEEEE...
EEER!
DONK
WH-WH-WH-WHAT'S GOING ON IN HERE ?!?
DRINKING-ING PARTY.
B-DUMP B-DUMP B-DUMP
"PARTY"?! IT LOOKS MORE LIKE A *WAKE*.
Y'RE MORE RIGHT THAN Y'KNOW.
YOU DON'T KNOW YET?
HUH?
WE HAVE LOST A GREAT INDIVIDUAL.

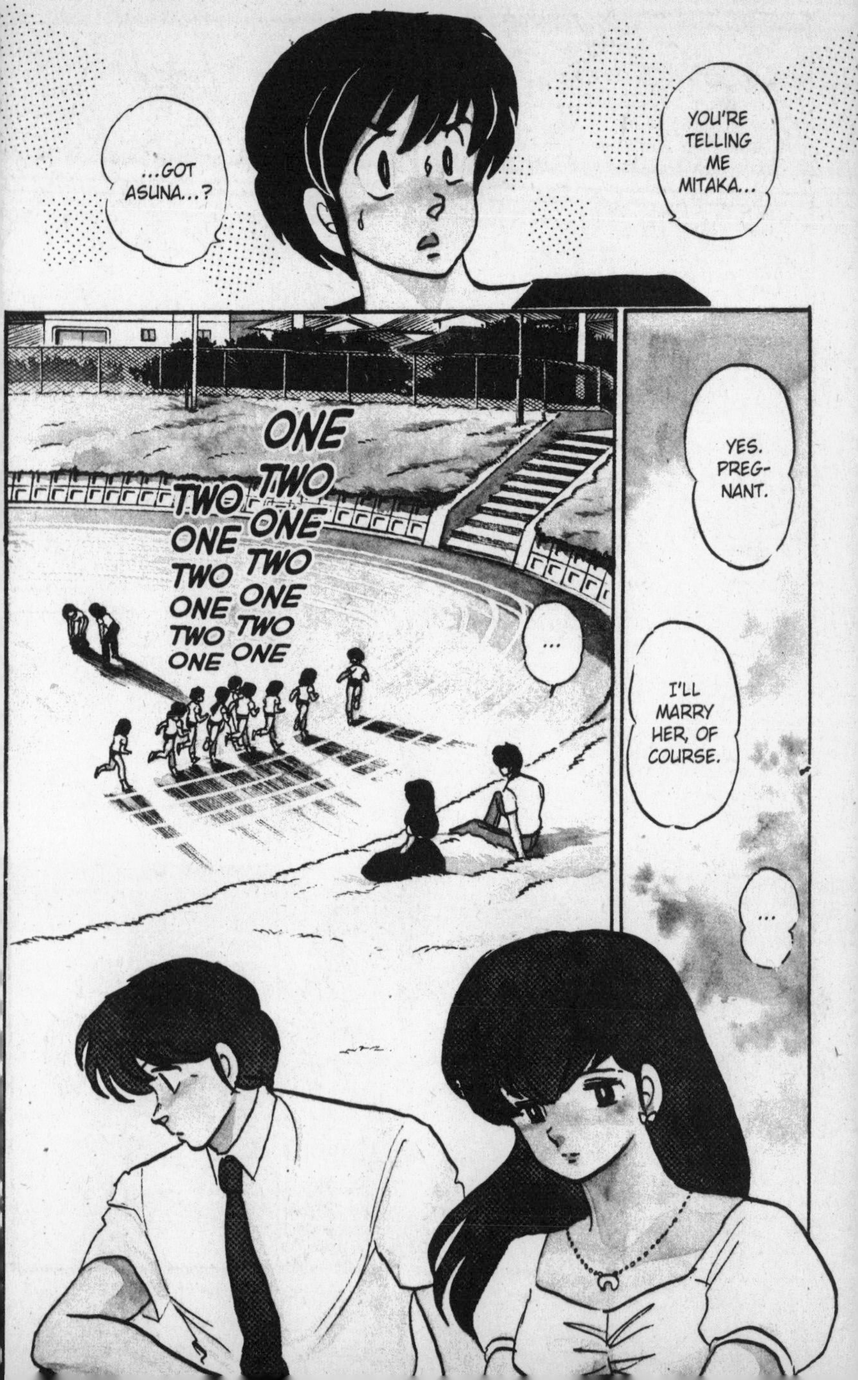
YOU'RE TELLING ME MITAKA...
...GOT ASUNA...?
YES. PREGNANT.
ONE TWO ONE TWO ONE TWO ONE
TWO ONE TWO ONE TWO ONE
...
I'LL MARRY HER, OF COURSE.
...

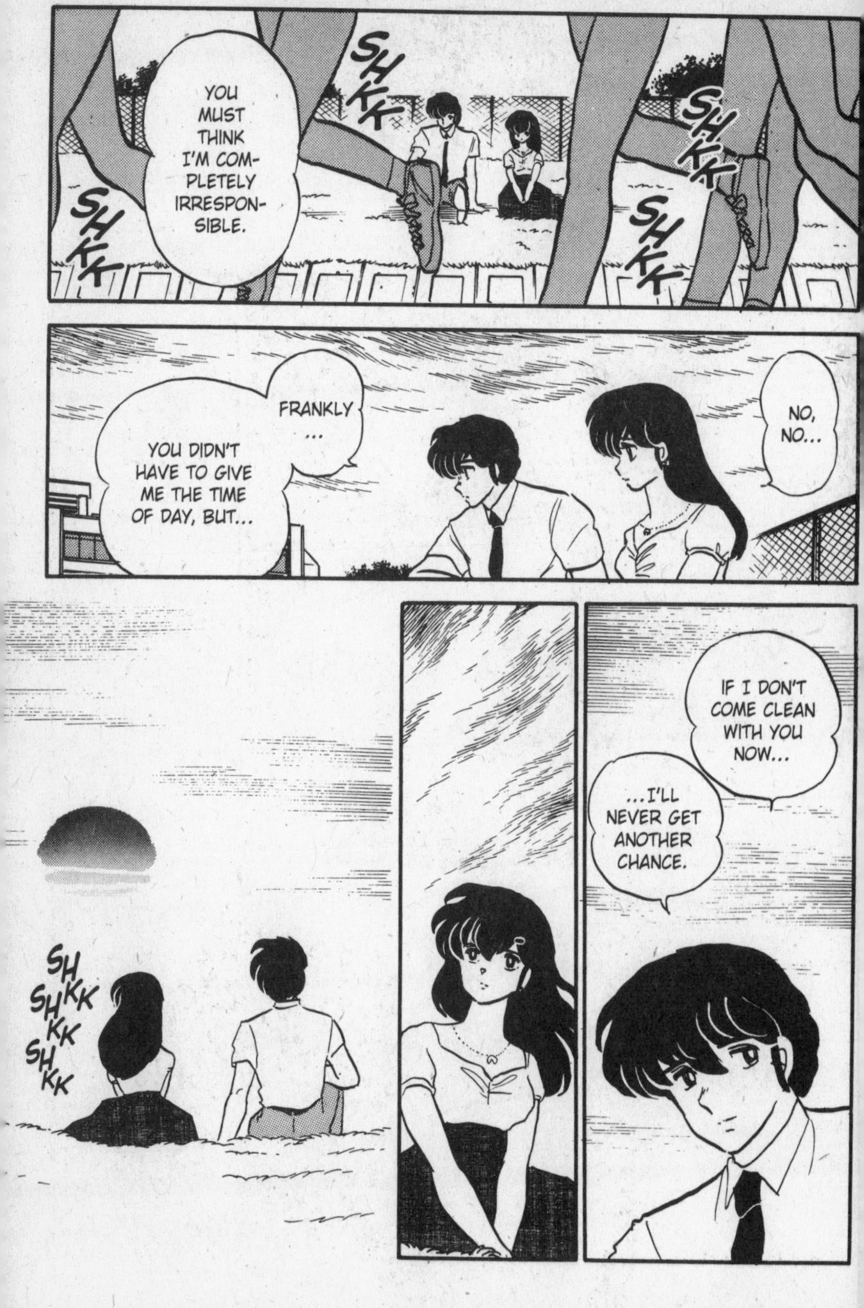
SHKK
YOU MUST THINK I'M COMPLETELY IRRESPONSIBLE.
SHKK
SHKK
SHKK
FRANKLY...
YOU DIDN'T HAVE TO GIVE ME THE TIME OF DAY, BUT...
NO, NO...
SHKK SHKK SHKK
IF I DON'T COME CLEAN WITH YOU NOW...
...I'LL NEVER GET ANOTHER CHANCE.

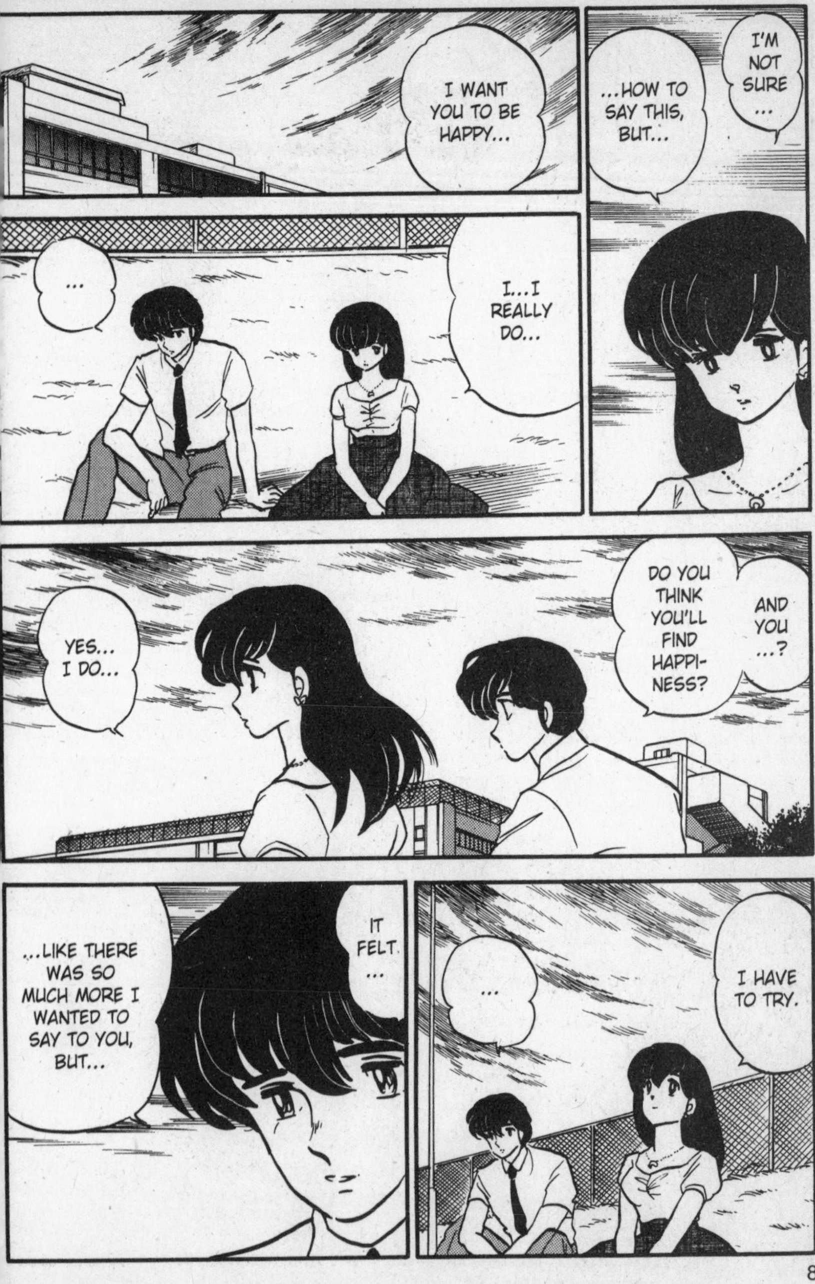
I'M NOT SURE ...
...HOW TO SAY THIS, BUT...
I WANT YOU TO BE HAPPY...
I...I REALLY DO...
...
AND YOU ...?
DO YOU THINK YOU'LL FIND HAPPINESS?
YES... I DO...
I HAVE TO TRY.
...
IT FELT ...
...LIKE THERE WAS SO MUCH MORE I WANTED TO SAY TO YOU, BUT...

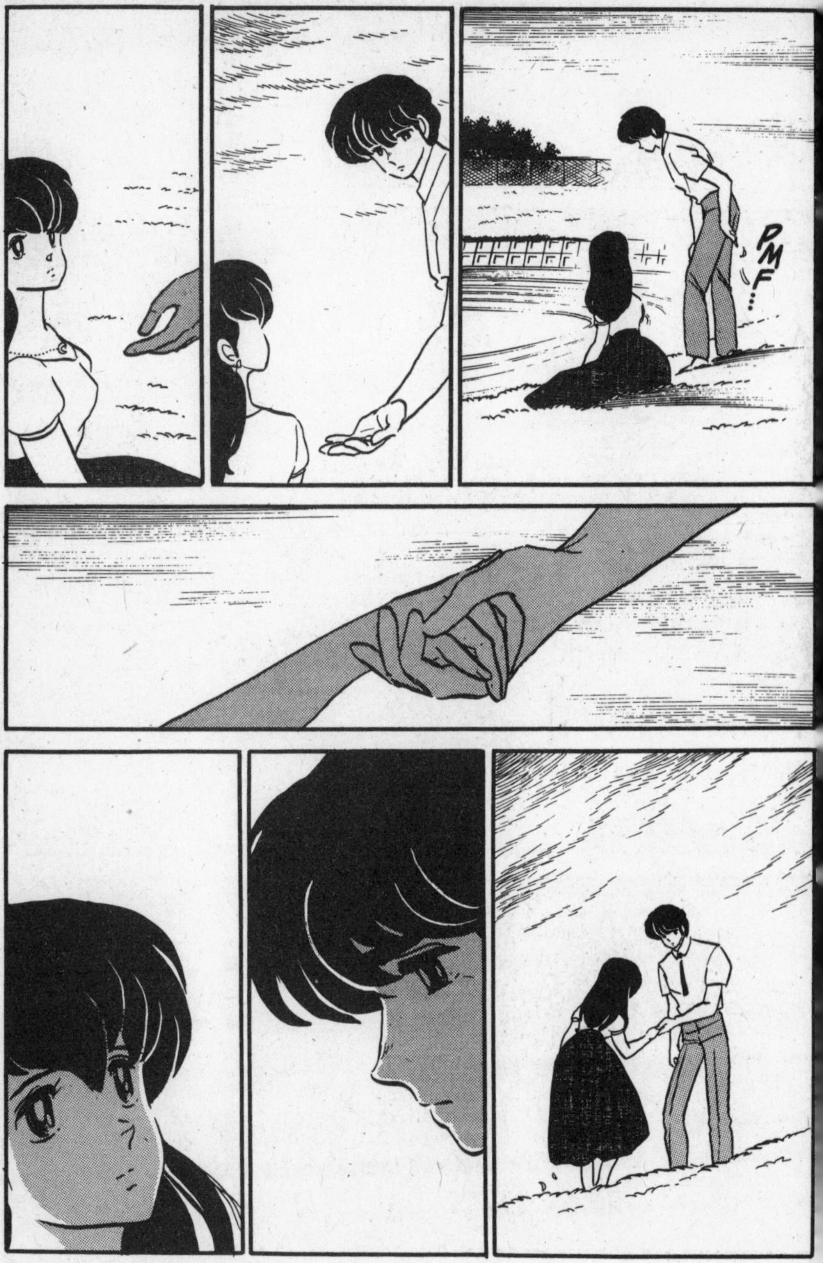
PMF...

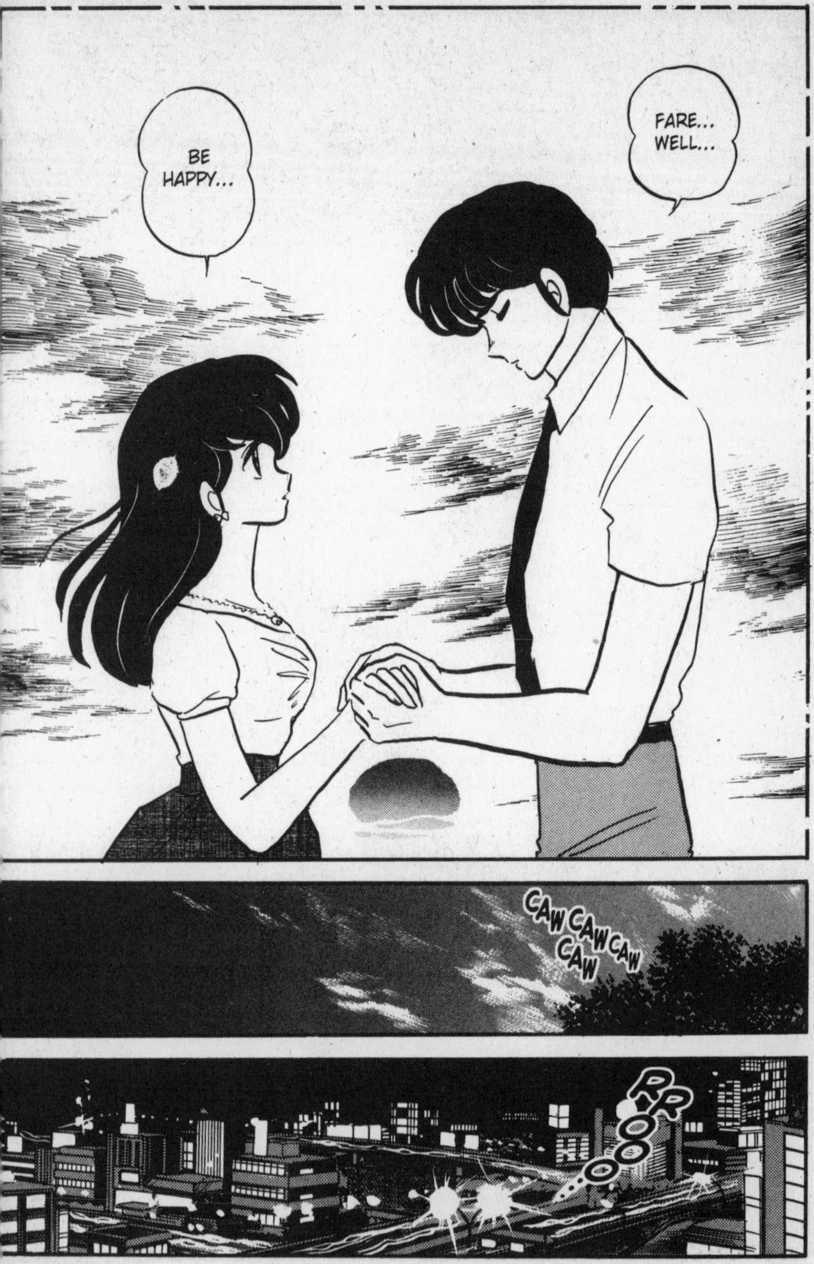
FARE... WELL...
BE HAPPY...
CAW CAW CAW CAW
RROOOO

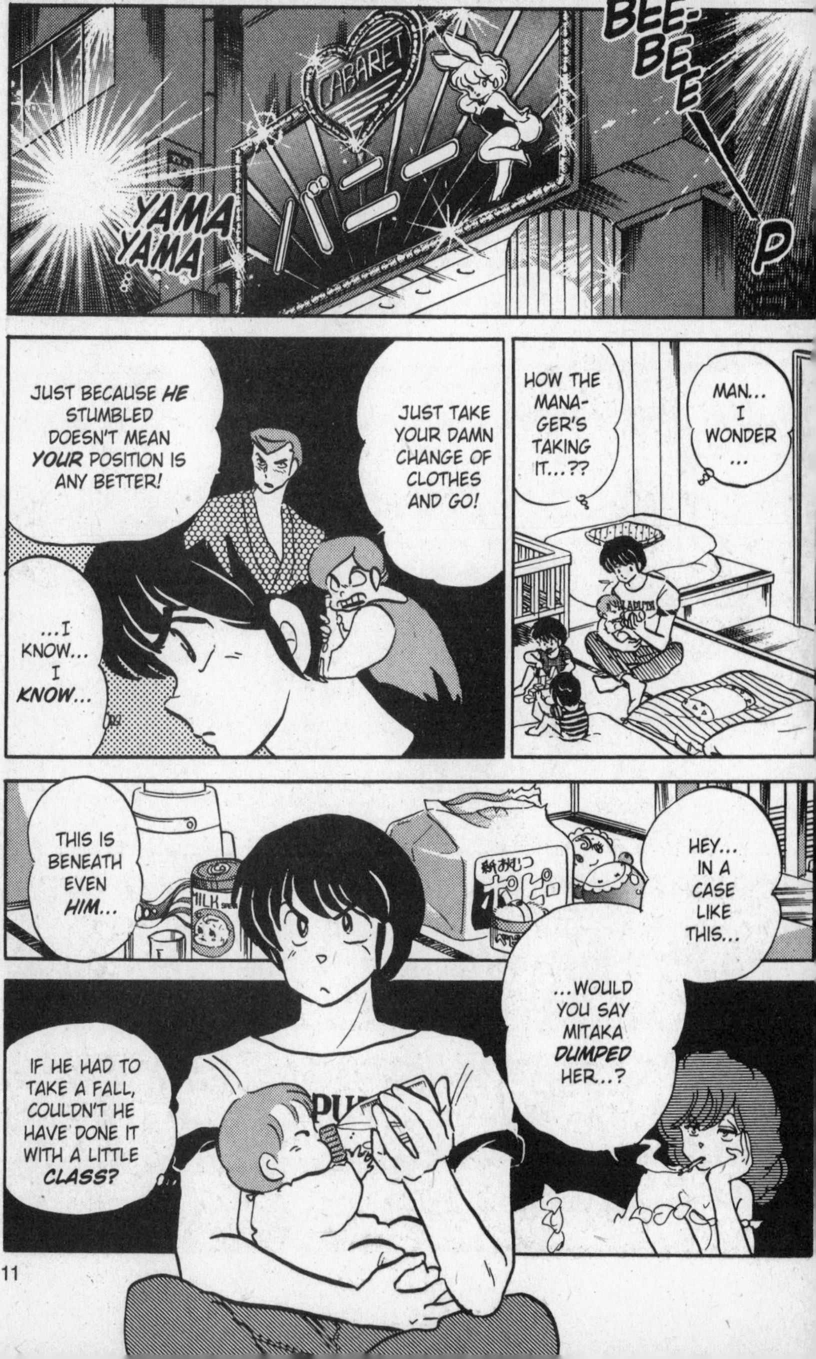
BEE-BEE-P
CABARET
バニー
YAMA YAMA
JUST BECAUSE HE STUMBLED DOESN'T MEAN YOUR POSITION IS ANY BETTER!
JUST TAKE YOUR DAMN CHANGE OF CLOTHES AND GO!
...I KNOW... I KNOW...
MAN... I WONDER...
HOW THE MANA-GER'S TAKING IT...??
HEY... IN A CASE LIKE THIS...
...WOULD YOU SAY MITAKA DUMPED HER...?
THIS IS BENEATH EVEN HIM...
IF HE HAD TO TAKE A FALL, COULDN'T HE HAVE DONE IT WITH A LITTLE CLASS?
MILK
ポピー

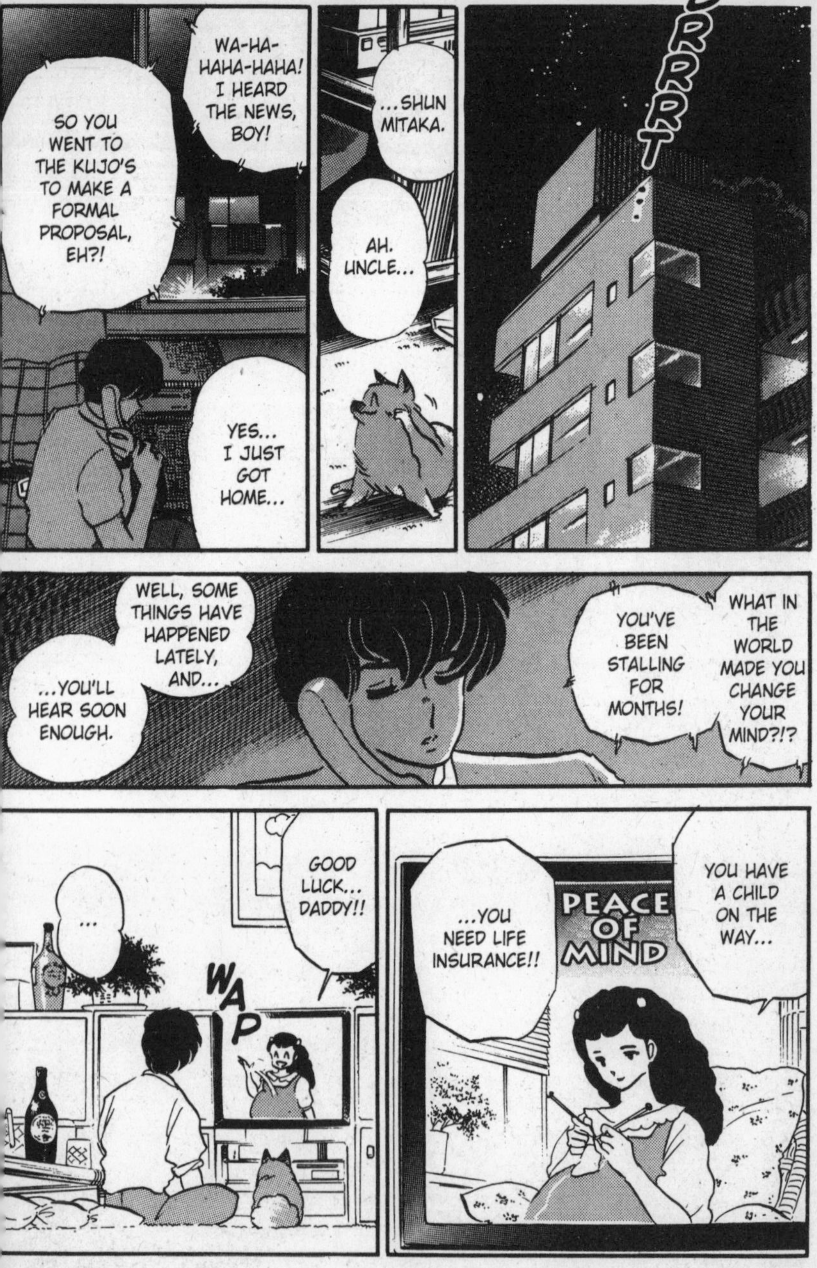
BRRRT
...SHUN MITAKA.
AH. UNCLE...
WA-HA-HAHA-HAHA! I HEARD THE NEWS, BOY!
SO YOU WENT TO THE KUJO'S TO MAKE A FORMAL PROPOSAL, EH?!
YES... I JUST GOT HOME...
WHAT IN THE WORLD MADE YOU CHANGE YOUR MIND?!?
YOU'VE BEEN STALLING FOR MONTHS!
WELL, SOME THINGS HAVE HAPPENED LATELY, AND...
...YOU'LL HEAR SOON ENOUGH.
YOU HAVE A CHILD ON THE WAY...
PEACE OF MIND
...YOU NEED LIFE INSURANCE!!
GOOD LUCK... DADDY!!
WAP
...

IT STILL DOESN'T FEEL REAL...

HAF HAF HAF HAF HAF

"DADDY," HUH ...??

PLEASE GRANT ME YOUR DAUGHTER'S HAND IN MARRIAGE.

I'M HAPPY ...

WHAT'S WRONG, ASUNA?

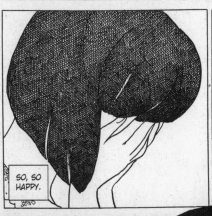

SO, SO HAPPY.

...MAKE SURE SHE STAYS THAT WAY.

IT'S UP TO ME TO...

13

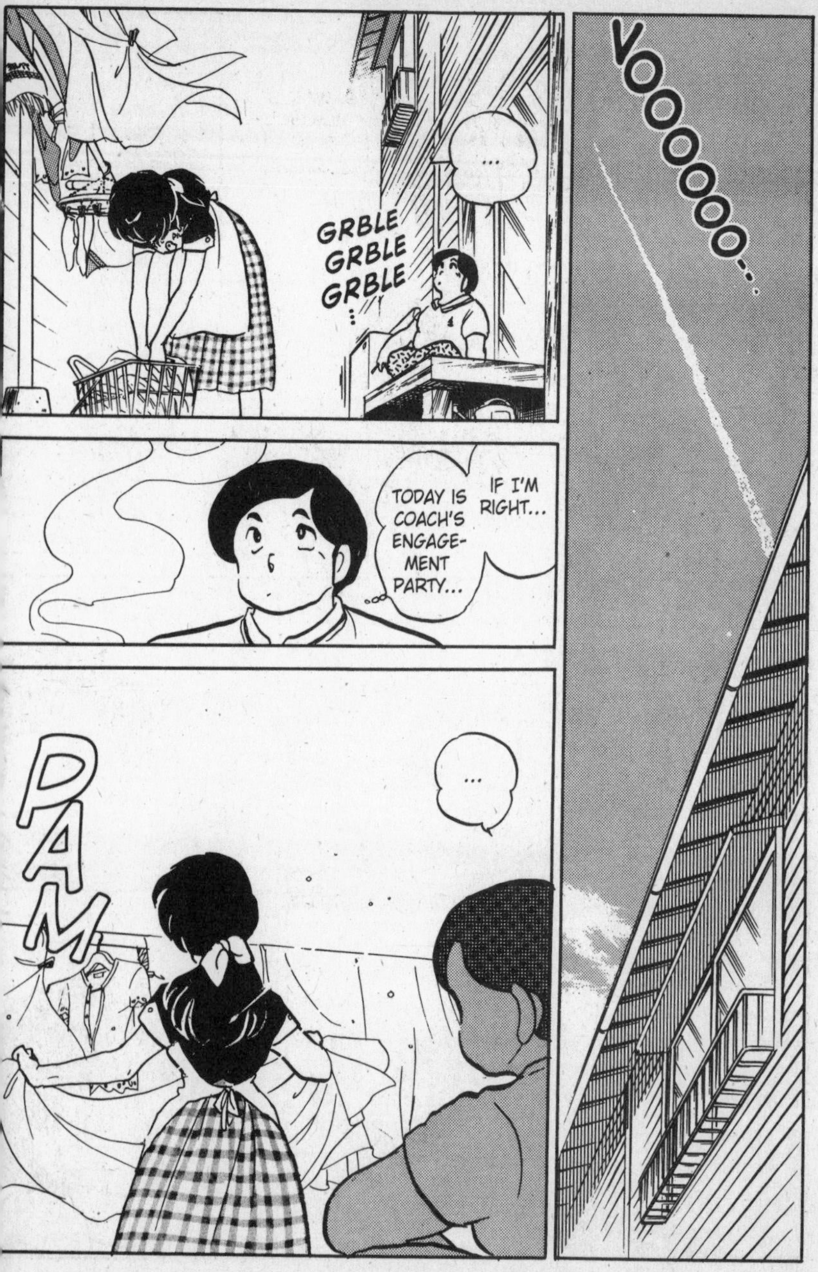
VOOOOOO...
...
GRBLE GRBLE GRBLE
IF I'M RIGHT...
TODAY IS COACH'S ENGAGEMENT PARTY...
...
PAM

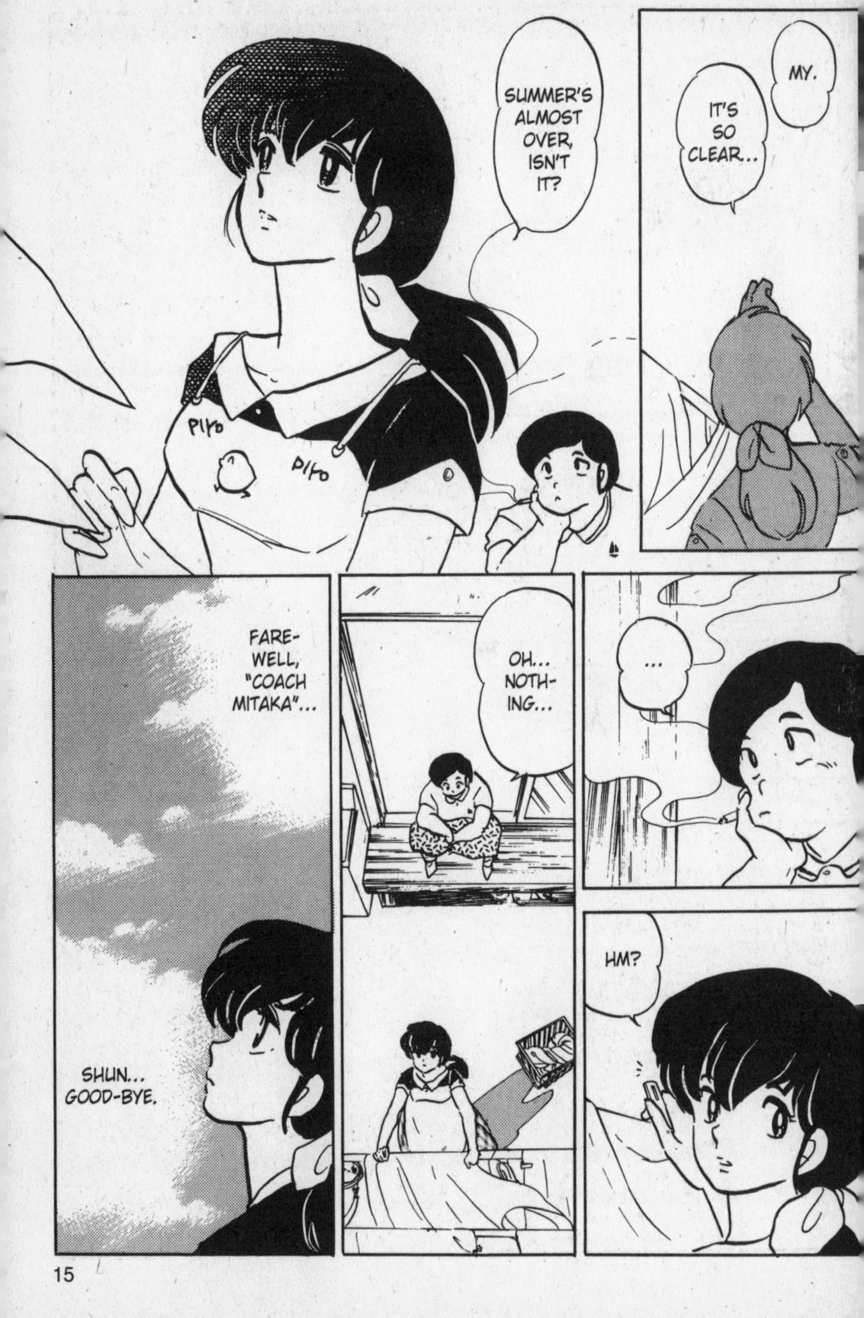
MY.
IT'S SO CLEAR...
SUMMER'S ALMOST OVER, ISN'T IT?
piyo
piyo
...
HM?
OH... NOTHING...
FARE-WELL, "COACH MITAKA"...
SHUN... GOOD-BYE.

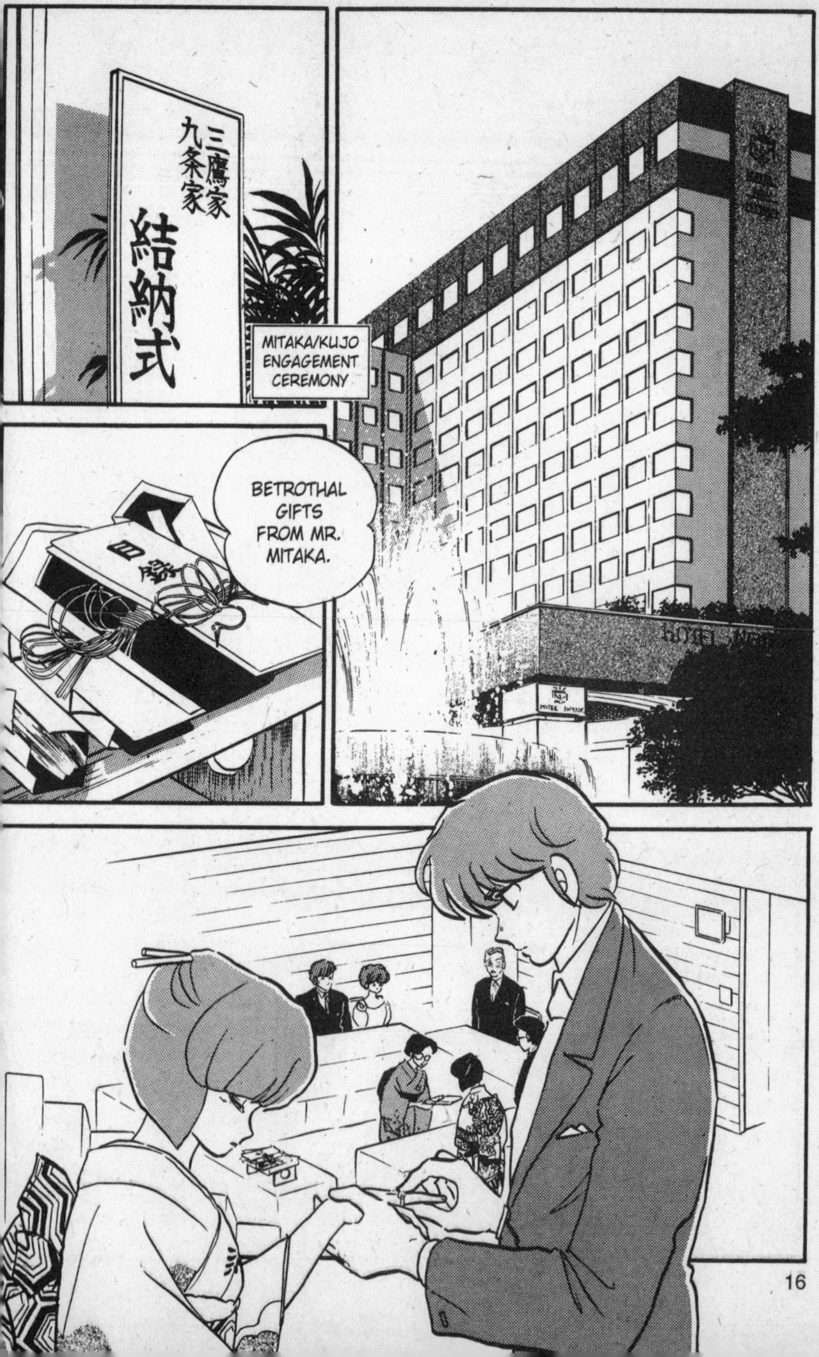
三鷹家
九条家
結納式
MITAKA/KUJO ENGAGEMENT CEREMONY
BETROTHAL GIFTS FROM MR. MITAKA.

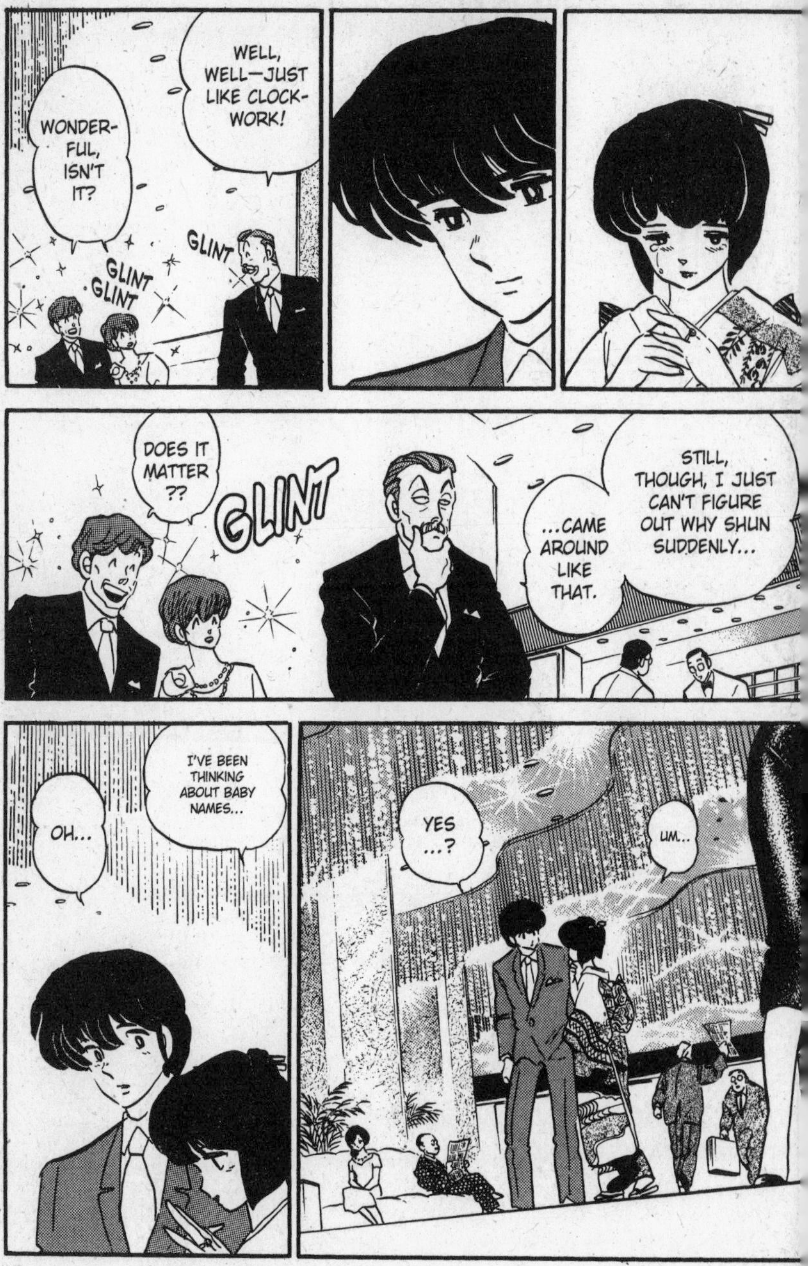
WELL, WELL—JUST LIKE CLOCK-WORK!
WONDER-FUL, ISN'T IT?
GLINT
GLINT GLINT
STILL, THOUGH, I JUST CAN'T FIGURE OUT WHY SHUN SUDDENLY...
...CAME AROUND LIKE THAT.
GLINT
DOES IT MATTER ??
UM...
YES ...?
I'VE BEEN THINKING ABOUT BABY NAMES...
OH...

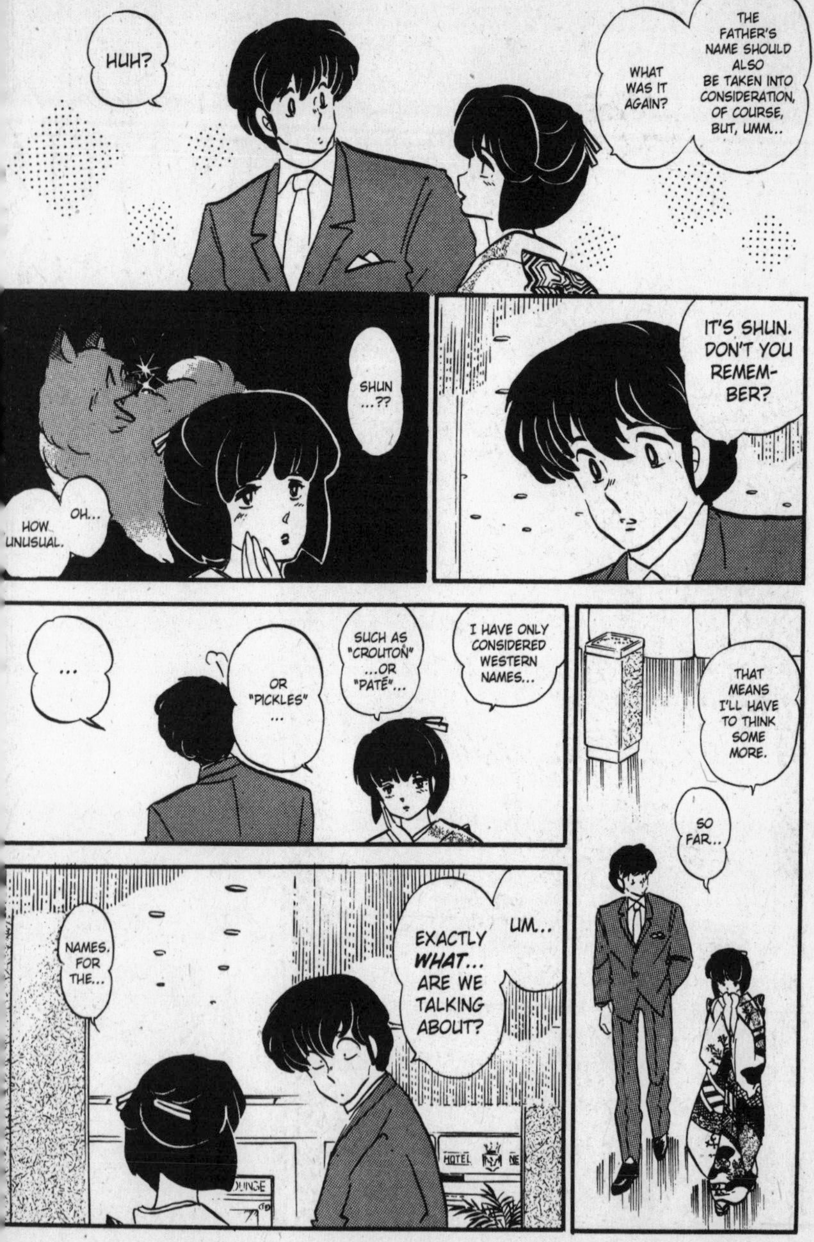
THE FATHER'S NAME SHOULD ALSO BE TAKEN INTO CONSIDERATION, OF COURSE, BUT, UMM..
WHAT WAS IT AGAIN?
HUH?
IT'S SHUN. DON'T YOU REMEMBER?
SHUN ...??
OH... HOW UNUSUAL.
THAT MEANS I'LL HAVE TO THINK SOME MORE.
SO FAR...
I HAVE ONLY CONSIDERED WESTERN NAMES...
SUCH AS "CROUTON" ...OR "PATÉ"...
OR "PICKLES" ...
...
UM...
EXACTLY *WHAT*... ARE WE TALKING ABOUT?
NAMES. FOR THE...
HOTEL
OUNGE

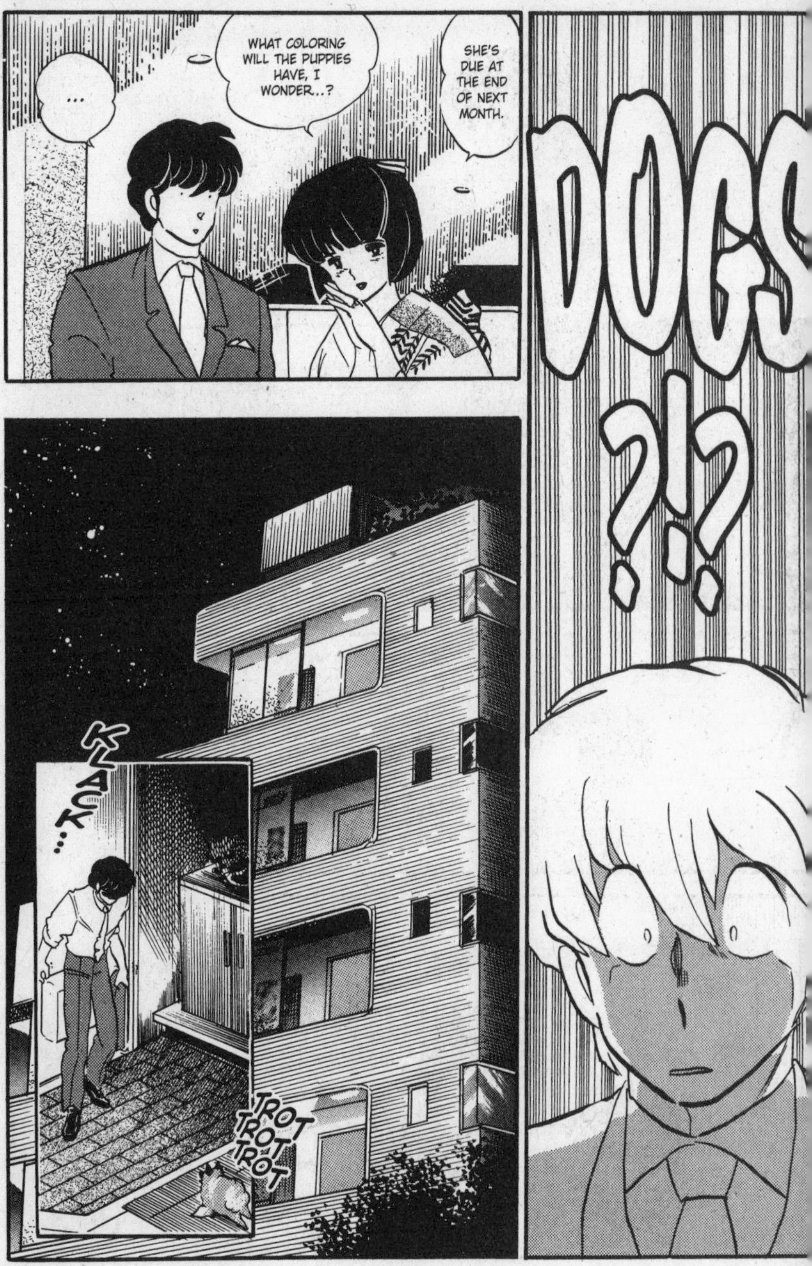

SHE'S DUE AT THE END OF NEXT MONTH.
WHAT COLORING WILL THE PUPPIES HAVE, I WONDER...?
...
DOGS ?!?
KLACK...
TROT TROT TROT

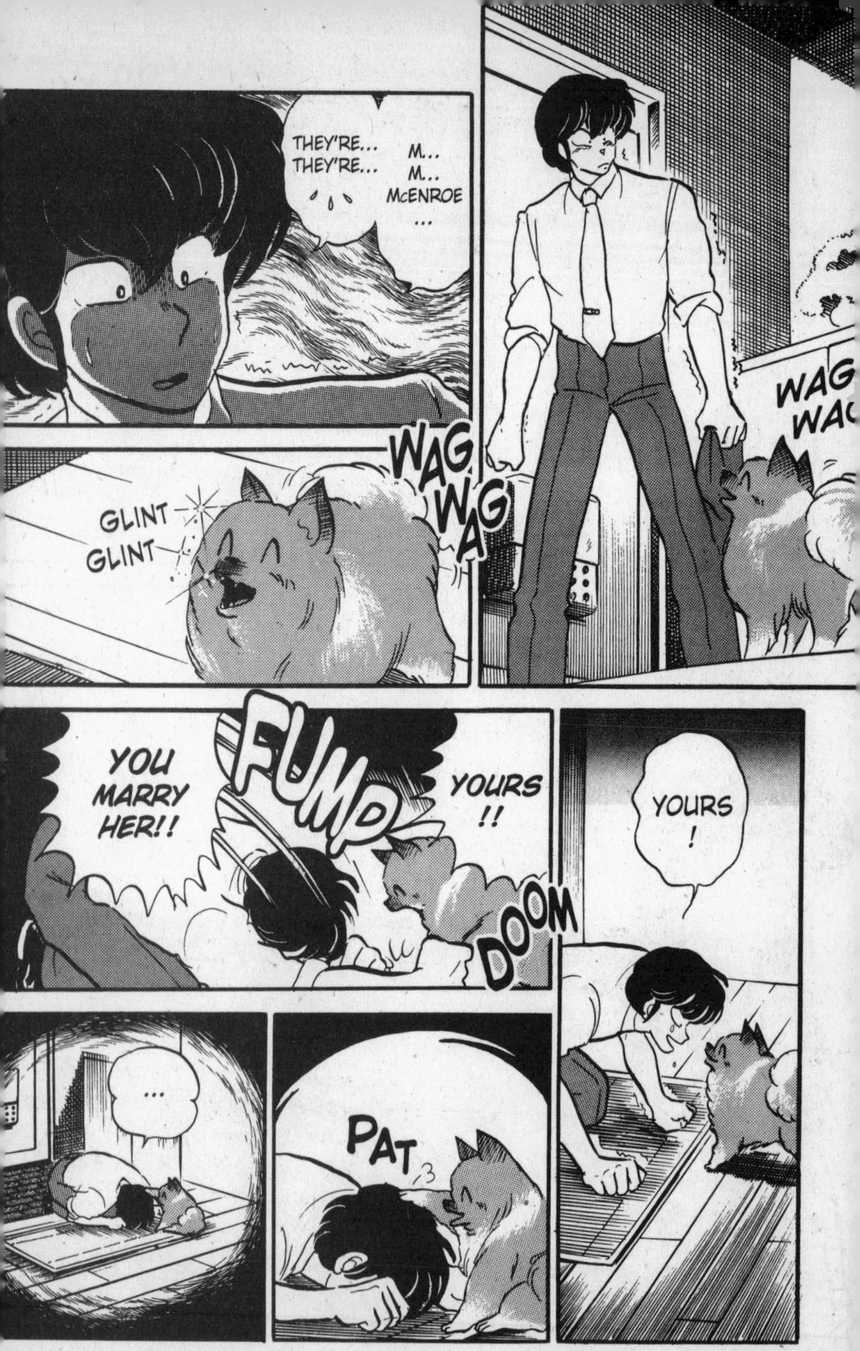

THEY'RE... THEY'RE...
M... M... McENROE ...
WAG WAG
WAG WAG
GLINT GLINT
YOU MARRY HER!!
FUMP
YOURS !!
DOOM
YOURS !
...
PAT

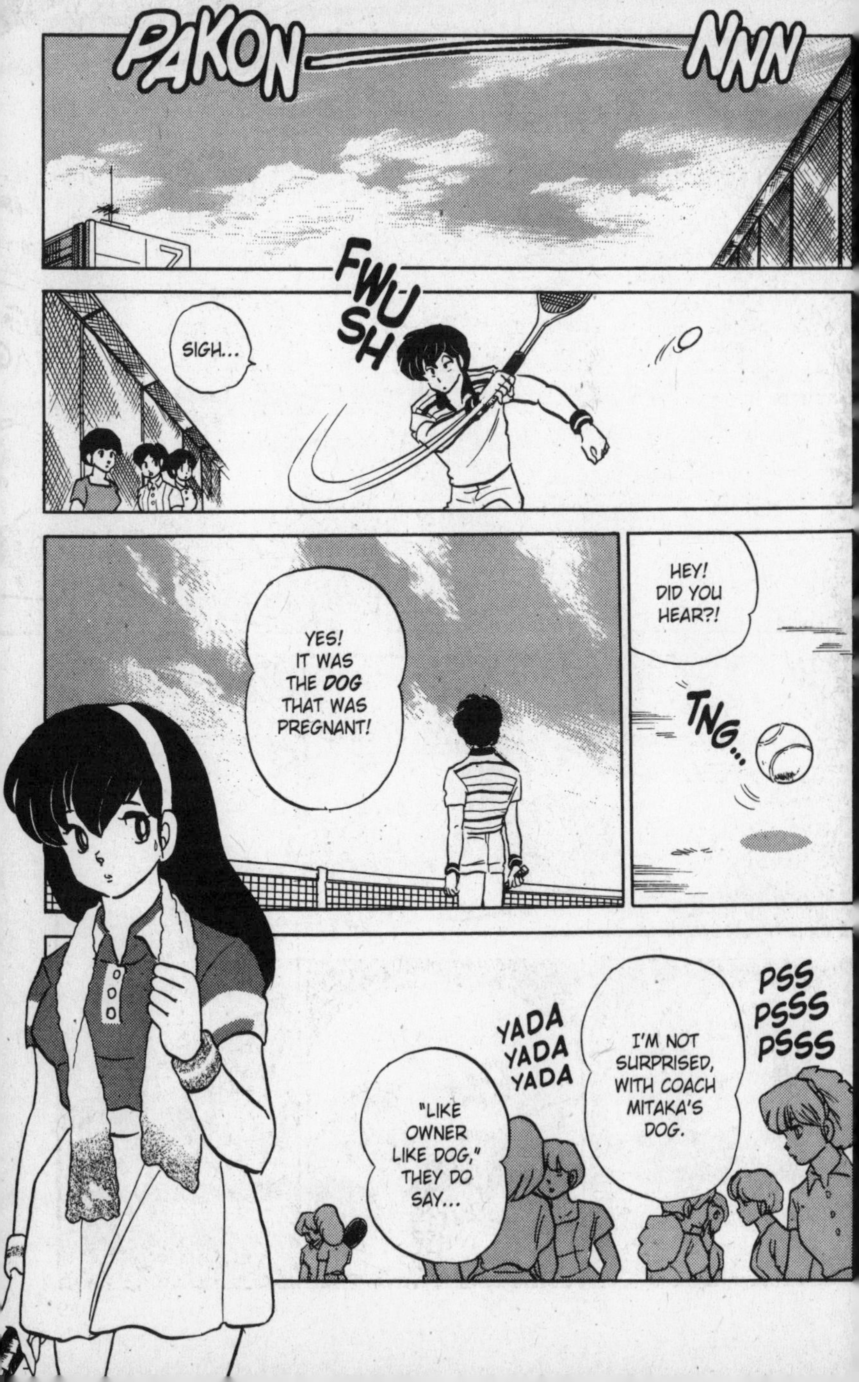
PAKON
NNN
FWUSH
SIGH...
HEY! DID YOU HEAR?!
TNG...
YES! IT WAS THE DOG THAT WAS PREGNANT!
PSS PSSS PSSS
I'M NOT SURPRISED, WITH COACH MITAKA'S DOG.
YADA YADA YADA
"LIKE OWNER LIKE DOG," THEY DO SAY...

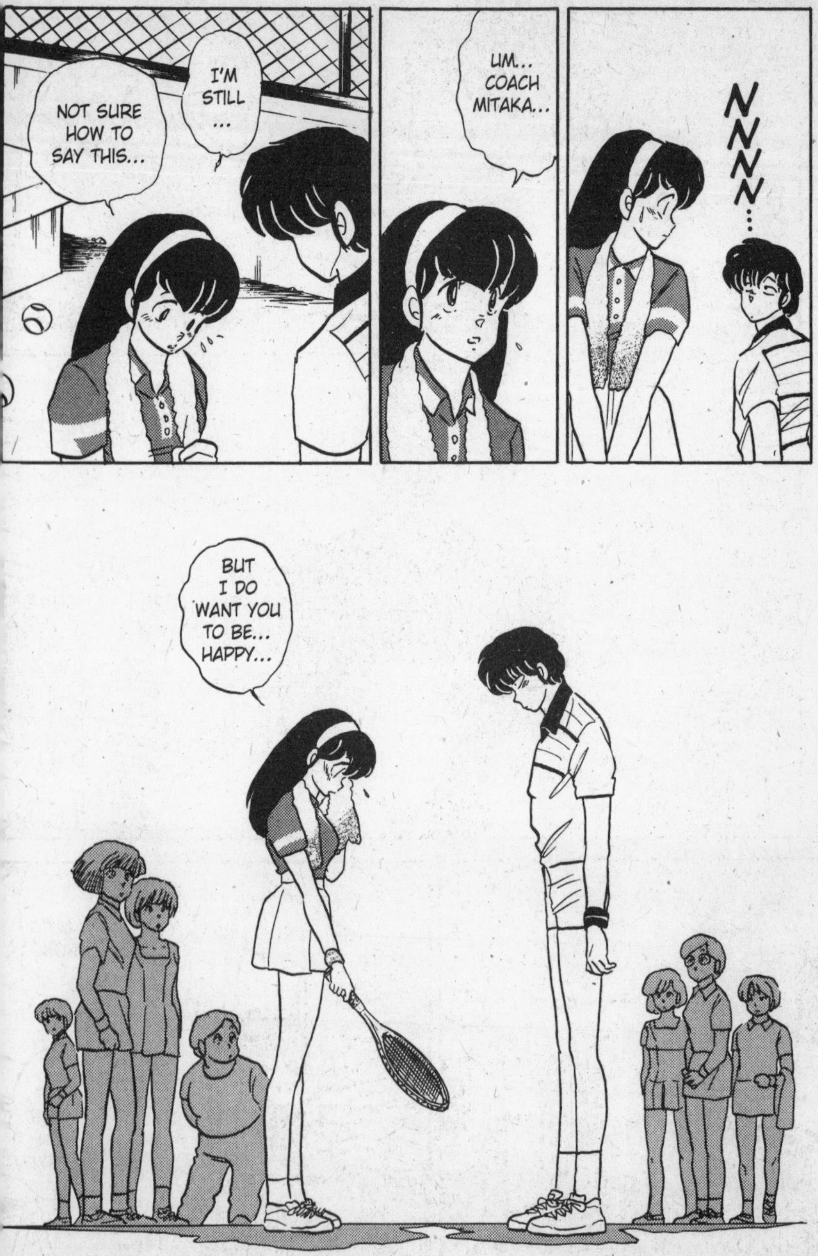
I'M STILL ...
NOT SURE HOW TO SAY THIS...
UM... COACH MITAKA...
NNNN...
BUT I DO WANT YOU TO BE... HAPPY...

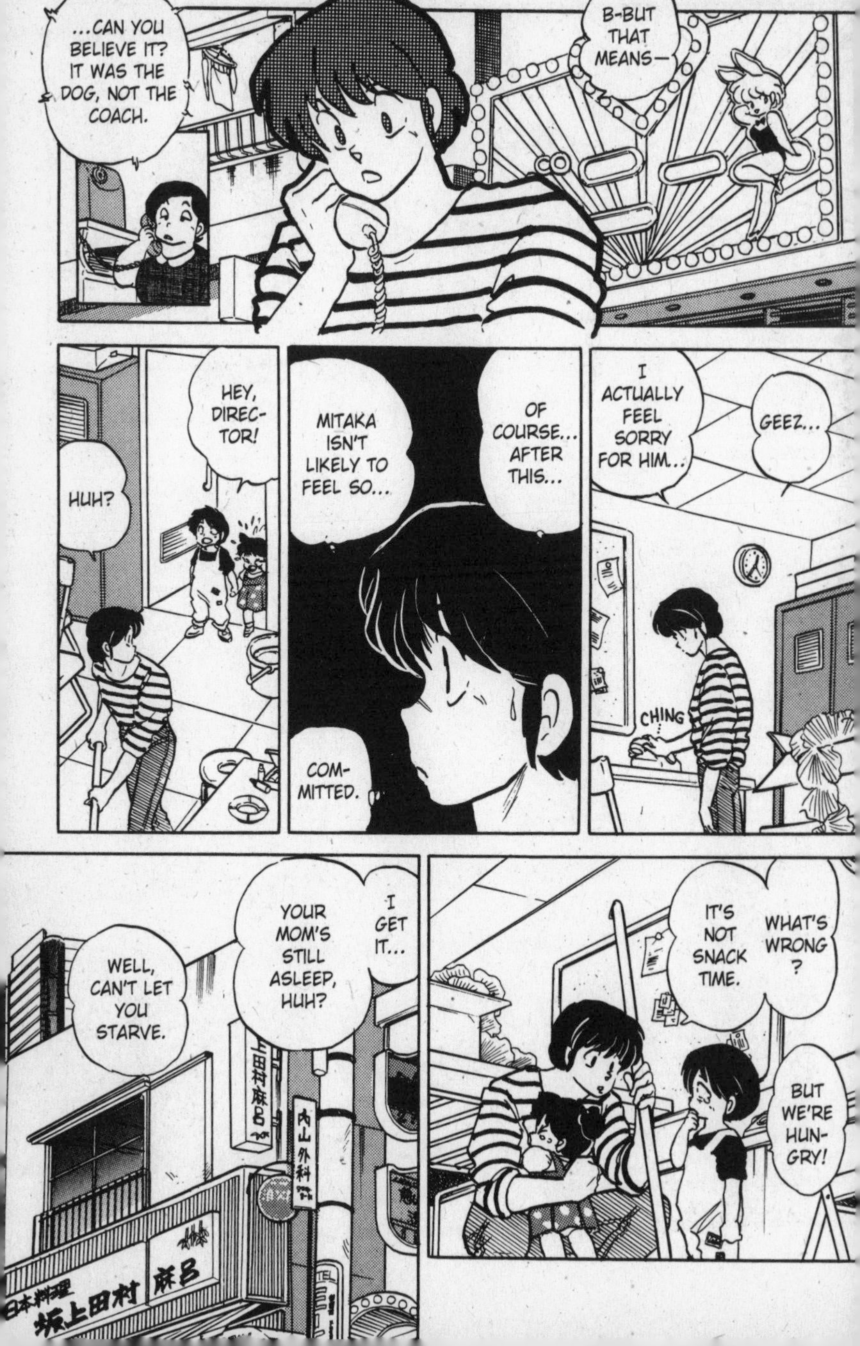
B-BUT THAT MEANS—
...CAN YOU BELIEVE IT? IT WAS THE DOG, NOT THE COACH.
GEEZ...
I ACTUALLY FEEL SORRY FOR HIM...
CHING
OF COURSE... AFTER THIS...
MITAKA ISN'T LIKELY TO FEEL SO...
COMMITTED.
HEY, DIRECTOR!
HUH?
WHAT'S WRONG?
IT'S NOT SNACK TIME.
BUT WE'RE HUNGRY!
I GET IT...
YOUR MOM'S STILL ASLEEP, HUH?
WELL, CAN'T LET YOU STARVE.
上田村麻呂
内山外科
日本料理
坂上田村 麻呂

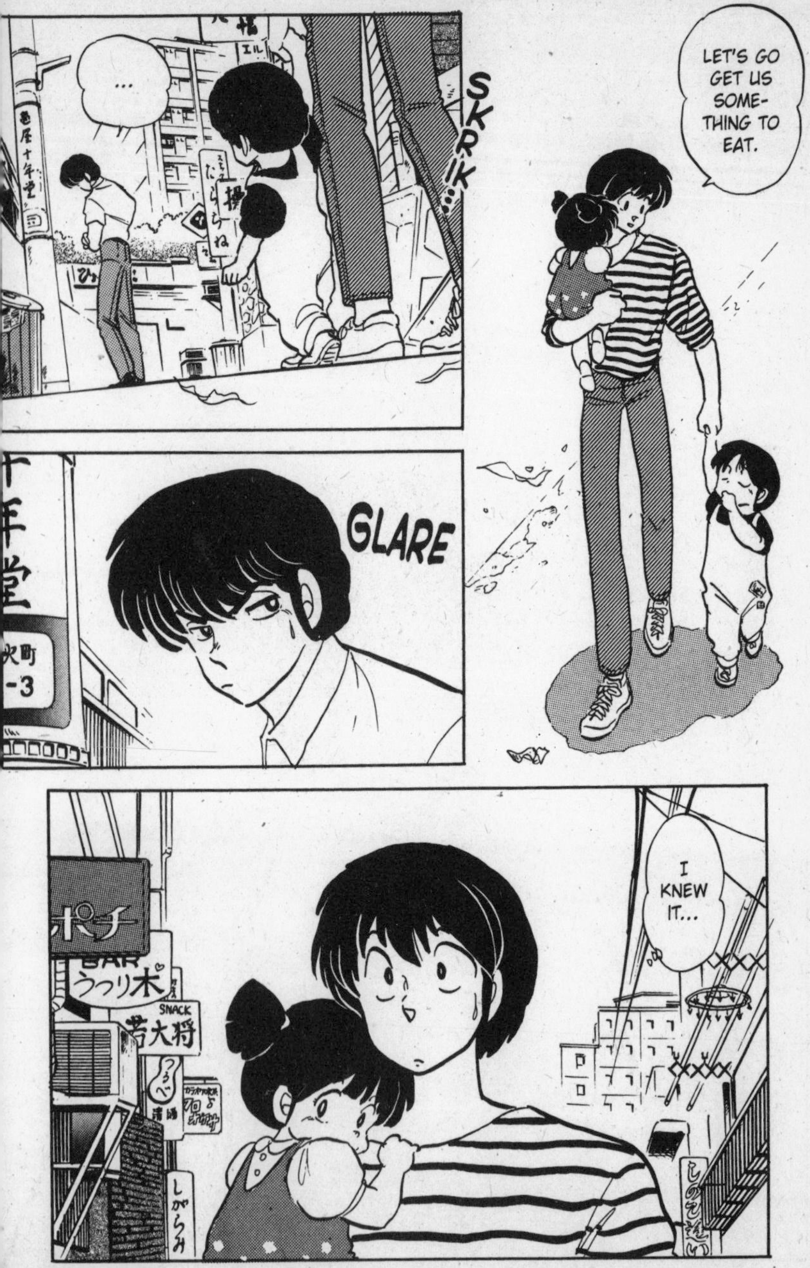
LET'S GO GET US SOME-THING TO EAT.
...
SKRIK!...
GLARE
BAR
SNACK
I KNEW IT...

PART TWO
ONE MORE ROUND

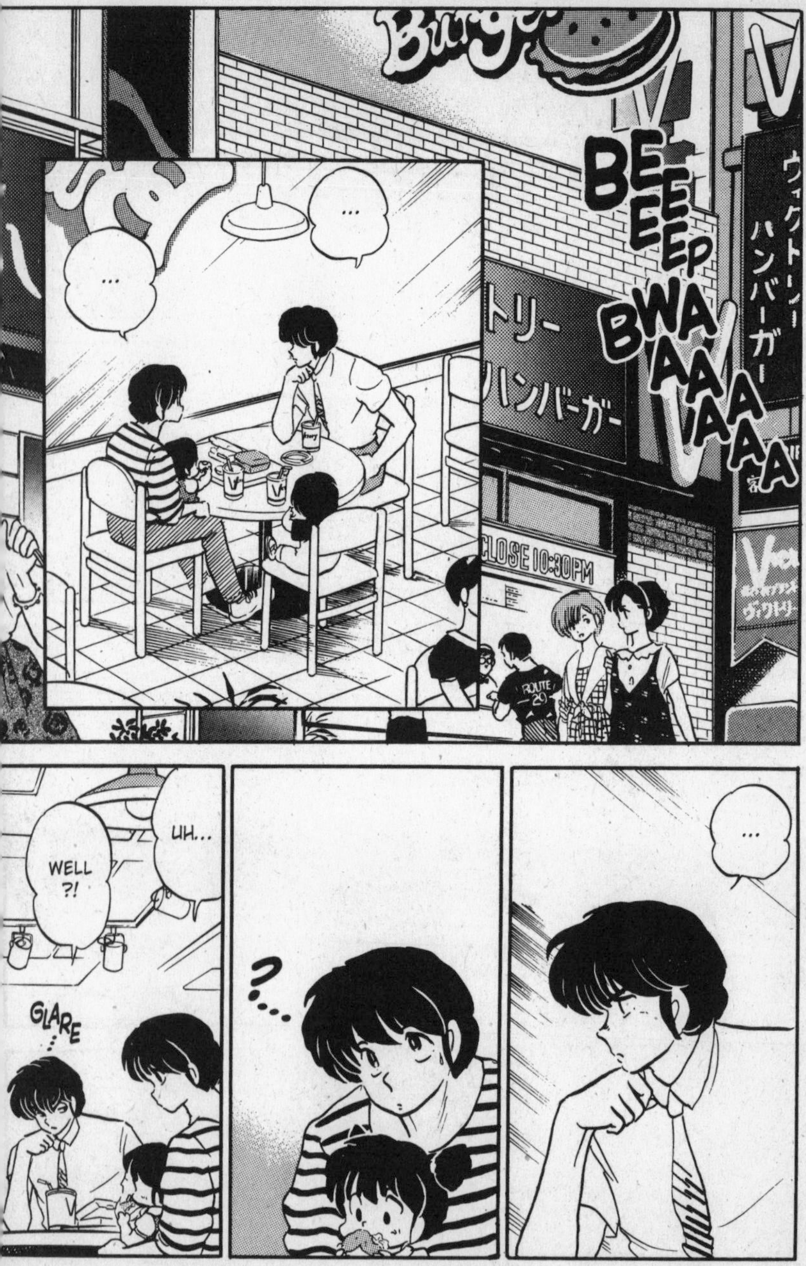

ウィクトリー ハンバーガー
BEEEEP
BWAAAAAAA
トリー ハンバーガー
CLOSE 10:30PM
ROUTE 20
...
...
...
?...
UH...
WELL ?!
GLARE

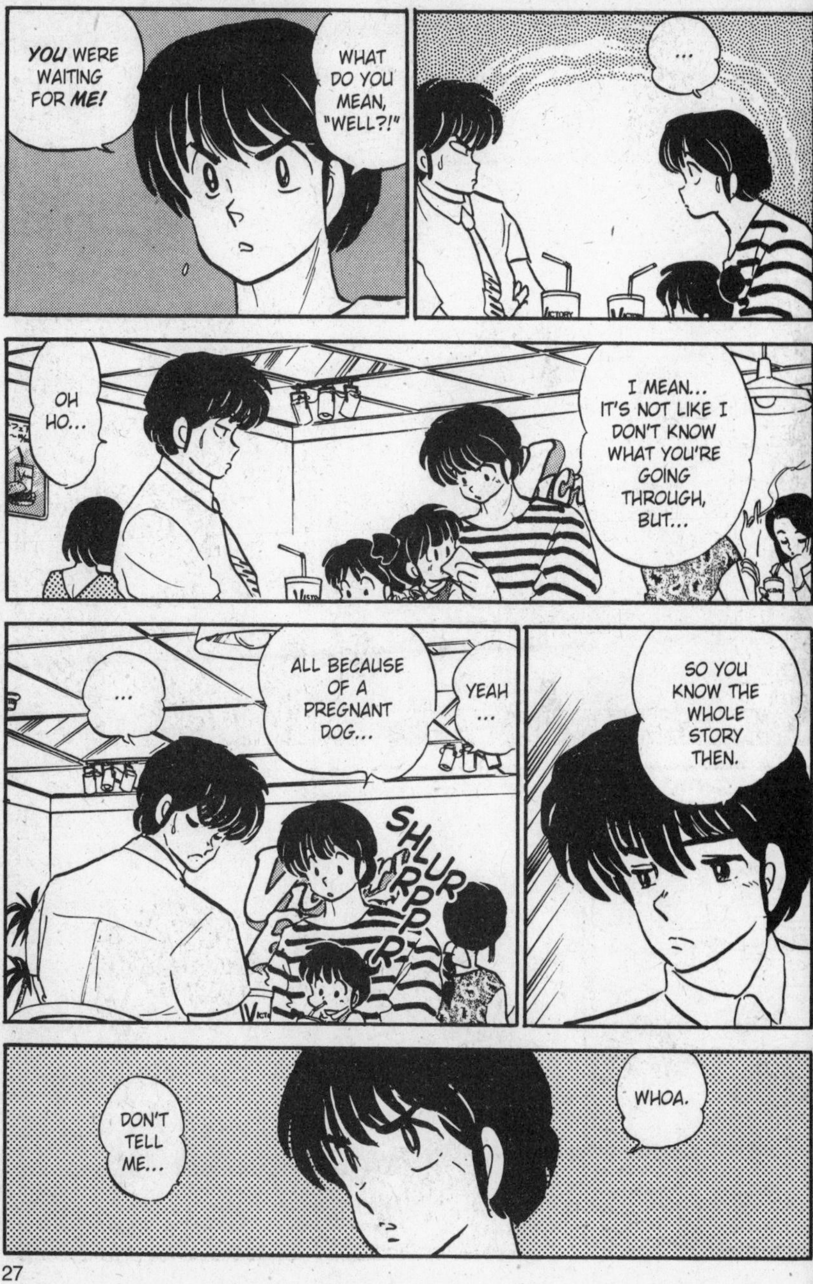
YOU WERE WAITING FOR ME!
WHAT DO YOU MEAN, "WELL?!"
...
OH HO...
I MEAN... IT'S NOT LIKE I DON'T KNOW WHAT YOU'RE GOING THROUGH, BUT...
...
ALL BECAUSE OF A PREGNANT DOG...
YEAH ...
SHLURRPPR
SO YOU KNOW THE WHOLE STORY THEN.
DON'T TELL ME...
WHOA.

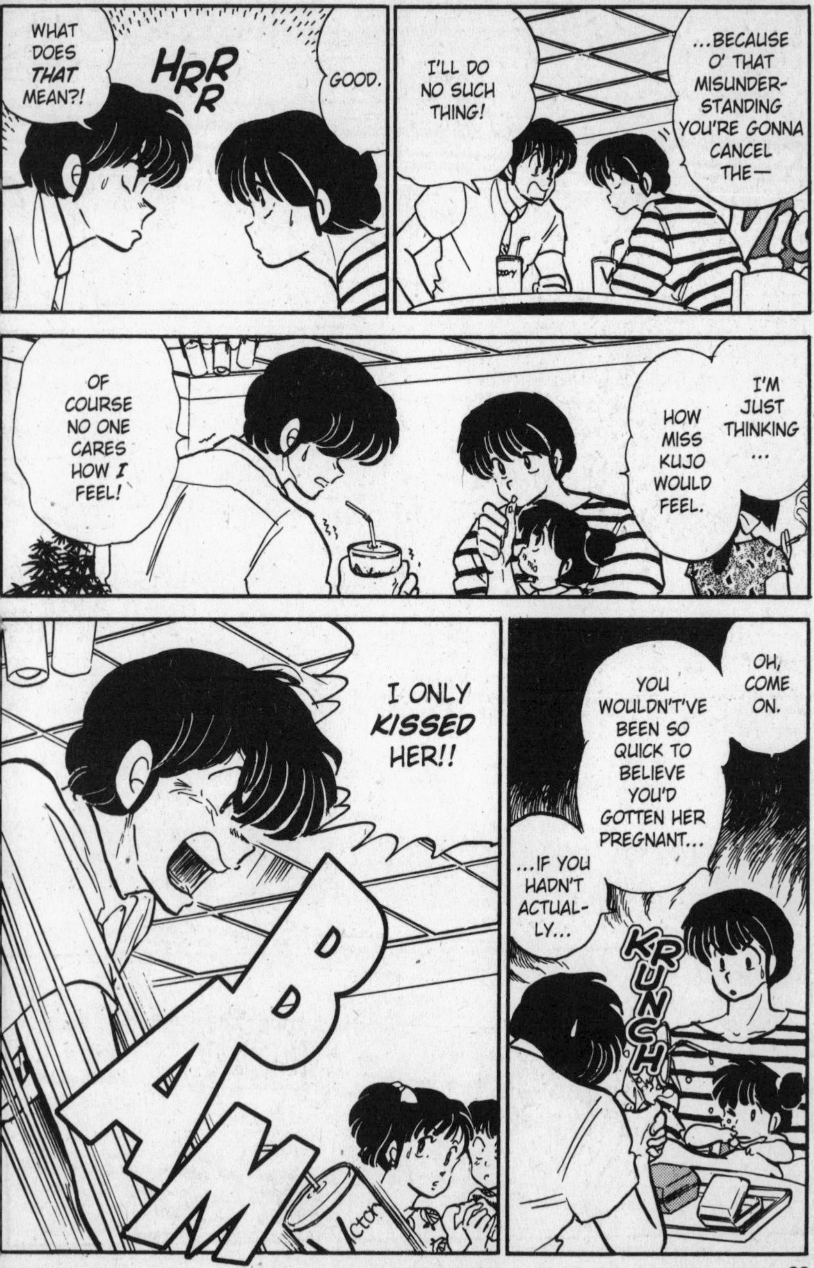

WHAT DOES THAT MEAN?!
HRRR
GOOD.
I'LL DO NO SUCH THING!
...BECAUSE O' THAT MISUNDER-STANDING YOU'RE GONNA CANCEL THE—
OF COURSE NO ONE CARES HOW I FEEL!
I'M JUST THINKING...
HOW MISS KUJO WOULD FEEL.
I ONLY KISSED HER!!
BAM
OH, COME ON.
YOU WOULDN'T'VE BEEN SO QUICK TO BELIEVE YOU'D GOTTEN HER PREGNANT...
...IF YOU HADN'T ACTUAL-LY...
KRUNCH

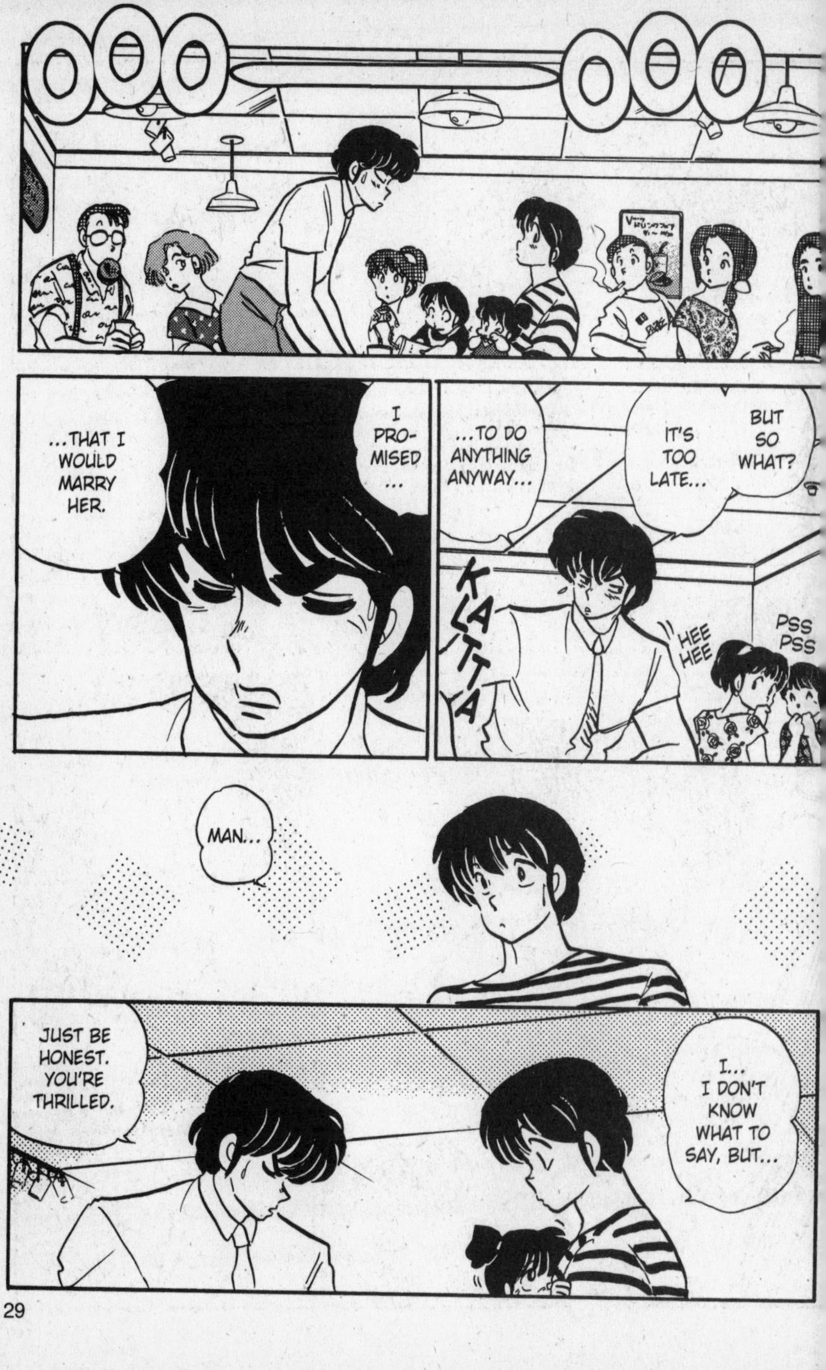
BUT SO WHAT?
IT'S TOO LATE...
...TO DO ANYTHING ANYWAY...
KLATTA
HEE HEE
PSS PSS
I PRO- MISED ...
...THAT I WOULD MARRY HER.
MAN...
I... I DON'T KNOW WHAT TO SAY, BUT...
JUST BE HONEST. YOU'RE THRILLED.

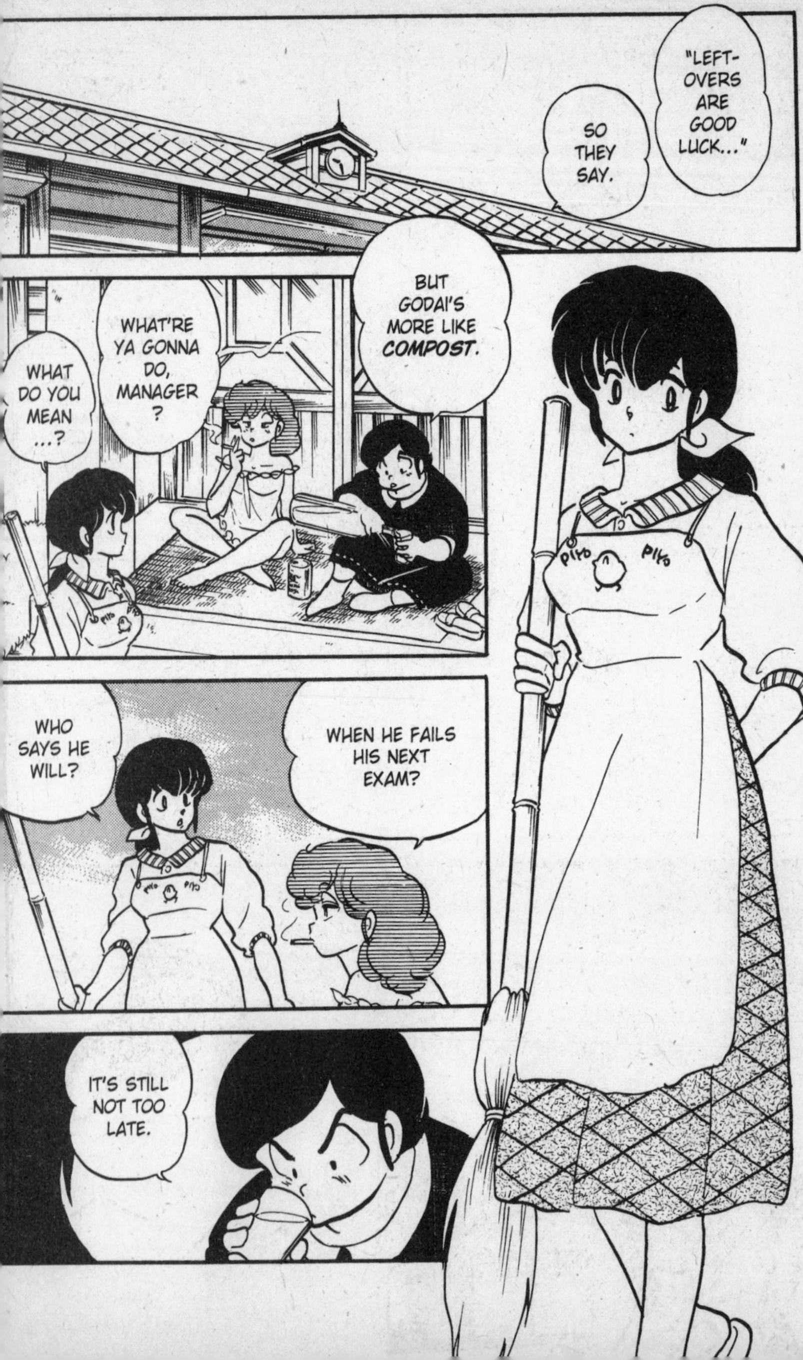
"LEFT-OVERS ARE GOOD LUCK..."
SO THEY SAY.
BUT GODAI'S MORE LIKE COMPOST.
WHAT DO YOU MEAN ...?
WHAT'RE YA GONNA DO, MANAGER?
WHEN HE FAILS HIS NEXT EXAM?
WHO SAYS HE WILL?
IT'S STILL NOT TOO LATE.

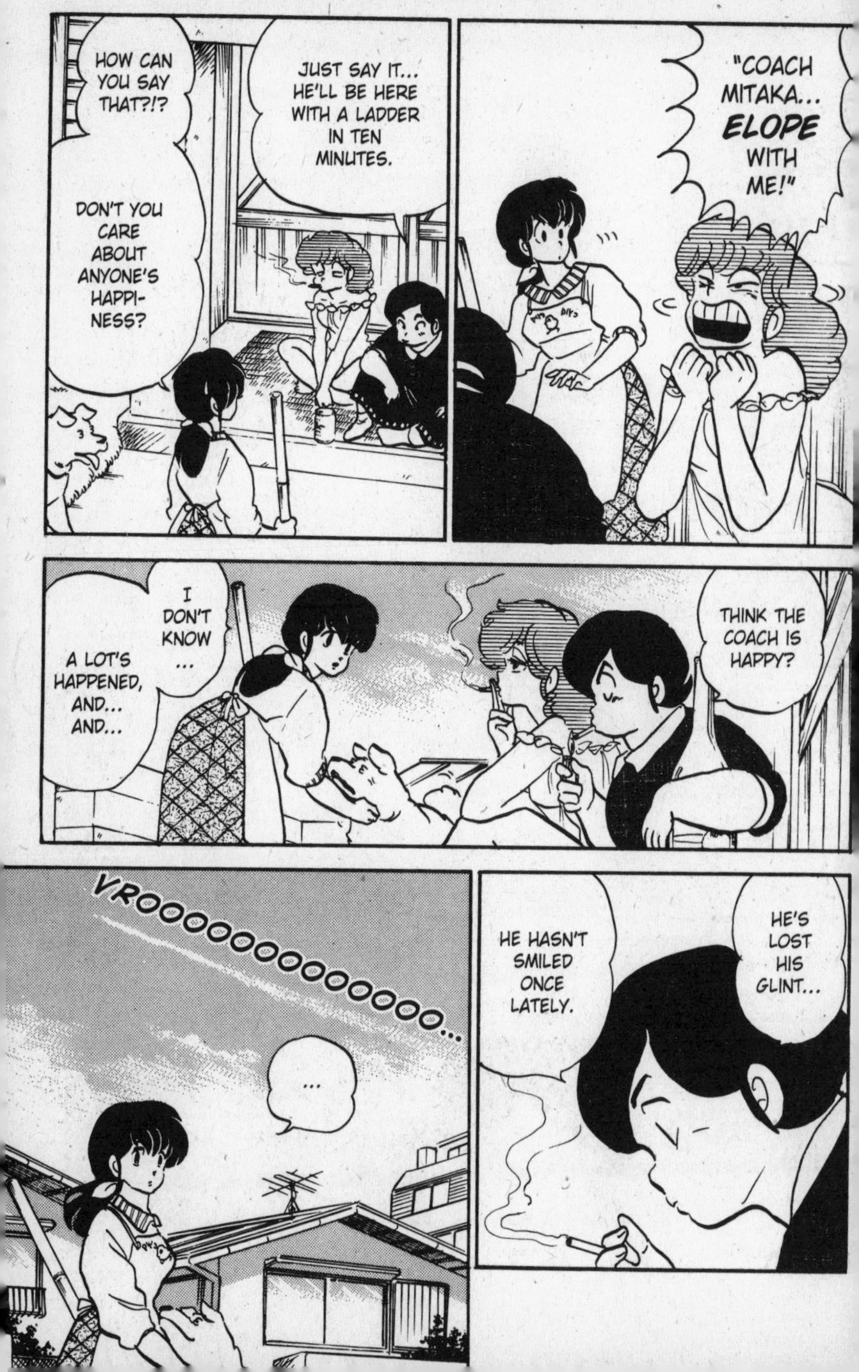
HOW CAN YOU SAY THAT?!?
DON'T YOU CARE ABOUT ANYONE'S HAPPI-NESS?
JUST SAY IT... HE'LL BE HERE WITH A LADDER IN TEN MINUTES.
"COACH MITAKA... ELOPE WITH ME!"
I DON'T KNOW ...
A LOT'S HAPPENED, AND... AND...
THINK THE COACH IS HAPPY?
VROOOOOOOOOOOOOOOO...
...
HE HASN'T SMILED ONCE LATELY.
HE'S LOST HIS GLINT...

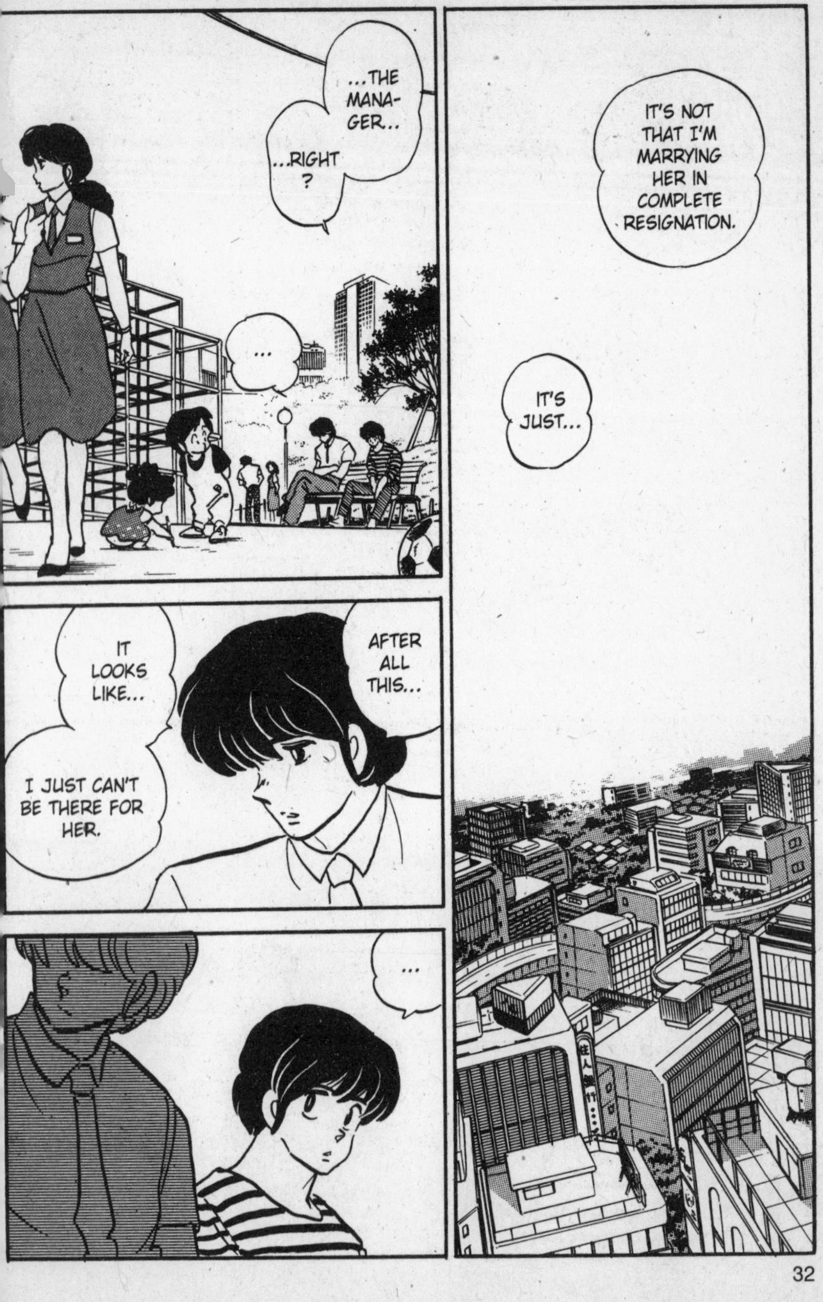
...THE MANA-GER...
...RIGHT?
...
AFTER ALL THIS...
IT LOOKS LIKE...
I JUST CAN'T BE THERE FOR HER.
...
IT'S NOT THAT I'M MARRYING HER IN COMPLETE RESIGNATION.
IT'S JUST...

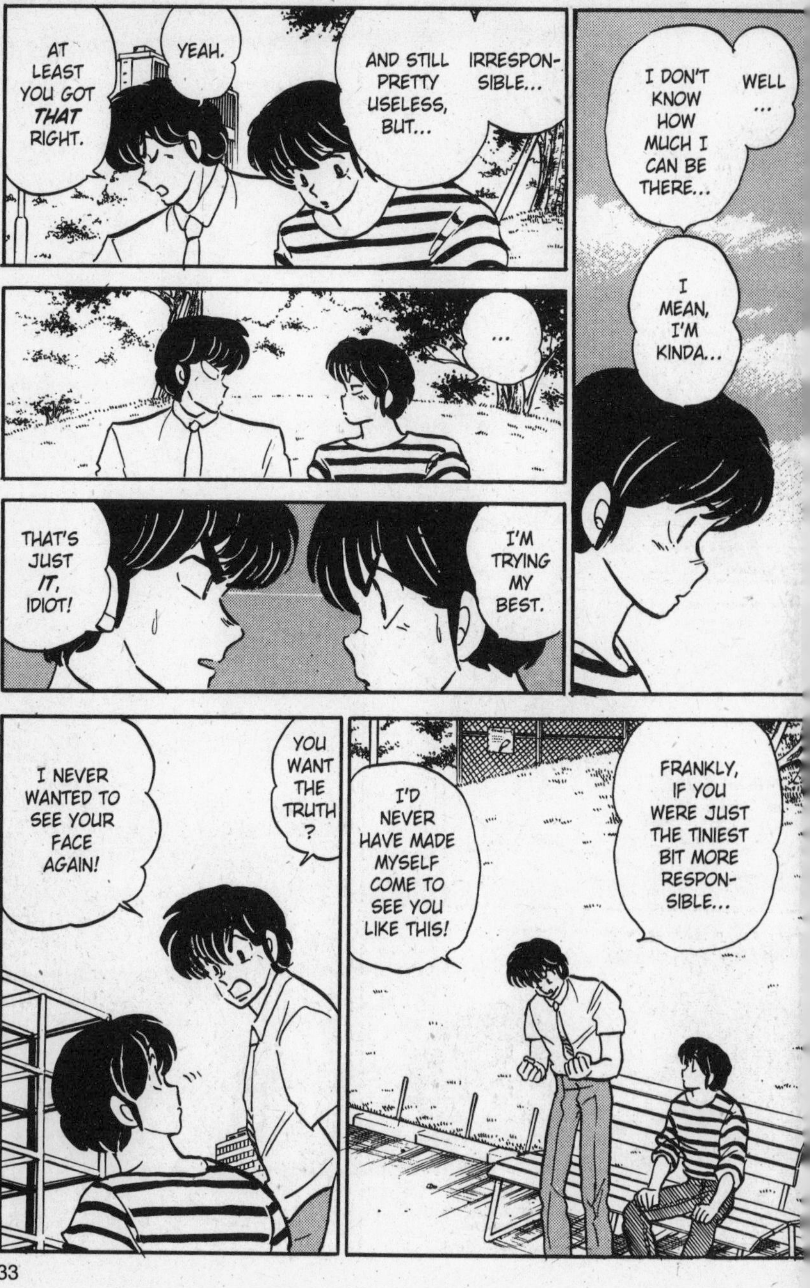
WELL ...
I DON'T KNOW HOW MUCH I CAN BE THERE...
I MEAN, I'M KINDA...
IRRESPON-SIBLE...
AND STILL PRETTY USELESS, BUT...
YEAH.
AT LEAST YOU GOT *THAT* RIGHT.
...
I'M TRYING MY BEST.
THAT'S JUST *IT*, IDIOT!
FRANKLY, IF YOU WERE JUST THE TINIEST BIT MORE RESPON-SIBLE...
I'D NEVER HAVE MADE MYSELF COME TO SEE YOU LIKE THIS!
YOU WANT THE TRUTH ?
I NEVER WANTED TO SEE YOUR FACE AGAIN!

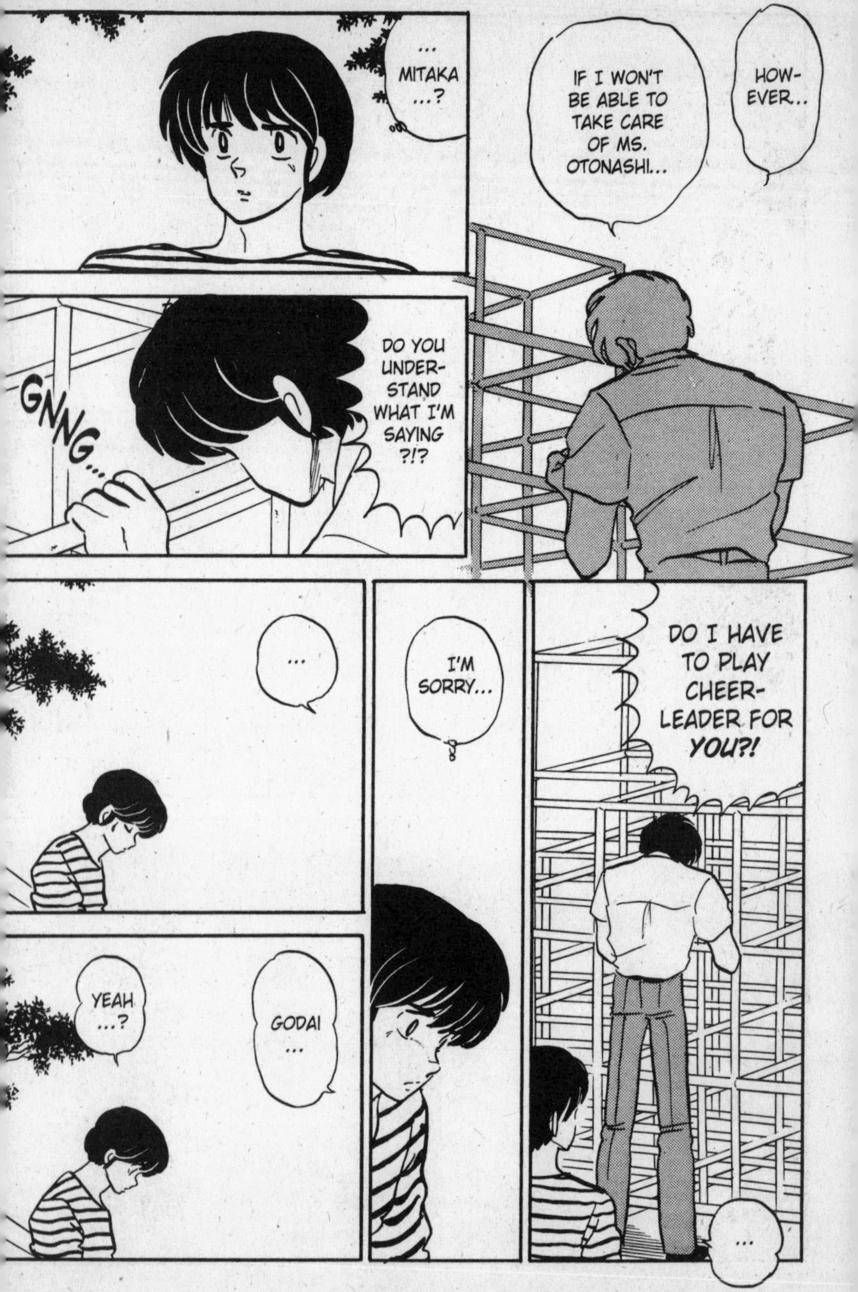

... MITAKA ...?
IF I WON'T BE ABLE TO TAKE CARE OF MS. OTONASHI...
HOW-EVER...
GNNG...
DO YOU UNDER-STAND WHAT I'M SAYING ?!?
DO I HAVE TO PLAY CHEER-LEADER FOR YOU?!
...
I'M SORRY...
...
YEAH ...?
GODAI ...

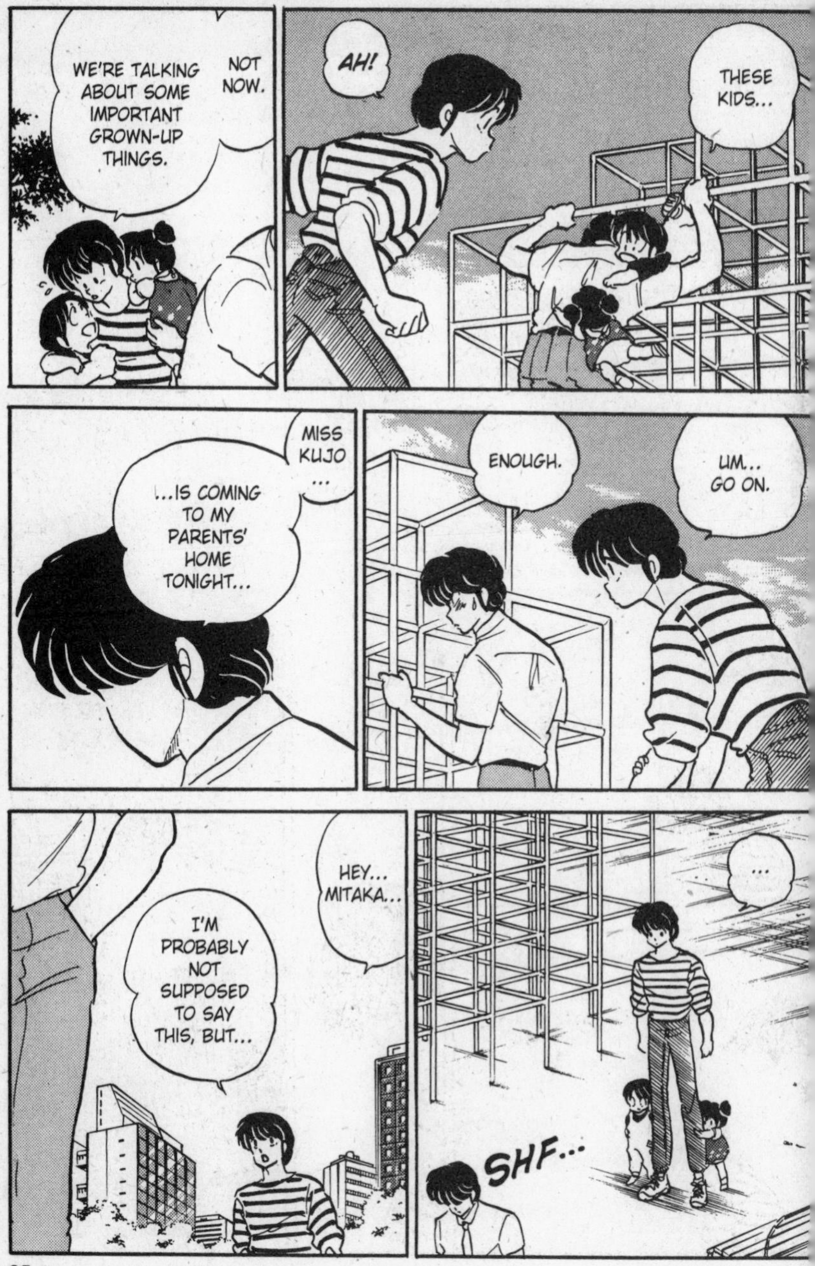
NOT NOW.
WE'RE TALKING ABOUT SOME IMPORTANT GROWN-UP THINGS.
AH!
THESE KIDS...
MISS KUJO ...
...IS COMING TO MY PARENTS' HOME TONIGHT...
ENOUGH.
UM... GO ON.
HEY... MITAKA...
I'M PROBABLY NOT SUPPOSED TO SAY THIS, BUT...
...
SHF...

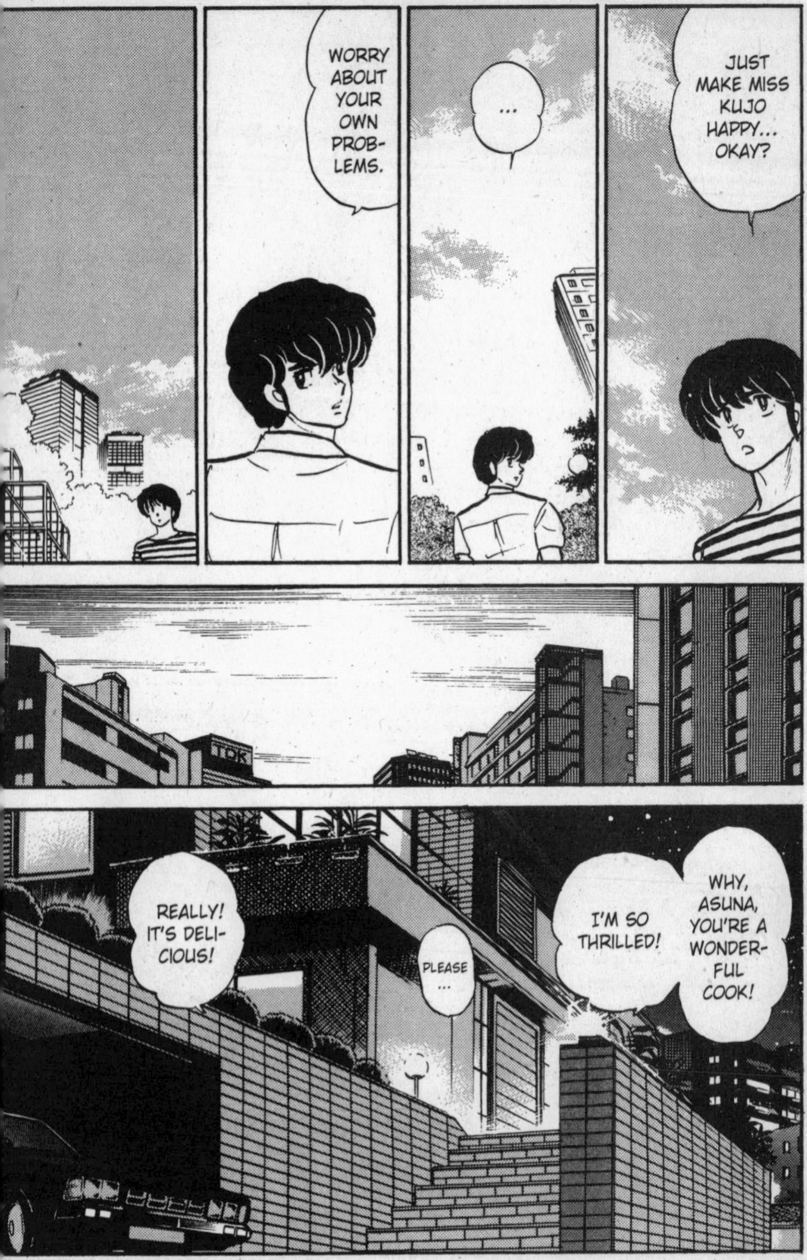
WORRY ABOUT YOUR OWN PROB-LEMS.
...
JUST MAKE MISS KUJO HAPPY... OKAY?
TDK
REALLY! IT'S DELI-CIOUS!
PLEASE ...
I'M SO THRILLED!
WHY, ASUNA, YOU'RE A WONDER-FUL COOK!

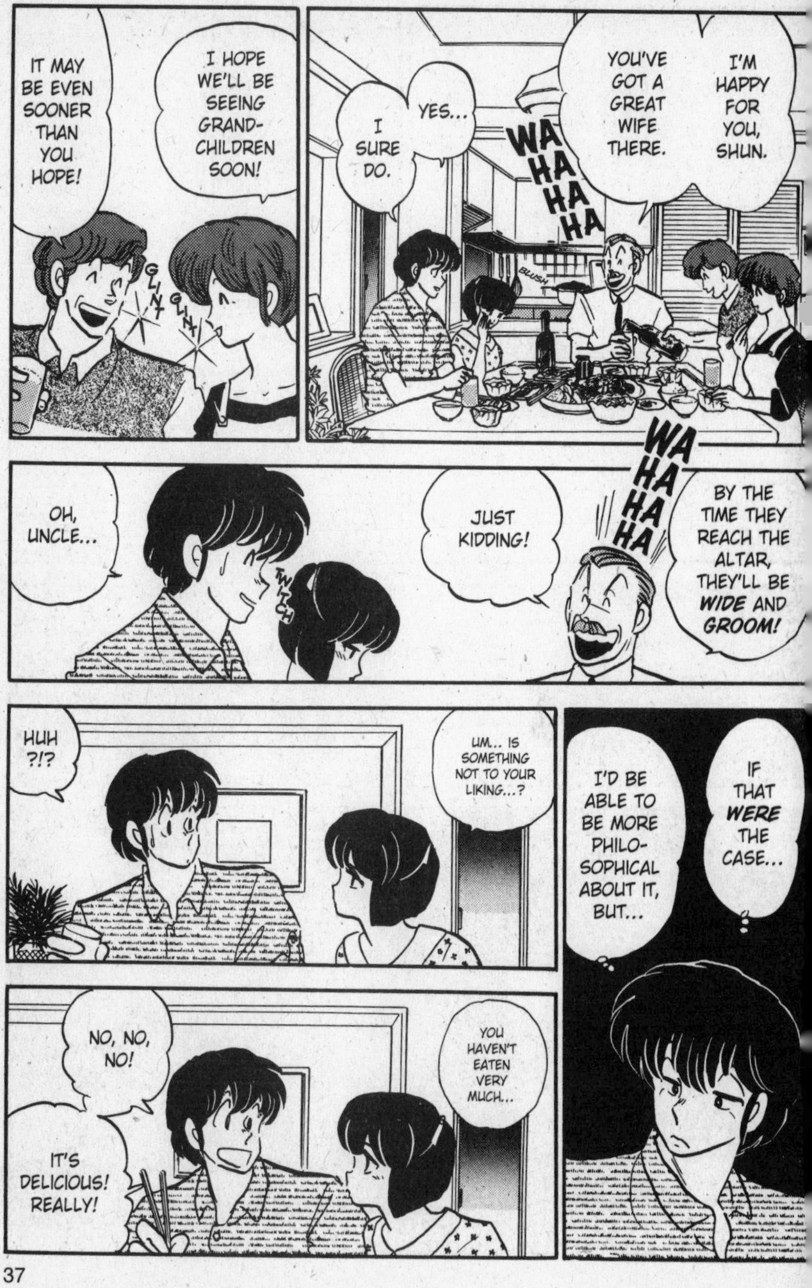

I HOPE WE'LL BE SEEING GRAND-CHILDREN SOON!
IT MAY BE EVEN SOONER THAN YOU HOPE!
GLINT
GLINT
I'M HAPPY FOR YOU, SHUN.
YOU'VE GOT A GREAT WIFE THERE.
WAHAHAHA
YES... I SURE DO.
BLUSH
WAHAHAHA
BY THE TIME THEY REACH THE ALTAR, THEY'LL BE *WIDE* AND *GROOM!*
JUST KIDDING!
OH, UNCLE...
TWITCH
IF THAT *WERE* THE CASE...
I'D BE ABLE TO BE MORE PHILO-SOPHICAL ABOUT IT, BUT...
UM... IS SOMETHING NOT TO YOUR LIKING...?
HUH ?!?
YOU HAVEN'T EATEN VERY MUCH...
NO, NO, NO!
IT'S DELICIOUS! REALLY!

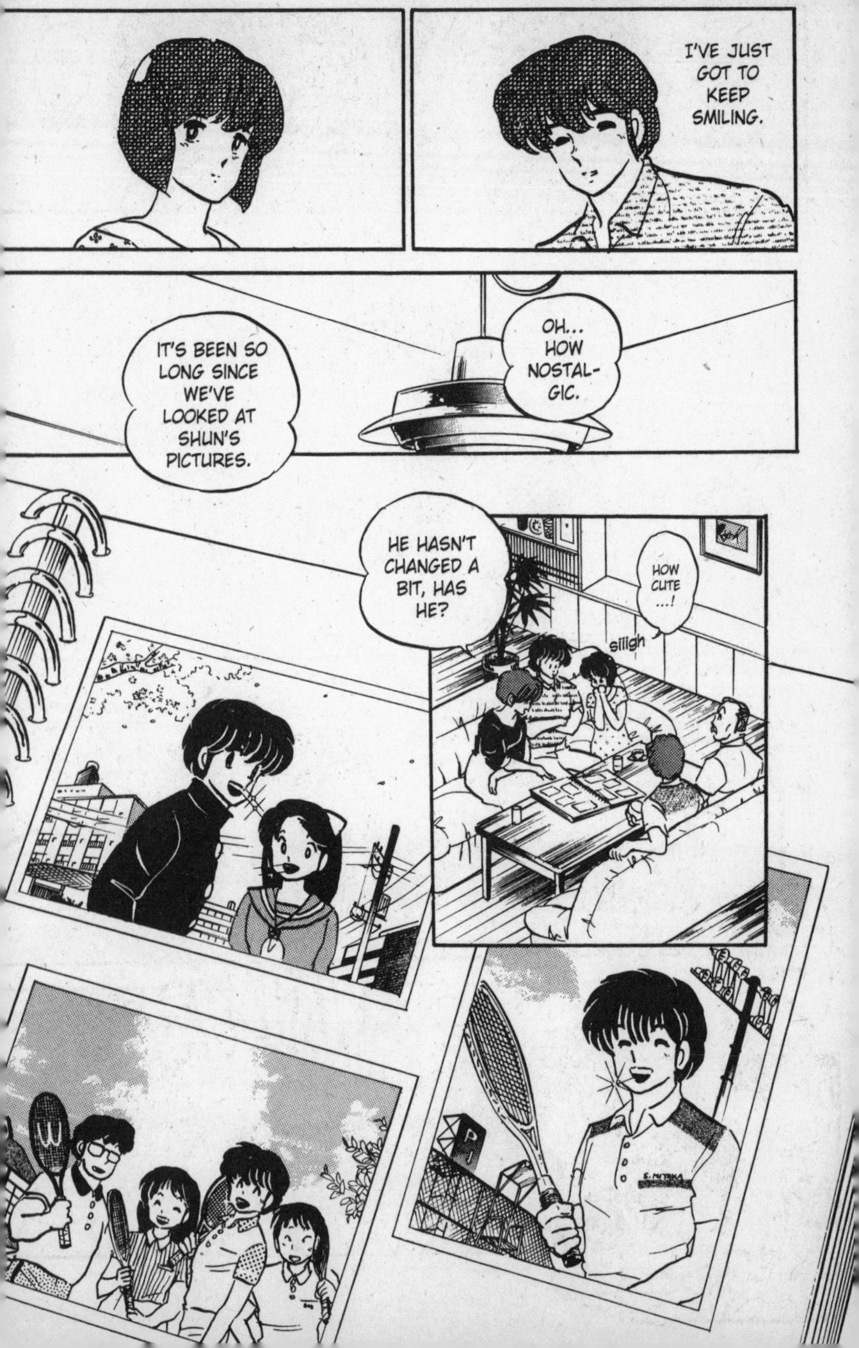
I'VE JUST GOT TO KEEP SMILING.
OH... HOW NOSTAL-GIC.
IT'S BEEN SO LONG SINCE WE'VE LOOKED AT SHUN'S PICTURES.
HOW CUTE ...!
siiigh
HE HASN'T CHANGED A BIT, HAS HE?

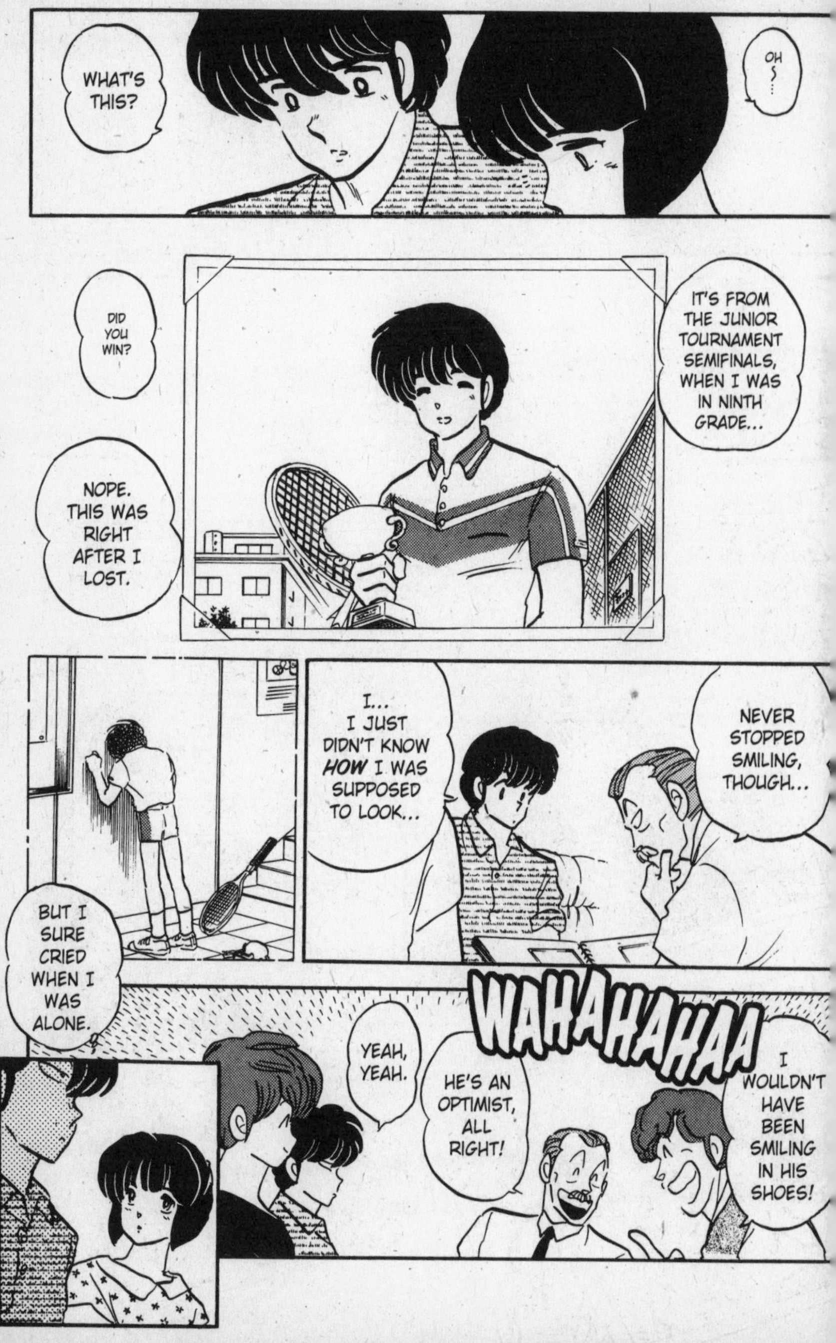
WHAT'S THIS?
OH...
DID YOU WIN?
IT'S FROM THE JUNIOR TOURNAMENT SEMIFINALS, WHEN I WAS IN NINTH GRADE...
NOPE. THIS WAS RIGHT AFTER I LOST.
BUT I SURE CRIED WHEN I WAS ALONE.
I... I JUST DIDN'T KNOW *HOW* I WAS SUPPOSED TO LOOK...
NEVER STOPPED SMILING, THOUGH...
WAHAHAHAA
YEAH, YEAH.
HE'S AN OPTIMIST, ALL RIGHT!
I WOULDN'T HAVE BEEN SMILING IN HIS SHOES!

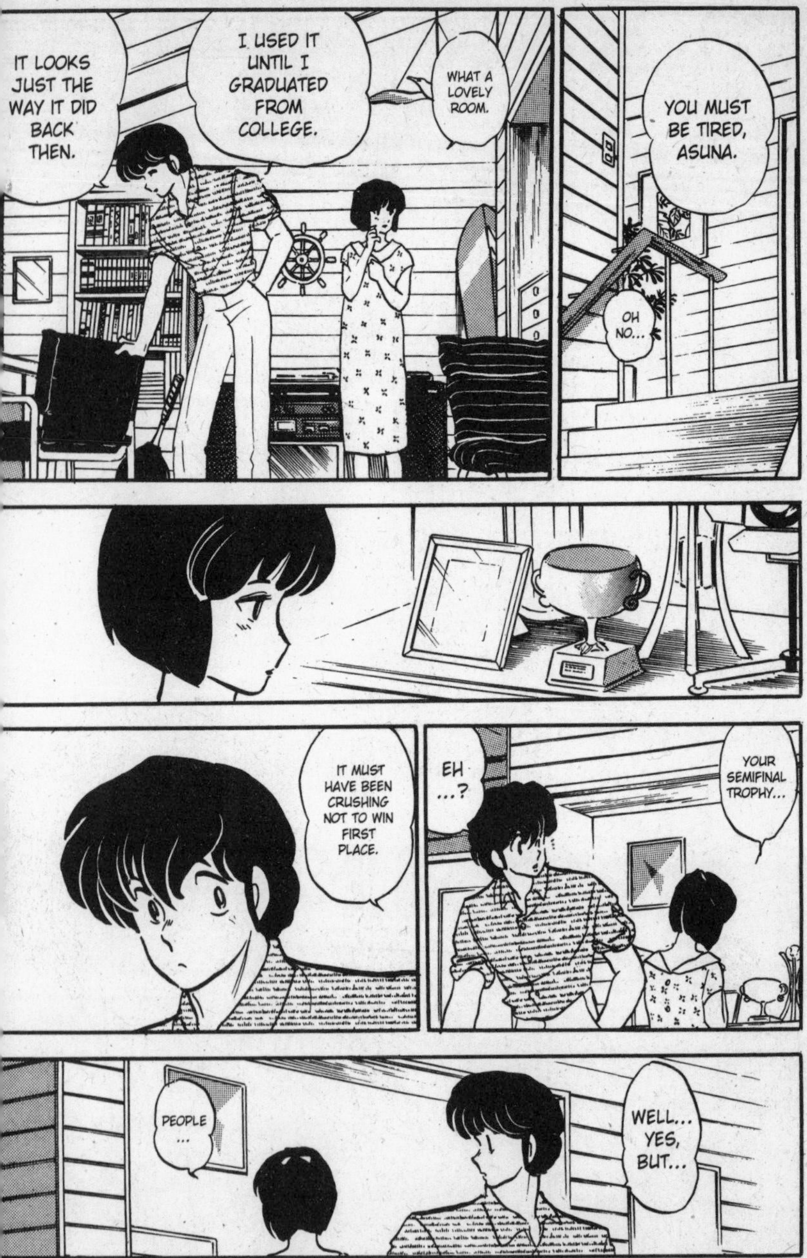
IT LOOKS JUST THE WAY IT DID BACK THEN.
I USED IT UNTIL I GRADUATED FROM COLLEGE.
WHAT A LOVELY ROOM.
YOU MUST BE TIRED, ASUNA.
OH NO...
IT MUST HAVE BEEN CRUSHING NOT TO WIN FIRST PLACE.
EH ...?
YOUR SEMIFINAL TROPHY...
PEOPLE ...
WELL... YES, BUT...

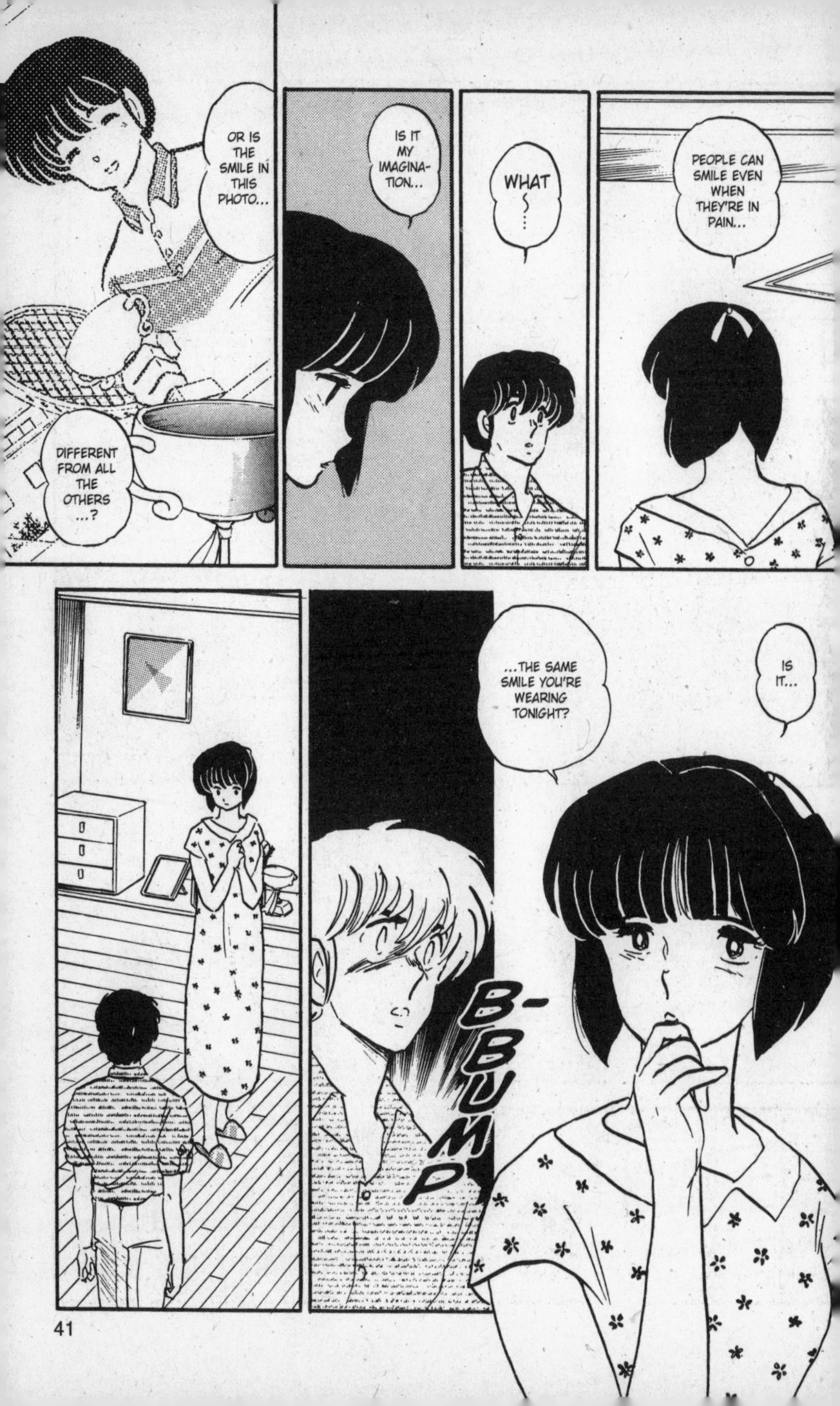
PEOPLE CAN SMILE EVEN WHEN THEY'RE IN PAIN...
WHAT ...
IS IT MY IMAGINATION...
OR IS THE SMILE IN THIS PHOTO...
DIFFERENT FROM ALL THE OTHERS ...?
IS IT...
...THE SAME SMILE YOU'RE WEARING TONIGHT?
B-BBUMP

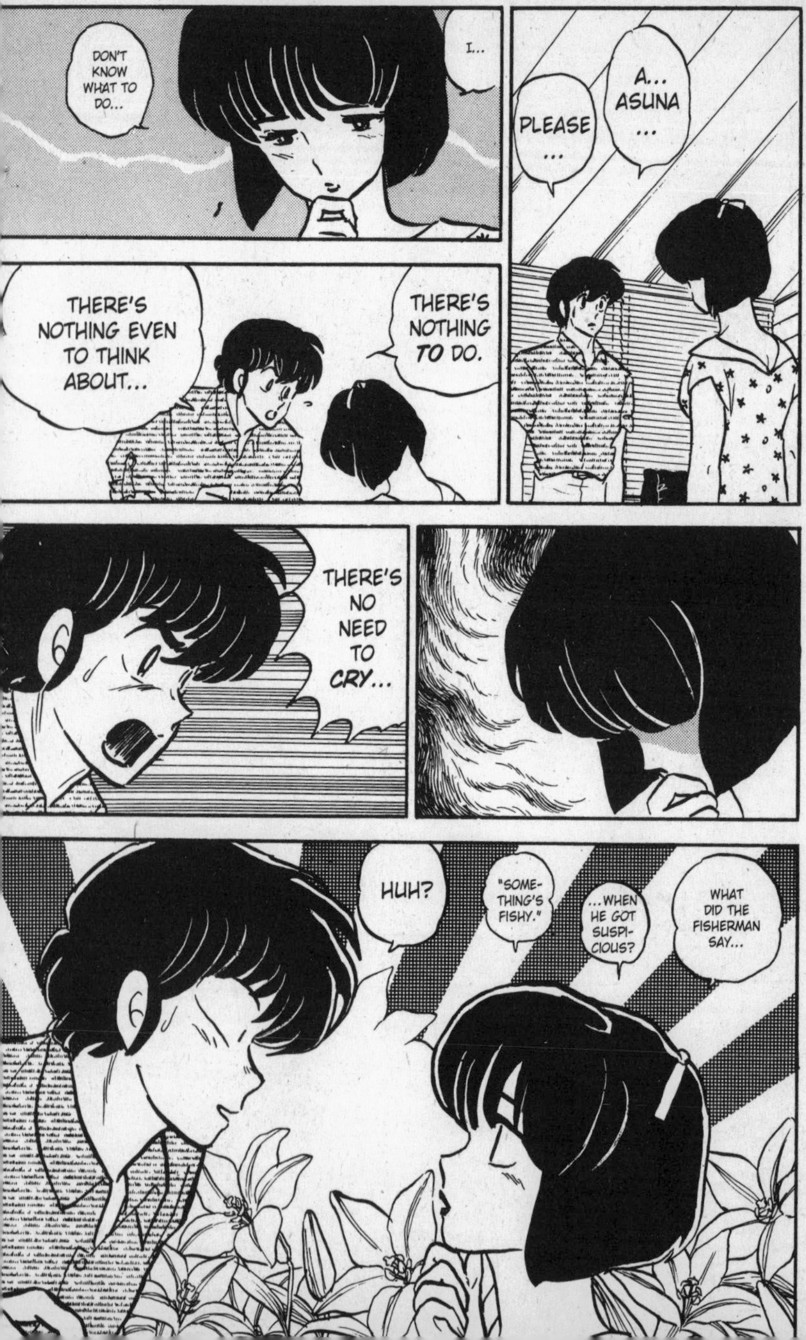
A... ASUNA ...
PLEASE ...
I...
DON'T KNOW WHAT TO DO...
THERE'S NOTHING TO DO.
THERE'S NOTHING EVEN TO THINK ABOUT...
THERE'S NO NEED TO CRY...
WHAT DID THE FISHERMAN SAY...
...WHEN HE GOT SUSPICIOUS?
"SOMETHING'S FISHY."
HUH?

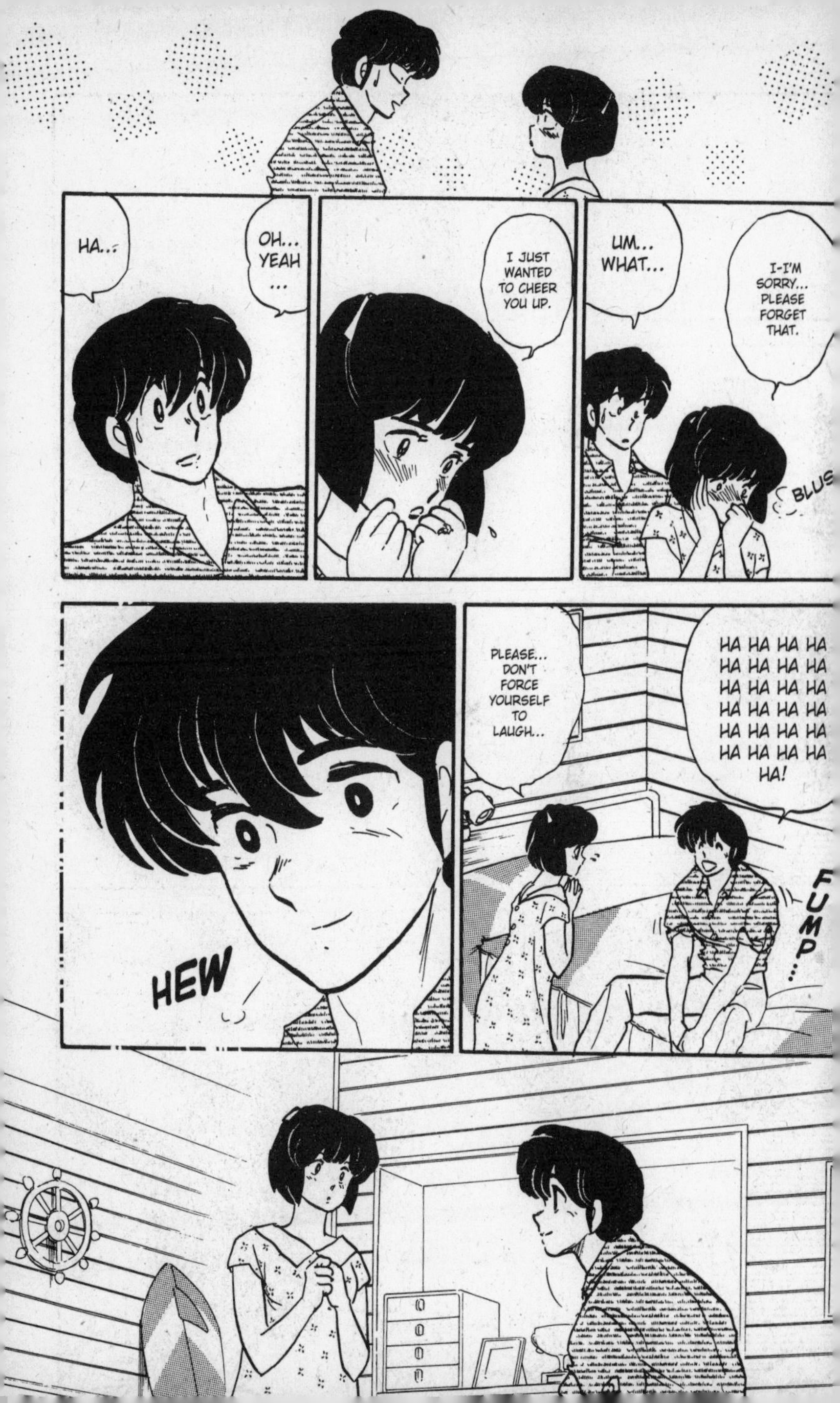
I-I'M SORRY... PLEASE FORGET THAT.
UM... WHAT...
I JUST WANTED TO CHEER YOU UP.
OH... YEAH ...
HA...
BLUS
HA HA HA HA HA HA HA HA HA HA HA HA HA HA HA HA HA HA HA HA HA HA HA HA HA!
FUMP...
PLEASE... DON'T FORCE YOURSELF TO LAUGH...
HEW

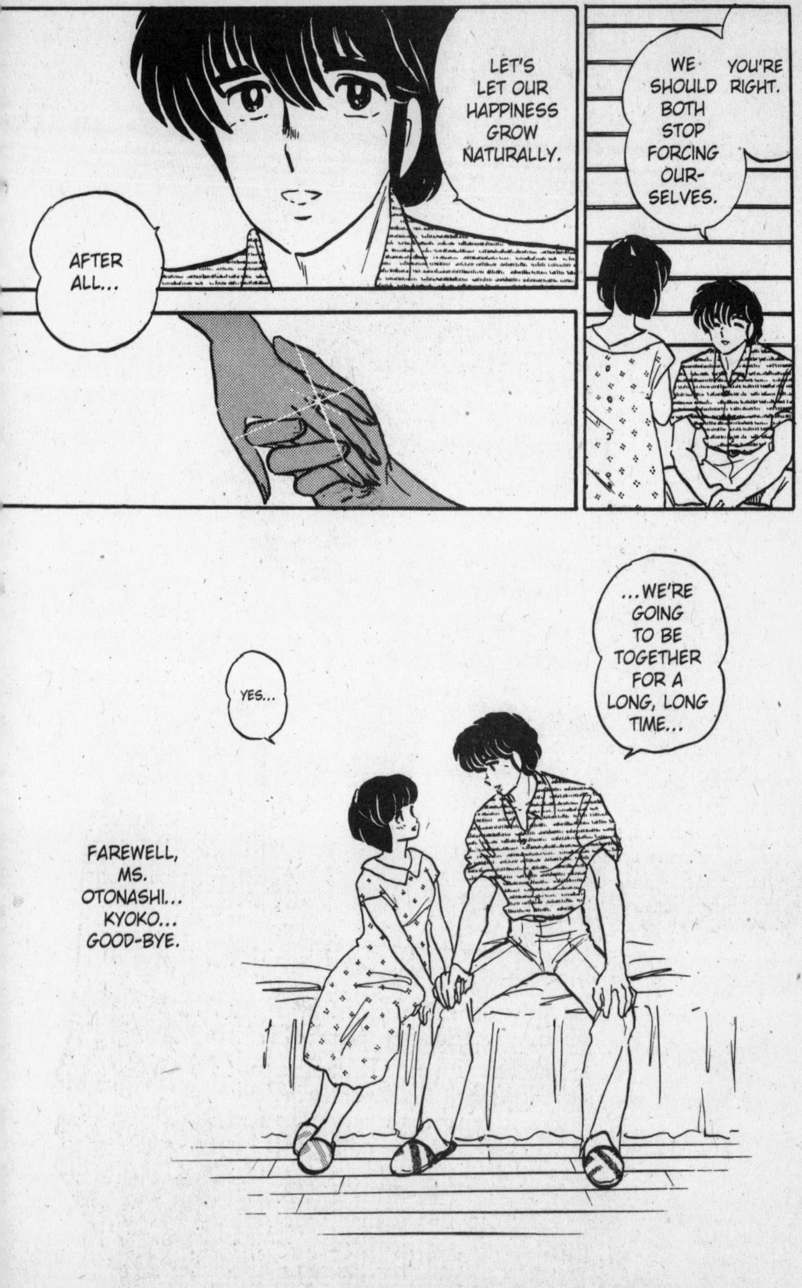
LET'S LET OUR HAPPINESS GROW NATURALLY.
AFTER ALL...
WE SHOULD BOTH STOP FORCING OURSELVES.
YOU'RE RIGHT.
...WE'RE GOING TO BE TOGETHER FOR A LONG, LONG TIME...
YES...
FAREWELL, MS. OTONASHI... KYOKO... GOOD-BYE.

PART THREE
TWISTS UPON TWISTS

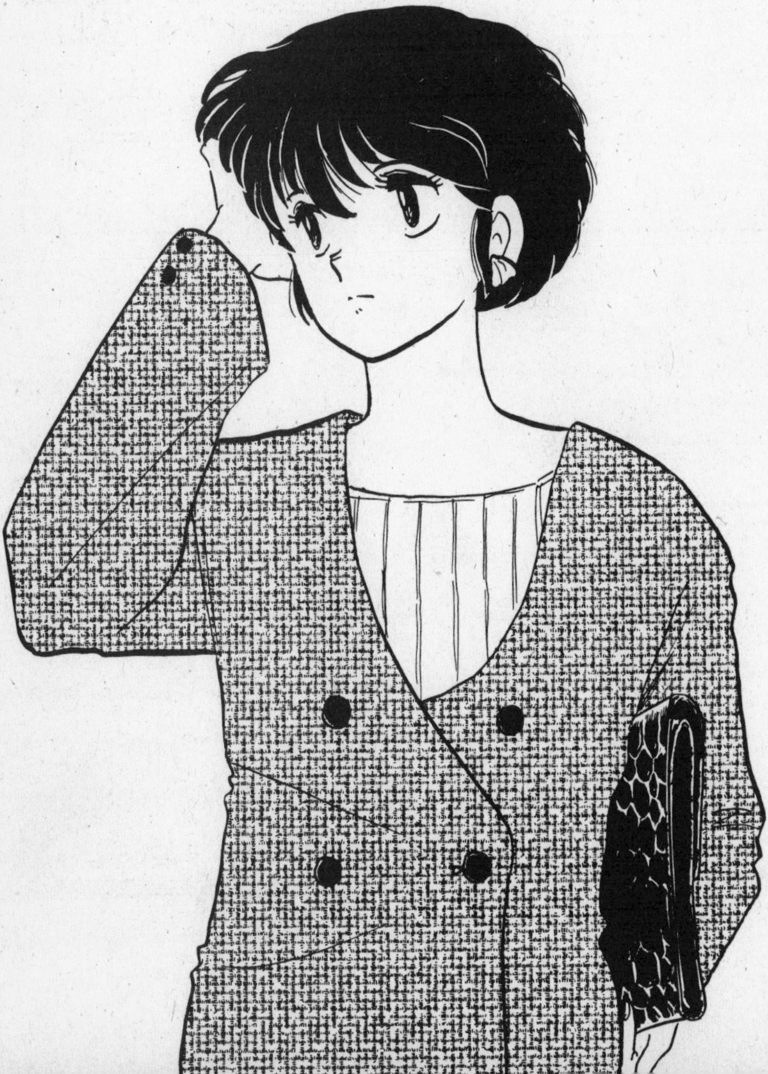

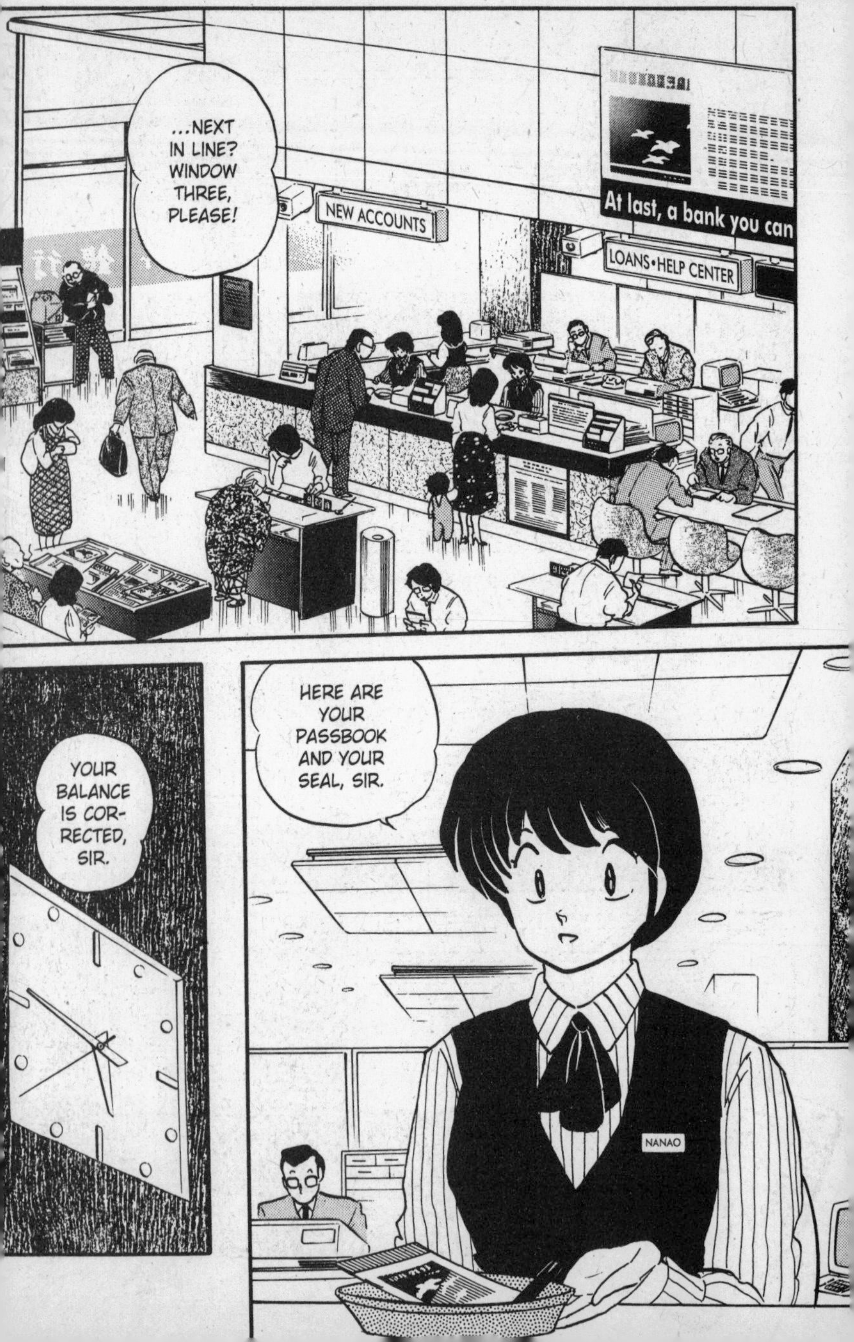
...NEXT IN LINE? WINDOW THREE, PLEASE!
NEW ACCOUNTS
At last, a bank you can
LOANS•HELP CENTER
YOUR BALANCE IS COR-RECTED, SIR.
HERE ARE YOUR PASSBOOK AND YOUR SEAL, SIR.
NANAO

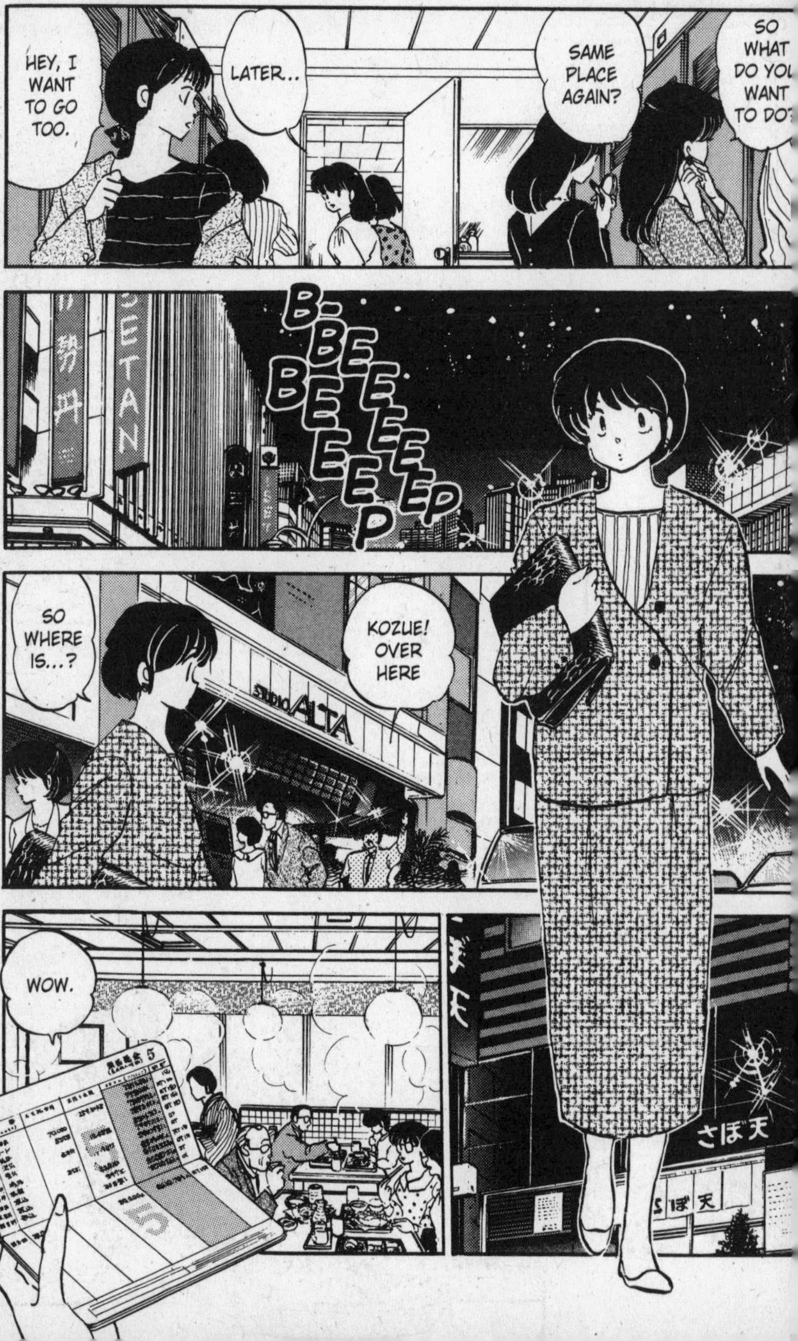

SO WHAT DO YOU WANT TO DO?
SAME PLACE AGAIN?
LATER...
HEY, I WANT TO GO TOO.
SETAN
B-BEEEEEP
BEEEEEP
KOZUE! OVER HERE
STUDIO ALTA
SO WHERE IS...?
さぼ天
さぼ天
WOW.

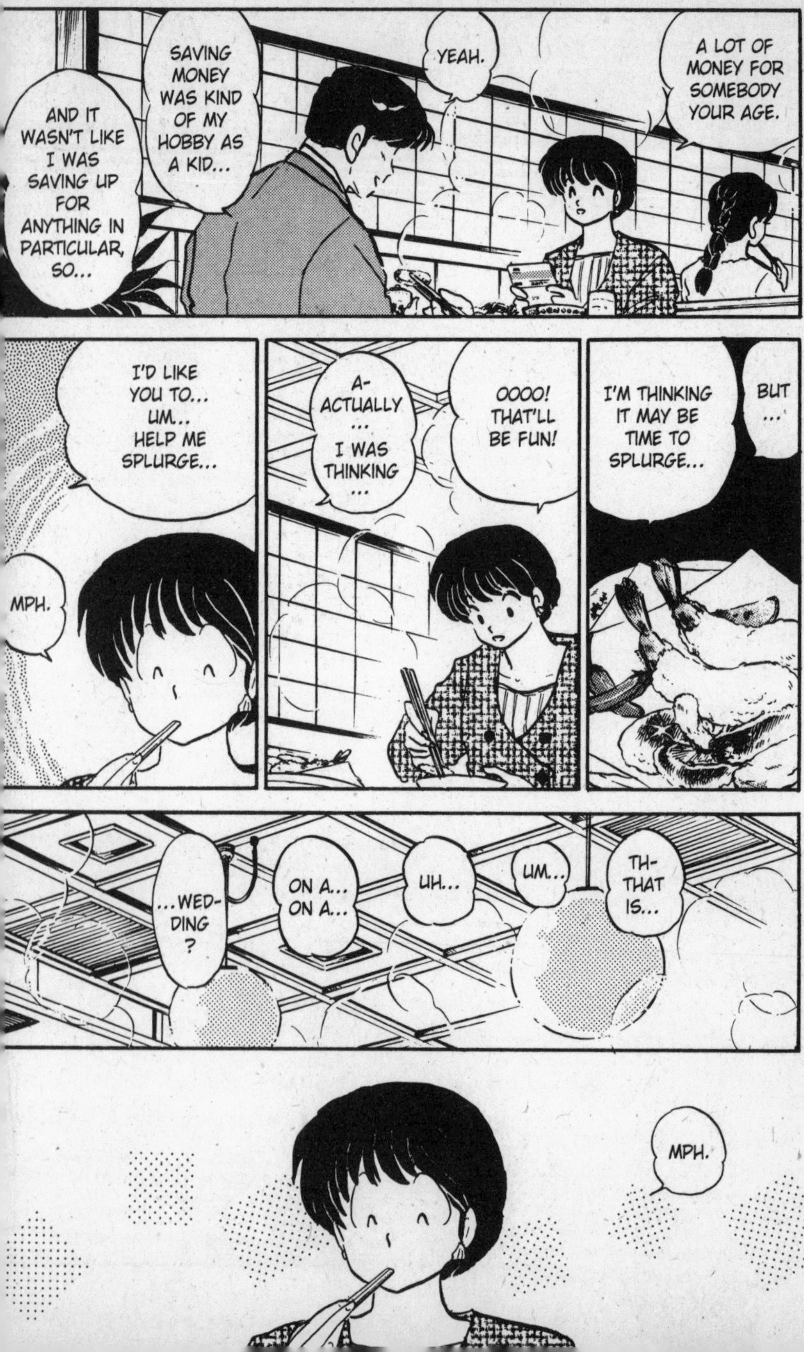
A LOT OF MONEY FOR SOMEBODY YOUR AGE.
YEAH.
SAVING MONEY WAS KIND OF MY HOBBY AS A KID...
AND IT WASN'T LIKE I WAS SAVING UP FOR ANYTHING IN PARTICULAR, SO...
BUT...
I'M THINKING IT MAY BE TIME TO SPLURGE...
OOOO! THAT'LL BE FUN!
A- ACTUALLY... I WAS THINKING...
I'D LIKE YOU TO... UM... HELP ME SPLURGE...
MPH.
TH- THAT IS...
UM...
UH...
ON A... ON A...
...WED-DING?
MPH.

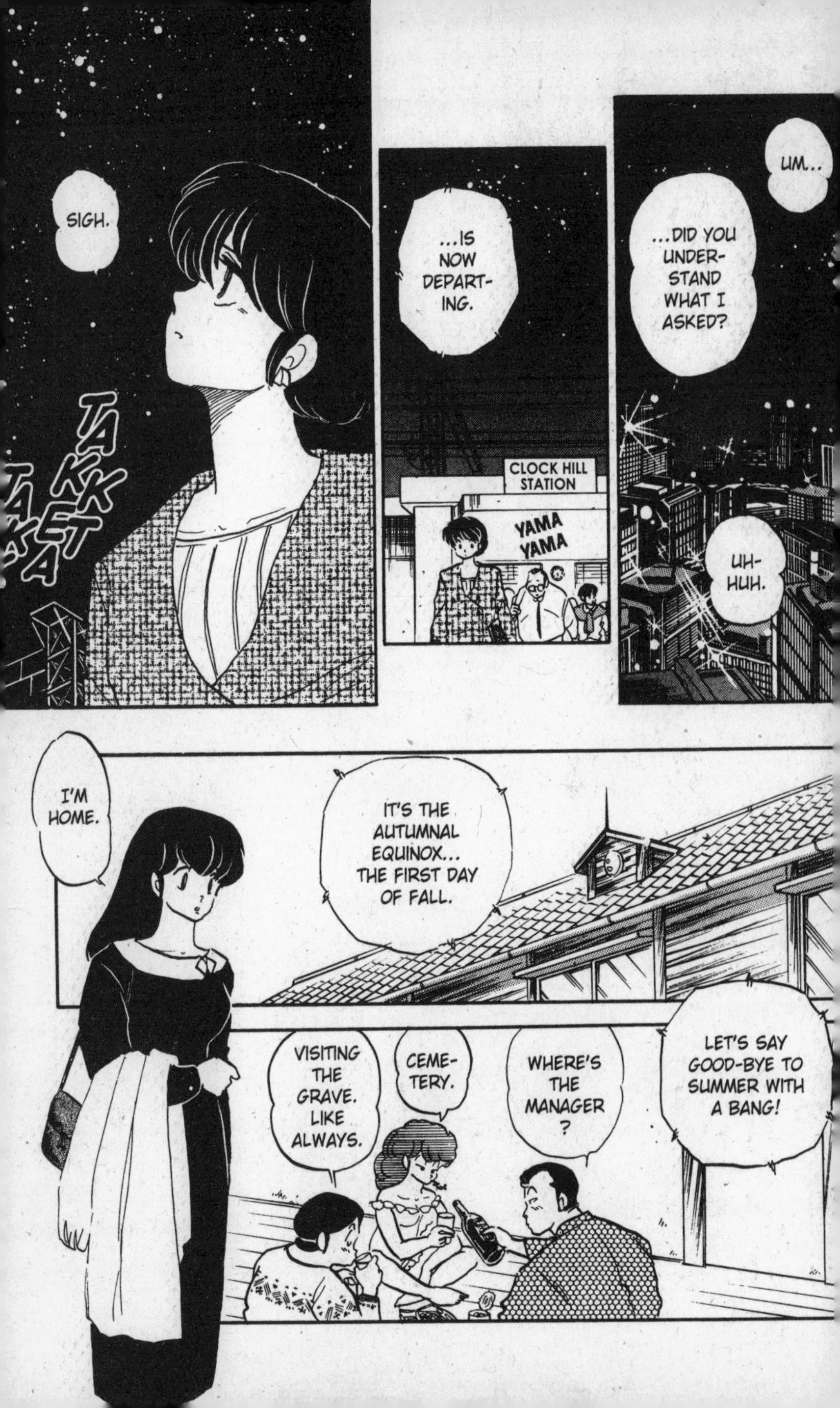
SIGH.
TAKKETA
...IS NOW DEPARTING.
CLOCK HILL STATION
YAMA YAMA
UM...
...DID YOU UNDERSTAND WHAT I ASKED?
UH-HUH.
I'M HOME.
IT'S THE AUTUMNAL EQUINOX... THE FIRST DAY OF FALL.
LET'S SAY GOOD-BYE TO SUMMER WITH A BANG!
WHERE'S THE MANAGER?
CEMETERY.
VISITING THE GRAVE. LIKE ALWAYS.

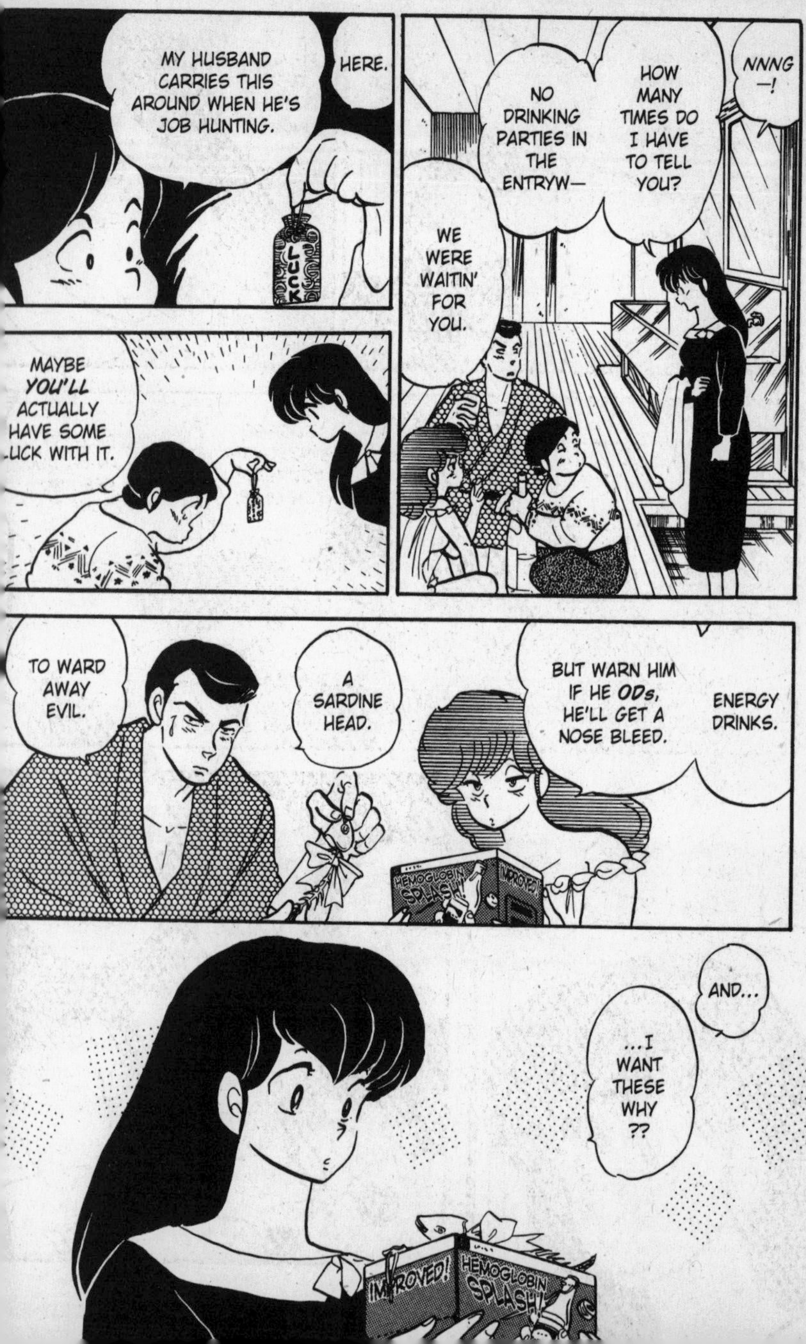
NNNG —!
HOW MANY TIMES DO I HAVE TO TELL YOU?
NO DRINKING PARTIES IN THE ENTRYW—
WE WERE WAITIN' FOR YOU.
HERE.
MY HUSBAND CARRIES THIS AROUND WHEN HE'S JOB HUNTING.
LUCK
MAYBE *YOU'LL* ACTUALLY HAVE SOME LUCK WITH IT.
ENERGY DRINKS.
BUT WARN HIM IF HE *ODs*, HE'LL GET A NOSE BLEED.
HEMOGLOBIN SPLASH!
IMPROVED!
A SARDINE HEAD.
TO WARD AWAY EVIL.
AND...
...I WANT THESE WHY ??
IMPROVED!
HEMOGLOBIN SPLASH!

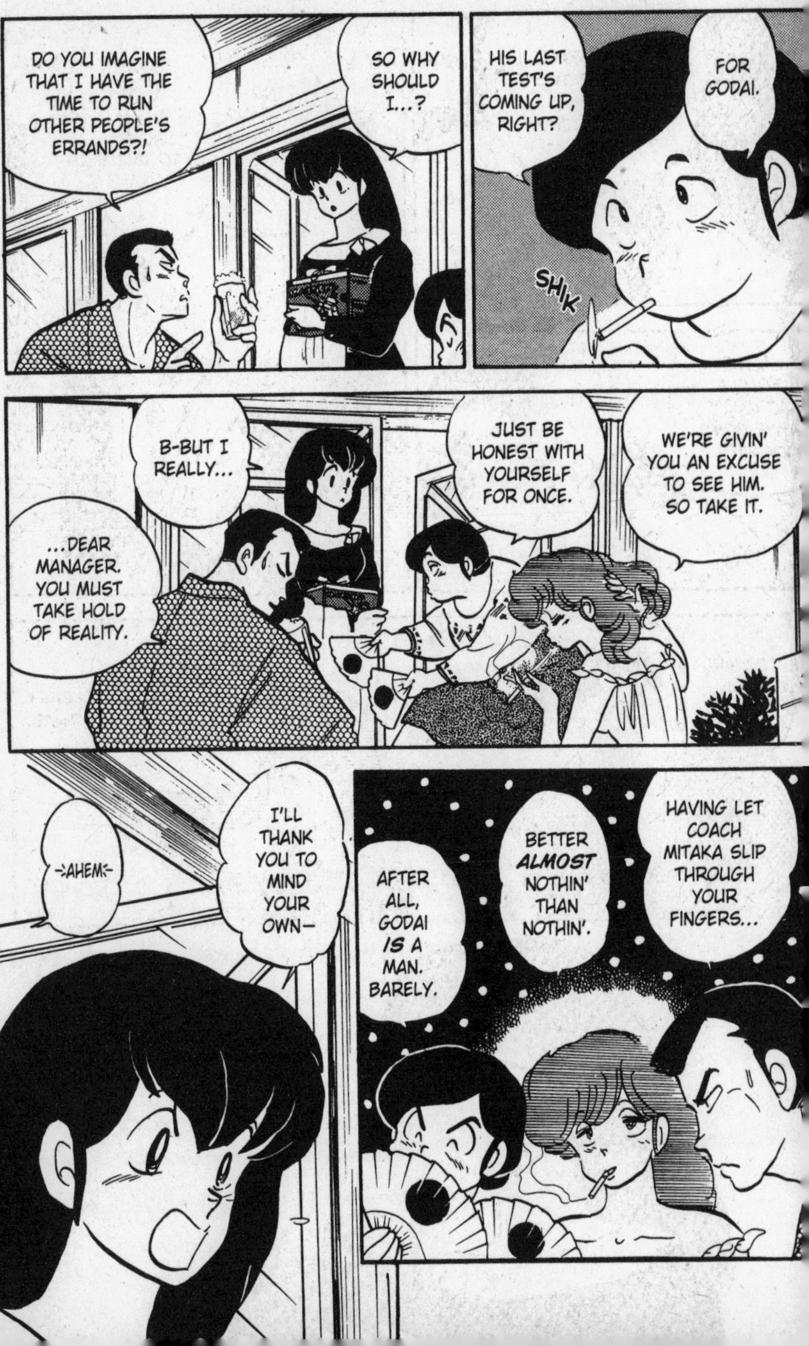
FOR GODAI.
HIS LAST TEST'S COMING UP, RIGHT?
SHIK
SO WHY SHOULD I...?
DO YOU IMAGINE THAT I HAVE THE TIME TO RUN OTHER PEOPLE'S ERRANDS?!
WE'RE GIVIN' YOU AN EXCUSE TO SEE HIM. SO TAKE IT.
JUST BE HONEST WITH YOURSELF FOR ONCE.
B-BUT I REALLY...
...DEAR MANAGER. YOU MUST TAKE HOLD OF REALITY.
HAVING LET COACH MITAKA SLIP THROUGH YOUR FINGERS...
BETTER *ALMOST* NOTHIN' THAN NOTHIN'.
AFTER ALL, GODAI *IS* A MAN. BARELY.
I'LL THANK YOU TO MIND YOUR OWN—
-AHEM-

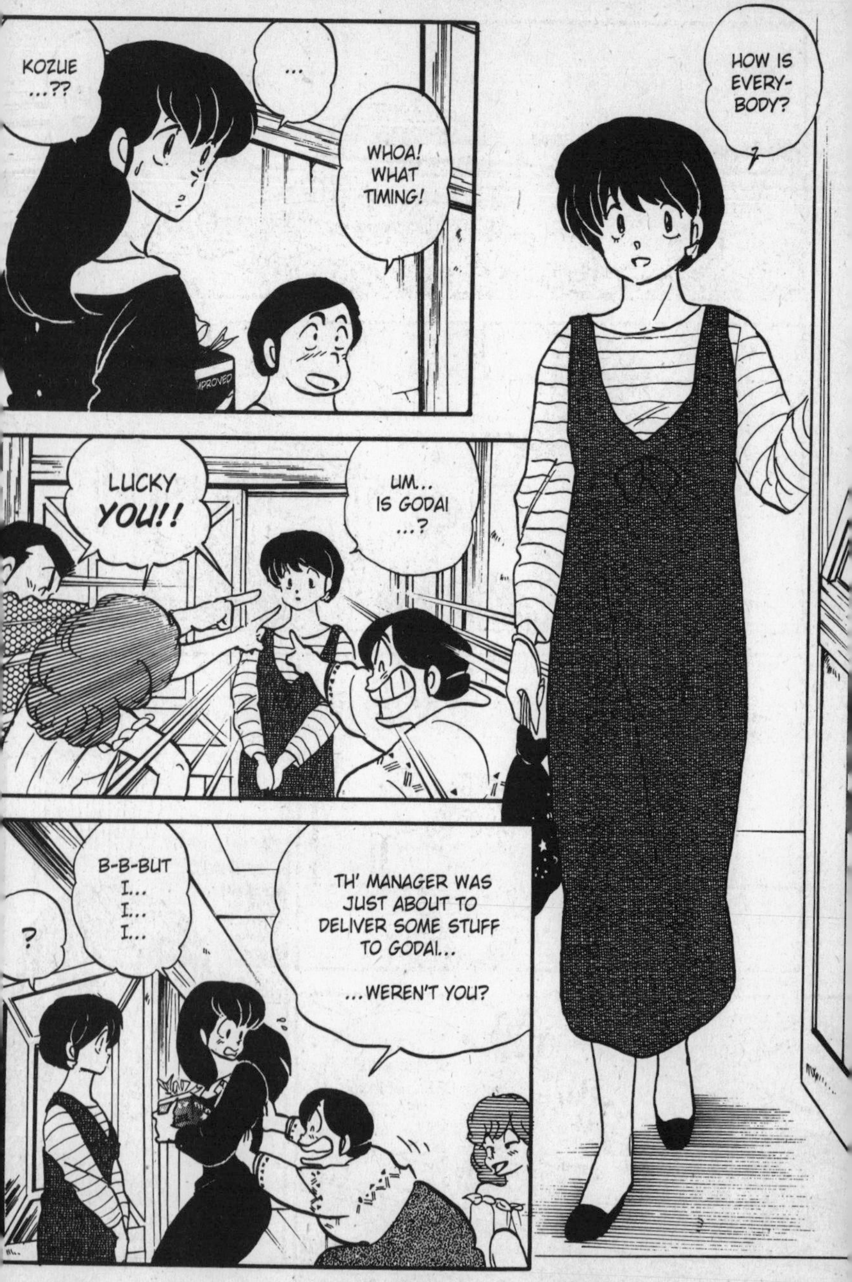

HOW IS EVERY-BODY?
KOZUE ...??
...
WHOA! WHAT TIMING!
IMPROVED
UM... IS GODAI ...?
LUCKY YOU!!
TH' MANAGER WAS JUST ABOUT TO DELIVER SOME STUFF TO GODAI... ...WEREN'T YOU?
B-B-BUT I... I... I...
?

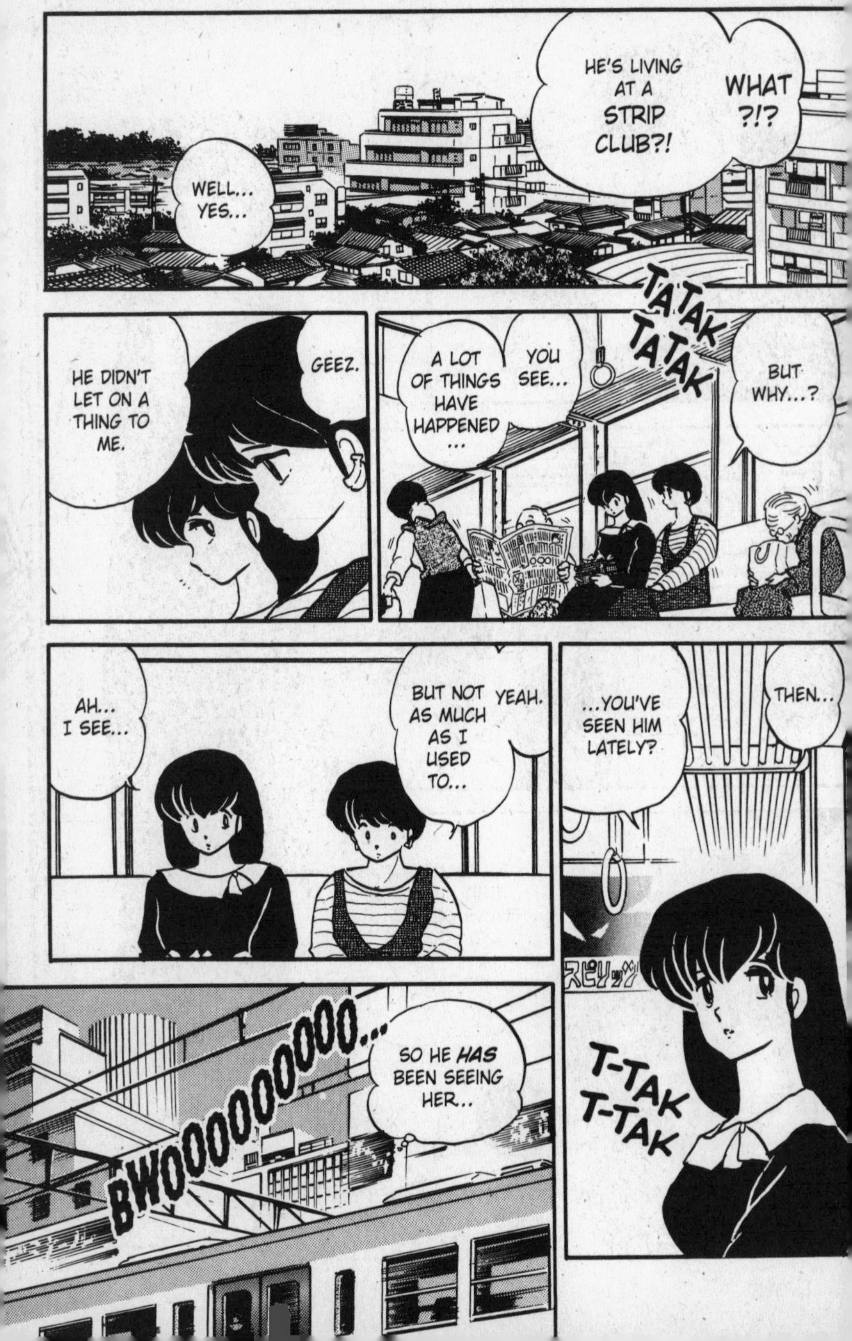
WHAT ?!?
HE'S LIVING AT A STRIP CLUB?!
WELL... YES...
BUT WHY...?
TATAK TATAK
YOU SEE...
A LOT OF THINGS HAVE HAPPENED ...
GEEZ.
HE DIDN'T LET ON A THING TO ME.
THEN...
...YOU'VE SEEN HIM LATELY?
T-TAK T-TAK
YEAH.
BUT NOT AS MUCH AS I USED TO...
AH... I SEE...
BWOOOOOOOOO...
SO HE *HAS* BEEN SEEING HER...

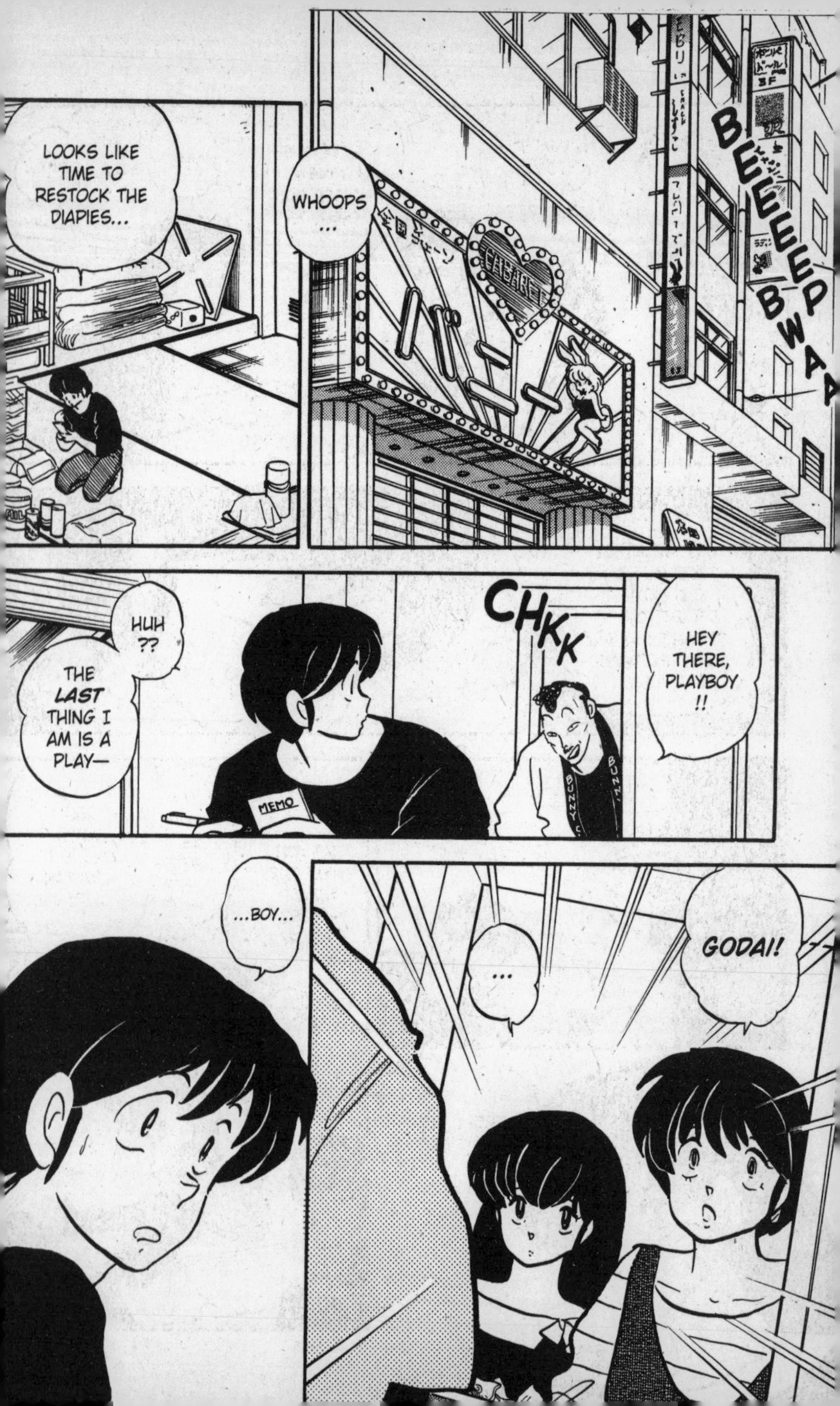
BEEEEEP BWAP
CABARET
WHOOPS ...
LOOKS LIKE TIME TO RESTOCK THE DIAPIES...
HEY THERE, PLAYBOY !!
CHKK
BUNNY
MEMO
HUH ??
THE *LAST* THING I AM IS A PLAY—
GODAI!
...
...BOY...

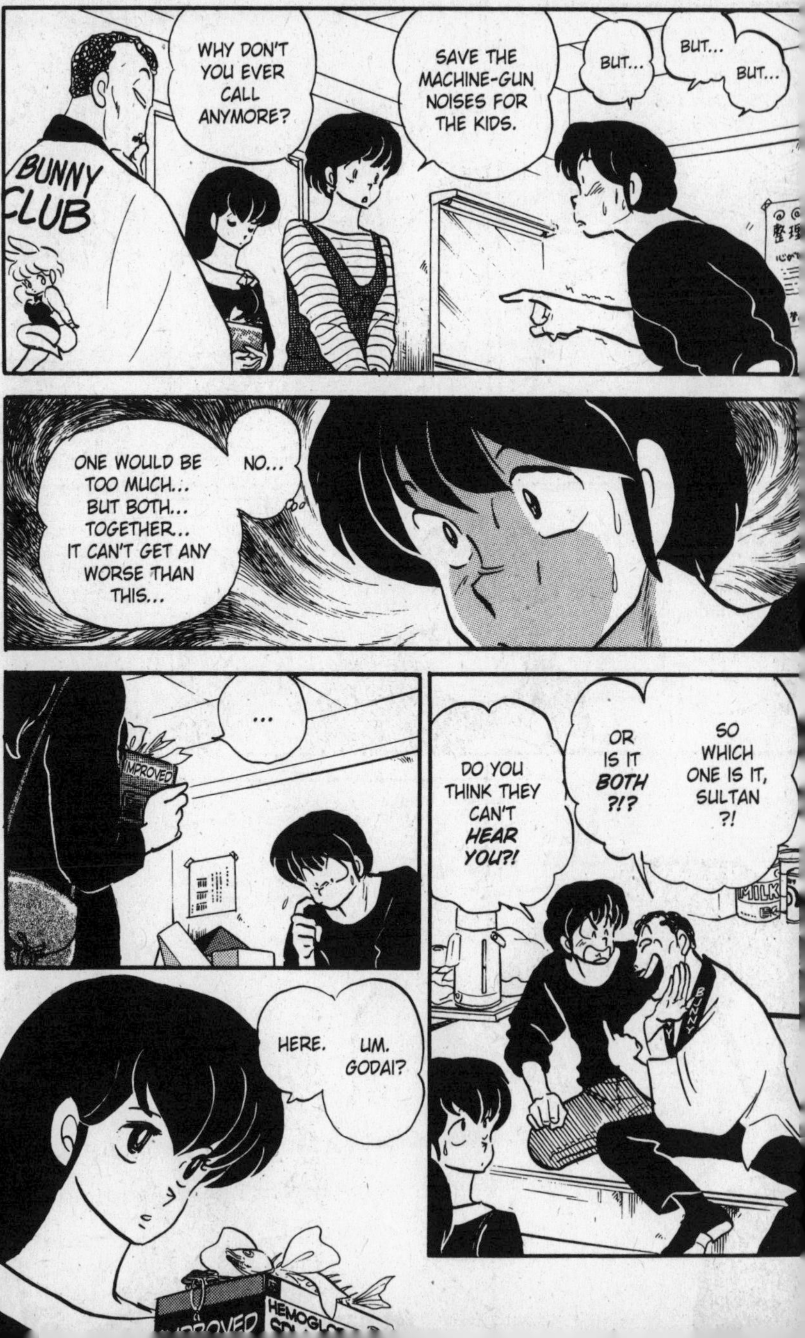
BUNNY CLUB
WHY DON'T YOU EVER CALL ANYMORE?
SAVE THE MACHINE-GUN NOISES FOR THE KIDS.
BUT...
BUT... BUT...
ONE WOULD BE TOO MUCH... BUT BOTH... TOGETHER... IT CAN'T GET ANY WORSE THAN THIS...
NO...
...
DO YOU THINK THEY CAN'T *HEAR YOU?!*
OR IS IT *BOTH ?!?*
SO WHICH ONE IS IT, SULTAN ?!
BUNNY
HERE.
UM. GODAI?

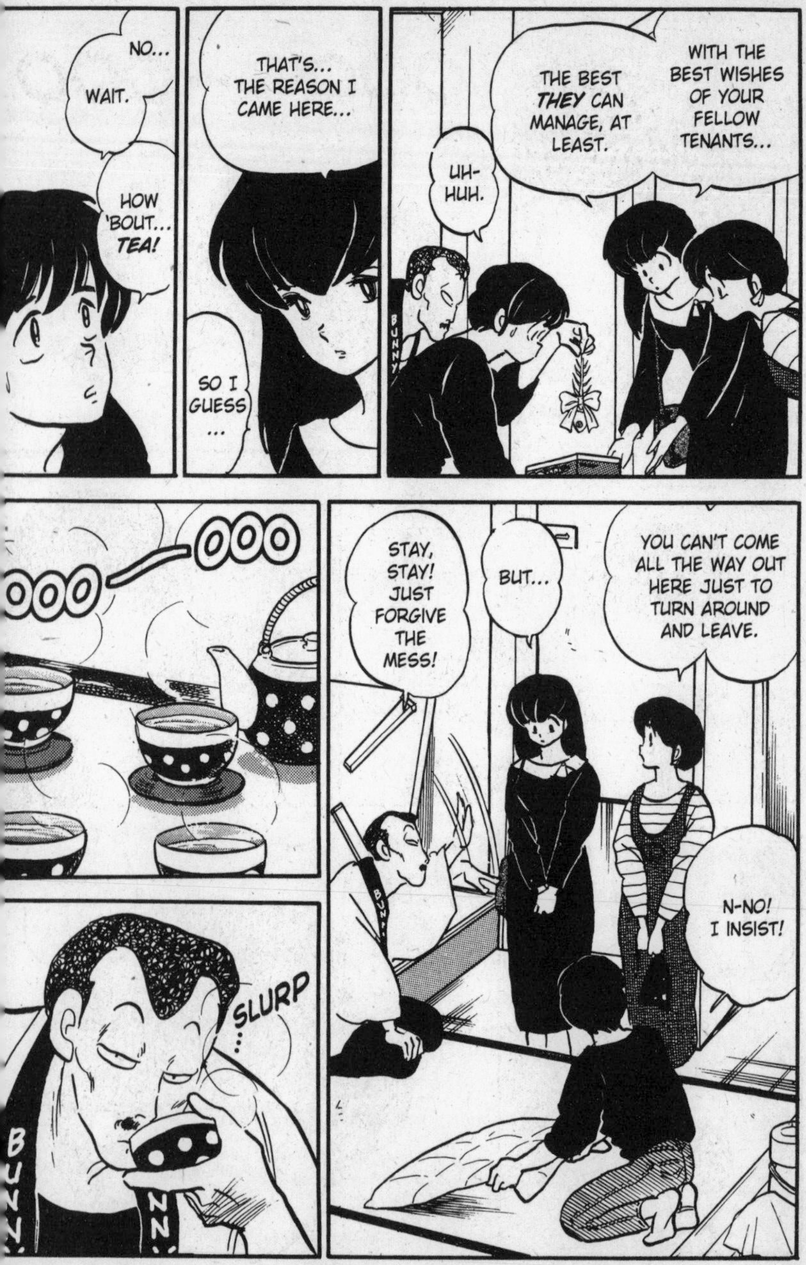
WITH THE BEST WISHES OF YOUR FELLOW TENANTS...
THE BEST *THEY* CAN MANAGE, AT LEAST.
UH-HUH.
THAT'S... THE REASON I CAME HERE...
SO I GUESS ...
NO...
WAIT.
HOW 'BOUT... *TEA!*
YOU CAN'T COME ALL THE WAY OUT HERE JUST TO TURN AROUND AND LEAVE.
BUT...
STAY, STAY! JUST FORGIVE THE MESS!
N-NO! I INSIST!
OOO—OOO
SLURP...
BUNNY

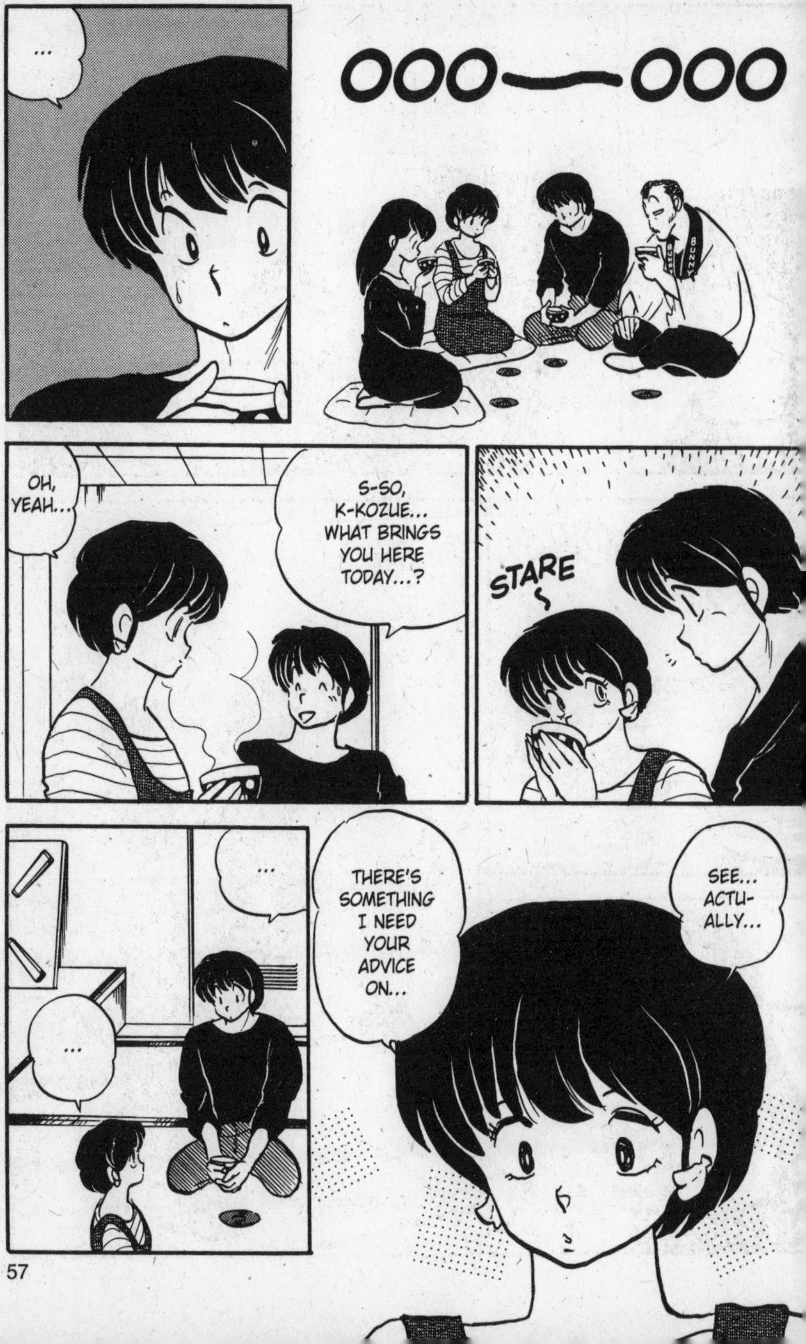
OOO——OOO
...
STARE
S-SO, K-KOZUE... WHAT BRINGS YOU HERE TODAY...?
OH, YEAH...
SEE... ACTU-ALLY...
THERE'S SOMETHING I NEED YOUR ADVICE ON...
...
...

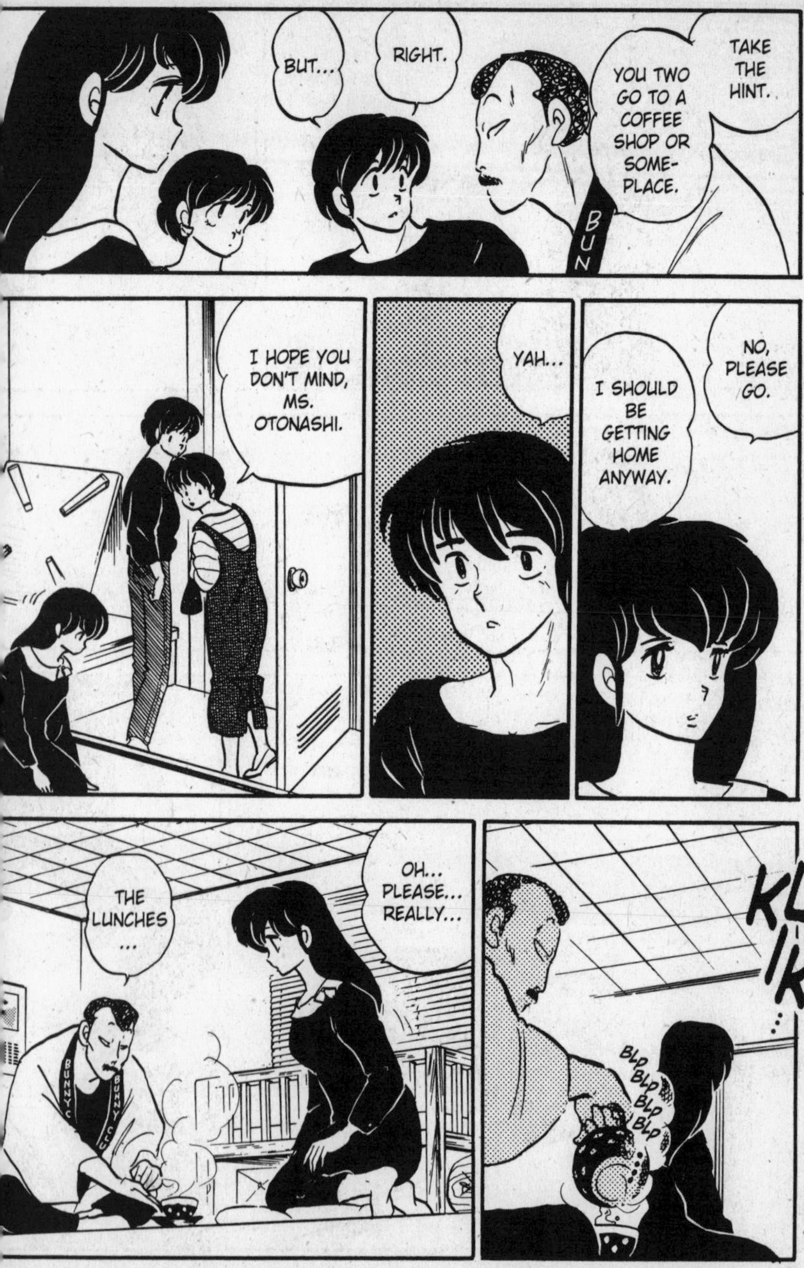

BUT...
RIGHT.
YOU TWO GO TO A COFFEE SHOP OR SOME-PLACE.
TAKE THE HINT.
BUN
I HOPE YOU DON'T MIND, MS. OTONASHI.
YAH...
I SHOULD BE GETTING HOME ANYWAY.
NO, PLEASE GO.
THE LUNCHES ...
OH... PLEASE... REALLY...
BUNNY C
KLIK...
BLP BLP BLP BLP

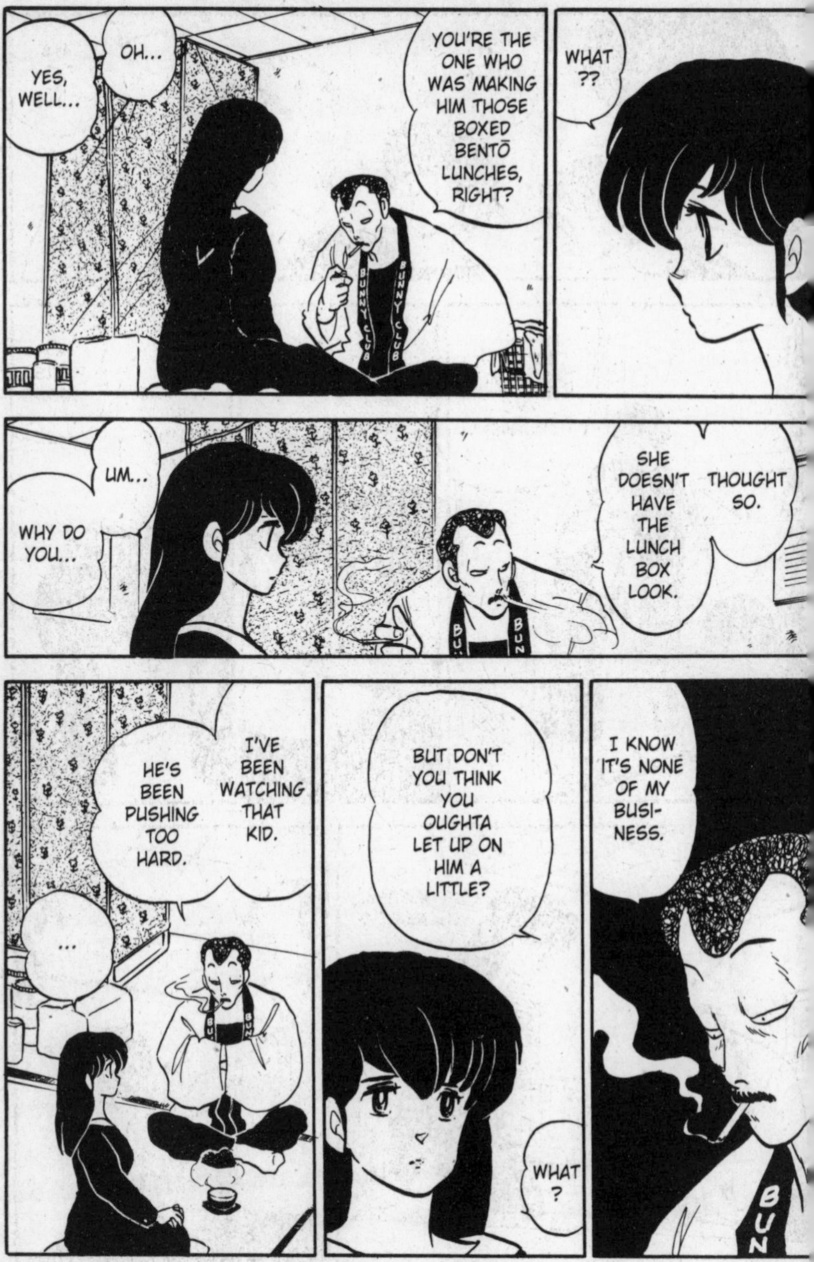

OH...
YES, WELL...
YOU'RE THE ONE WHO WAS MAKING HIM THOSE BOXED BENTŌ LUNCHES, RIGHT?
BUNNY CLUB
BUNNY CLUB
WHAT ??
UM...
WHY DO YOU...
SHE DOESN'T HAVE THE LUNCH BOX LOOK.
THOUGHT SO.
I'VE BEEN WATCHING THAT KID.
HE'S BEEN PUSHING TOO HARD.
...
BUT DON'T YOU THINK YOU OUGHTA LET UP ON HIM A LITTLE?
WHAT ?
I KNOW IT'S NONE OF MY BUSI-NESS.

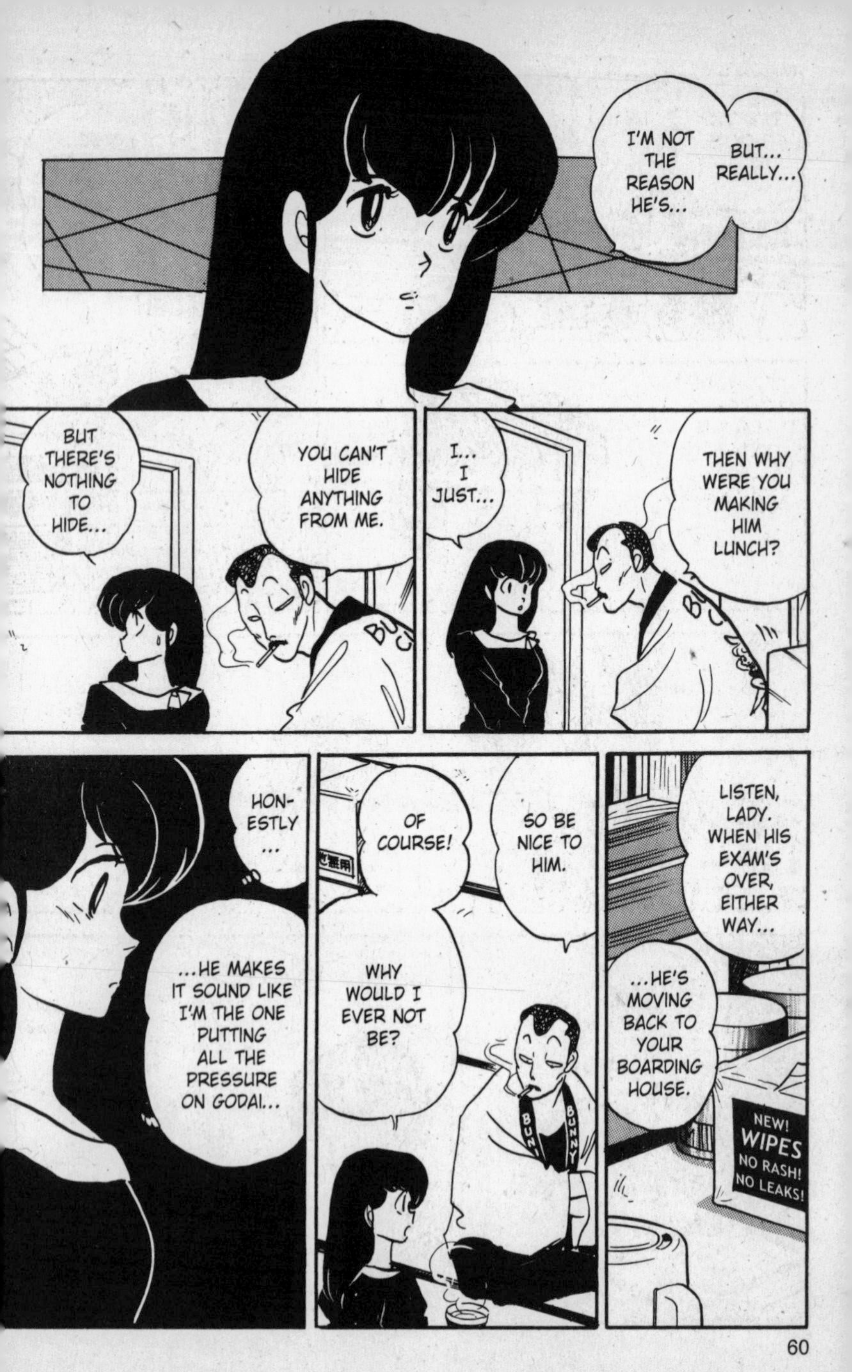

BUT... REALLY...
I'M NOT THE REASON HE'S...
THEN WHY WERE YOU MAKING HIM LUNCH?
I... I JUST...
YOU CAN'T HIDE ANYTHING FROM ME.
BUT THERE'S NOTHING TO HIDE...
LISTEN, LADY. WHEN HIS EXAM'S OVER, EITHER WAY...
...HE'S MOVING BACK TO YOUR BOARDING HOUSE.
NEW! WIPES NO RASH! NO LEAKS!
SO BE NICE TO HIM.
OF COURSE!
WHY WOULD I EVER NOT BE?
HON- ESTLY ...
...HE MAKES IT SOUND LIKE I'M THE ONE PUTTING ALL THE PRESSURE ON GODAI...

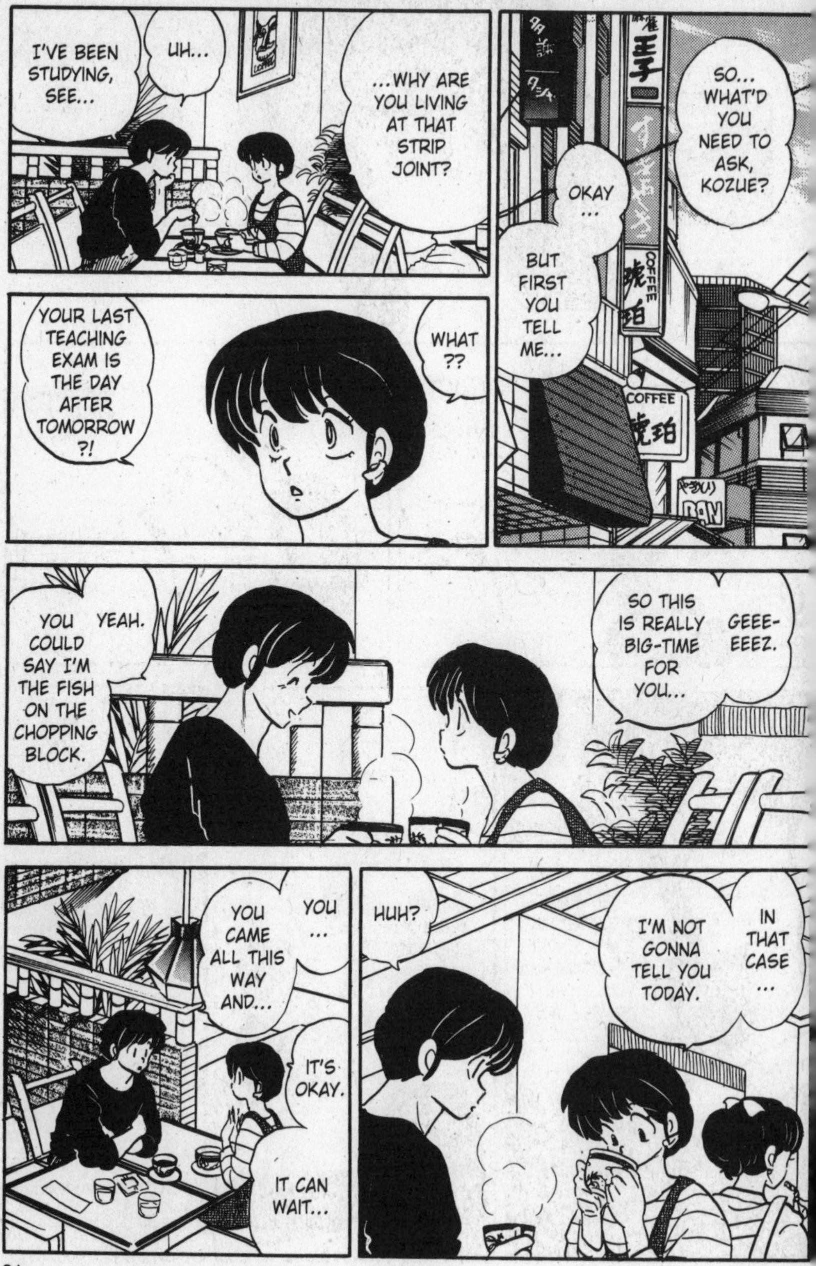

SO... WHAT'D YOU NEED TO ASK, KOZUE?
OKAY ...
BUT FIRST YOU TELL ME...
COFFEE
COFFEE
...WHY ARE YOU LIVING AT THAT STRIP JOINT?
UH...
I'VE BEEN STUDYING, SEE...
WHAT ??
YOUR LAST TEACHING EXAM IS THE DAY AFTER TOMORROW ?!
GEEE-EEEZ.
SO THIS IS REALLY BIG-TIME FOR YOU...
YEAH.
YOU COULD SAY I'M THE FISH ON THE CHOPPING BLOCK.
IN THAT CASE ...
I'M NOT GONNA TELL YOU TODAY.
HUH?
YOU ...
YOU CAME ALL THIS WAY AND...
IT'S OKAY.
IT CAN WAIT...

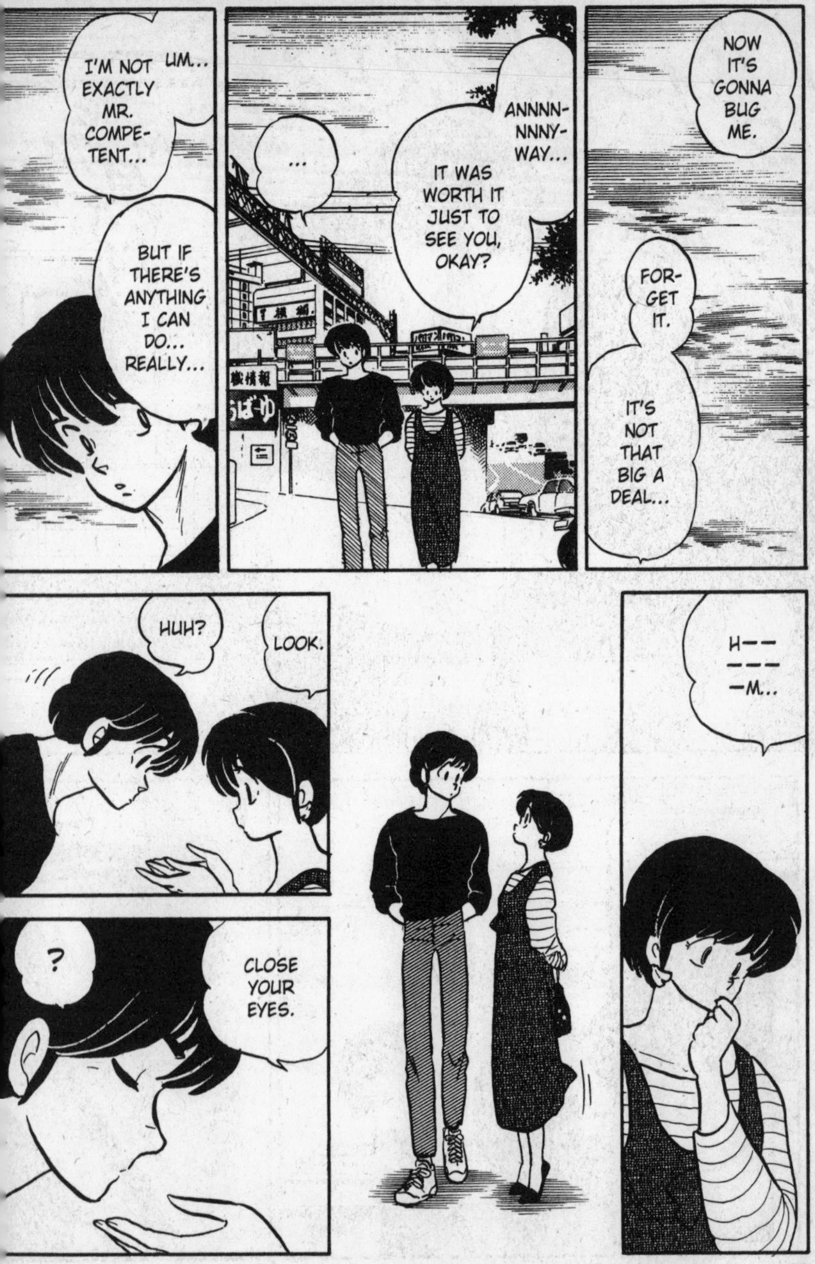
UM...
I'M NOT EXACTLY MR. COMPETENT...
BUT IF THERE'S ANYTHING I CAN DO... REALLY...
...
ANNNN-NNNY-WAY...
IT WAS WORTH IT JUST TO SEE YOU, OKAY?
NOW IT'S GONNA BUG ME.
FOR-GET IT.
IT'S NOT THAT BIG A DEAL...
HUH?
LOOK.
?
CLOSE YOUR EYES.
H-----M...

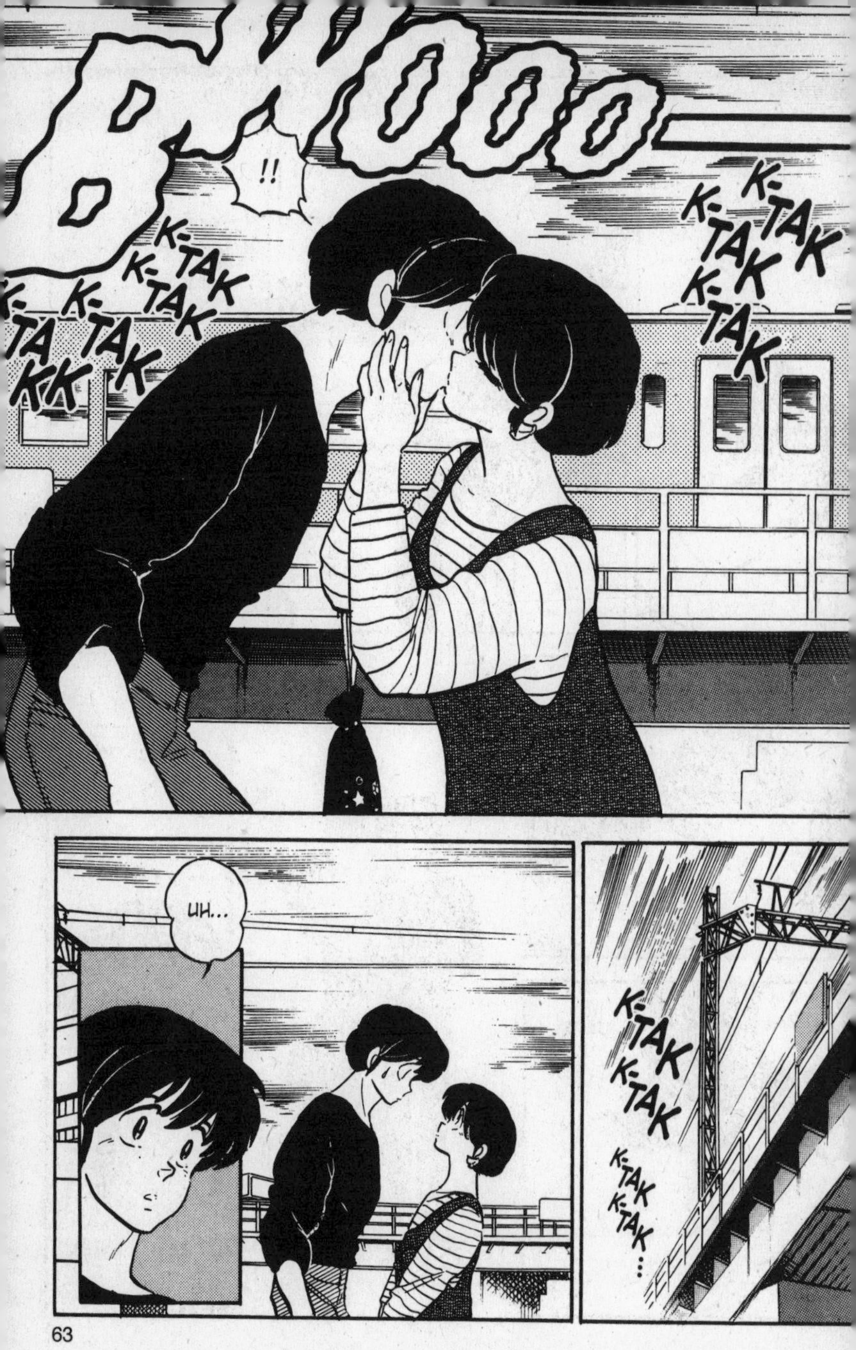
B'WOOO
!!
K-TAK K-TAK K-TAK K-TAK
K-TAK K-TAK K-TAK K-TAK K-TAK K-TAKK
uh...
K-TAK K-TAK K-TAK K-TAK...

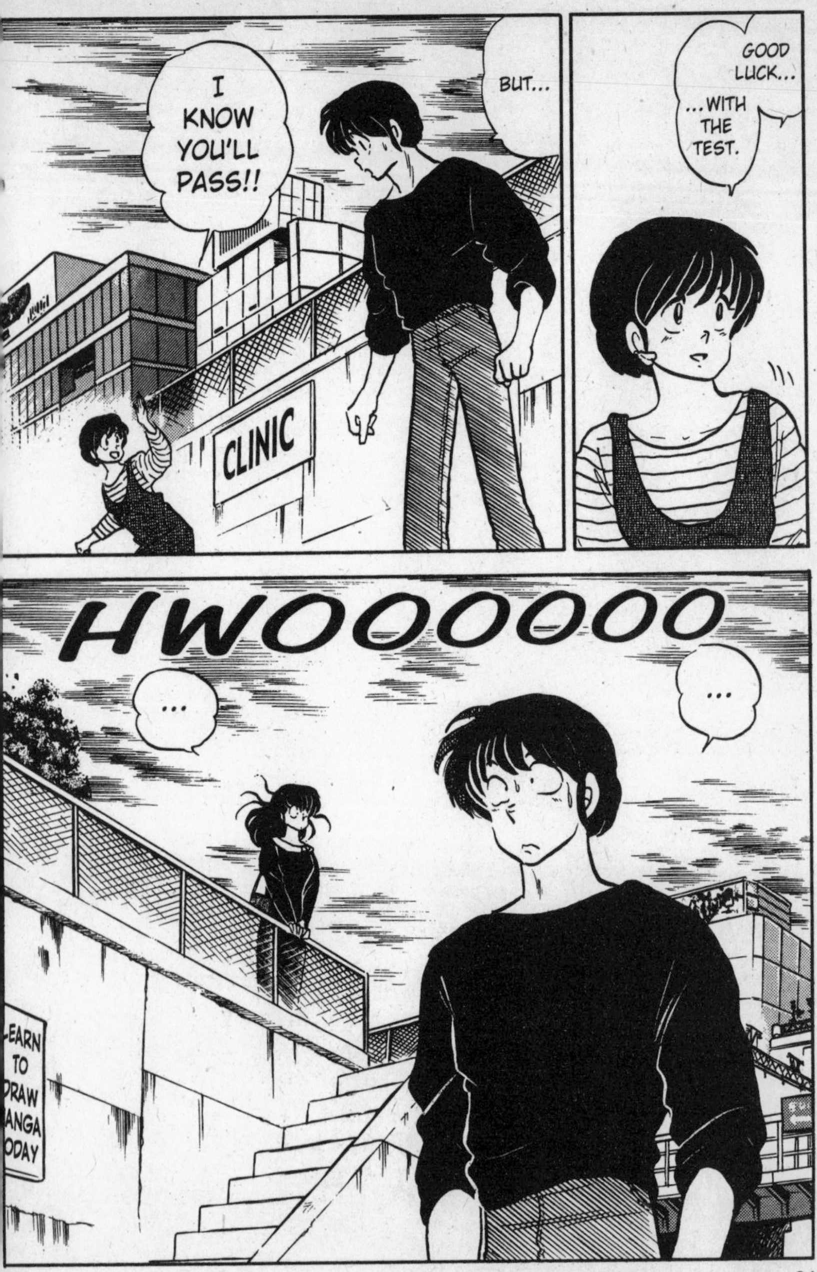
GOOD LUCK...
...WITH THE TEST.
BUT...
I KNOW YOU'LL PASS!!
CLINIC
HWOOOOOO
...
...
EARN TO DRAW ANGA ODAY

HAH
HAH
HAH

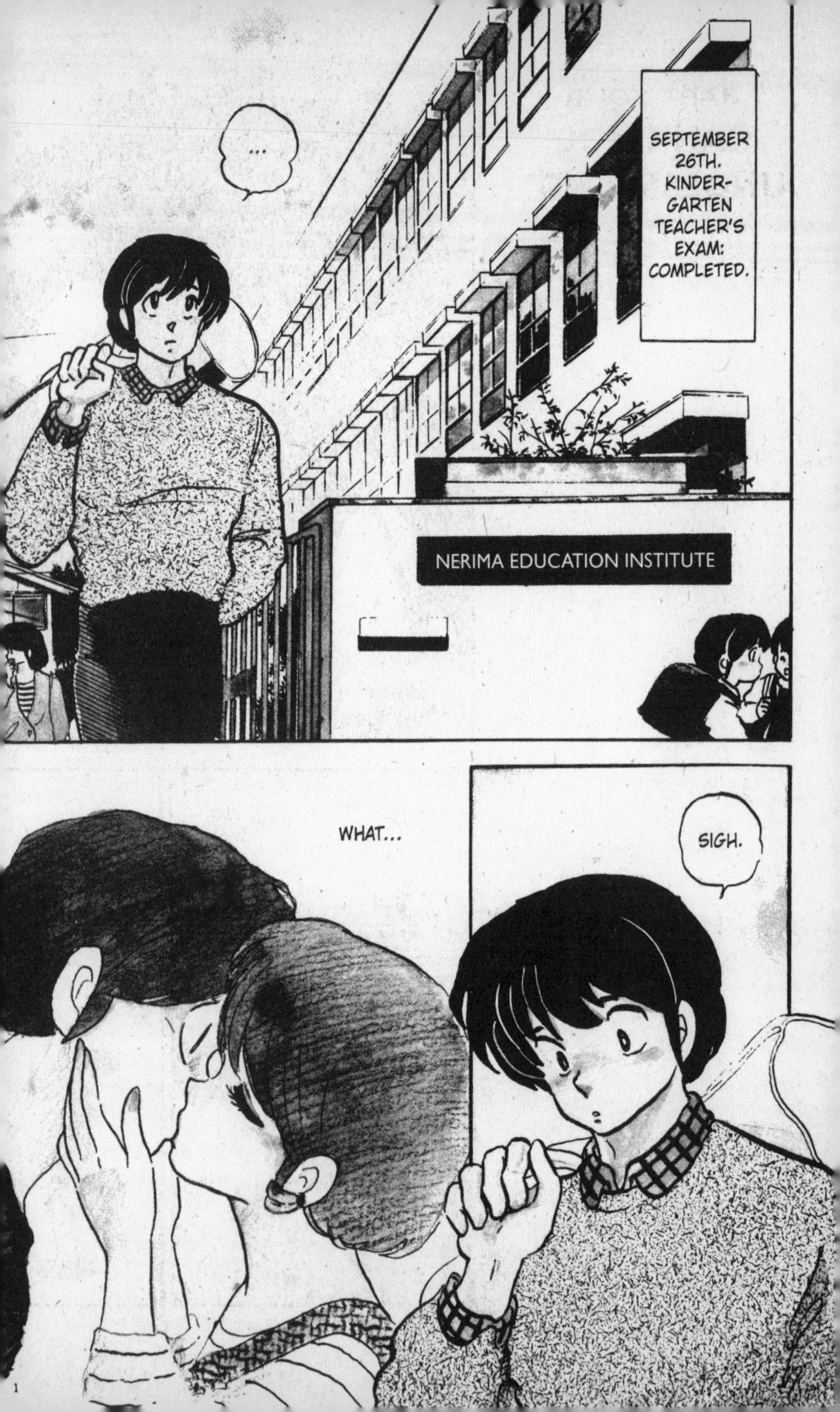
SEPTEMBER 26TH. KINDER-GARTEN TEACHER'S EXAM: COMPLETED.
...
NERIMA EDUCATION INSTITUTE
SIGH.
WHAT...

PART FOUR
CAN'T YOU UNDERSTAND?

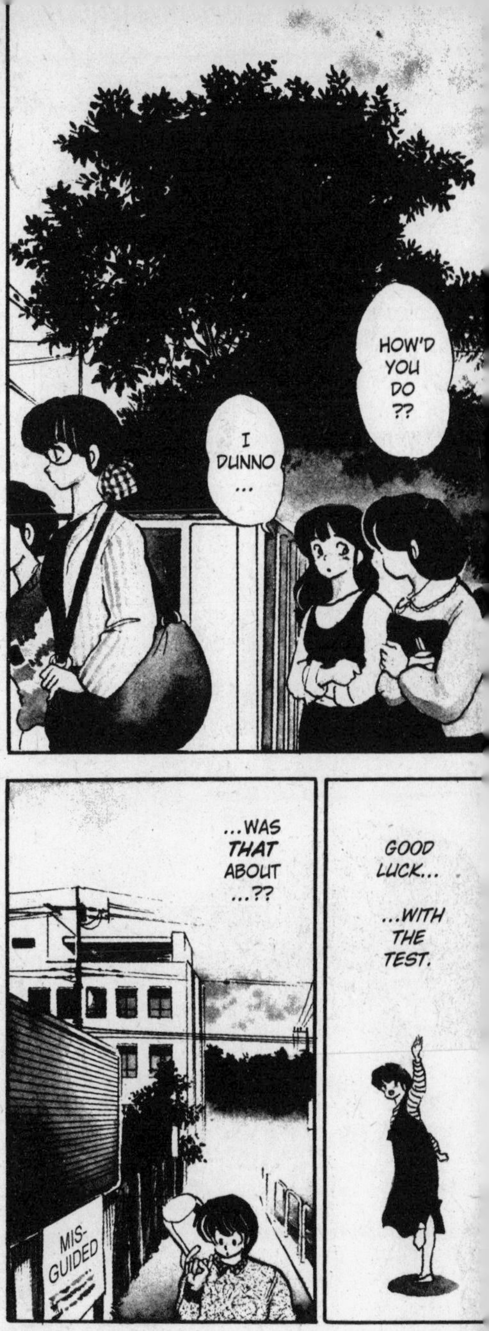
HOW'D YOU DO ??
I DUNNO ...
GOOD LUCK...
...WITH THE TEST.
...WAS *THAT* ABOUT ...??
MIS-GUIDED

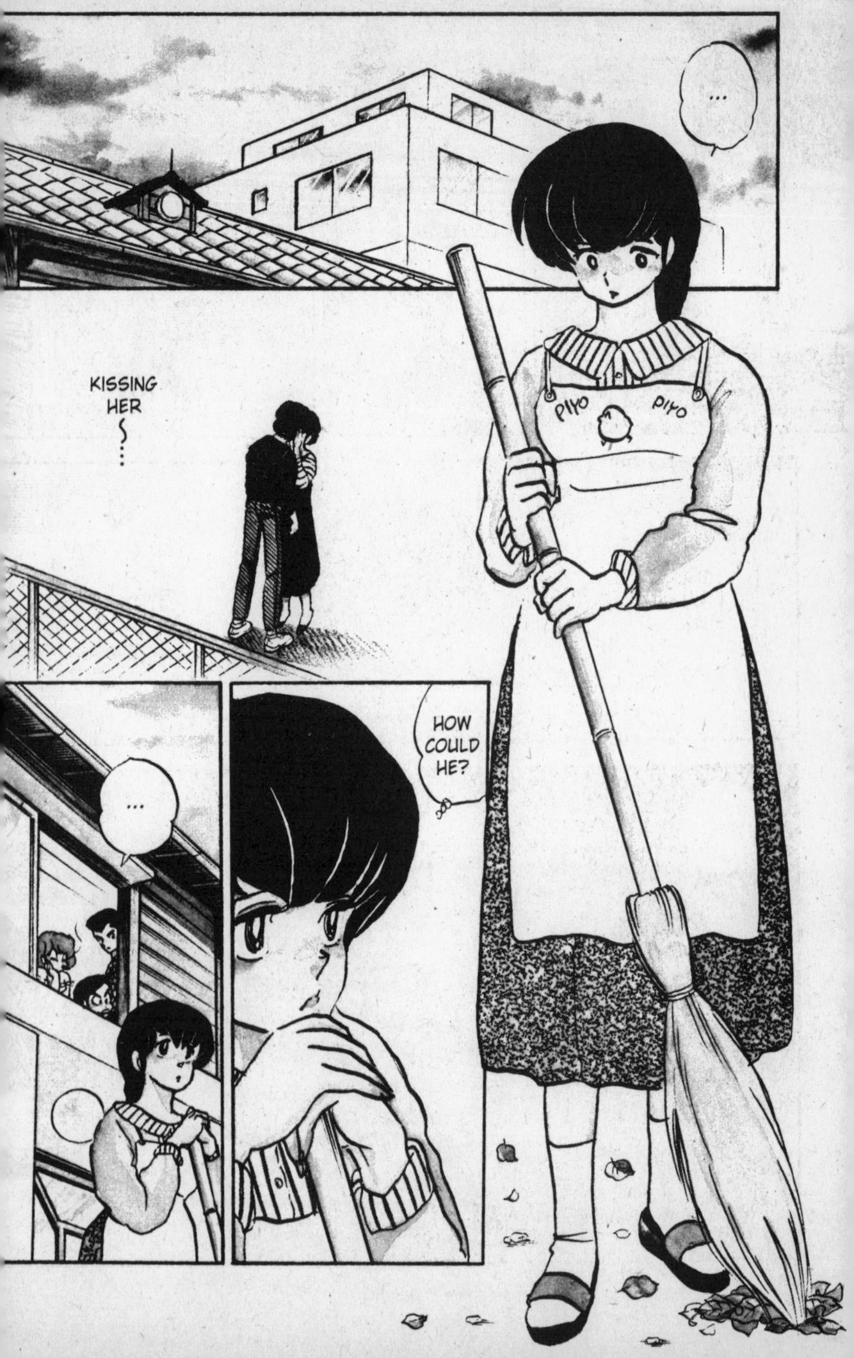

...
KISSING HER
HOW COULD HE?
...
PIYO PIYO

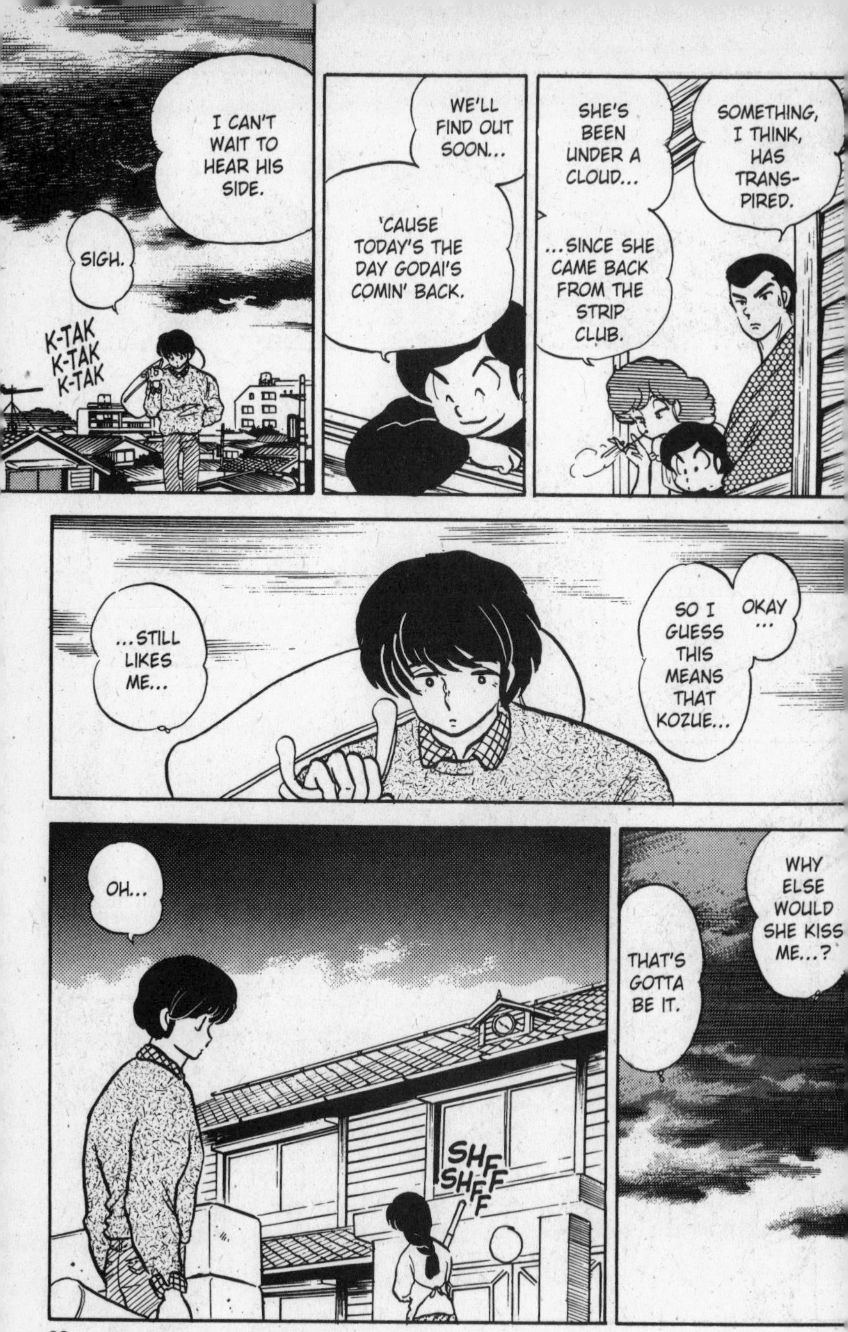
SOMETHING, I THINK, HAS TRANSPIRED.
SHE'S BEEN UNDER A CLOUD...
...SINCE SHE CAME BACK FROM THE STRIP CLUB.
WE'LL FIND OUT SOON...
'CAUSE TODAY'S THE DAY GODAI'S COMIN' BACK.
I CAN'T WAIT TO HEAR HIS SIDE.
SIGH.
K-TAK K-TAK K-TAK
OKAY...
SO I GUESS THIS MEANS THAT KOZUE...
...STILL LIKES ME...
WHY ELSE WOULD SHE KISS ME...?
THAT'S GOTTA BE IT.
OH...
SHFF SHFF

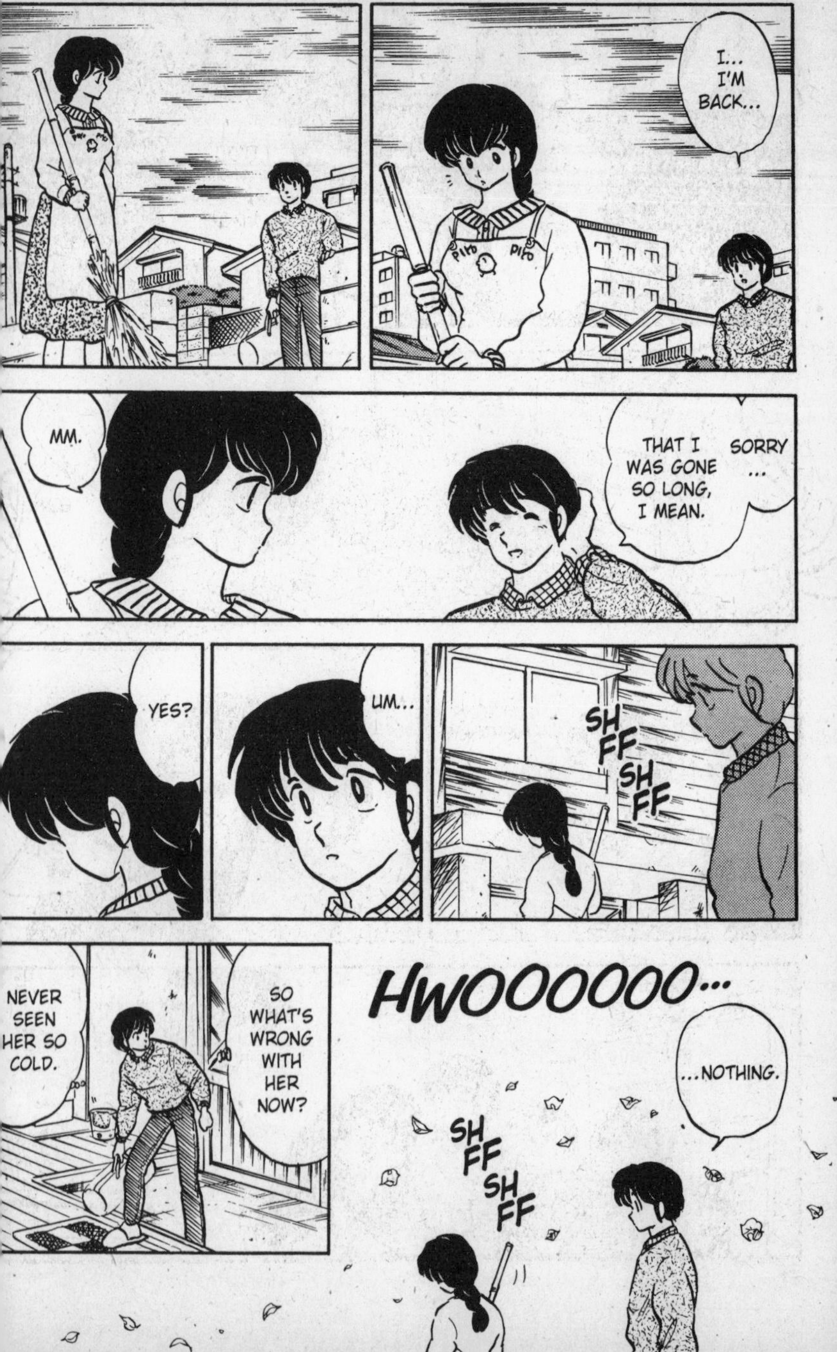
I... I'M BACK...
SORRY... THAT I WAS GONE SO LONG, I MEAN.
MM.
UM...
YES?
SH FF SH FF
HWOOOOOO...
...NOTHING.
SH FF SH FF
SO WHAT'S WRONG WITH HER NOW?
NEVER SEEN HER SO COLD.

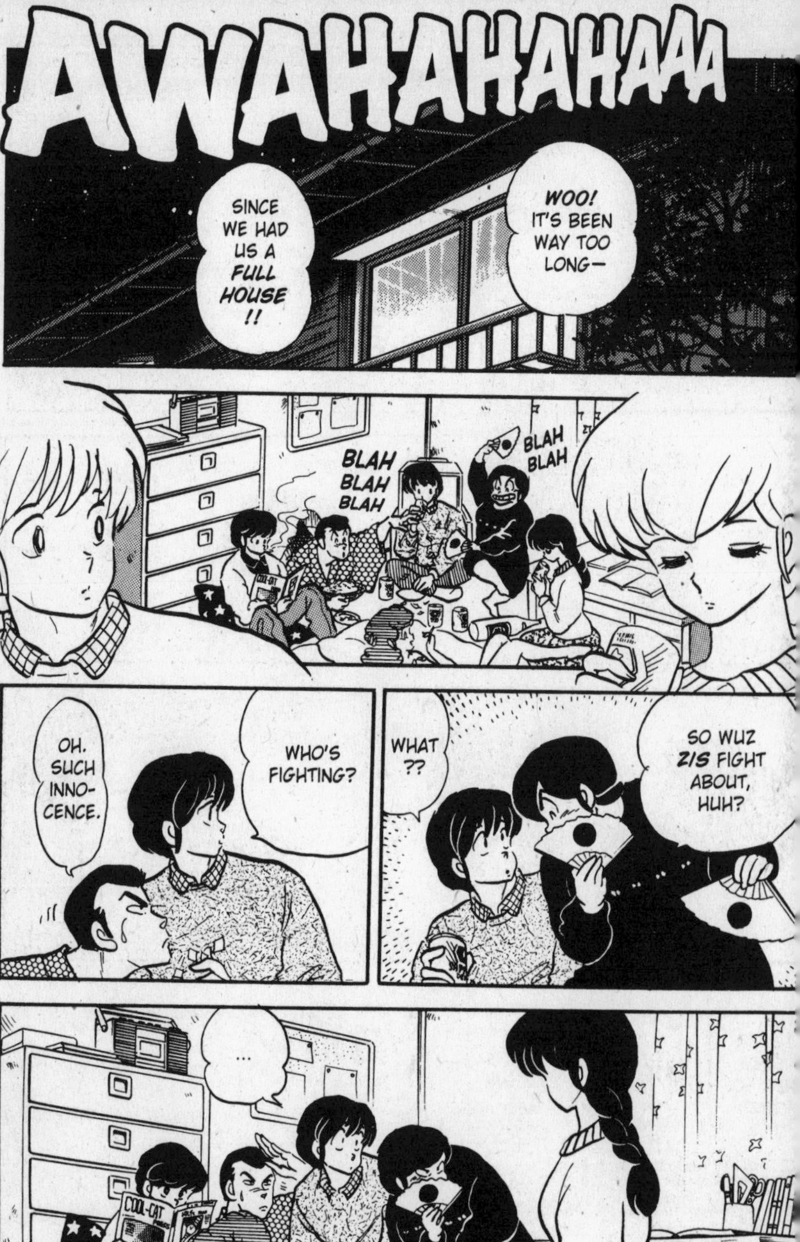

AWAHAHAHAAA
SINCE WE HAD US A FULL HOUSE !!
WOO! IT'S BEEN WAY TOO LONG—
BLAH BLAH BLAH
BLAH BLAH
OH. SUCH INNO-CENCE.
WHO'S FIGHTING?
WHAT ??
SO WUZ ZIS FIGHT ABOUT, HUH?
...
COOL-CAT

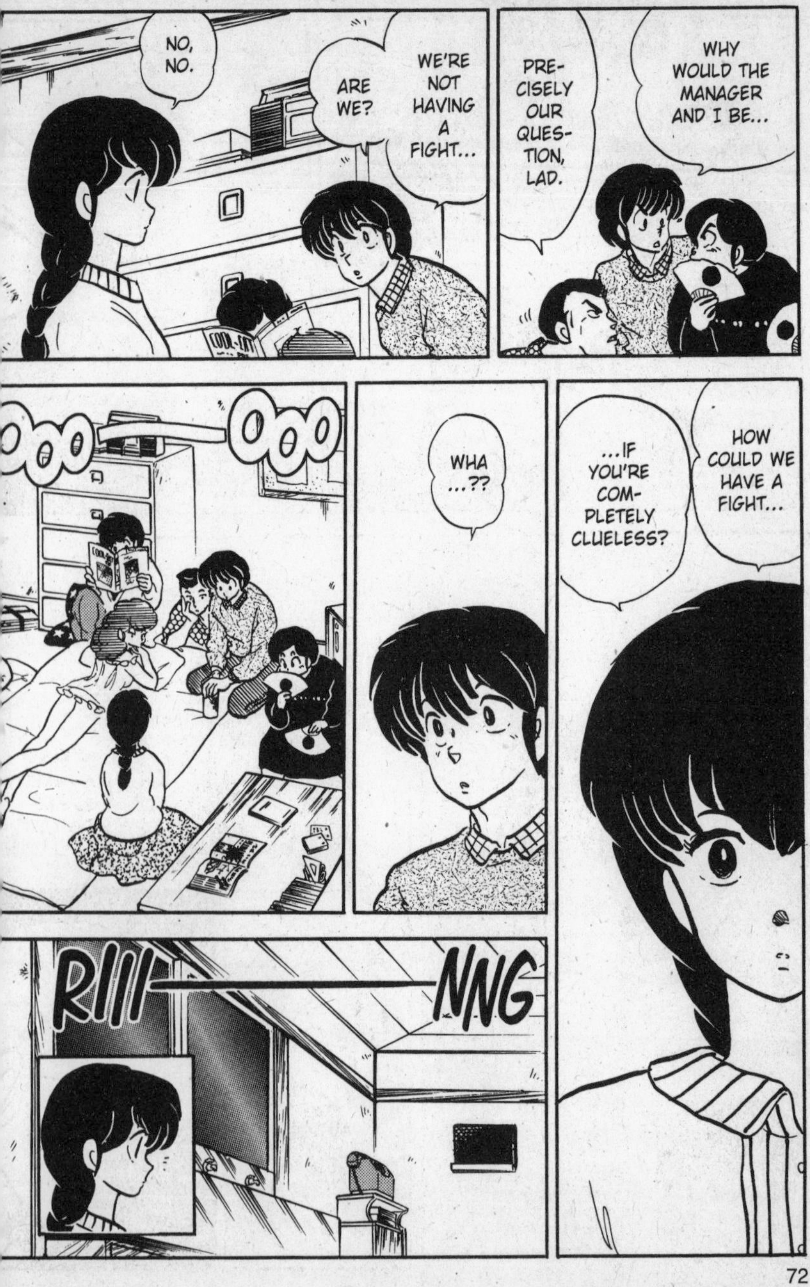
WE'RE NOT HAVING A FIGHT...
ARE WE?
NO, NO.
WHY WOULD THE MANAGER AND I BE...
PRE-CISELY OUR QUES-TION, LAD.
OOO
OOO
WHA ...??
HOW COULD WE HAVE A FIGHT...
...IF YOU'RE COM-PLETELY CLUELESS?
RIII
NNG

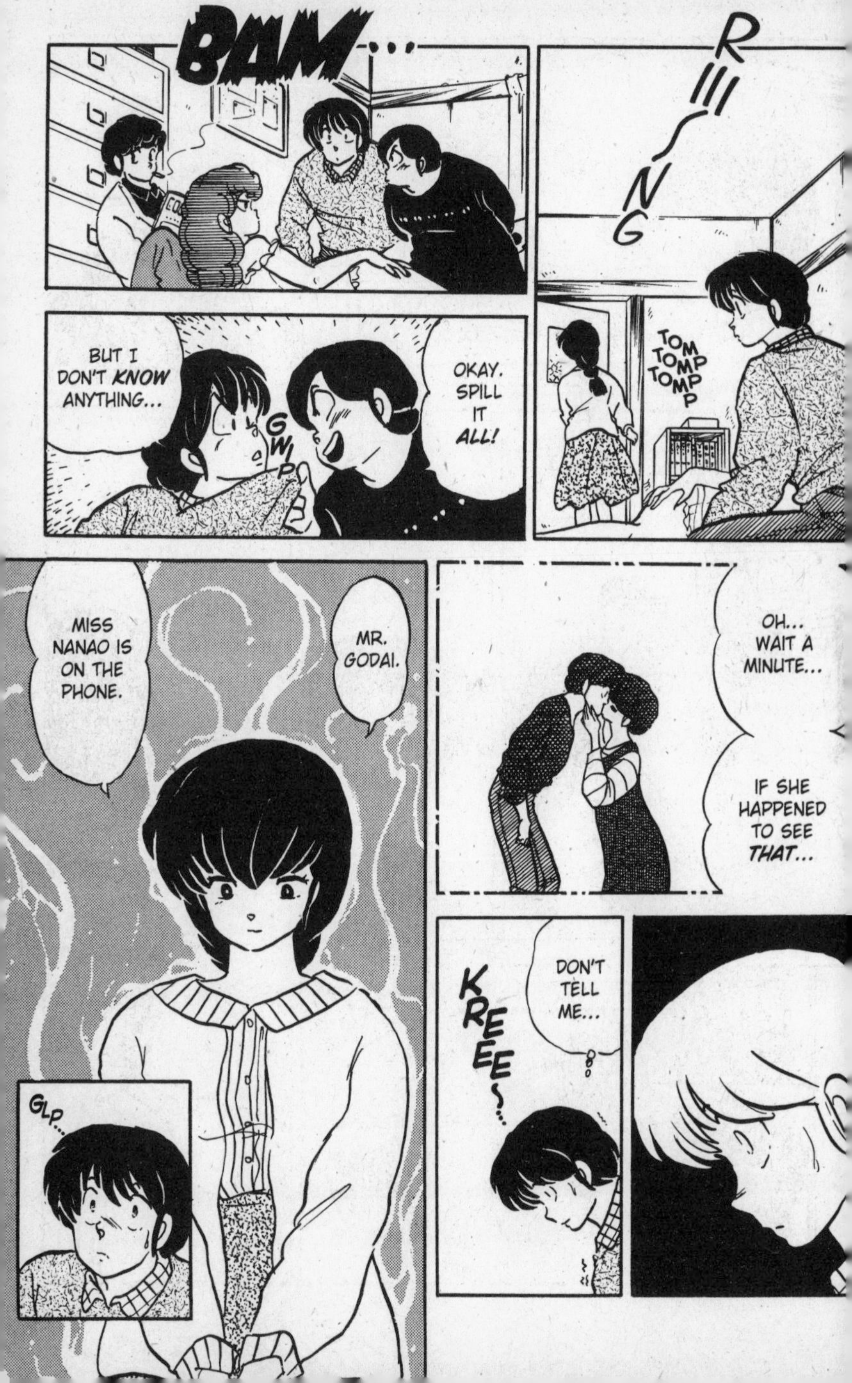
BAM...
BUT I DON'T *KNOW* ANYTHING...
GWIP
OKAY. SPILL IT *ALL!*
RIIING
TOM TOMP TOMP
MR. GODAI.
MISS NANAO IS ON THE PHONE.
GLP...
OH... WAIT A MINUTE...
IF SHE HAPPENED TO SEE *THAT*...
DON'T TELL ME...
KREEE...

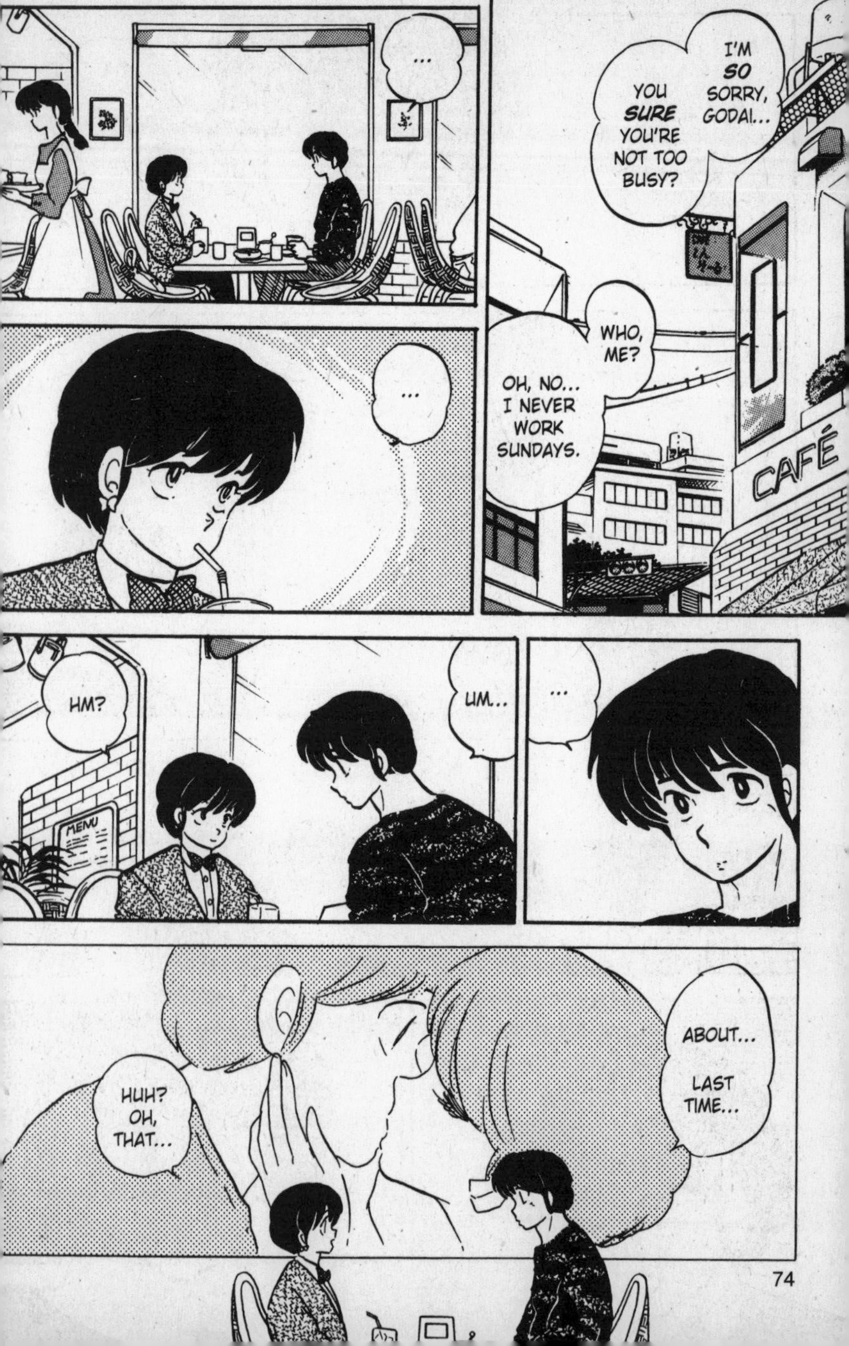
I'M SO SORRY, GODAI...
YOU SURE YOU'RE NOT TOO BUSY?
CAFÉ
WHO, ME?
OH, NO... I NEVER WORK SUNDAYS.
...
...
...
UM...
HM?
MENU
ABOUT... LAST TIME...
HUH? OH, THAT...

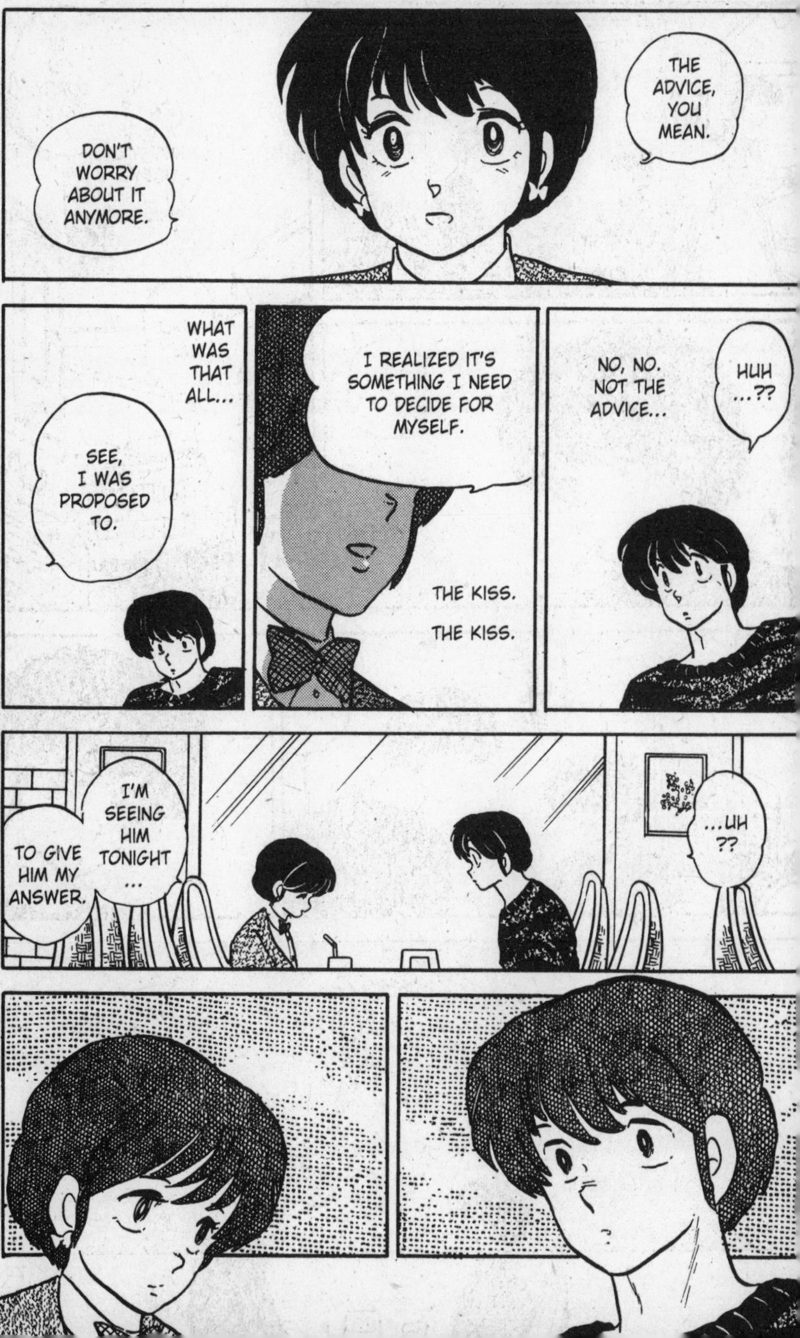

THE ADVICE, YOU MEAN.
DON'T WORRY ABOUT IT ANYMORE.
HUH ...??
NO, NO. NOT THE ADVICE...
THE KISS.
THE KISS.
I REALIZED IT'S SOMETHING I NEED TO DECIDE FOR MYSELF.
WHAT WAS THAT ALL...
SEE, I WAS PROPOSED TO.
...UH ??
I'M SEEING HIM TONIGHT ...
TO GIVE HIM MY ANSWER.

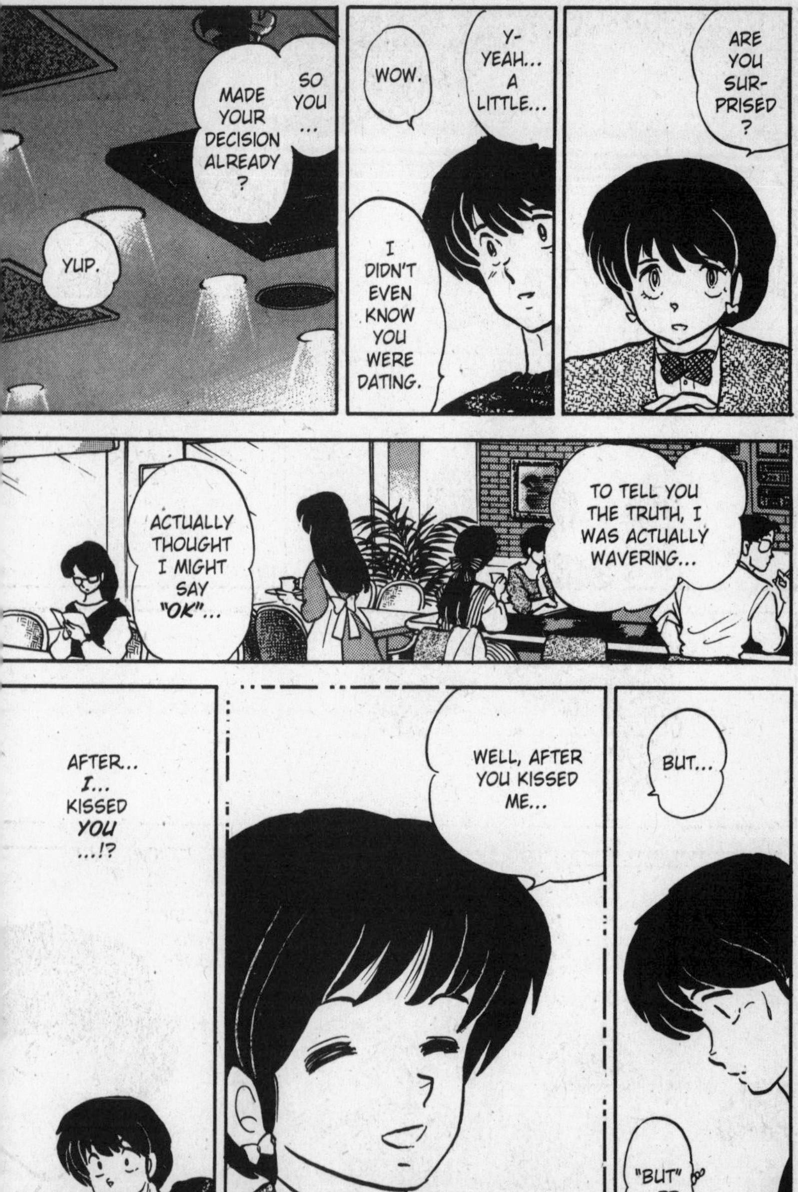

ARE YOU SUR-PRISED?
Y-YEAH... A LITTLE...
I DIDN'T EVEN KNOW YOU WERE DATING.
WOW.
SO YOU...
MADE YOUR DECISION ALREADY?
YUP.
TO TELL YOU THE TRUTH, I WAS ACTUALLY WAVERING...
ACTUALLY THOUGHT I MIGHT SAY "OK"...
BUT...
"BUT"...??
WELL, AFTER YOU KISSED ME...
AFTER... *I*... KISSED *YOU*...!?

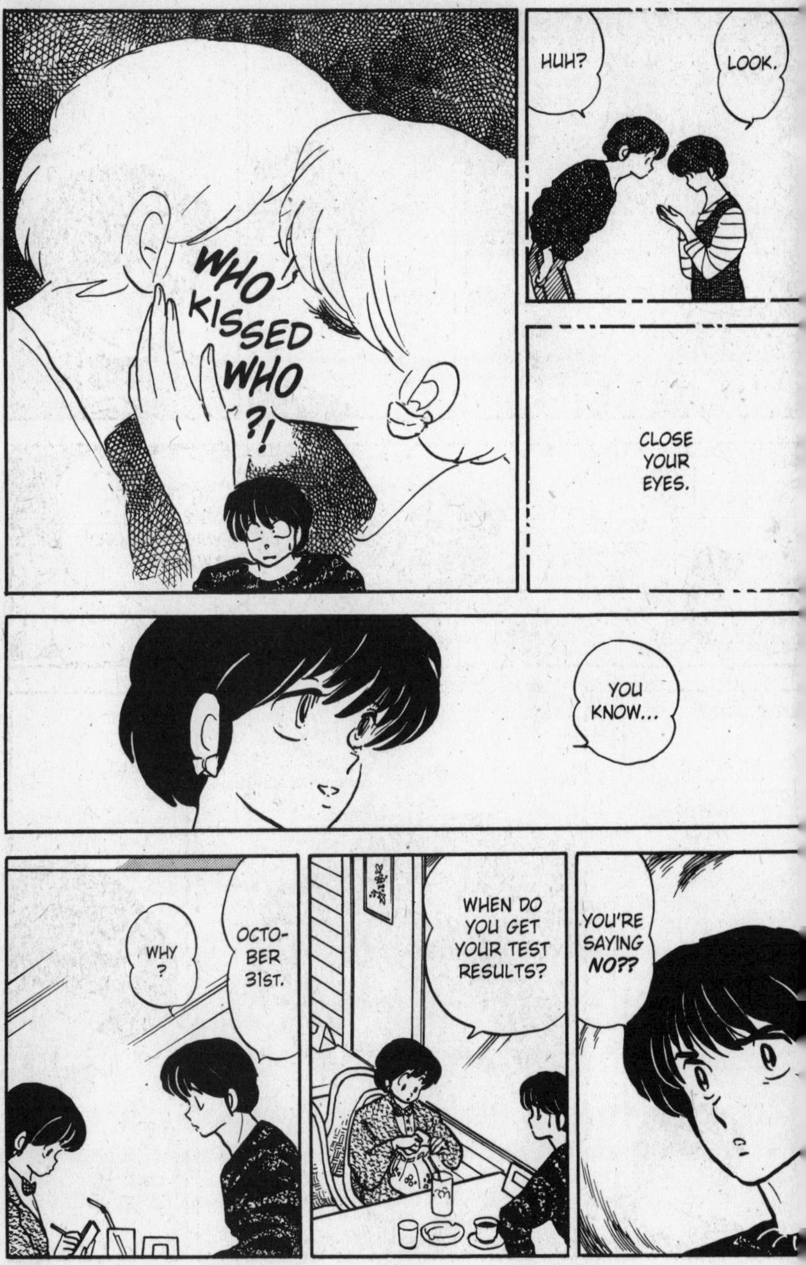
LOOK.
HUH?
CLOSE YOUR EYES.
WHO KISSED WHO ?!
YOU KNOW...
YOU'RE SAYING NO??
WHEN DO YOU GET YOUR TEST RESULTS?
OCTOBER 31ST.
WHY ?

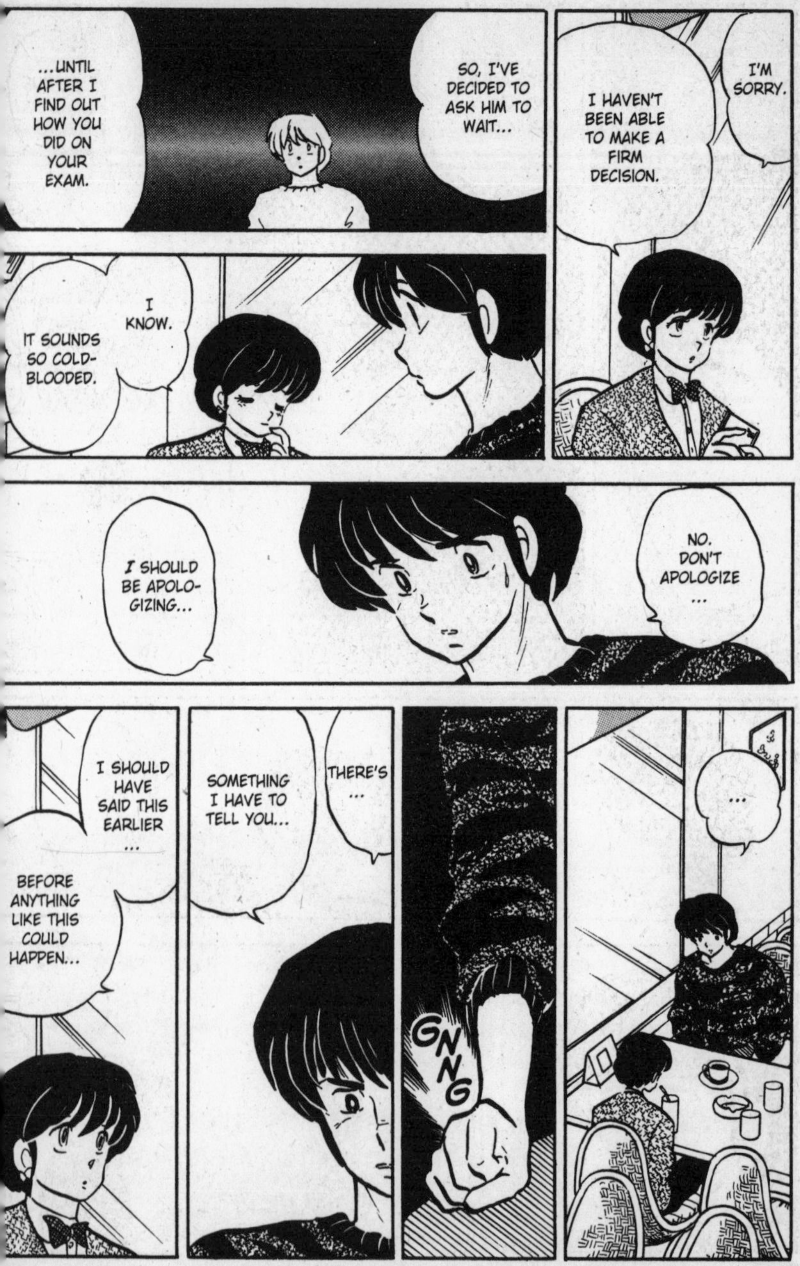
I'M SORRY.
I HAVEN'T BEEN ABLE TO MAKE A FIRM DECISION.
SO, I'VE DECIDED TO ASK HIM TO WAIT...
...UNTIL AFTER I FIND OUT HOW YOU DID ON YOUR EXAM.
I KNOW.
IT SOUNDS SO COLD-BLOODED.
NO. DON'T APOLOGIZE ...
I SHOULD BE APOLOGIZING...
...
GNNG
THERE'S ...
SOMETHING I HAVE TO TELL YOU...
I SHOULD HAVE SAID THIS EARLIER ...
BEFORE ANYTHING LIKE THIS COULD HAPPEN...

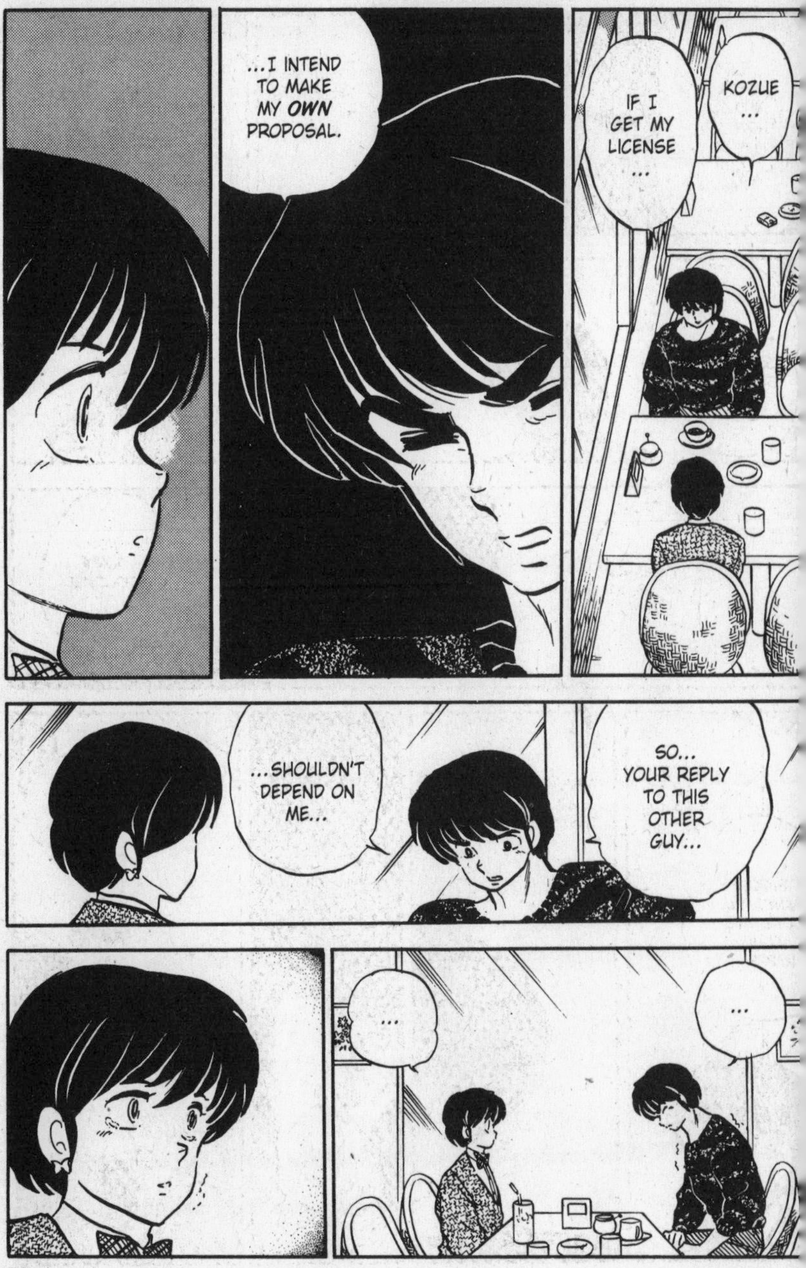
KOZUE ...
IF I GET MY LICENSE ...
...I INTEND TO MAKE MY OWN PROPOSAL.
SO... YOUR REPLY TO THIS OTHER GUY...
...SHOULDN'T DEPEND ON ME...
...
...

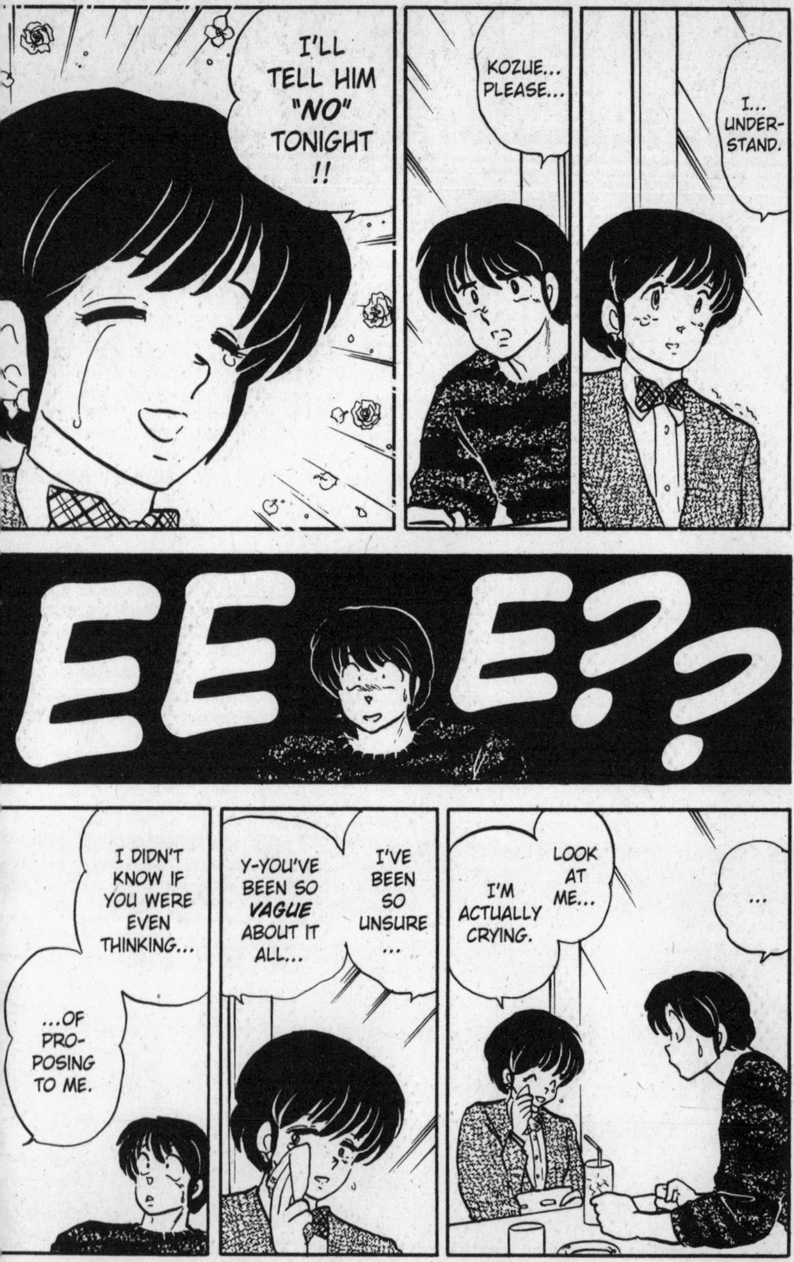

I'LL TELL HIM "*NO*" TONIGHT !!
KOZUE... PLEASE...
I... UNDER-STAND.
EEE??
I DIDN'T KNOW IF YOU WERE EVEN THINKING...
...OF PRO-POSING TO ME.
Y-YOU'VE BEEN SO *VAGUE* ABOUT IT ALL...
I'VE BEEN SO UNSURE...
LOOK AT ME...
I'M ACTUALLY CRYING.
...

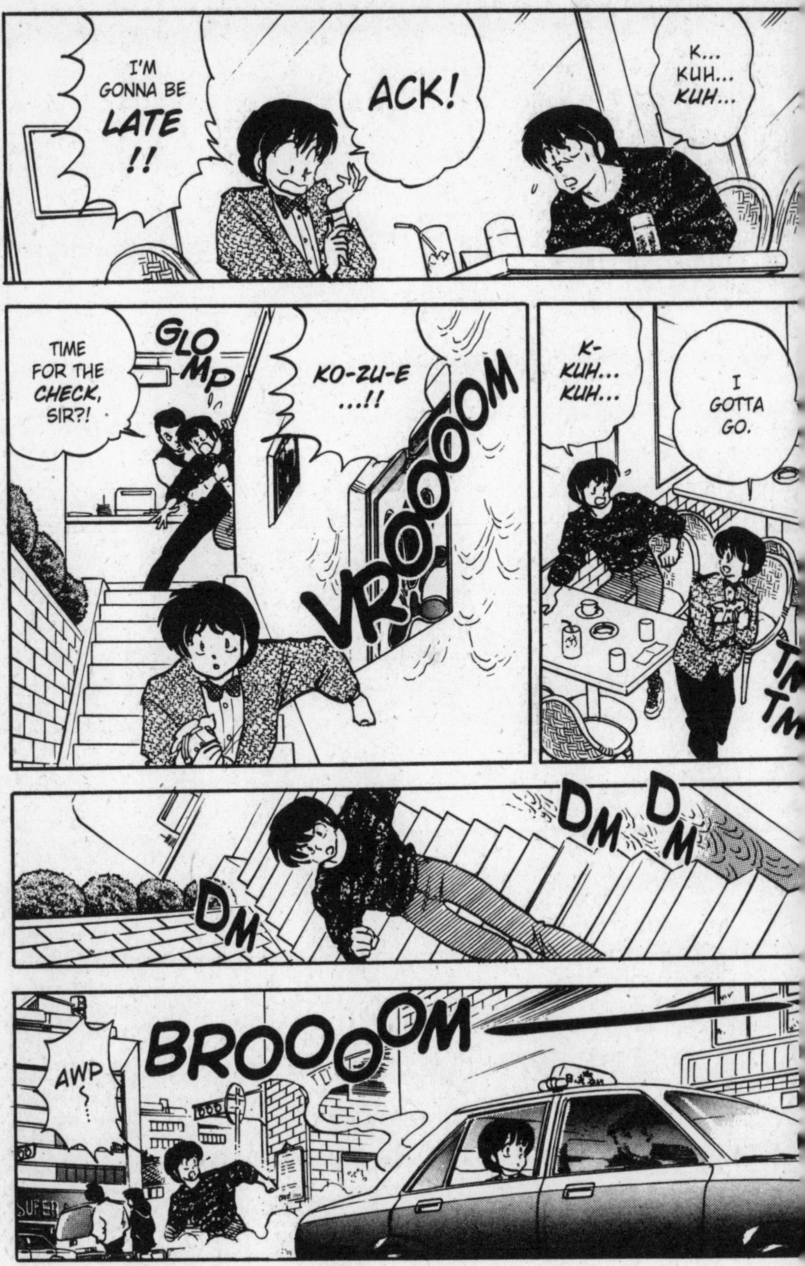
I'M GONNA BE LATE!!
ACK!
K... KUH... KUH...
TIME FOR THE CHECK, SIR?!
GLOMP
KO-ZU-E ...!!
VROOOOOM
K- KUH... KUH...
I GOTTA GO.
DM
DM
DM
AWP
BROOOOM

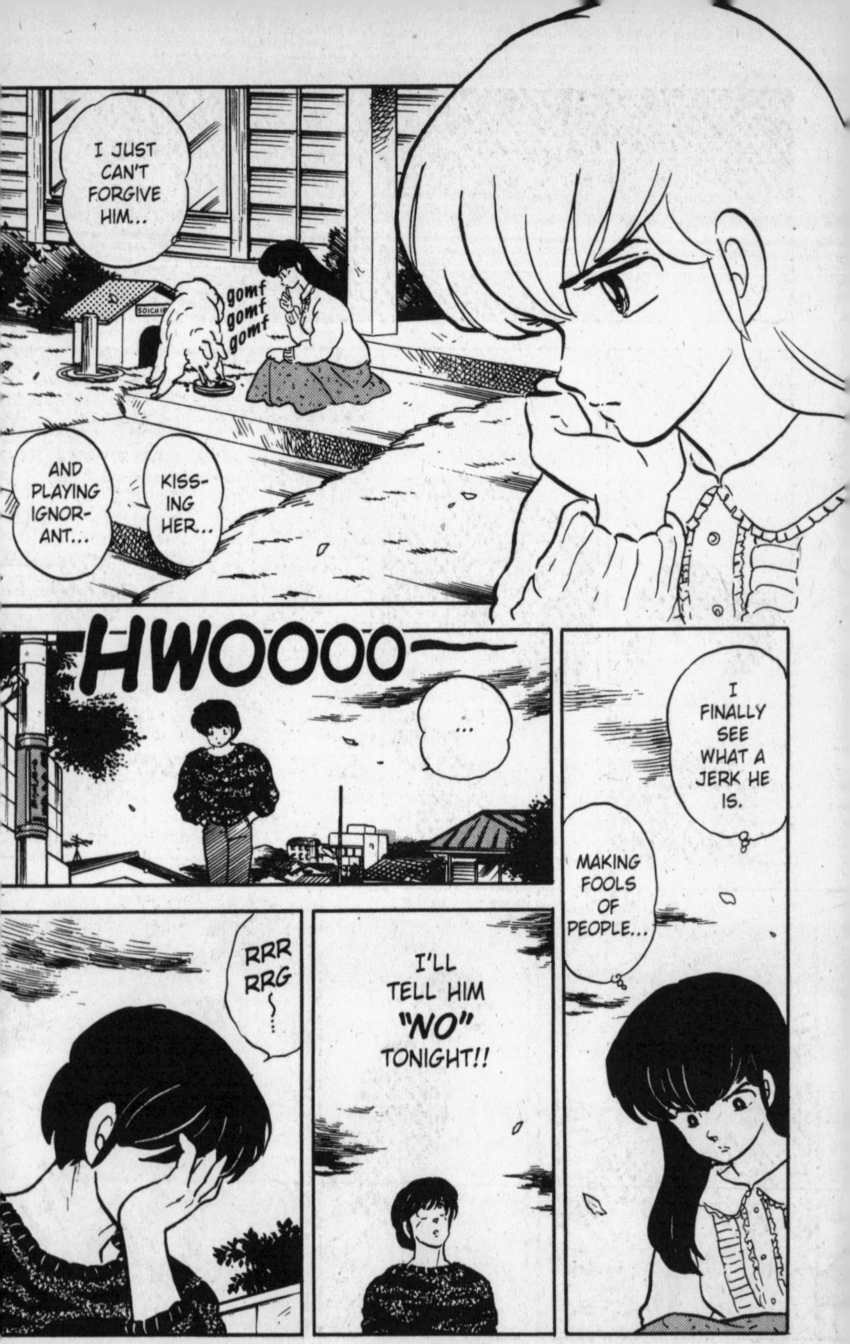
I JUST CAN'T FORGIVE HIM...
gomf gomf gomf
KISS-ING HER...
AND PLAYING IGNOR-ANT...
HWOOOO—
...
I FINALLY SEE WHAT A JERK HE IS.
MAKING FOOLS OF PEOPLE...
I'LL TELL HIM "NO" TONIGHT!!
RRR RRG~...

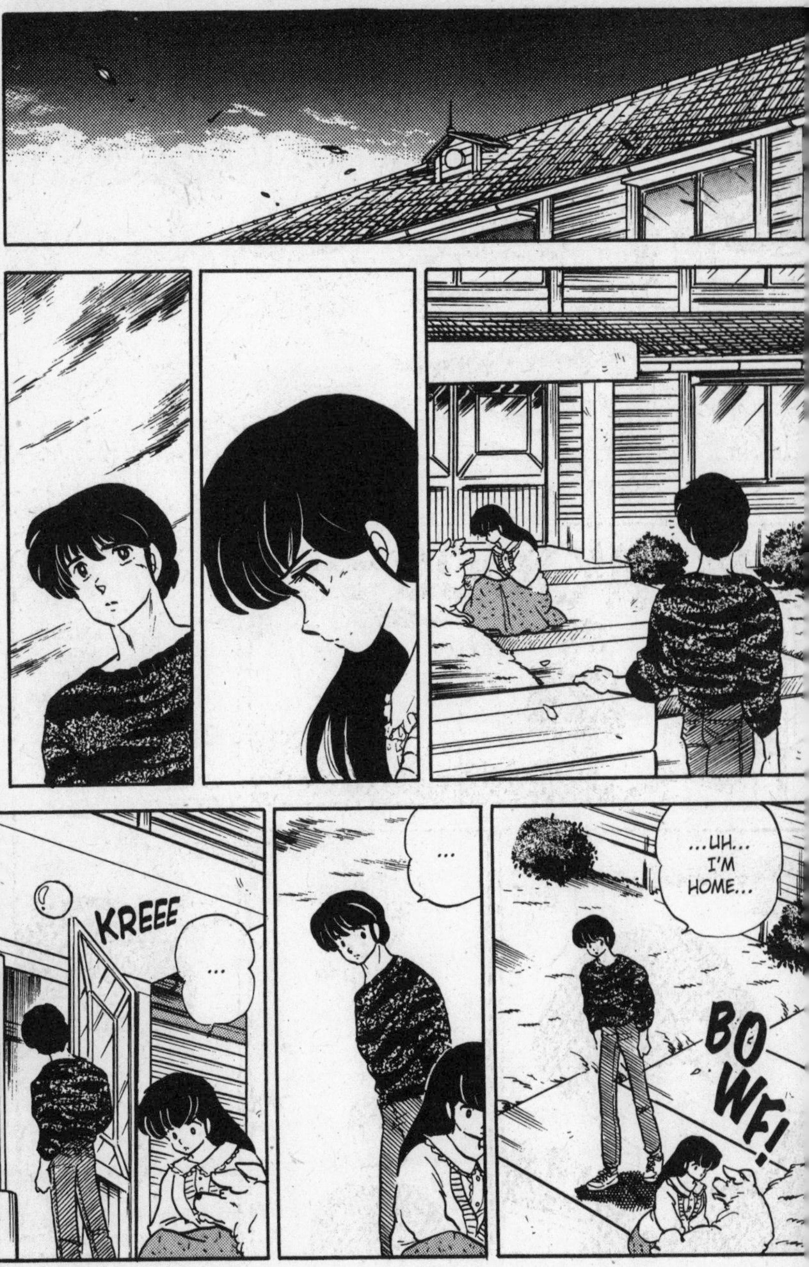
KREEE
...
...
...UH... I'M HOME...
BOWF!

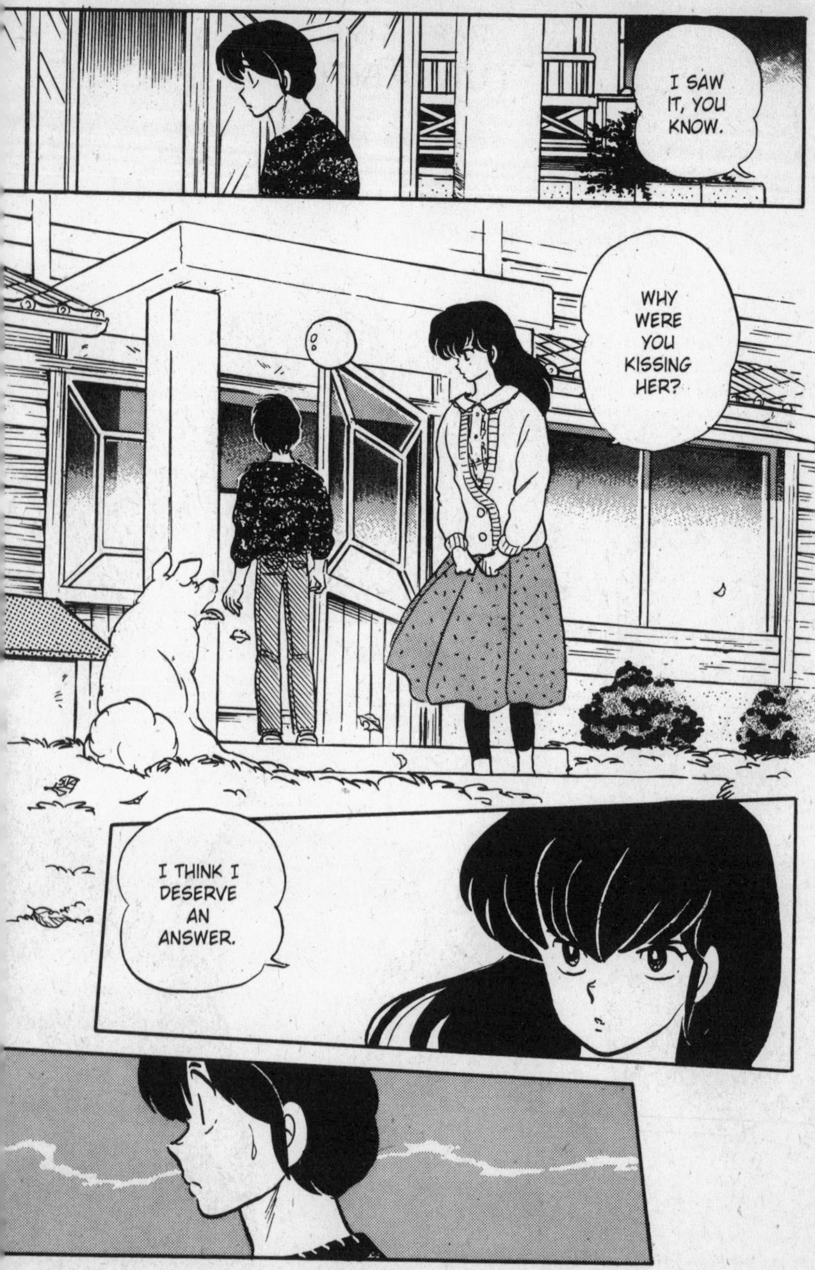
I SAW IT, YOU KNOW.
WHY WERE YOU KISSING HER?
I THINK I DESERVE AN ANSWER.

PART FIVE

TURNABOUT

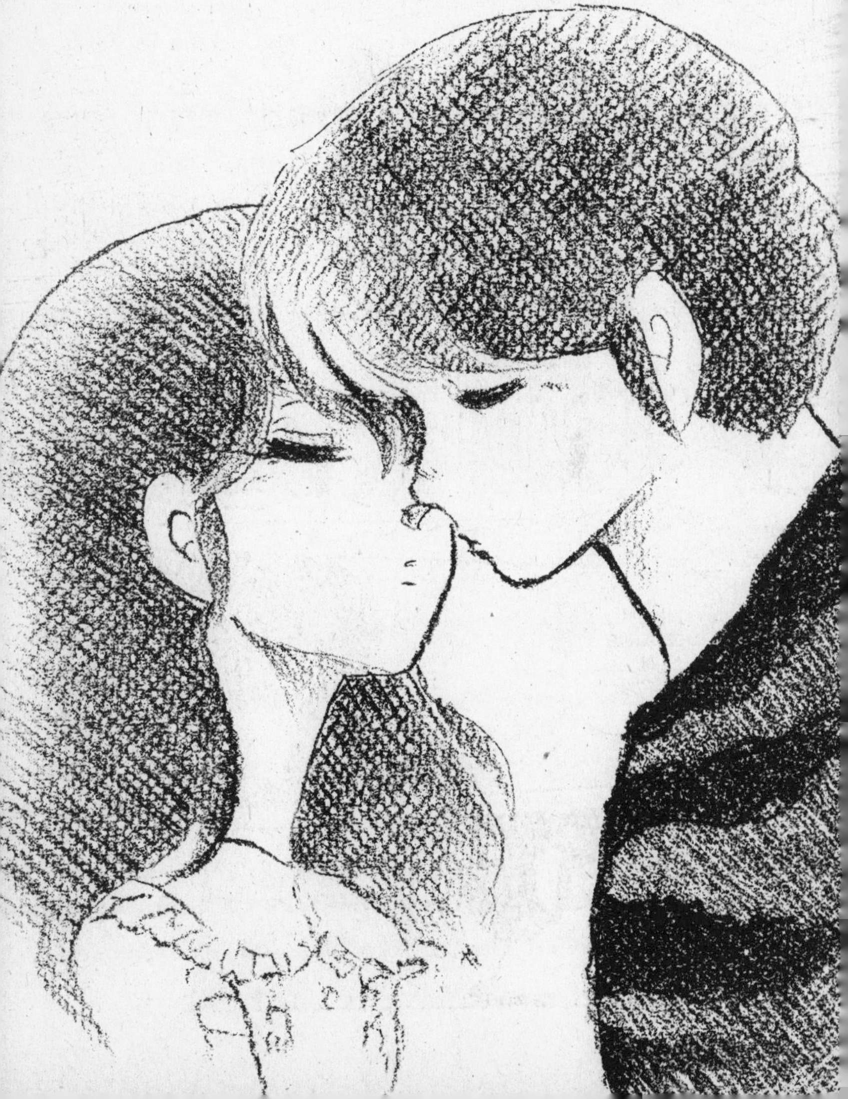

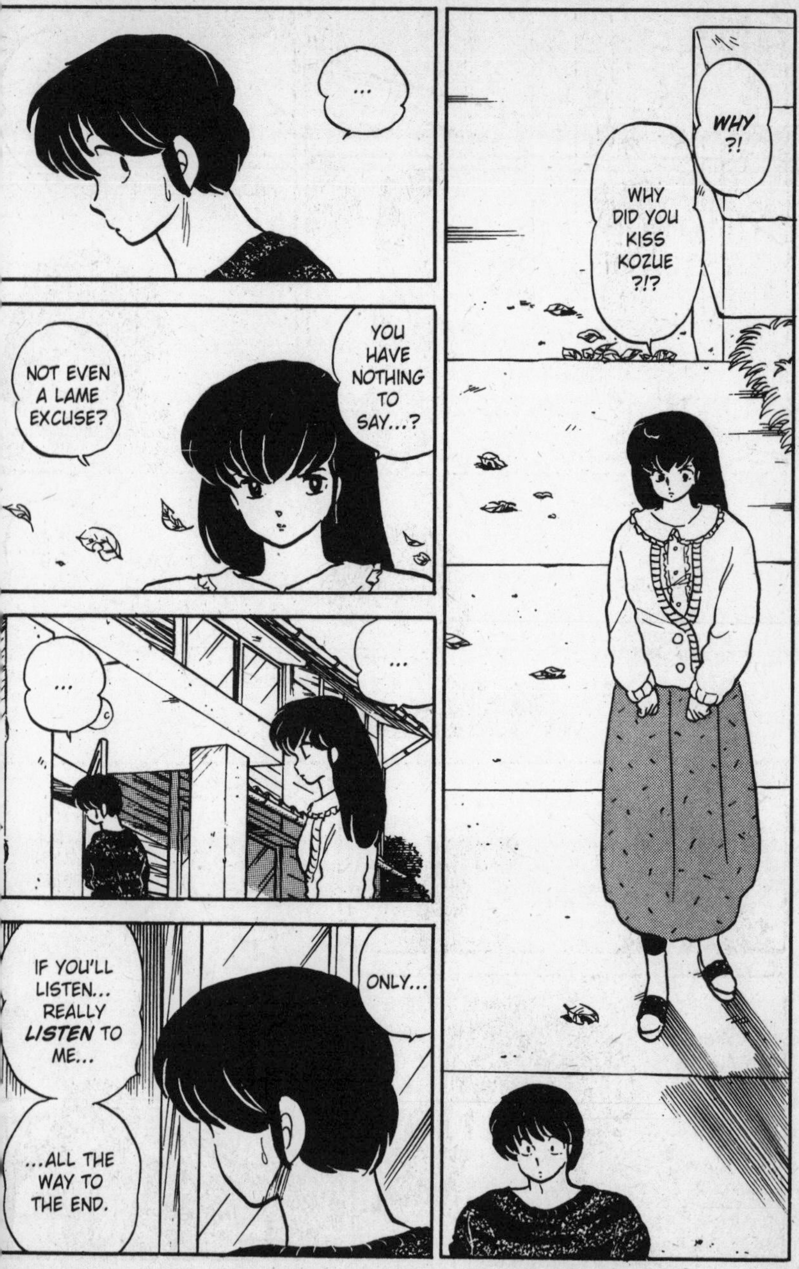

WHY?!
WHY DID YOU KISS KOZUE?!?
...
YOU HAVE NOTHING TO SAY...?
NOT EVEN A LAME EXCUSE?
...
...
ONLY...
IF YOU'LL LISTEN... REALLY *LISTEN* TO ME...
...ALL THE WAY TO THE END.

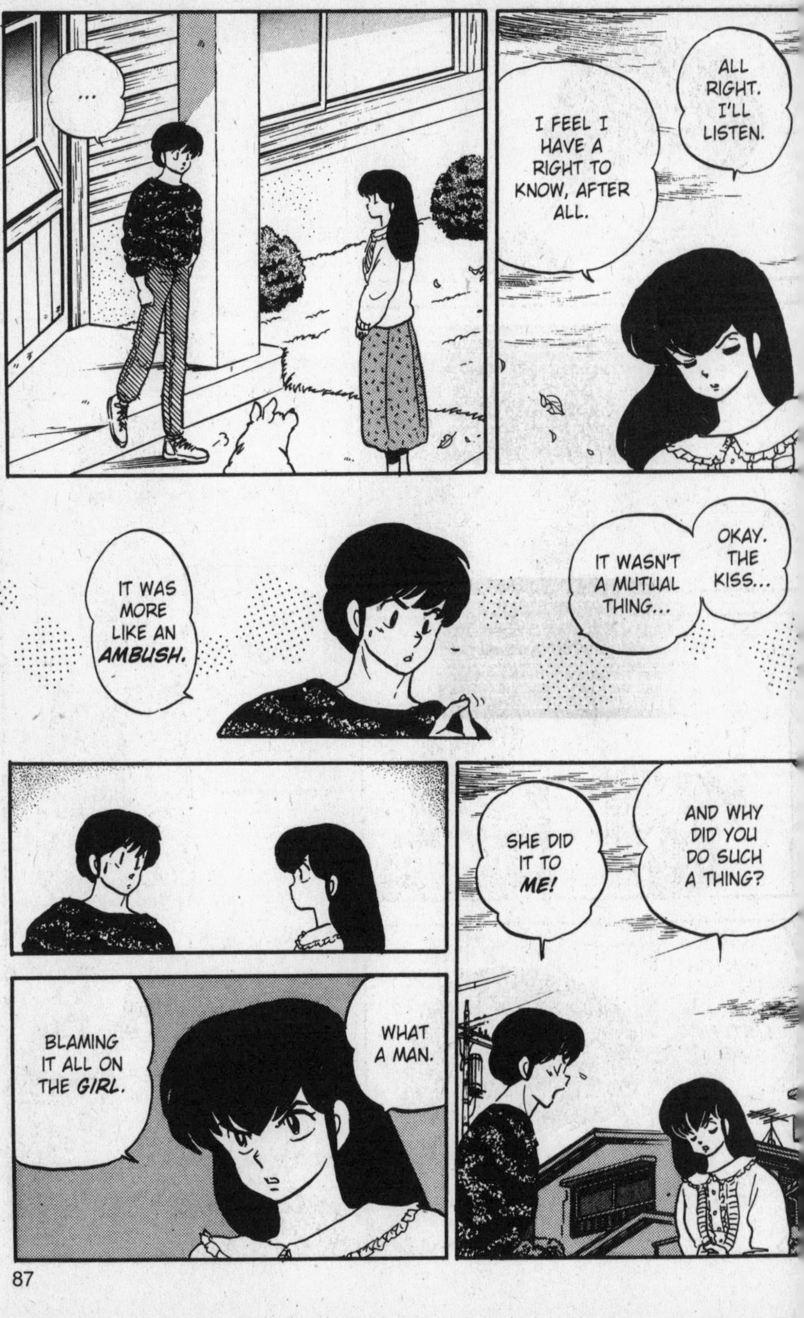
ALL RIGHT. I'LL LISTEN.
I FEEL I HAVE A RIGHT TO KNOW, AFTER ALL.
...
OKAY. THE KISS...
IT WASN'T A MUTUAL THING...
IT WAS MORE LIKE AN ***AMBUSH***.
AND WHY DID YOU DO SUCH A THING?
SHE DID IT TO ***ME!***
WHAT A MAN.
BLAMING IT ALL ON THE ***GIRL***.

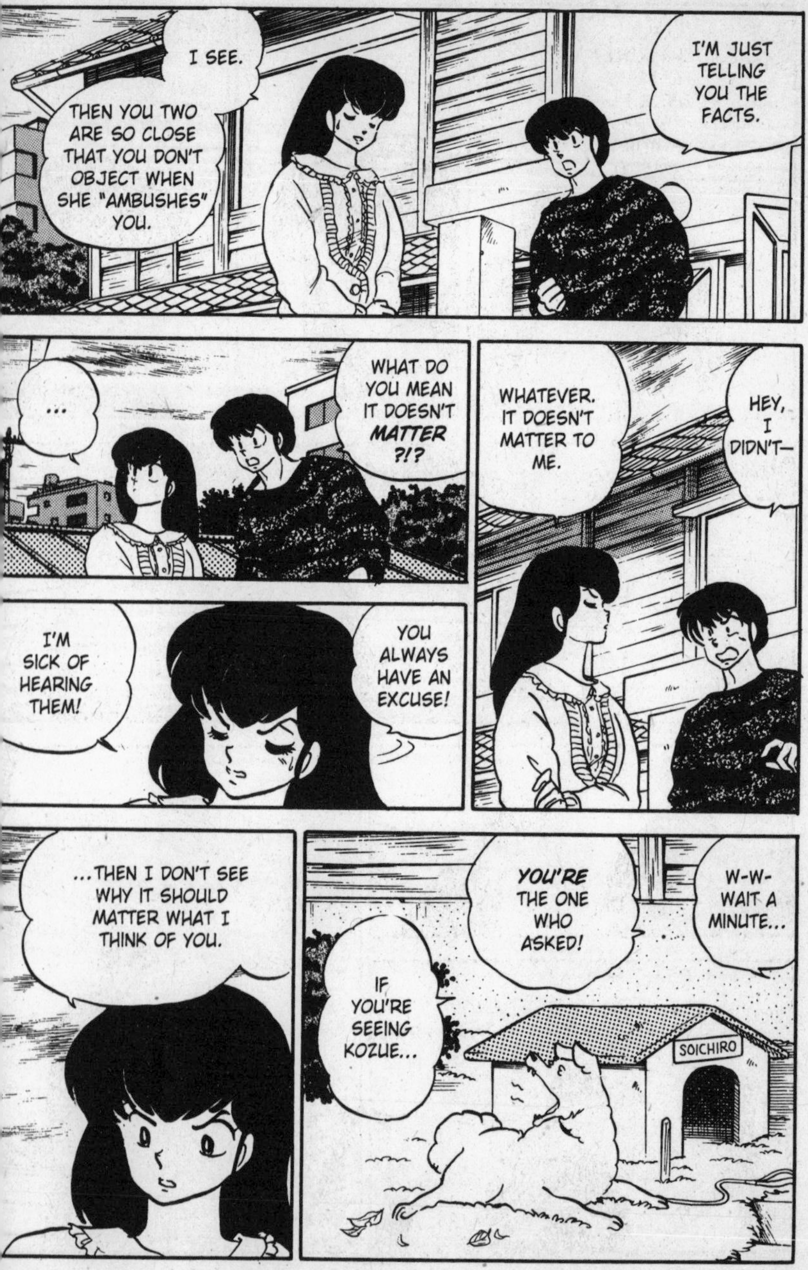
I'M JUST TELLING YOU THE FACTS.
I SEE.
THEN YOU TWO ARE SO CLOSE THAT YOU DON'T OBJECT WHEN SHE "AMBUSHES" YOU.
HEY, I DIDN'T—
WHATEVER. IT DOESN'T MATTER TO ME.
WHAT DO YOU MEAN IT DOESN'T *MATTER* ?!?
...
YOU ALWAYS HAVE AN EXCUSE!
I'M SICK OF HEARING THEM!
W-W-WAIT A MINUTE...
YOU'RE THE ONE WHO ASKED!
SOICHIRO
IF YOU'RE SEEING KOZUE...
...THEN I DON'T SEE WHY IT SHOULD MATTER WHAT I THINK OF YOU.

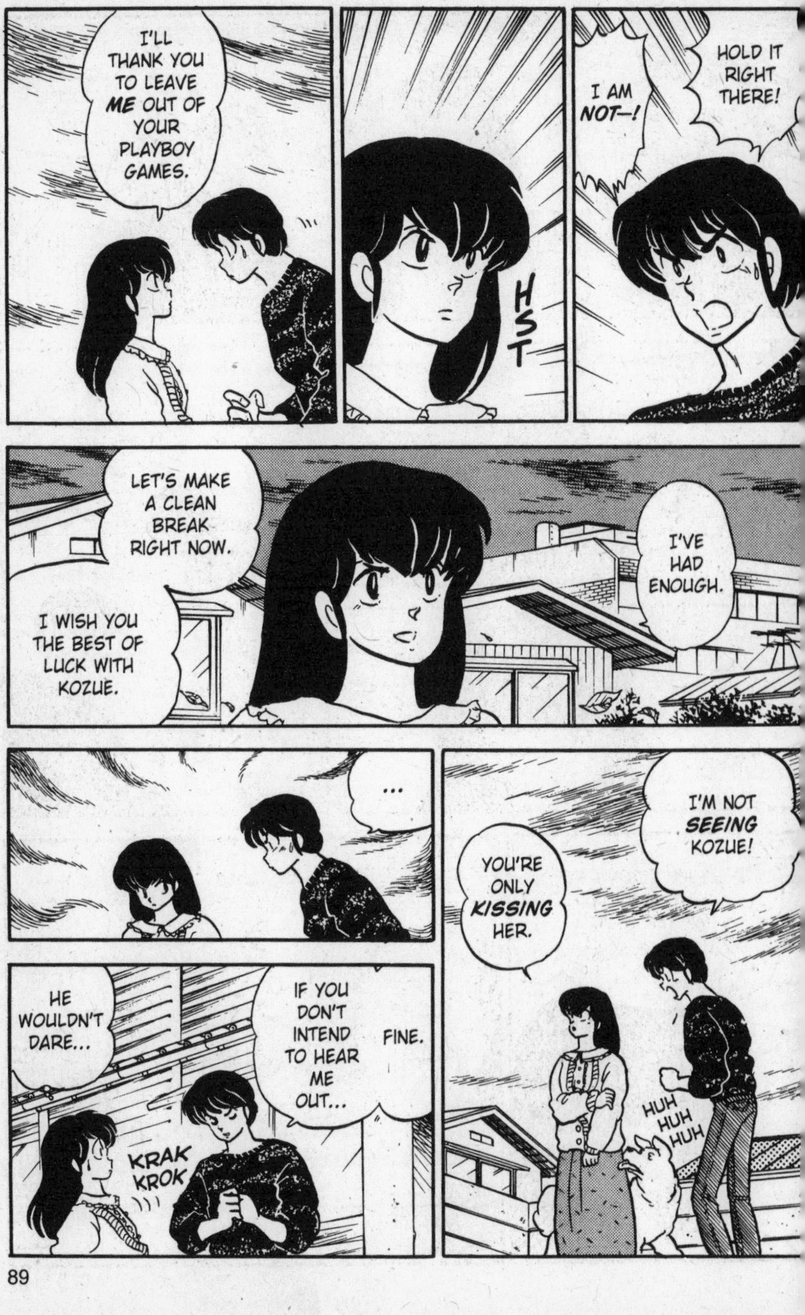
I'LL THANK YOU TO LEAVE ME OUT OF YOUR PLAYBOY GAMES.
HST
I AM NOT—!
HOLD IT RIGHT THERE!
LET'S MAKE A CLEAN BREAK RIGHT NOW.
I WISH YOU THE BEST OF LUCK WITH KOZUE.
I'VE HAD ENOUGH.
...
HE WOULDN'T DARE...
IF YOU DON'T INTEND TO HEAR ME OUT...
FINE.
KRAK KROK
I'M NOT SEEING KOZUE!
YOU'RE ONLY KISSING HER.
HUH HUH HUH

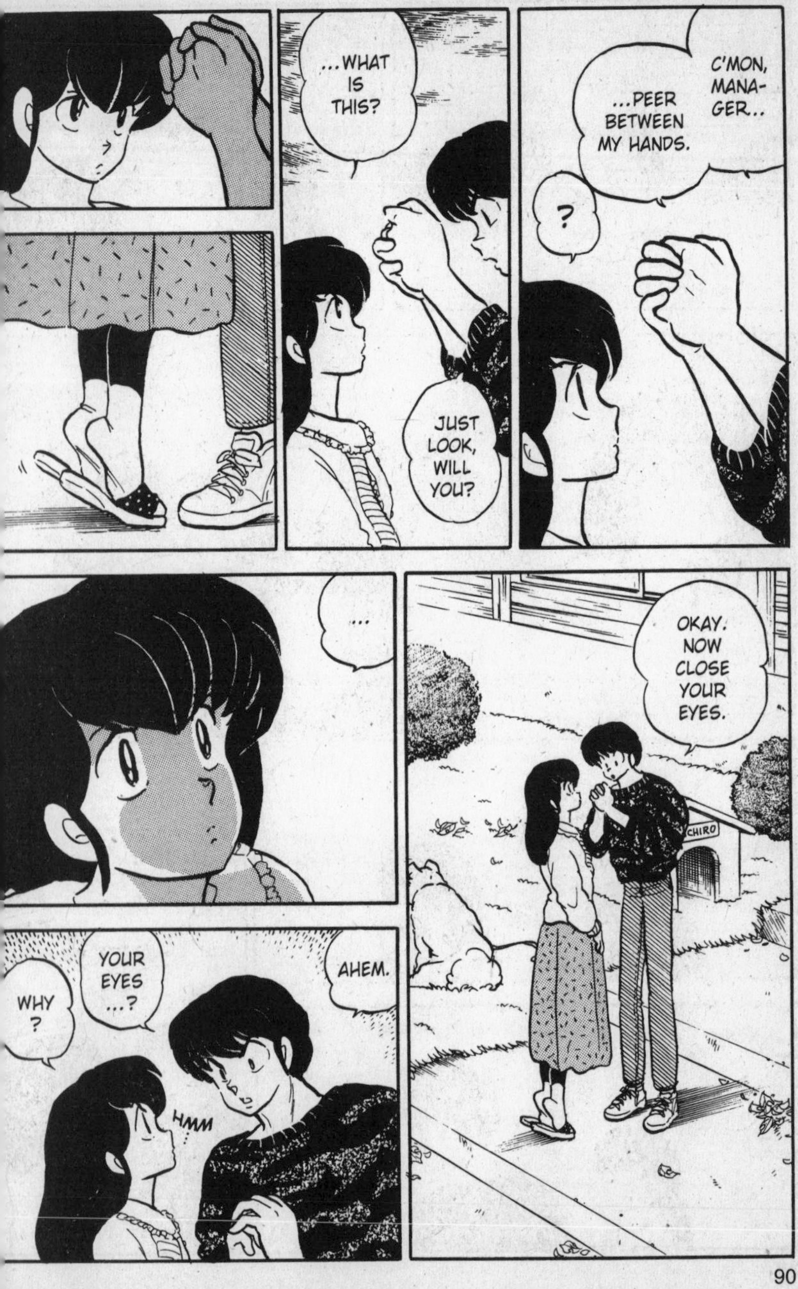
C'MON, MANAGER...
...PEER BETWEEN MY HANDS.
?
...WHAT IS THIS?
JUST LOOK, WILL YOU?
OKAY. NOW CLOSE YOUR EYES.
CHIRO
...
AHEM.
YOUR EYES ...?
WHY ?
HMM

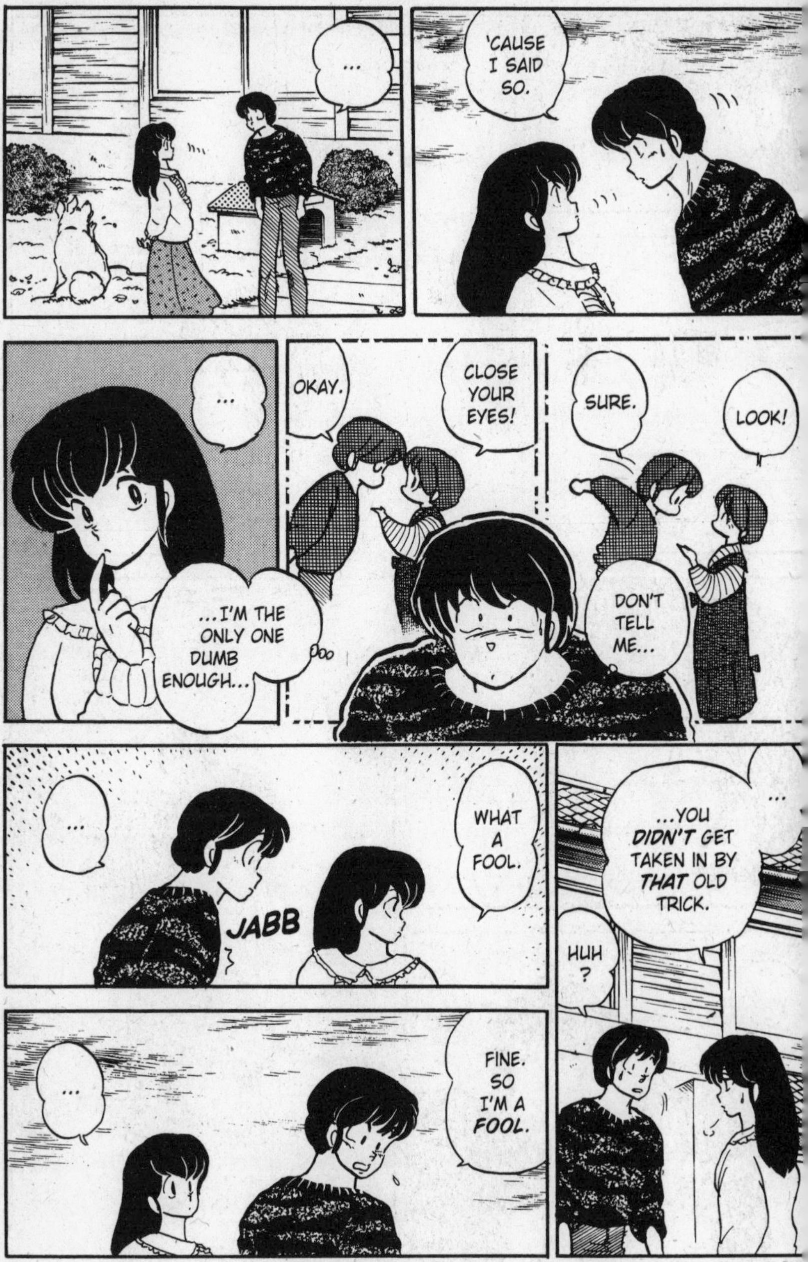
...
'CAUSE I SAID SO.
...
...I'M THE ONLY ONE DUMB ENOUGH...
OKAY.
CLOSE YOUR EYES!
SURE.
LOOK!
DON'T TELL ME...
...
WHAT A FOOL.
JABB
...
FINE. SO I'M A FOOL.
...
...YOU DIDN'T GET TAKEN IN BY THAT OLD TRICK.
HUH?

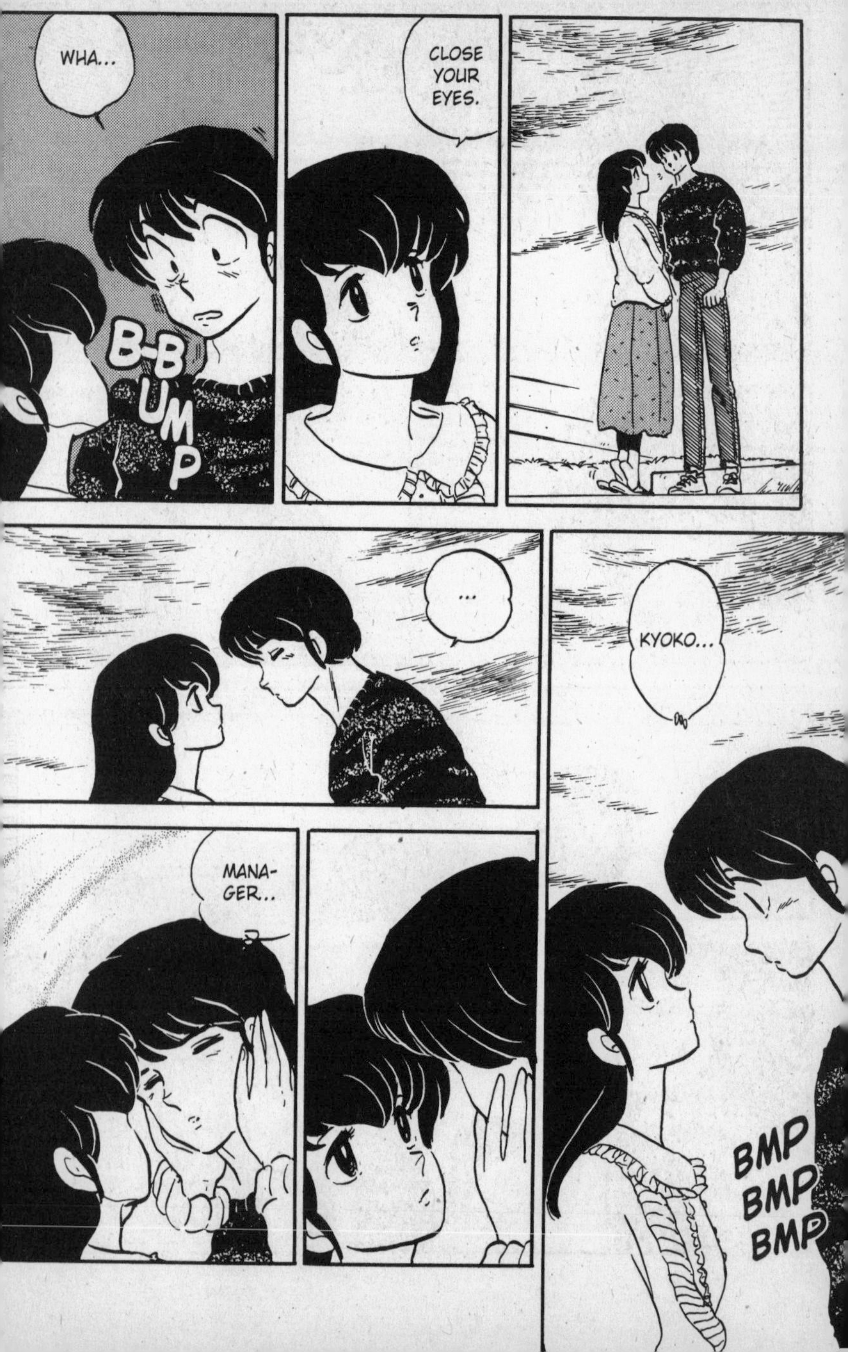
WHA...
B-BUMP
CLOSE YOUR EYES.
...
MANA-GER...
KYOKO...
BMP BMP BMP

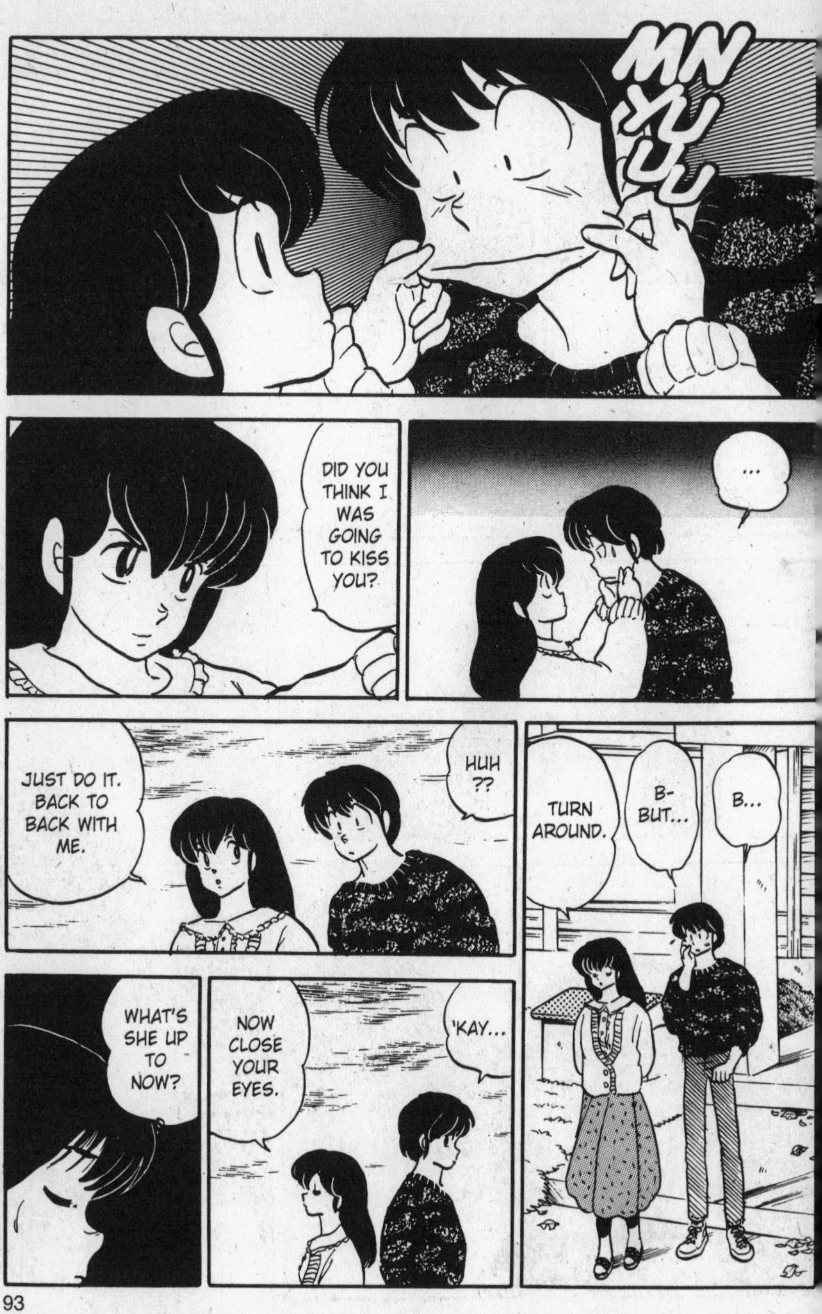
MN YUUU
DID YOU THINK I WAS GOING TO KISS YOU?
...
TURN AROUND.
B- BUT...
B...
JUST DO IT. BACK TO BACK WITH ME.
HUH ??
NOW CLOSE YOUR EYES.
'KAY...
WHAT'S SHE UP TO NOW?

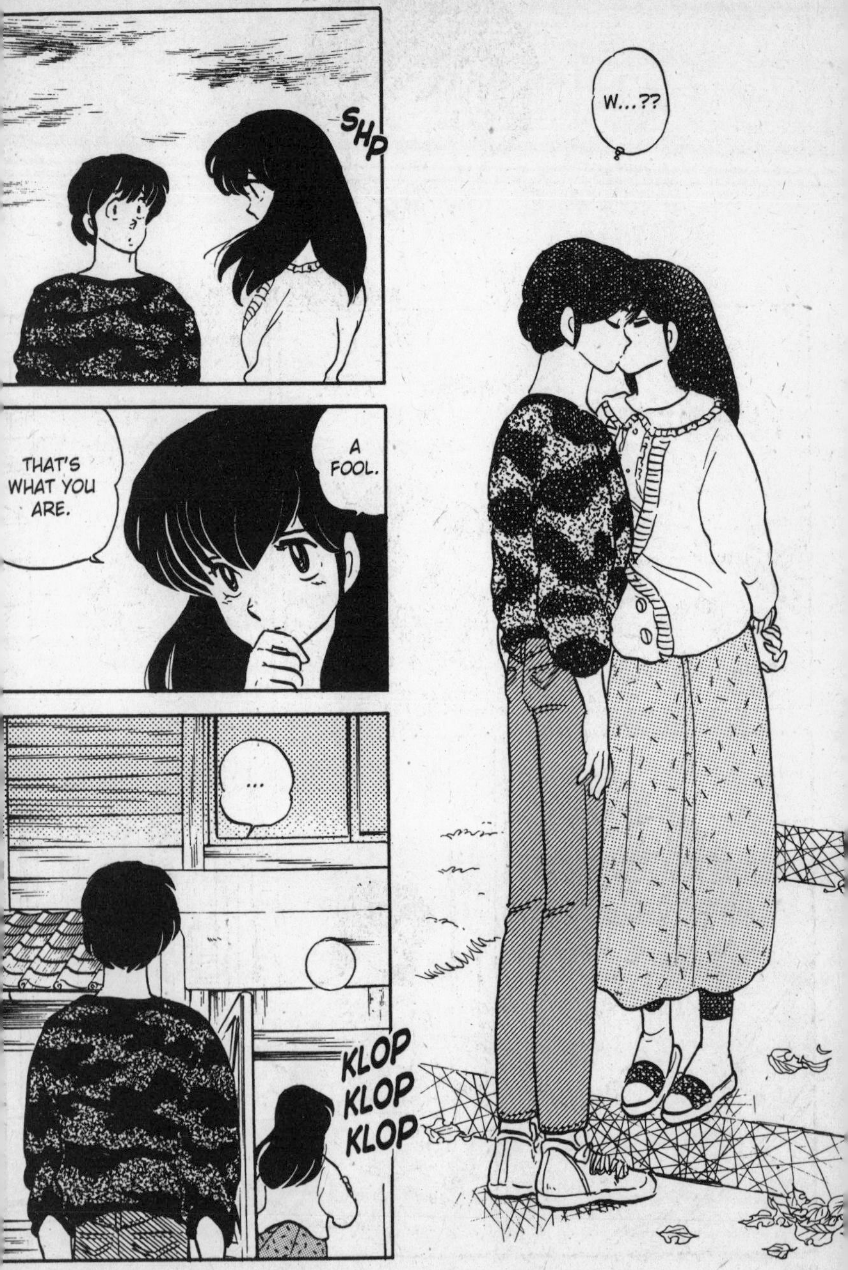
SHP
A FOOL.
THAT'S WHAT YOU ARE.
...
KLOP KLOP KLOP
W...??

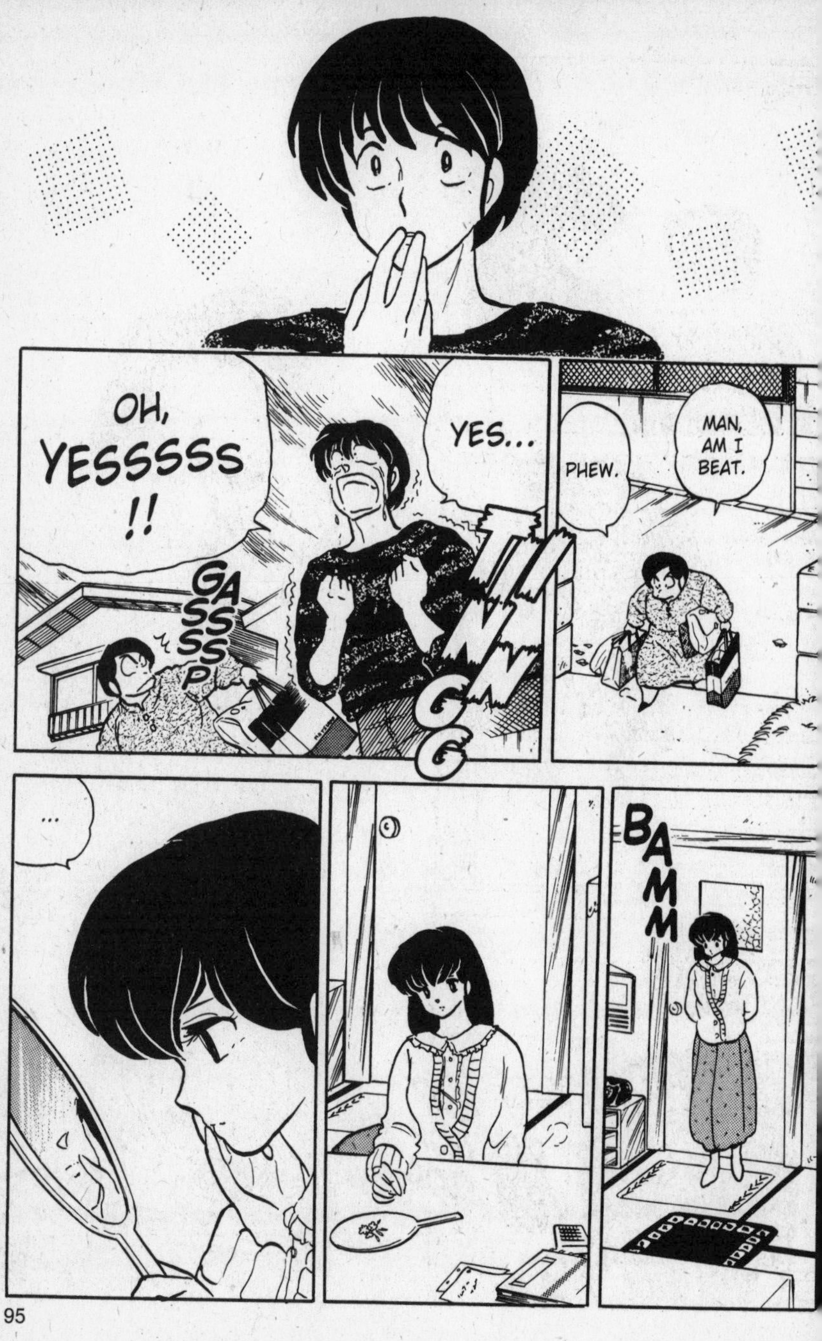
MAN, AM I BEAT.
PHEW.
YES...
OH, YESSSSS!!
GASSSSSP
TINNNGG
BAMM
...

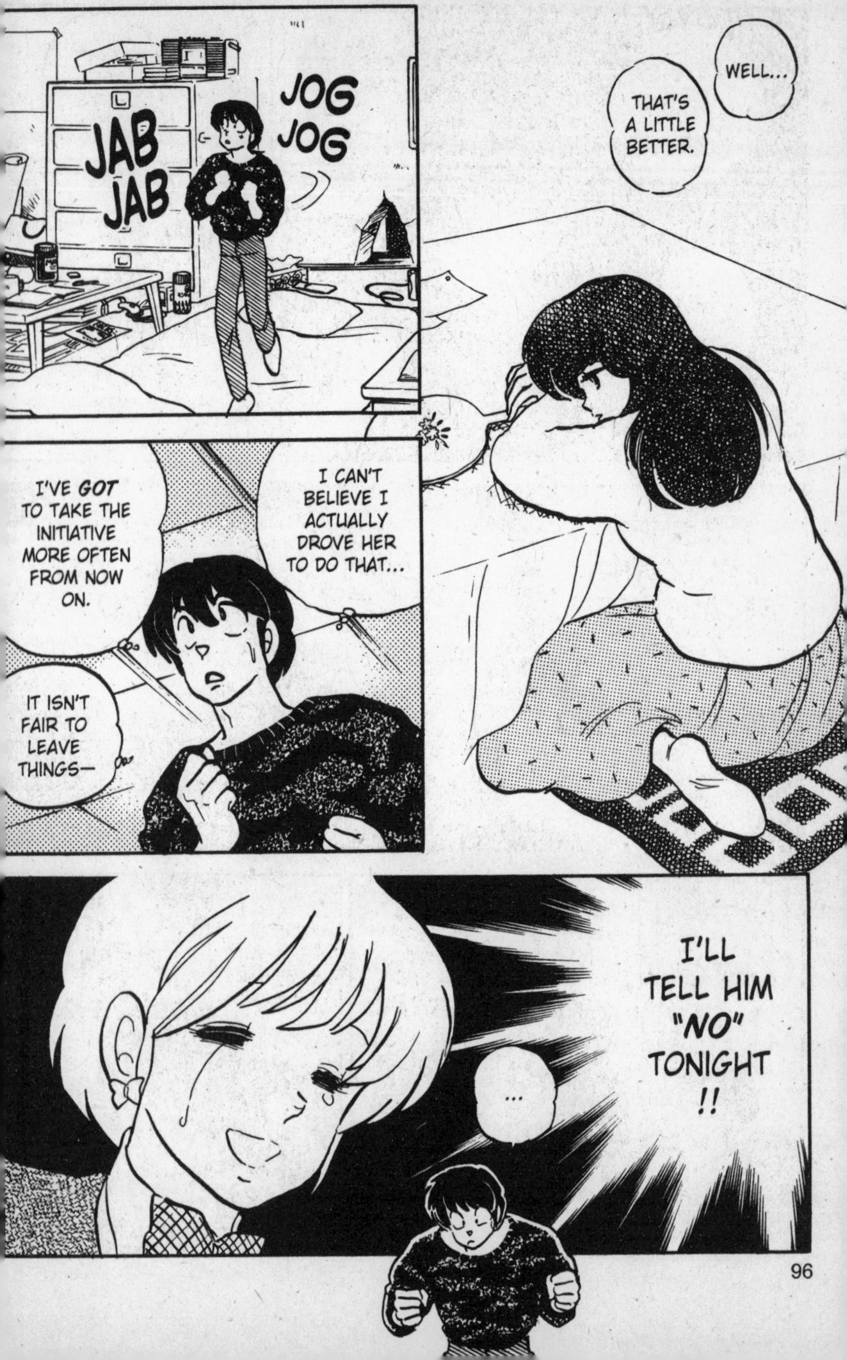

WELL...
THAT'S A LITTLE BETTER.
JOG JOG
JAB JAB
I CAN'T BELIEVE I ACTUALLY DROVE HER TO DO THAT...
I'VE *GOT* TO TAKE THE INITIATIVE MORE OFTEN FROM NOW ON.
IT ISN'T FAIR TO LEAVE THINGS—
I'LL TELL HIM "*NO*" TONIGHT !!
...

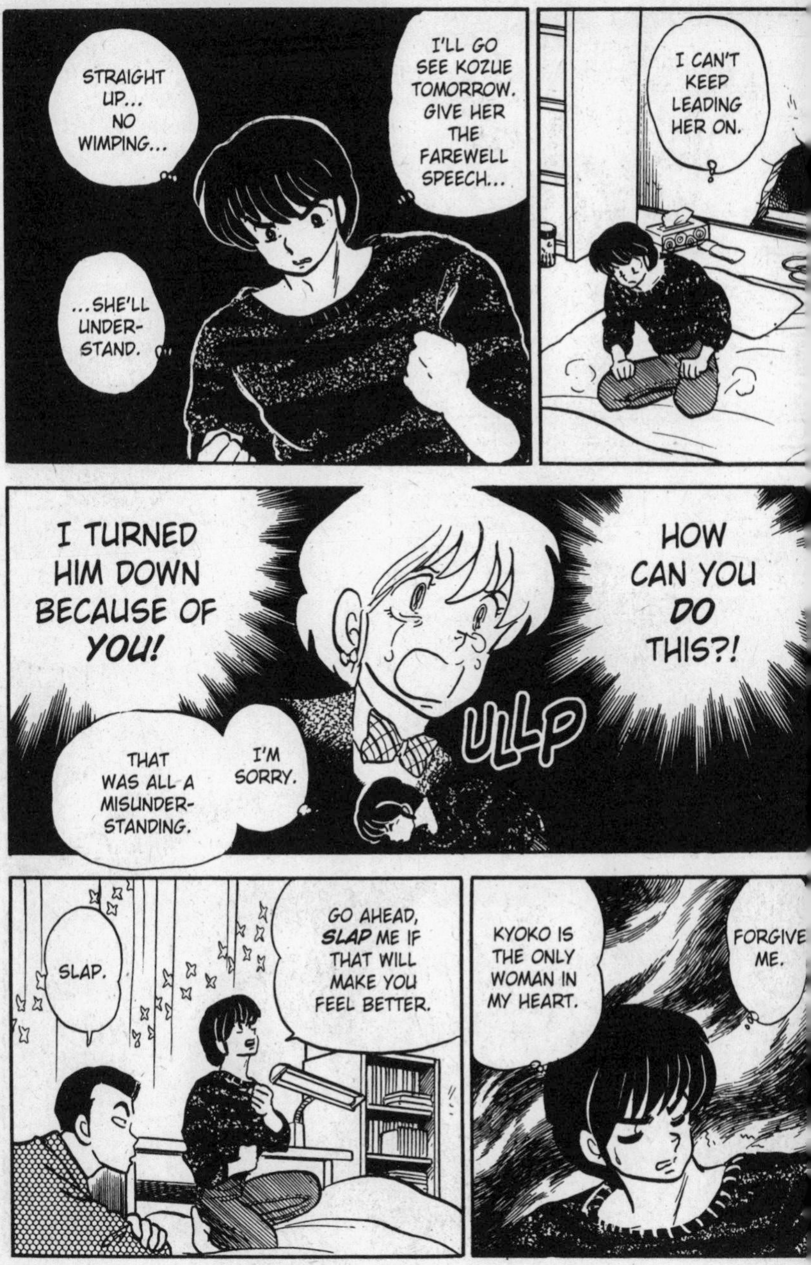
I CAN'T KEEP LEADING HER ON.
I'LL GO SEE KOZUE TOMORROW. GIVE HER THE FAREWELL SPEECH...
STRAIGHT UP... NO WIMPING...
...SHE'LL UNDER-STAND.
HOW CAN YOU DO THIS?!
I TURNED HIM DOWN BECAUSE OF YOU!
ULLP
I'M SORRY.
THAT WAS ALL A MISUNDER-STANDING.
FORGIVE ME.
KYOKO IS THE ONLY WOMAN IN MY HEART.
GO AHEAD, SLAP ME IF THAT WILL MAKE YOU FEEL BETTER.
SLAP.

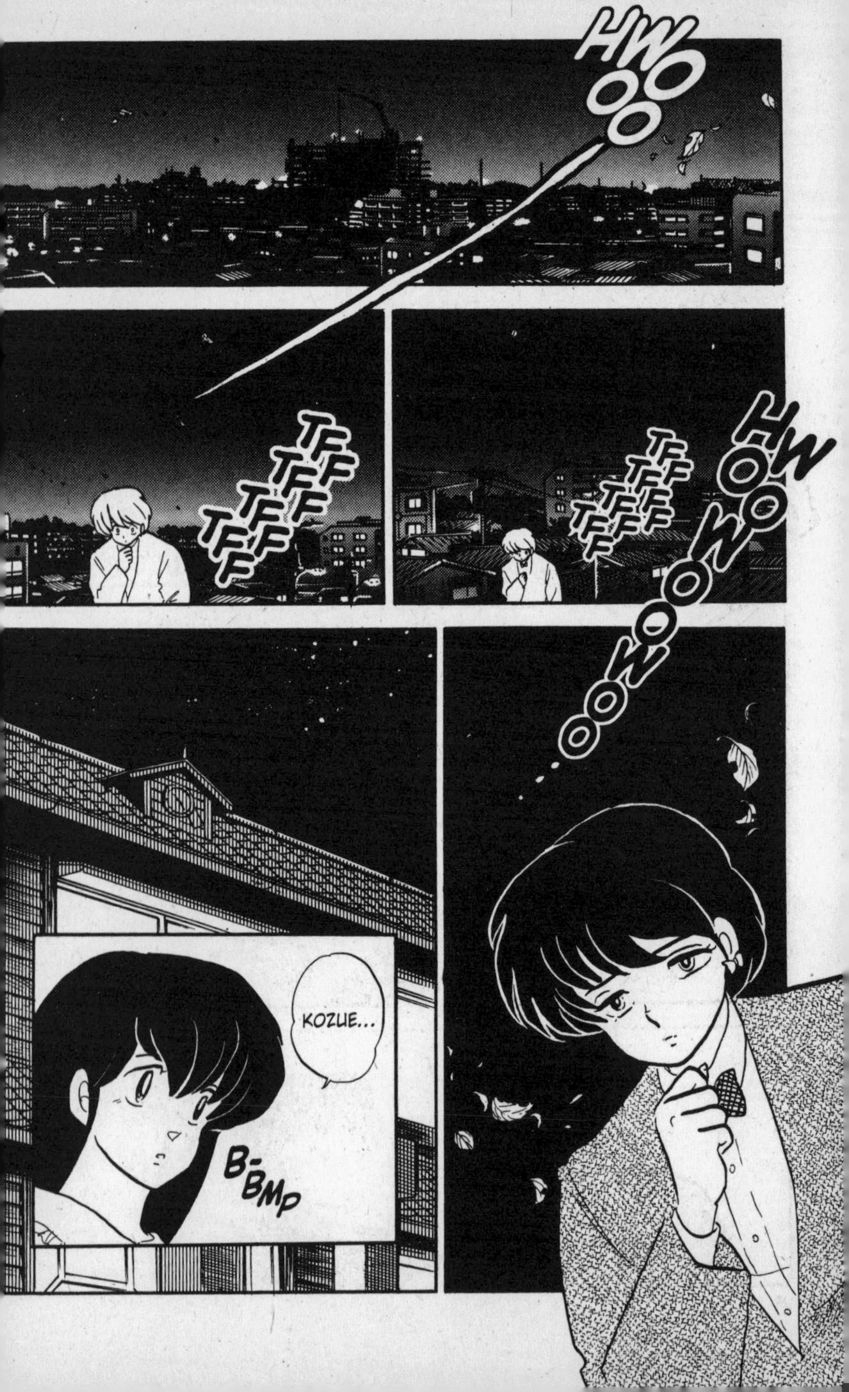

HWOOO
TFF TFF TFF TFF
HWOOWOOWOOWOOO...
TFF TFF TFF TFF
KOZUE...
B-BMP

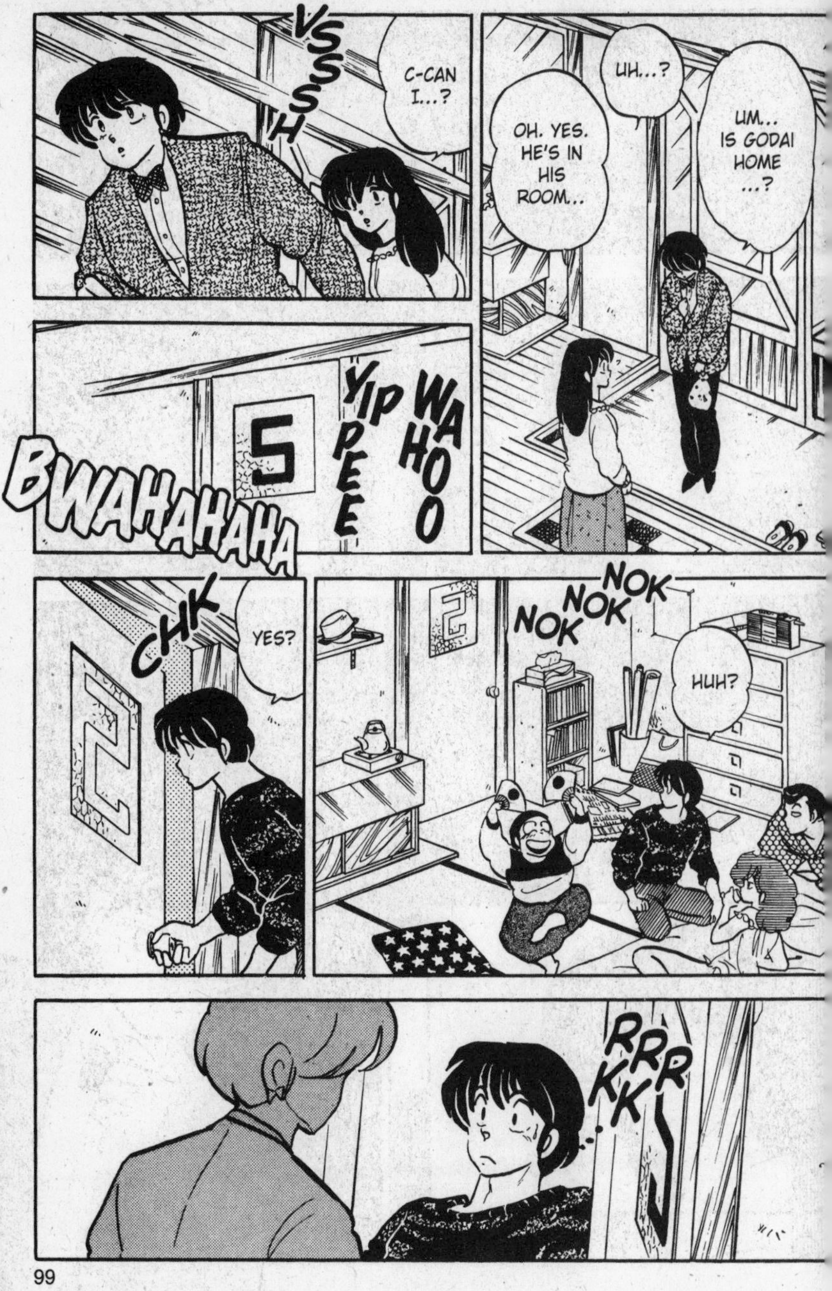
UM... IS GODAI HOME ...?
UH...?
OH. YES. HE'S IN HIS ROOM...
VSSSH
C-CAN I...?
WAHOO
YIPPEEE
BWAHAHAHA
NOK NOK NOK
HUH?
CHK
YES?
RRRKK

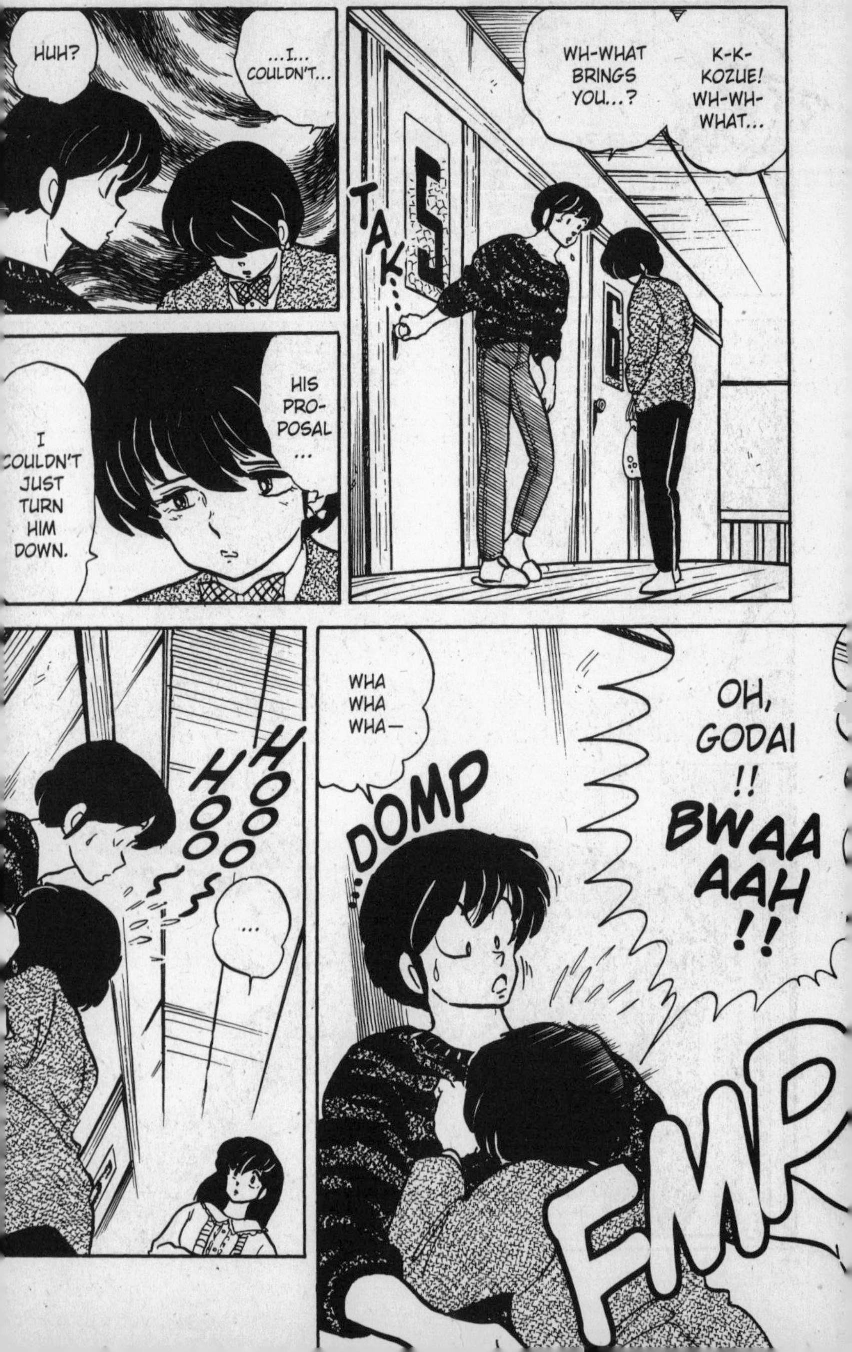
K-K-KOZUE! WH-WH-WHAT...
WH-WHAT BRINGS YOU...?
TAK...
...I... COULDN'T...
HUH?
HIS PROPOSAL...
I COULDN'T JUST TURN HIM DOWN.
OH, GODAI!!
BWAAAAH!!
FMP
DOMP
WHA WHA WHA—
HOOOO
HOOOO
...

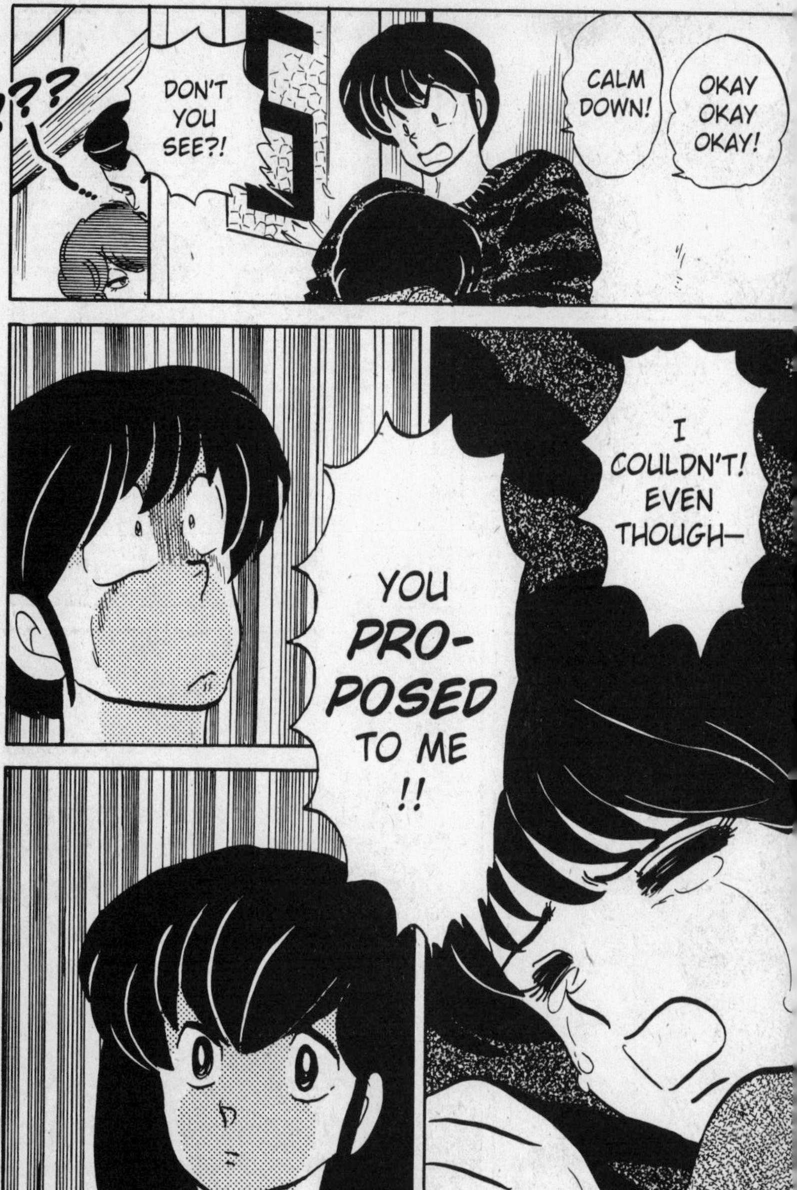
OKAY OKAY OKAY!
CALM DOWN!
DON'T YOU SEE?!
???
I COULDN'T! EVEN THOUGH—
YOU PROPOSED TO ME !!

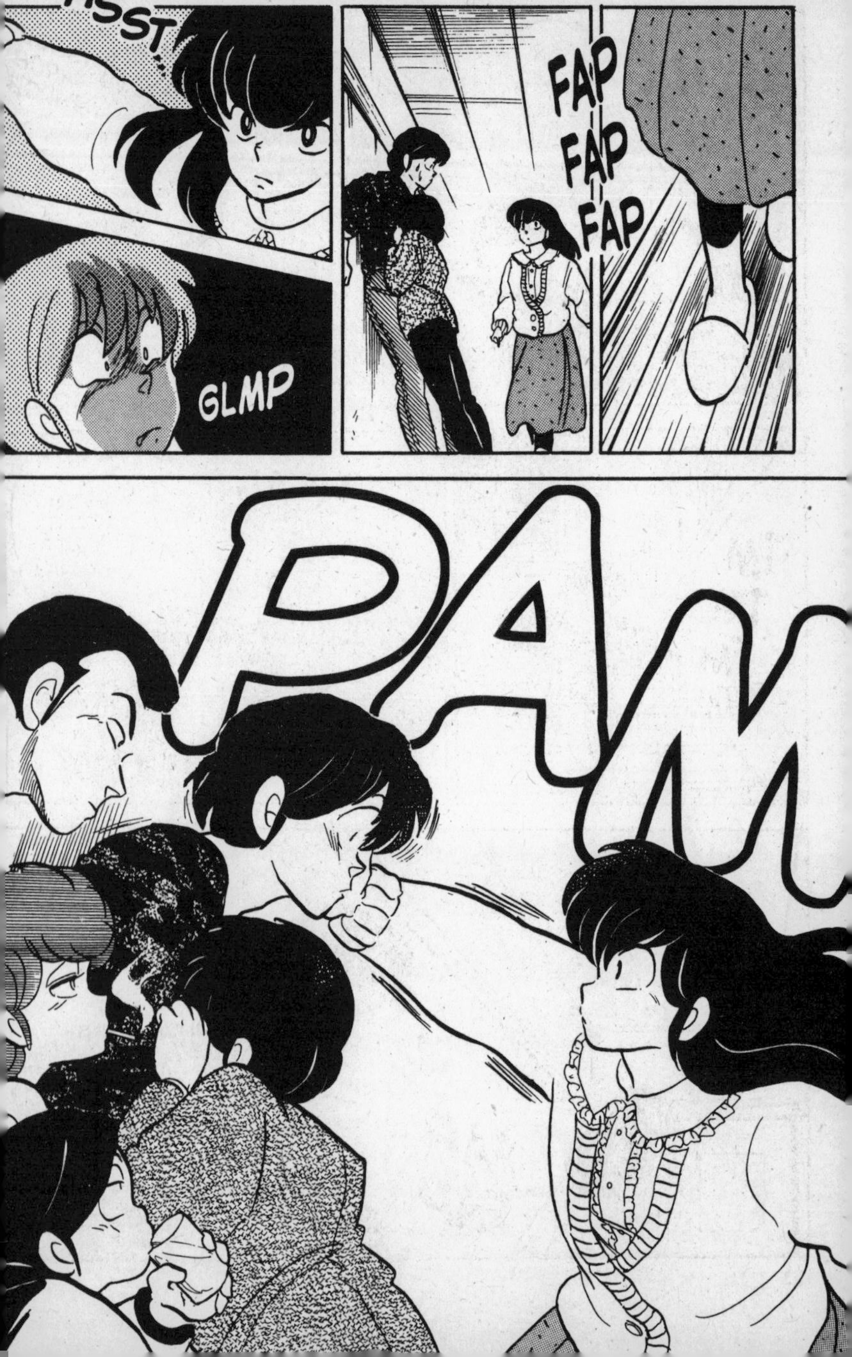
FAP
FAP
FAP
HSST
GLMP
PAM

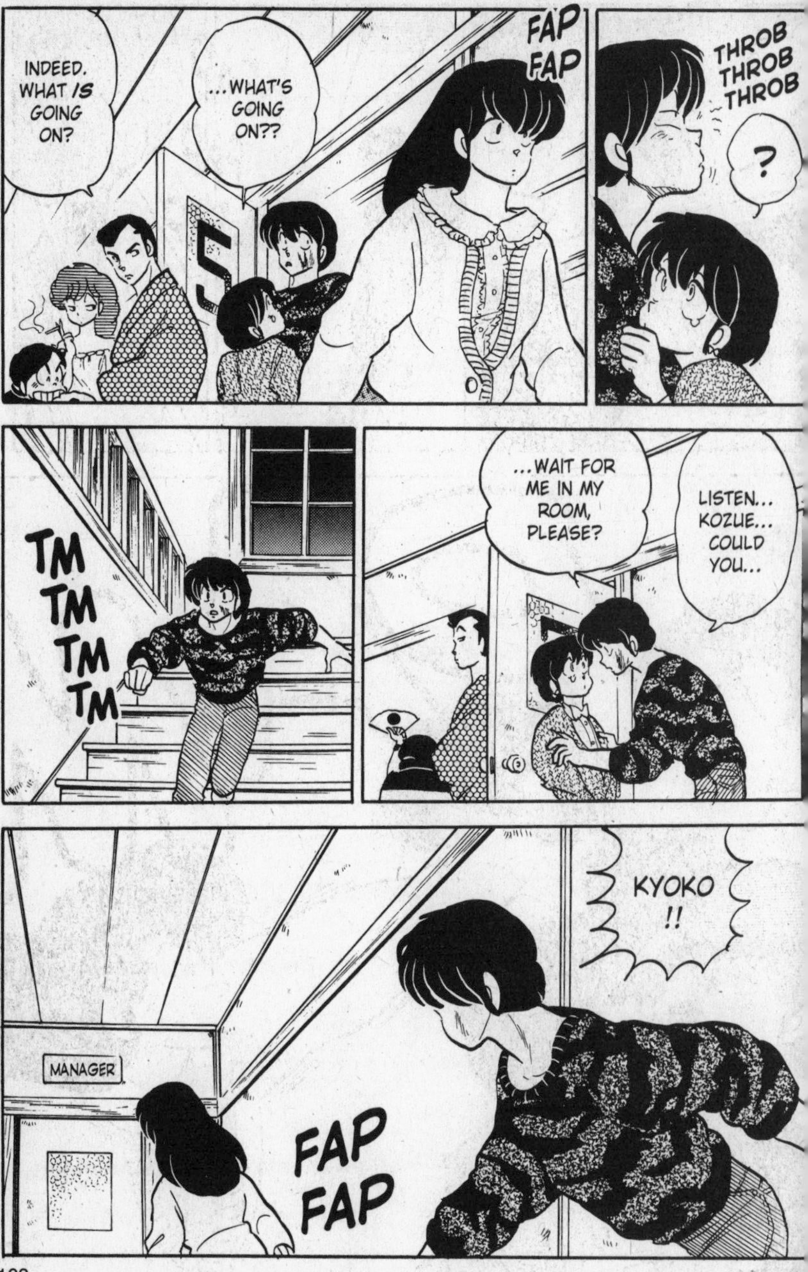
INDEED. WHAT IS GOING ON?
...WHAT'S GOING ON??
FAP FAP
THROB THROB THROB
?
TM TM TM TM
...WAIT FOR ME IN MY ROOM, PLEASE?
LISTEN... KOZUE... COULD YOU...
MANAGER
FAP FAP
KYOKO !!

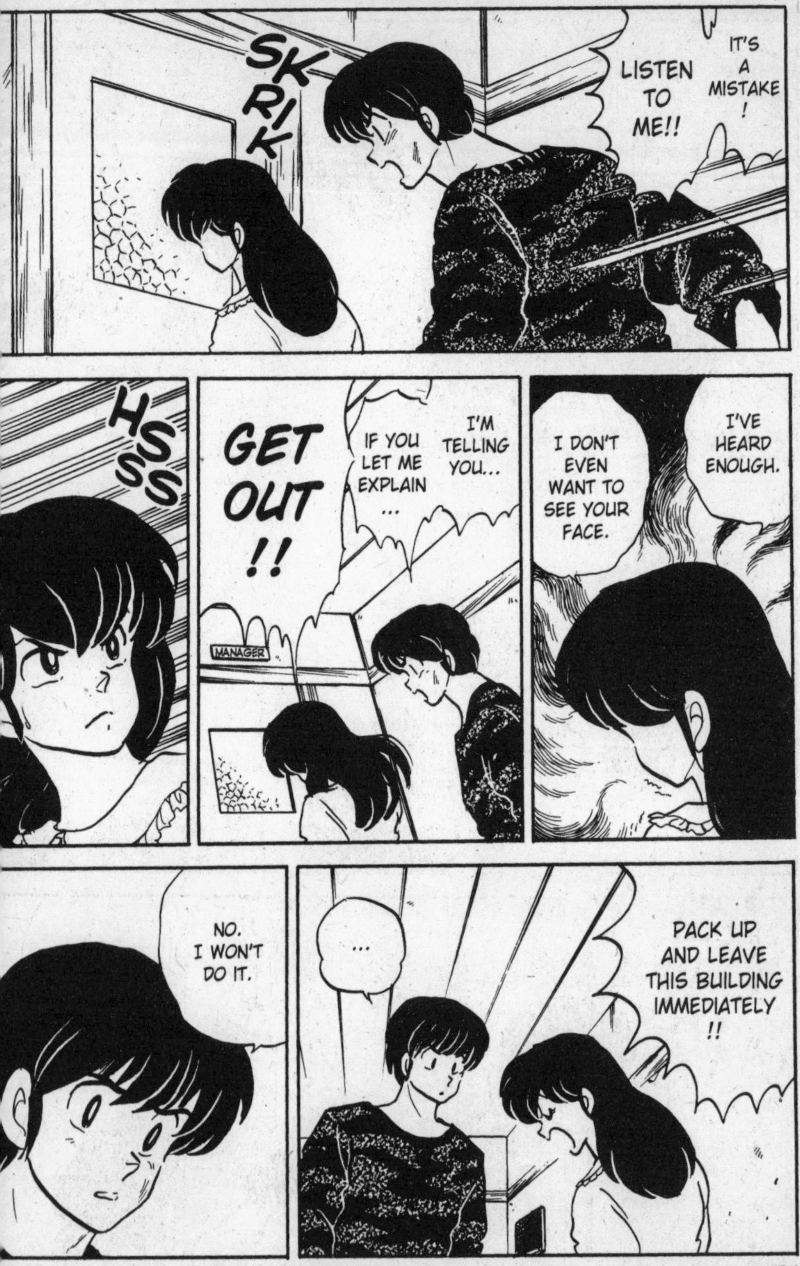

IT'S A MISTAKE!
LISTEN TO ME!!
SKRIK
I'VE HEARD ENOUGH.
I DON'T EVEN WANT TO SEE YOUR FACE.
I'M TELLING YOU...
IF YOU LET ME EXPLAIN ...
GET OUT!!
MANAGER
HSSSS
PACK UP AND LEAVE THIS BUILDING IMMEDIATELY!!
...
NO. I WON'T DO IT.

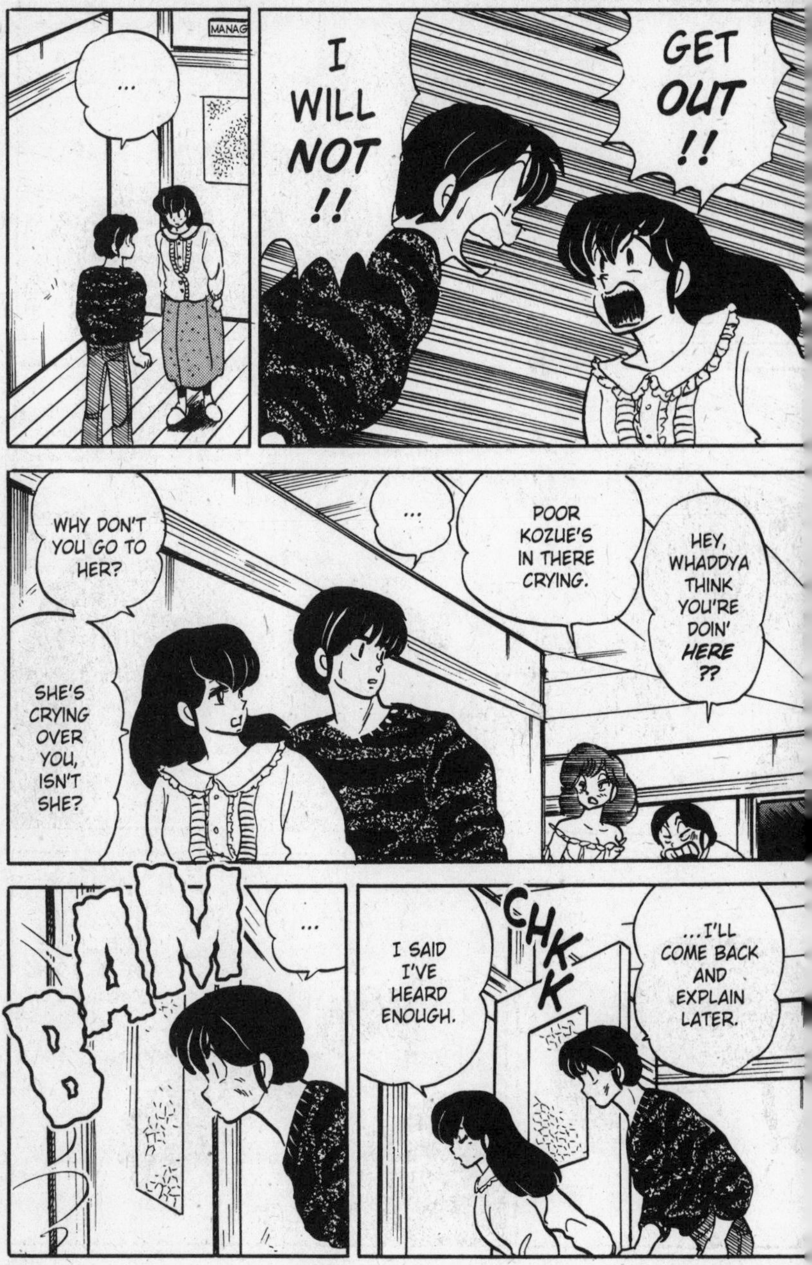
GET OUT!!
I WILL NOT!!
...
MANAG
HEY, WHADDYA THINK YOU'RE DOIN' HERE??
POOR KOZUE'S IN THERE CRYING.
...
WHY DON'T YOU GO TO HER?
SHE'S CRYING OVER YOU, ISN'T SHE?
...I'LL COME BACK AND EXPLAIN LATER.
CHKK
I SAID I'VE HEARD ENOUGH.
...
BAM

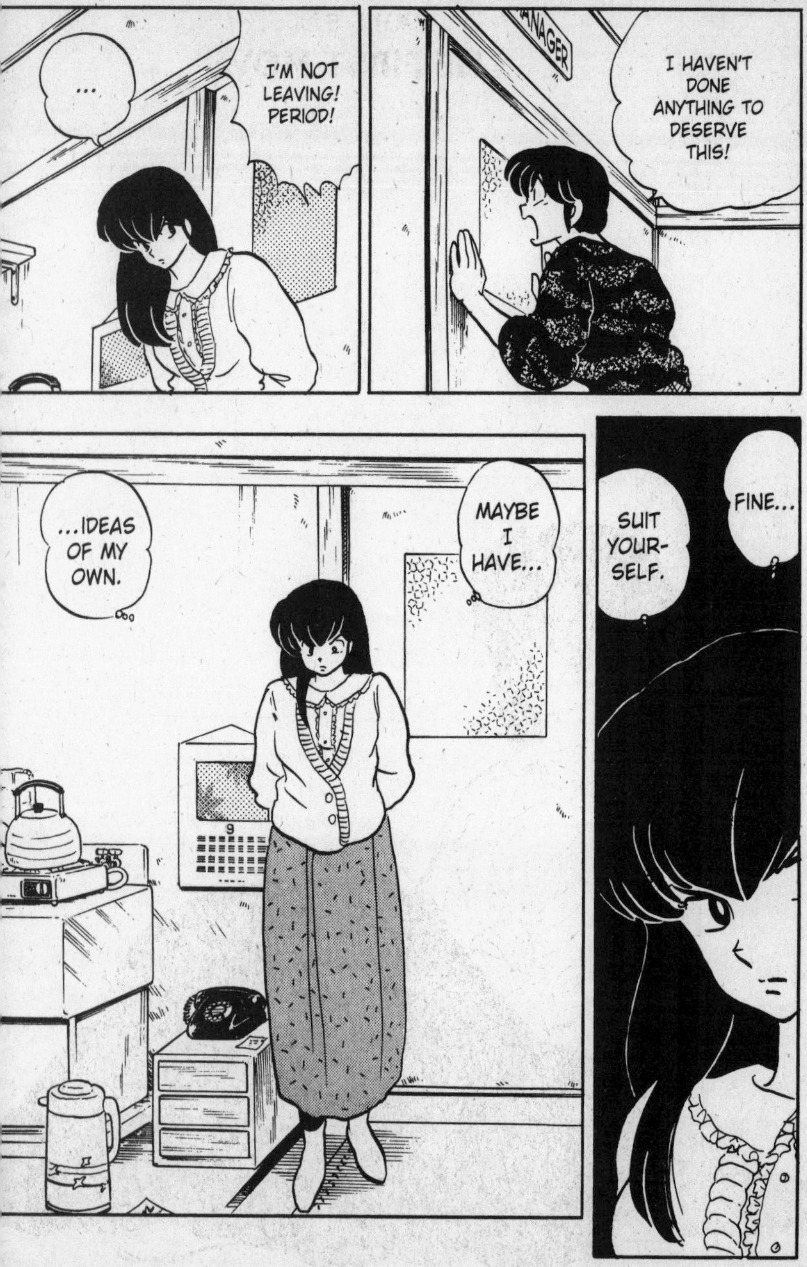
...
I'M NOT LEAVING! PERIOD!
MANAGER
I HAVEN'T DONE ANYTHING TO DESERVE THIS!
MAYBE I HAVE...
...IDEAS OF MY OWN.
FINE...
SUIT YOURSELF.

PART SIX

THE FIRST MOVE

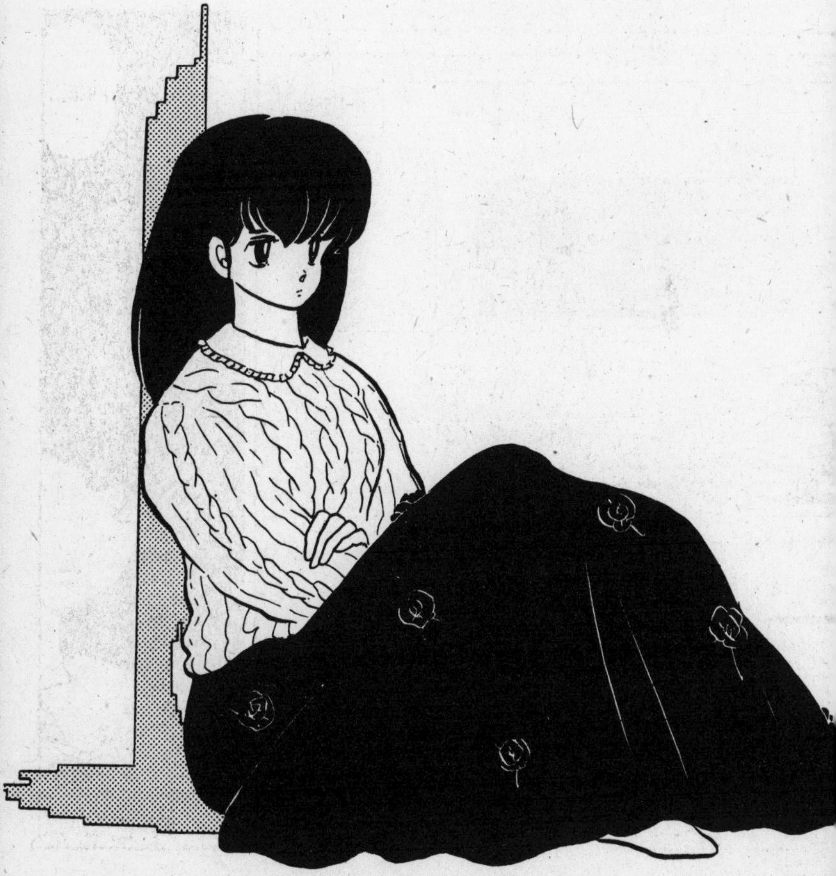

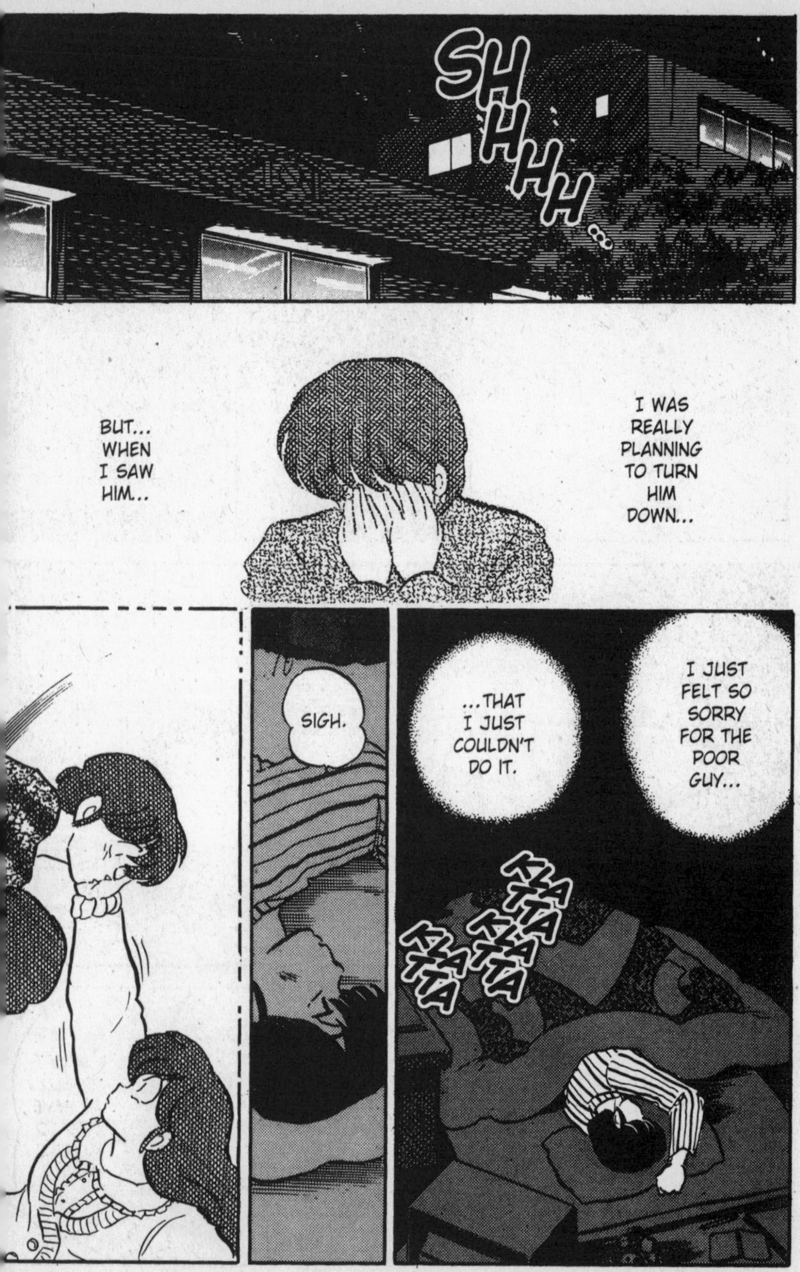
SHHHH...
I WAS REALLY PLANNING TO TURN HIM DOWN...
BUT... WHEN I SAW HIM...
I JUST FELT SO SORRY FOR THE POOR GUY...
...THAT I JUST COULDN'T DO IT.
KLATTA KLATTA KLATTA
SIGH.

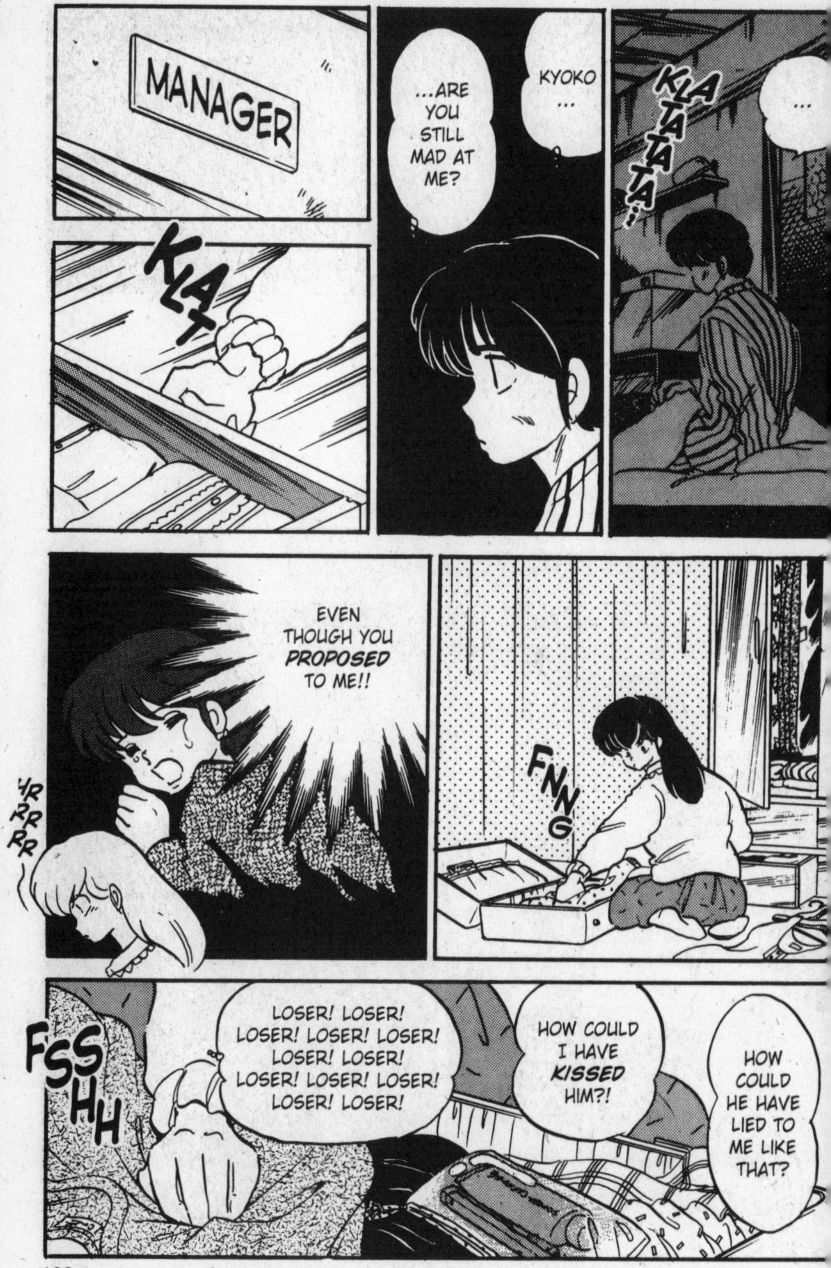
...
KLATATATA...
KYOKO ...
...ARE YOU STILL MAD AT ME?
MANAGER
KLAT
FNNG
EVEN THOUGH YOU PROPOSED TO ME!!
HRRRRR
HOW COULD HE HAVE LIED TO ME LIKE THAT?
HOW COULD I HAVE KISSED HIM?!
LOSER! LOSER! LOSER! LOSER! LOSER! LOSER! LOSER! LOSER! LOSER! LOSER! LOSER! LOSER!
FSSHH

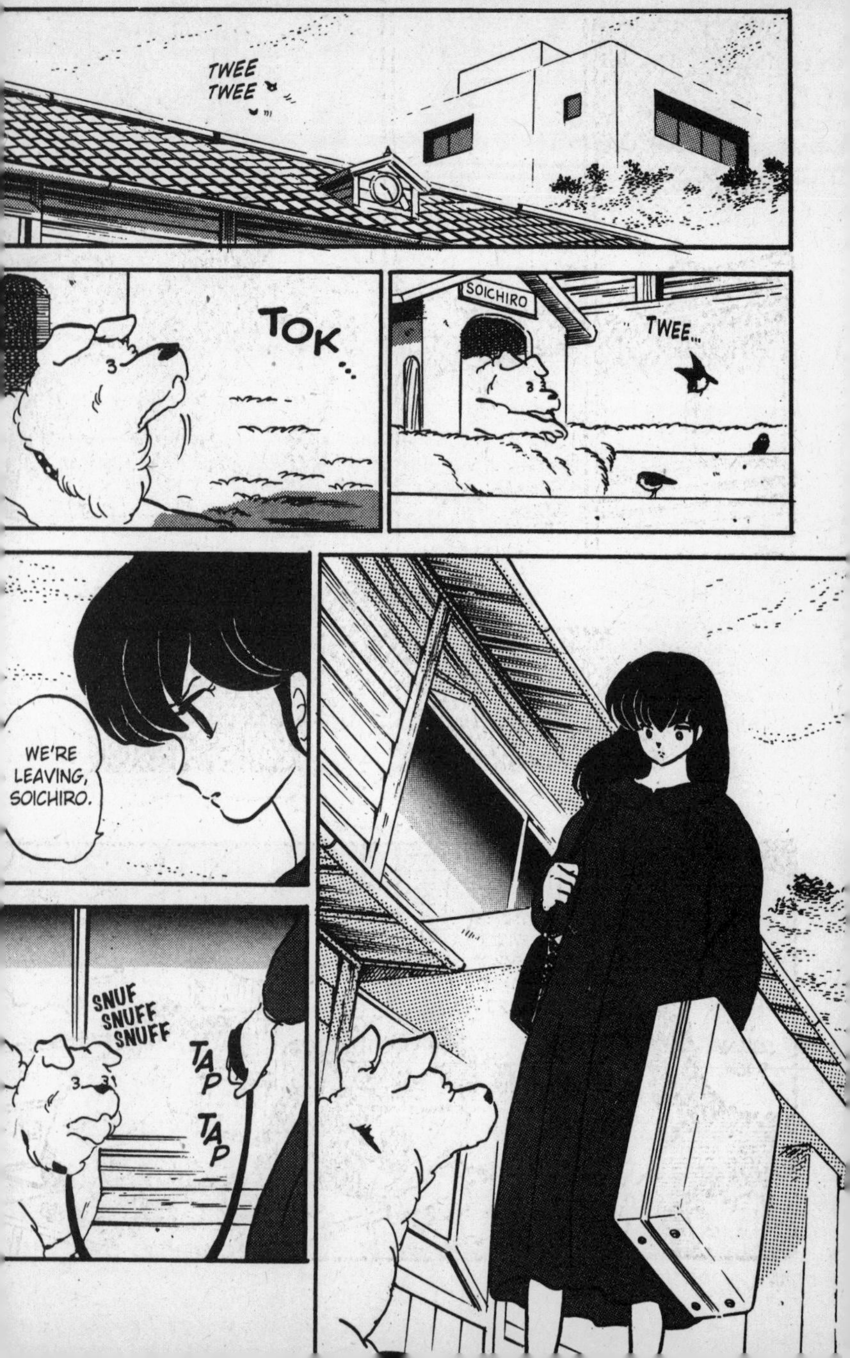
TWEE
TWEE
SOICHIRO
TWEE...
TOK...
WE'RE LEAVING, SOICHIRO.
SNUF SNUFF SNUFF
TAP TAP

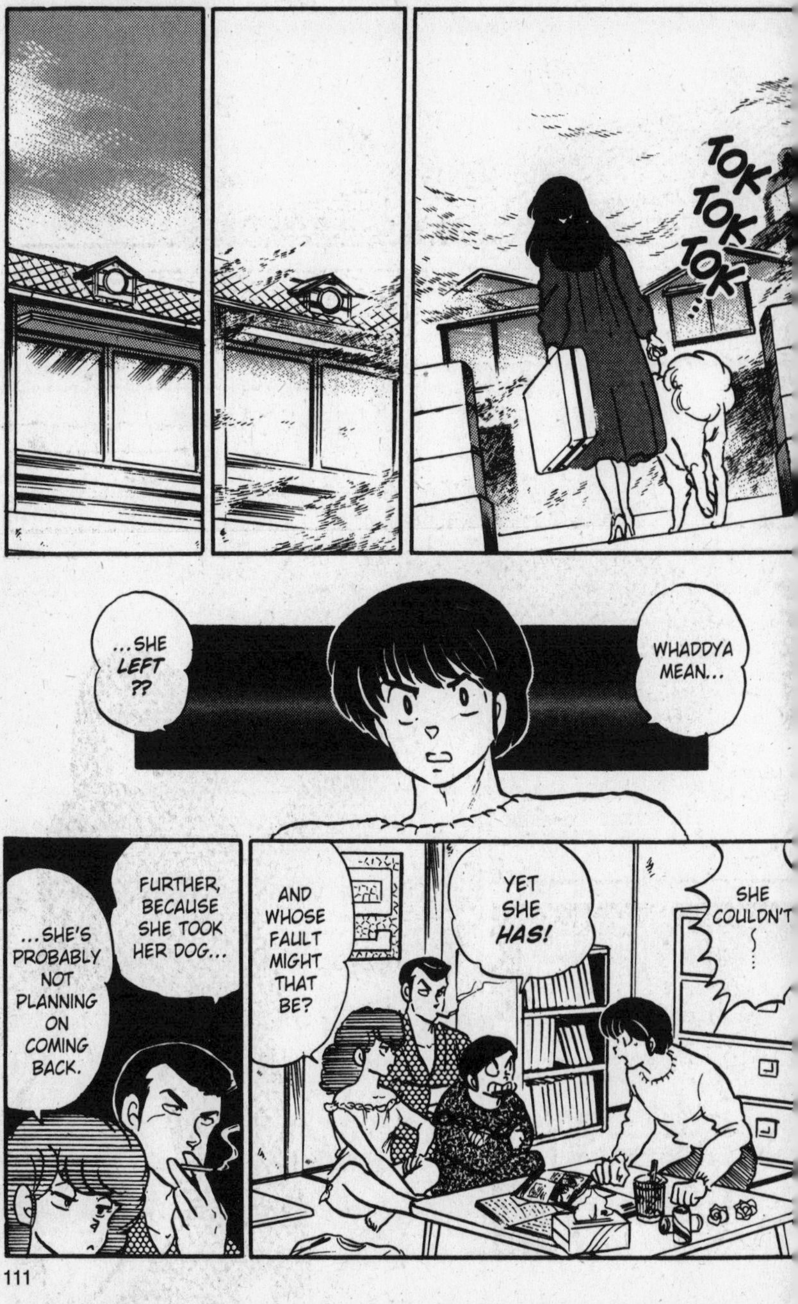
TOK TOK TOK...
WHADDYA MEAN...
...SHE LEFT ??
SHE COULDN'T...
YET SHE HAS!
AND WHOSE FAULT MIGHT THAT BE?
FURTHER, BECAUSE SHE TOOK HER DOG...
...SHE'S PROBABLY NOT PLANNING ON COMING BACK.

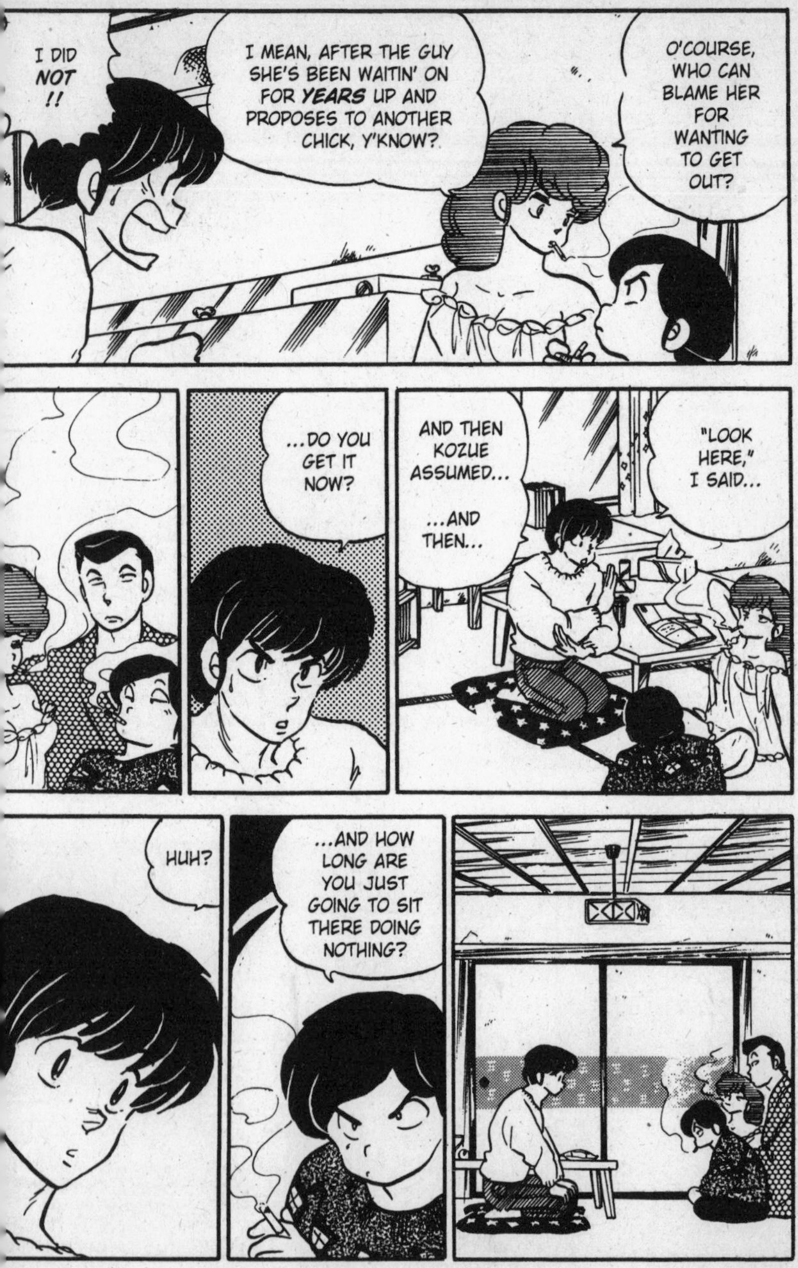
O'COURSE, WHO CAN BLAME HER FOR WANTING TO GET OUT?
I MEAN, AFTER THE GUY SHE'S BEEN WAITIN' ON FOR **YEARS** UP AND PROPOSES TO ANOTHER CHICK, Y'KNOW?
I DID **NOT** !!
"LOOK HERE," I SAID...
AND THEN KOZUE ASSUMED... ...AND THEN...
...DO YOU GET IT NOW?
...AND HOW LONG ARE YOU JUST GOING TO SIT THERE DOING NOTHING?
HUH?

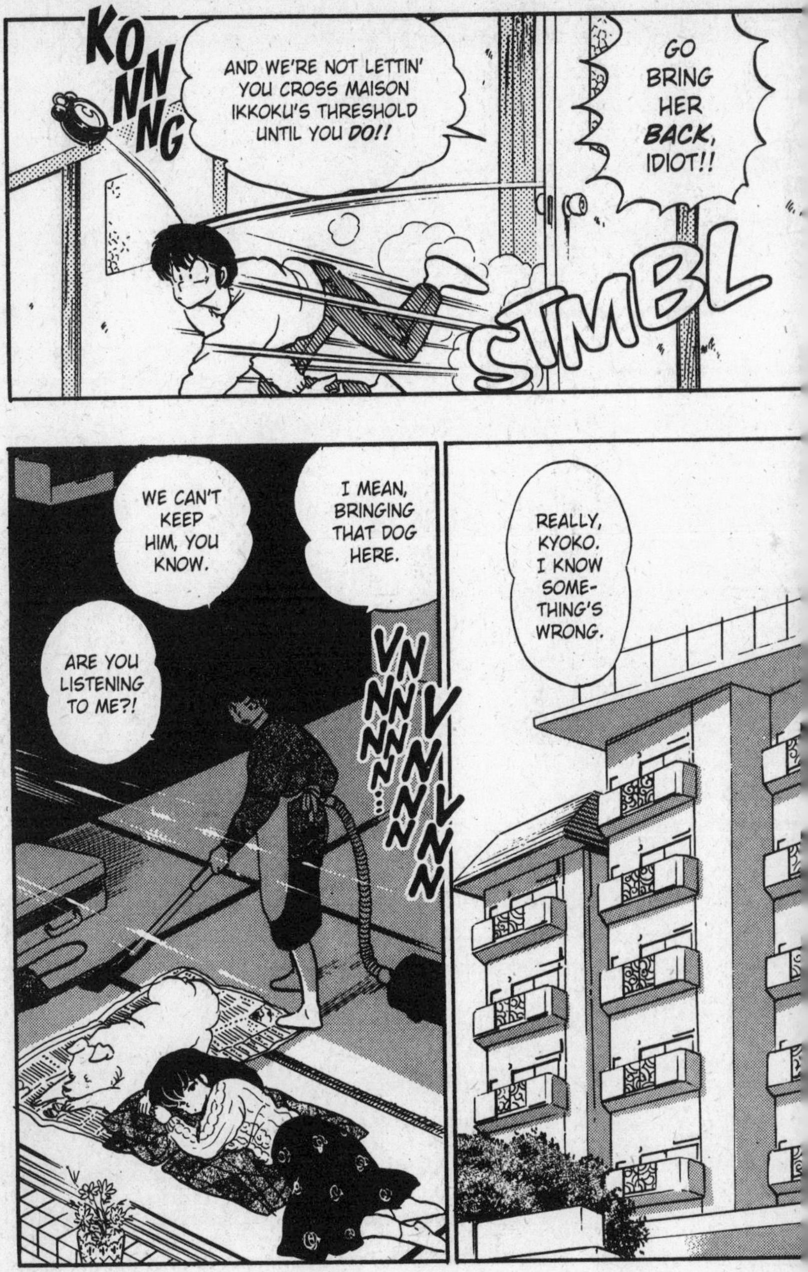
GO BRING HER BACK, IDIOT!!
AND WE'RE NOT LETTIN' YOU CROSS MAISON IKKOKU'S THRESHOLD UNTIL YOU DO!!
KONNNG
STMBL
REALLY, KYOKO. I KNOW SOME-THING'S WRONG.
I MEAN, BRINGING THAT DOG HERE.
WE CAN'T KEEP HIM, YOU KNOW.
ARE YOU LISTENING TO ME?!
VNNNNN...
VNNNNN
VNNNN

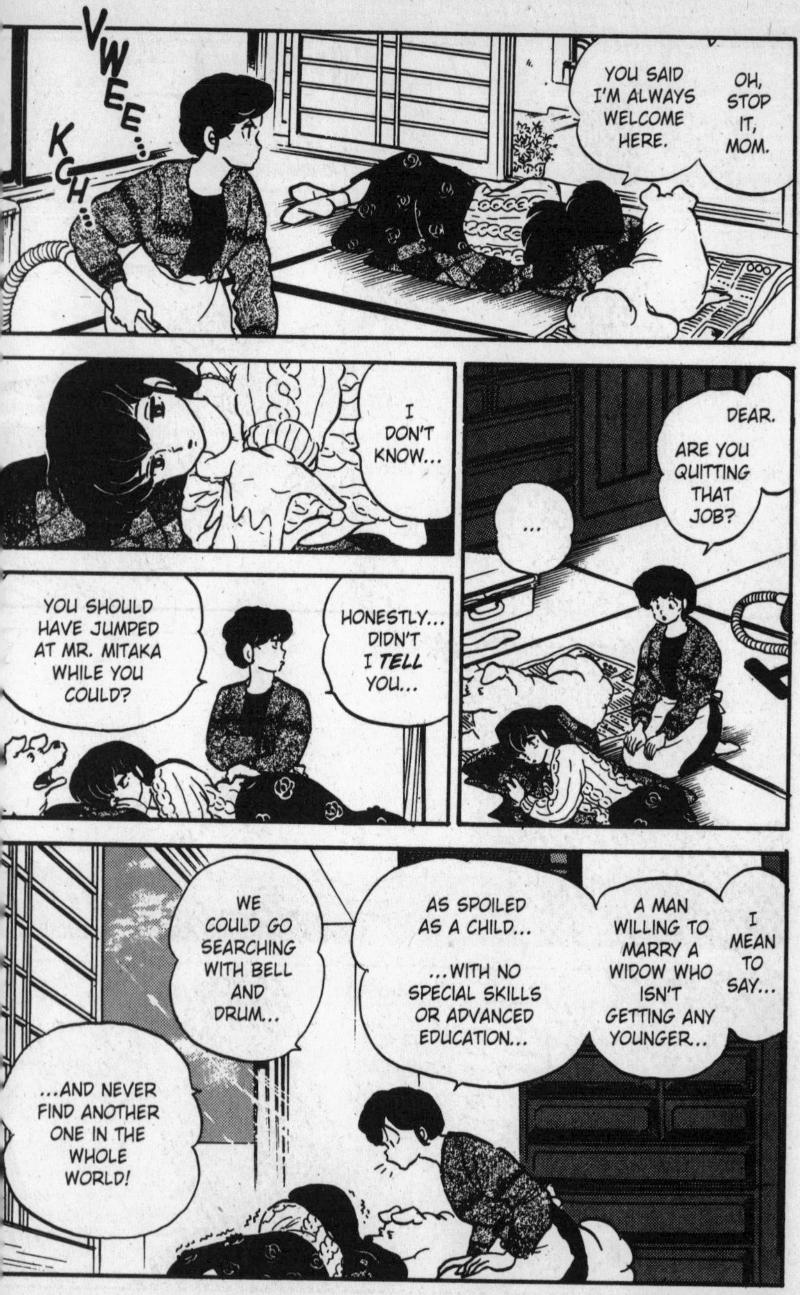
VWEE...
KCH...
OH, STOP IT, MOM.
YOU SAID I'M ALWAYS WELCOME HERE.
DEAR.
ARE YOU QUITTING THAT JOB?
...
I DON'T KNOW...
HONESTLY... DIDN'T I *TELL* YOU...
YOU SHOULD HAVE JUMPED AT MR. MITAKA WHILE YOU COULD?
I MEAN TO SAY...
A MAN WILLING TO MARRY A WIDOW WHO ISN'T GETTING ANY YOUNGER...
AS SPOILED AS A CHILD...
...WITH NO SPECIAL SKILLS OR ADVANCED EDUCATION...
WE COULD GO SEARCHING WITH BELL AND DRUM...
...AND NEVER FIND ANOTHER ONE IN THE WHOLE WORLD!

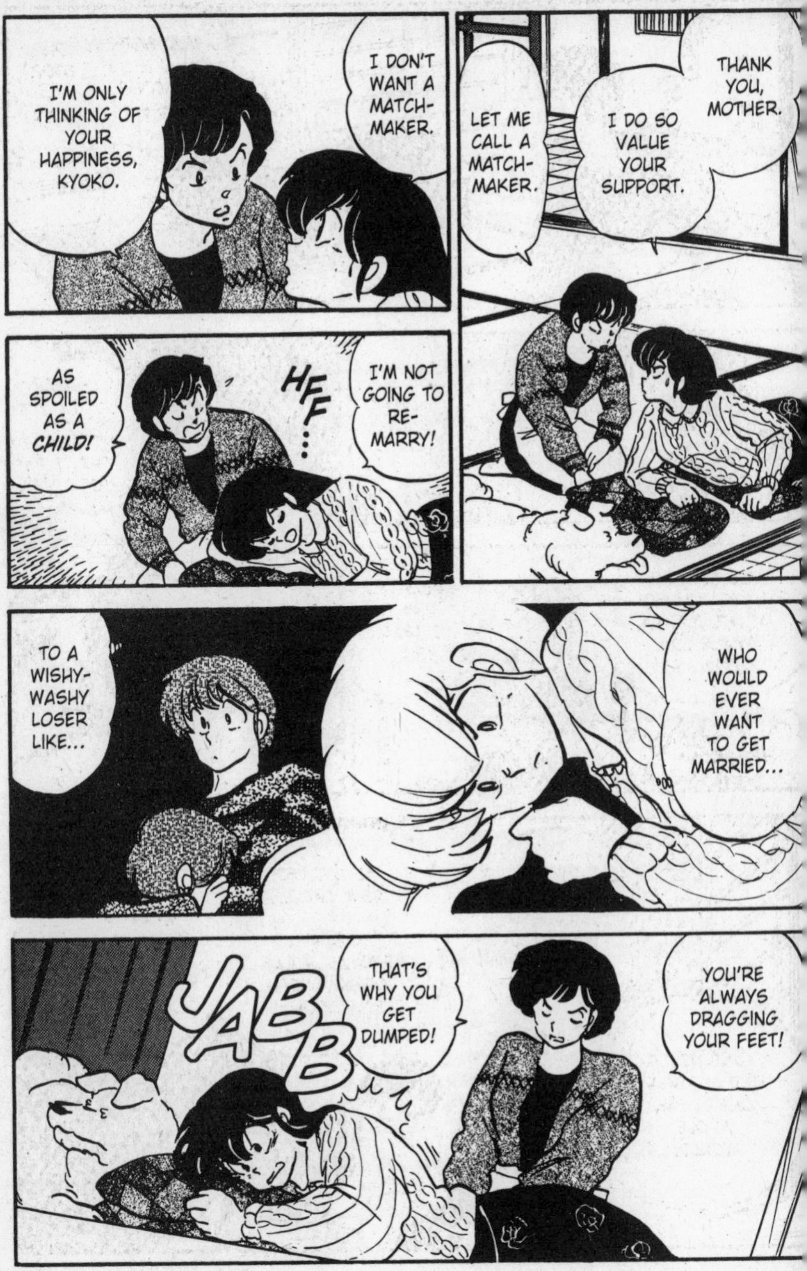

THANK YOU, MOTHER.
I DO SO VALUE YOUR SUPPORT.
LET ME CALL A MATCH-MAKER.
I DON'T WANT A MATCH-MAKER.
I'M ONLY THINKING OF YOUR HAPPINESS, KYOKO.
I'M NOT GOING TO RE-MARRY!
HFF...
AS SPOILED AS A CHILD!
WHO WOULD EVER WANT TO GET MARRIED...
TO A WISHY-WASHY LOSER LIKE...
YOU'RE ALWAYS DRAGGING YOUR FEET!
THAT'S WHY YOU GET DUMPED!
JABB

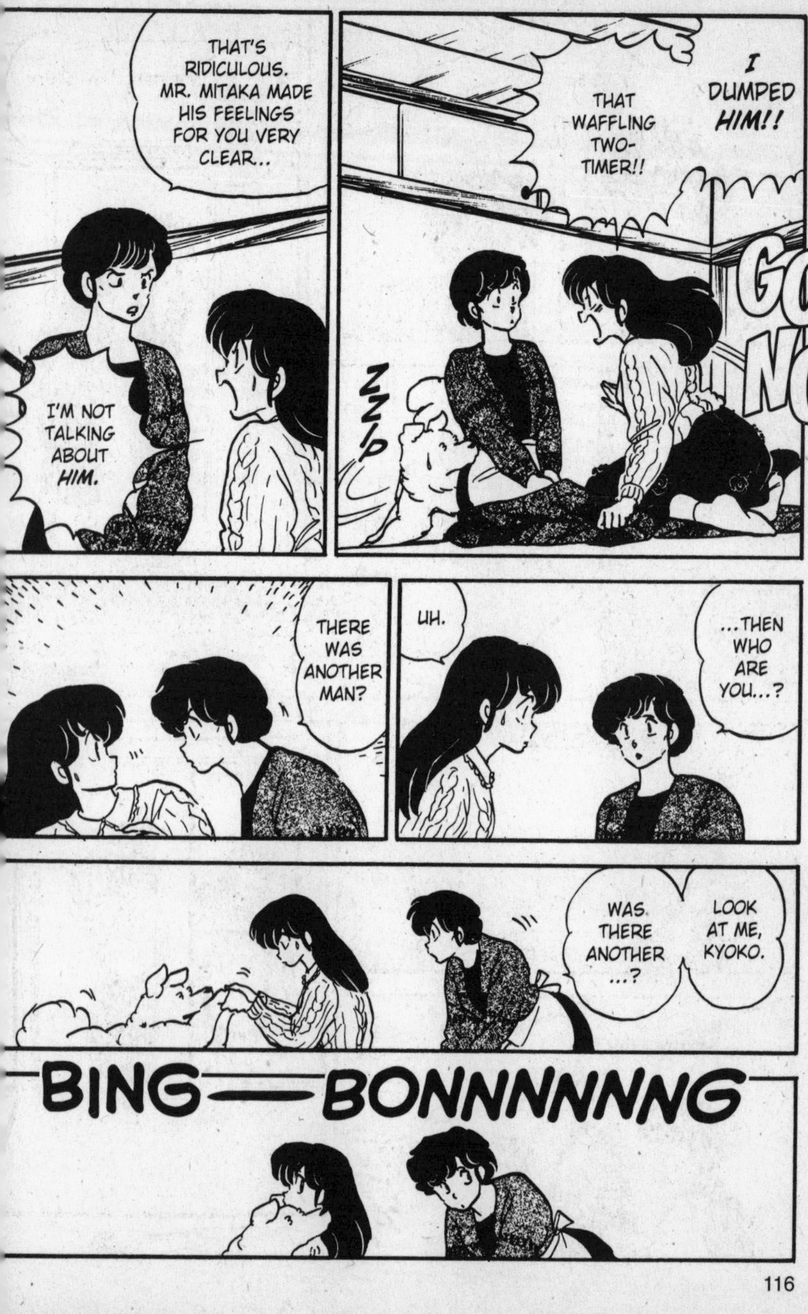
THAT'S RIDICULOUS. MR. MITAKA MADE HIS FEELINGS FOR YOU VERY CLEAR...
I'M NOT TALKING ABOUT HIM.
I DUMPED HIM!!
THAT WAFFLING TWO-TIMER!!
GONG
ZZZ
THERE WAS ANOTHER MAN?
...THEN WHO ARE YOU...?
UH.
LOOK AT ME, KYOKO.
WAS THERE ANOTHER ...?
BING—BONNNNNNG

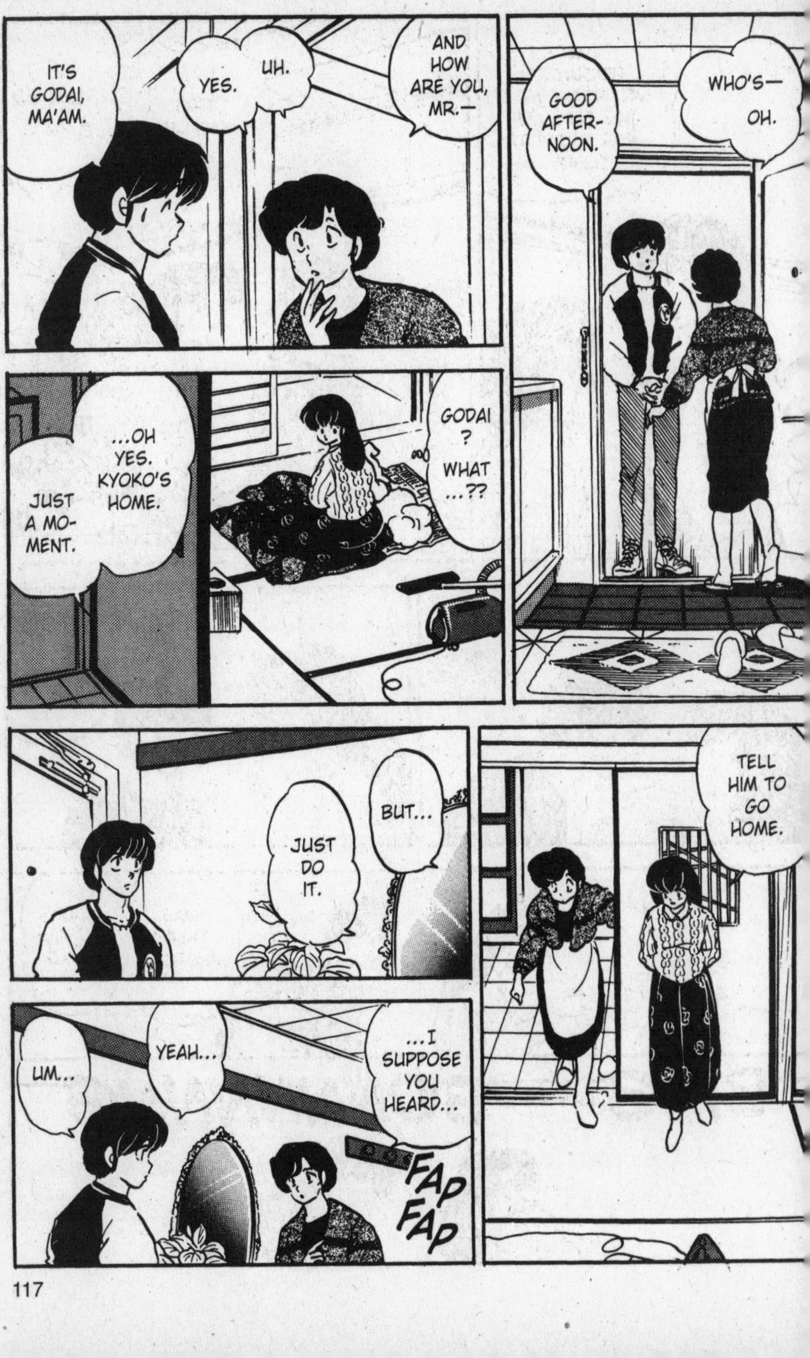
WHO'S— OH.
GOOD AFTERNOON.
AND HOW ARE YOU, MR.—
UH. YES.
IT'S GODAI, MA'AM.
GODAI? WHAT...??
...OH YES. KYOKO'S HOME.
JUST A MOMENT.
TELL HIM TO GO HOME.
BUT...
JUST DO IT.
...I SUPPOSE YOU HEARD...
YEAH...
UM...
FAP FAP

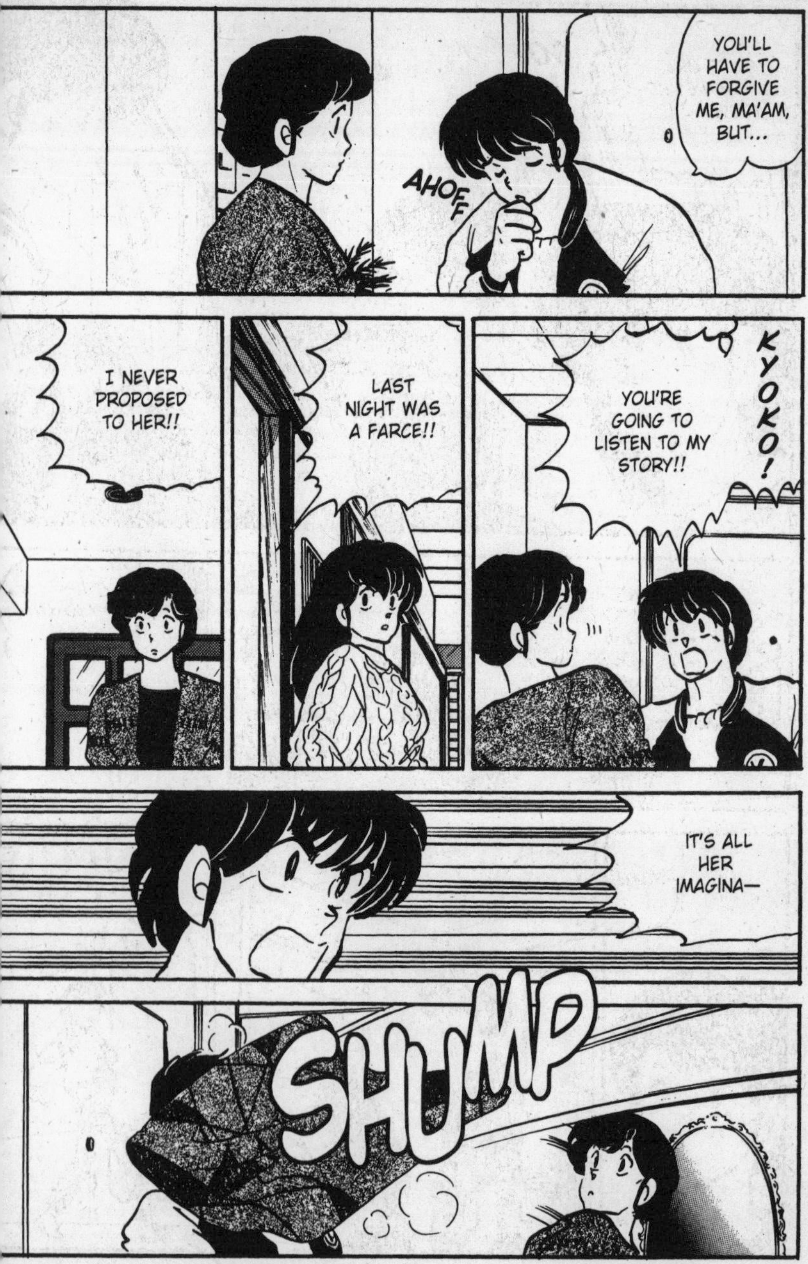
YOU'LL HAVE TO FORGIVE ME, MA'AM, BUT...
AHOFF
I NEVER PROPOSED TO HER!!
LAST NIGHT WAS A FARCE!!
KYOKO!
YOU'RE GOING TO LISTEN TO MY STORY!!
IT'S ALL HER IMAGINA—
SHUMP

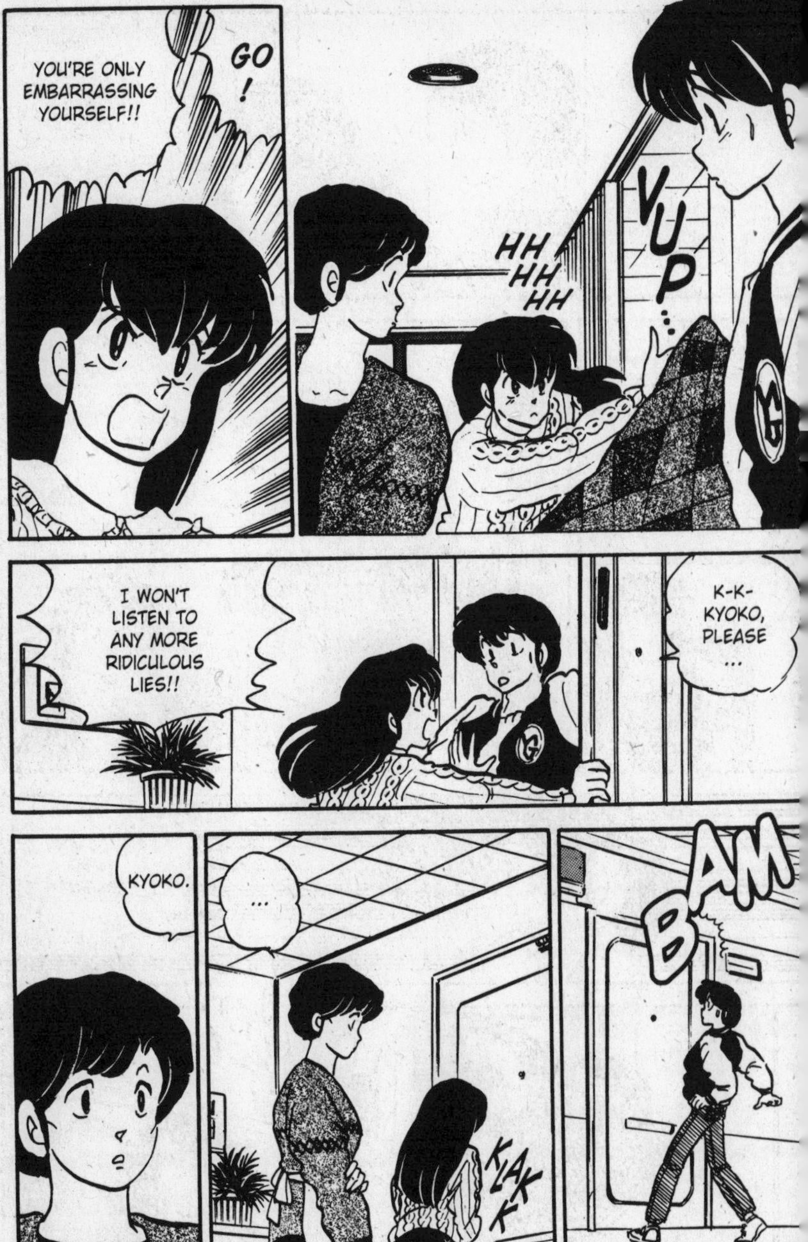
VUP...
HH HH HH
GO!
YOU'RE ONLY EMBARRASSING YOURSELF!!
K-K-KYOKO, PLEASE ...
I WON'T LISTEN TO ANY MORE RIDICULOUS LIES!!
BAM
...
KLAK KLAK
KYOKO.

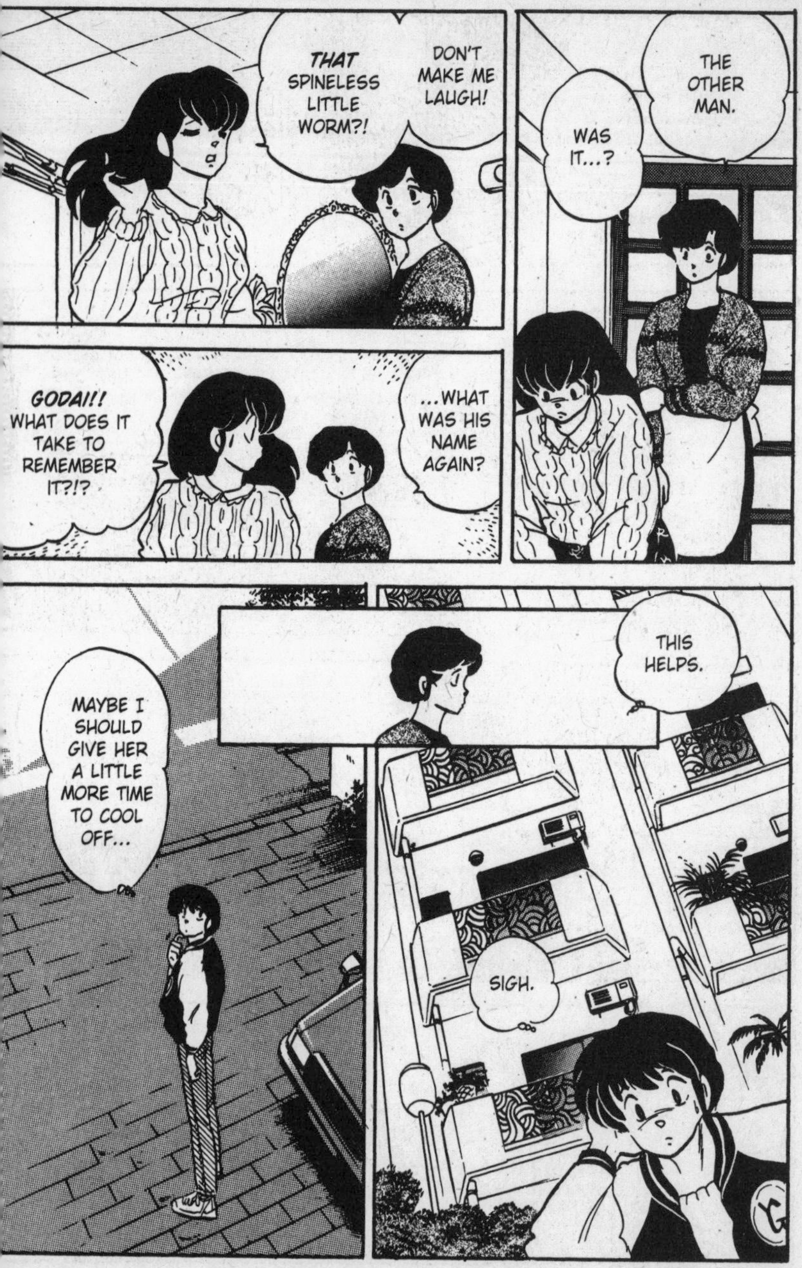
THAT SPINELESS LITTLE WORM?!
DON'T MAKE ME LAUGH!
WAS IT...?
THE OTHER MAN.
...WHAT WAS HIS NAME AGAIN?
GODAI!! WHAT DOES IT TAKE TO REMEMBER IT?!?
MAYBE I SHOULD GIVE HER A LITTLE MORE TIME TO COOL OFF...
THIS HELPS.
SIGH.

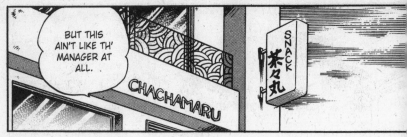

BUT THIS AIN'T LIKE TH' MANAGER AT ALL.

CHACHAMARU

AKEMI, CAN YOU PLEASE WORK?!

INDEED.

I THOUGHT SHE HAD A WORKIN' WOMAN'S PRIDE.

I MEAN, DITCHIN' HER JOB LIKE THAT?

TH' BOTTOM LINE IS...

SHE RAN OUT...

NOR TO EXTORT RENT PAYMENTS.

NOBODY TO DAMPEN OUR PARTIES FOR A LITTLE WHILE.

SO LOOK AT THE BRIGHT SIDE.

WE ARE NEEDED NOW MORE THAN EVER.

...CUZ OF A DELICATE EMOTIONAL PROBL'M.

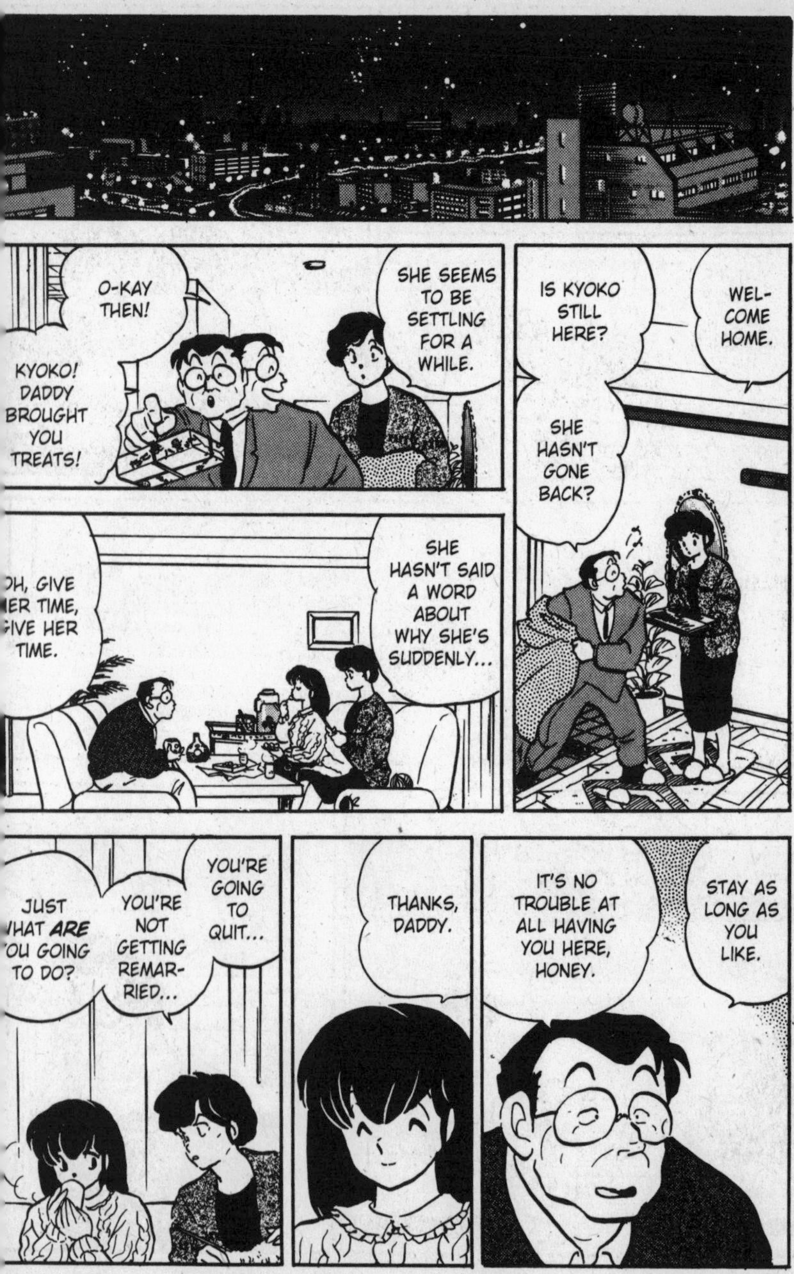
WEL-COME HOME.
IS KYOKO STILL HERE?
SHE HASN'T GONE BACK?
SHE SEEMS TO BE SETTLING FOR A WHILE.
O-KAY THEN!
KYOKO! DADDY BROUGHT YOU TREATS!
SHE HASN'T SAID A WORD ABOUT WHY SHE'S SUDDENLY...
H, GIVE ER TIME, IVE HER TIME.
STAY AS LONG AS YOU LIKE.
IT'S NO TROUBLE AT ALL HAVING YOU HERE, HONEY.
THANKS, DADDY.
YOU'RE GOING TO QUIT...
YOU'RE NOT GETTING REMAR-RIED...
JUST HAT *ARE* OU GOING TO DO?

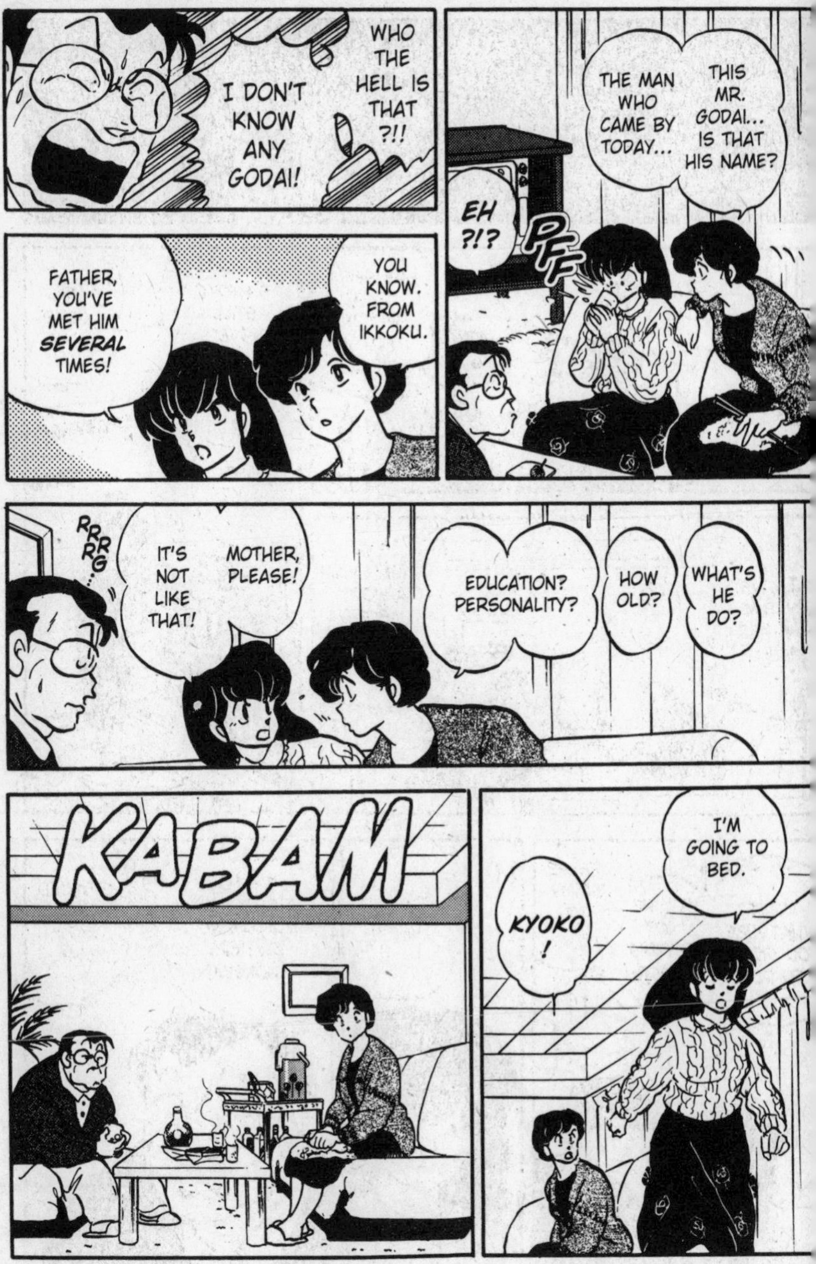
I DON'T KNOW ANY GODAI!
WHO THE HELL IS THAT?!!
THE MAN WHO CAME BY TODAY...
THIS MR. GODAI... IS THAT HIS NAME?
EH ?!?
PFF
FATHER, YOU'VE MET HIM SEVERAL TIMES!
YOU KNOW. FROM IKKOKU.
RRRG...
MOTHER, PLEASE!
IT'S NOT LIKE THAT!
EDUCATION? PERSONALITY?
HOW OLD?
WHAT'S HE DO?
KABAM
I'M GOING TO BED.
KYOKO!

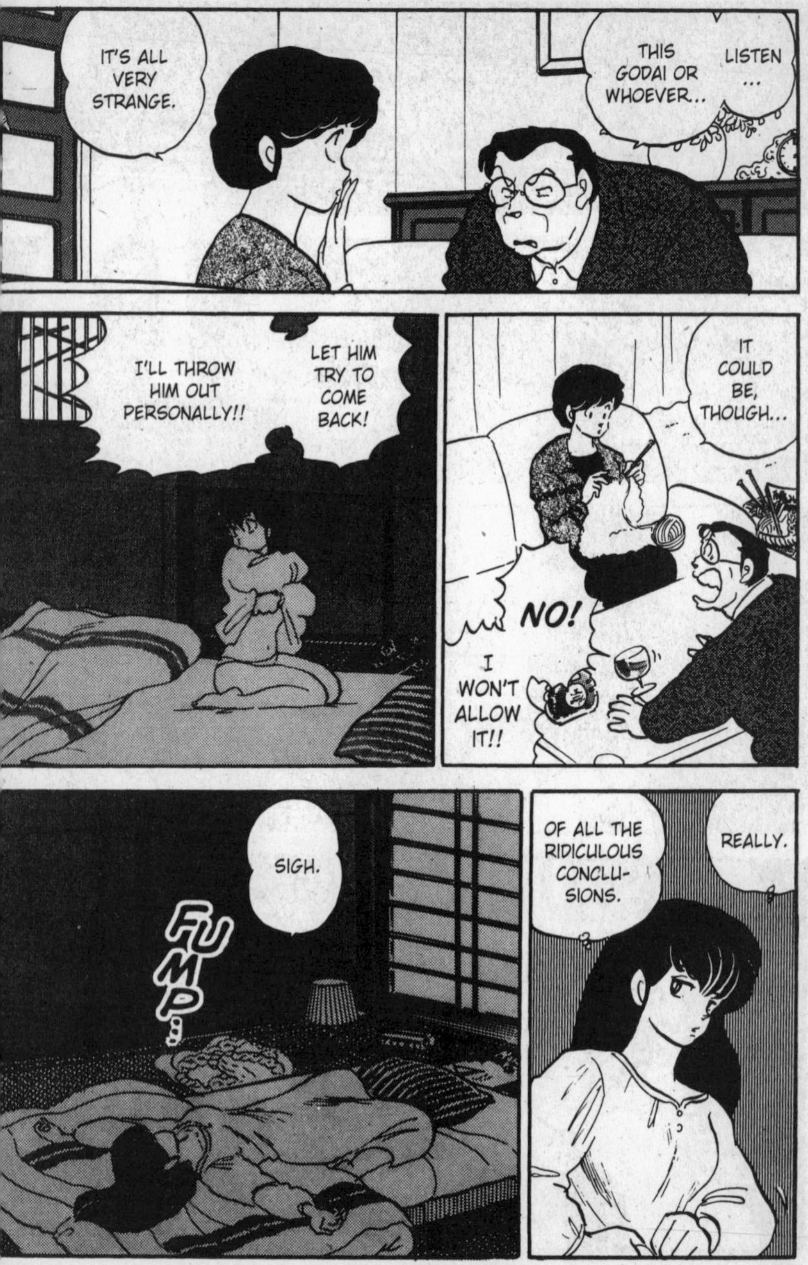
IT'S ALL VERY STRANGE.
LISTEN ...
THIS GODAI OR WHOEVER...
IT COULD BE, THOUGH...
NO!
I WON'T ALLOW IT!!
LET HIM TRY TO COME BACK!
I'LL THROW HIM OUT PERSONALLY!!
REALLY.
OF ALL THE RIDICULOUS CONCLU-SIONS.
SIGH.
FUMP...

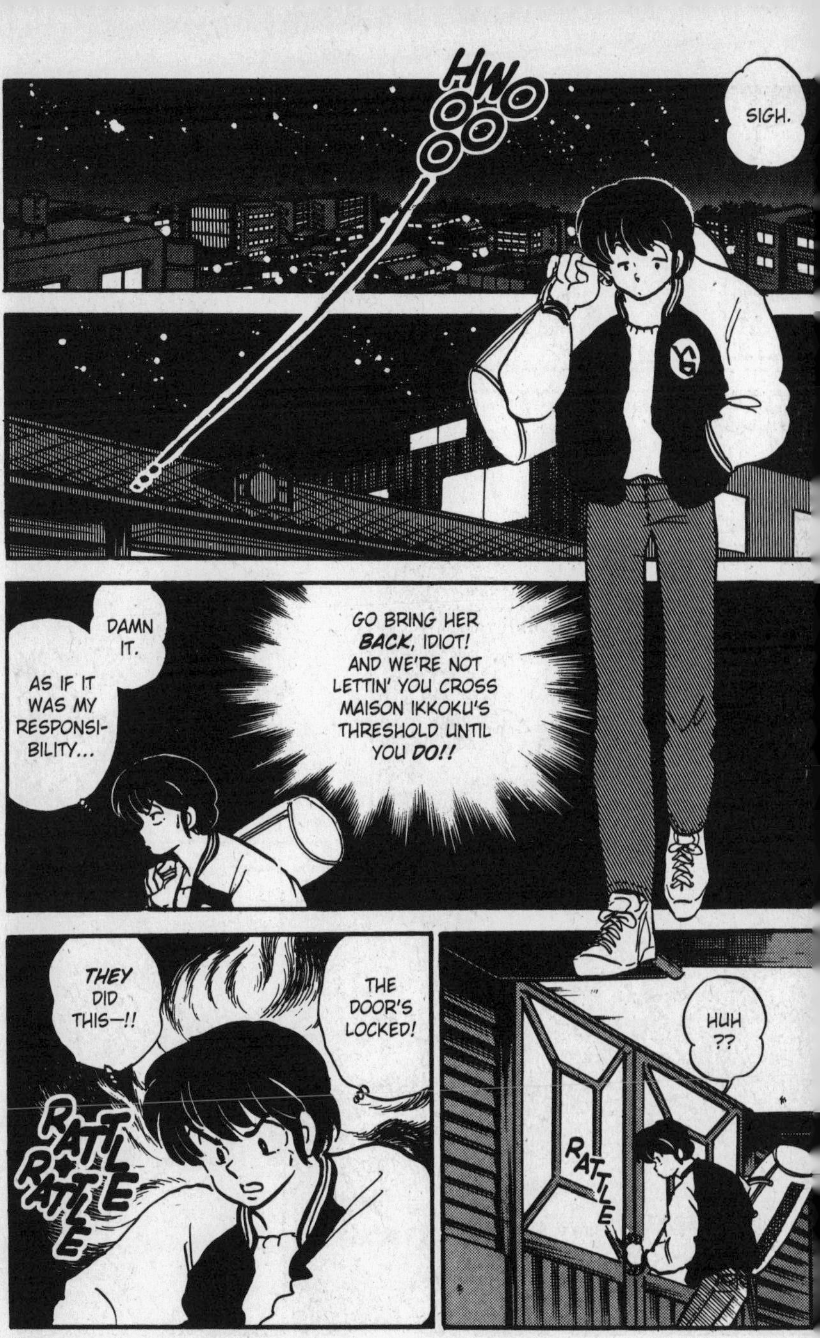
SIGH.
HWOOOO
GO BRING HER BACK, IDIOT! AND WE'RE NOT LETTIN' YOU CROSS MAISON IKKOKU'S THRESHOLD UNTIL YOU DO!!
DAMN IT.
AS IF IT WAS MY RESPONSI-BILITY...
HUH ??
RATTLE
THE DOOR'S LOCKED!
THEY DID THIS—!!
RATTLE RATTLE

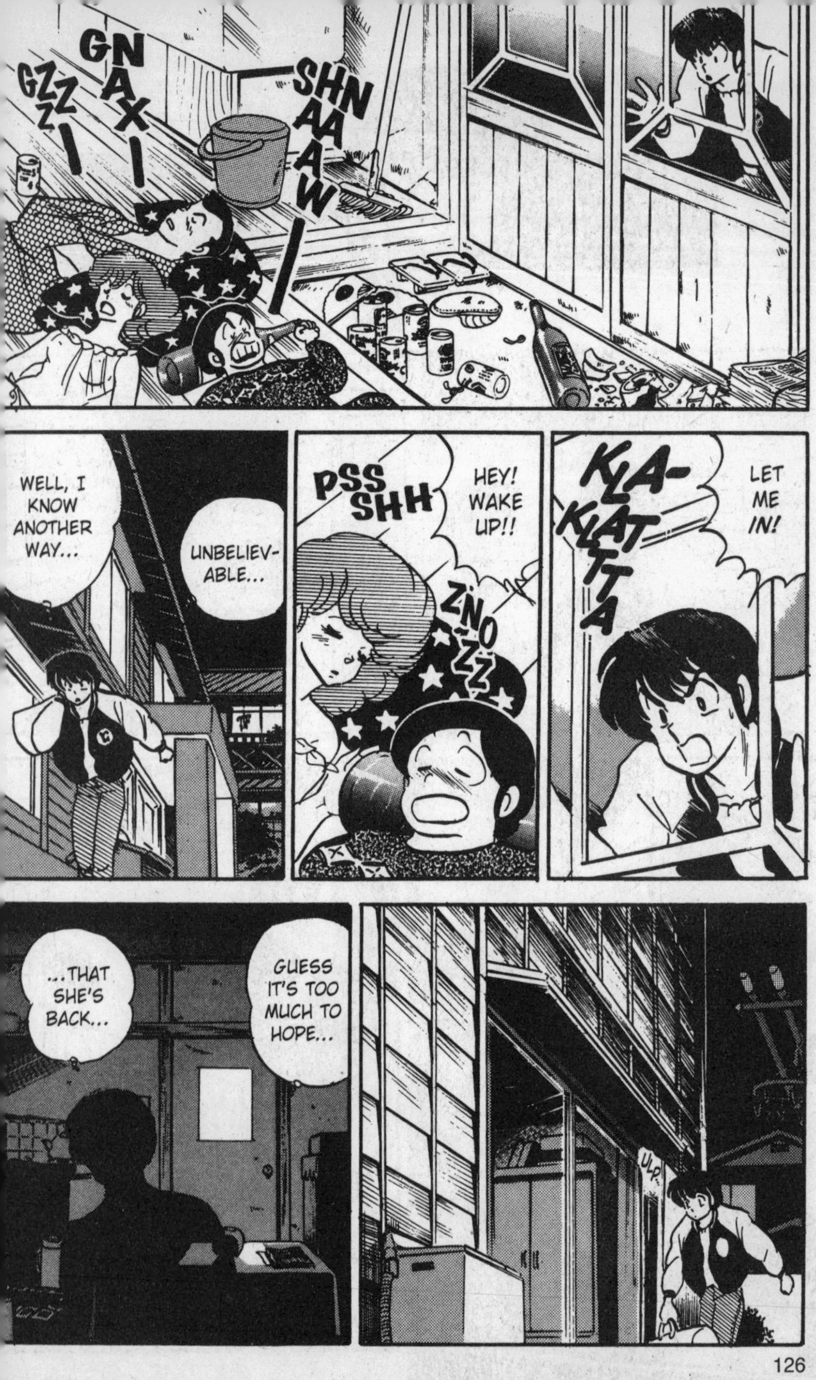
GZZZ
GNAXI
SHNAAAW
LET ME IN!
KLA-KLATTA
HEY! WAKE UP!!
PSSSHH
ZNOZZ
UNBELIEVABLE...
WELL, I KNOW ANOTHER WAY...
ULP
GUESS IT'S TOO MUCH TO HOPE...
...THAT SHE'S BACK...

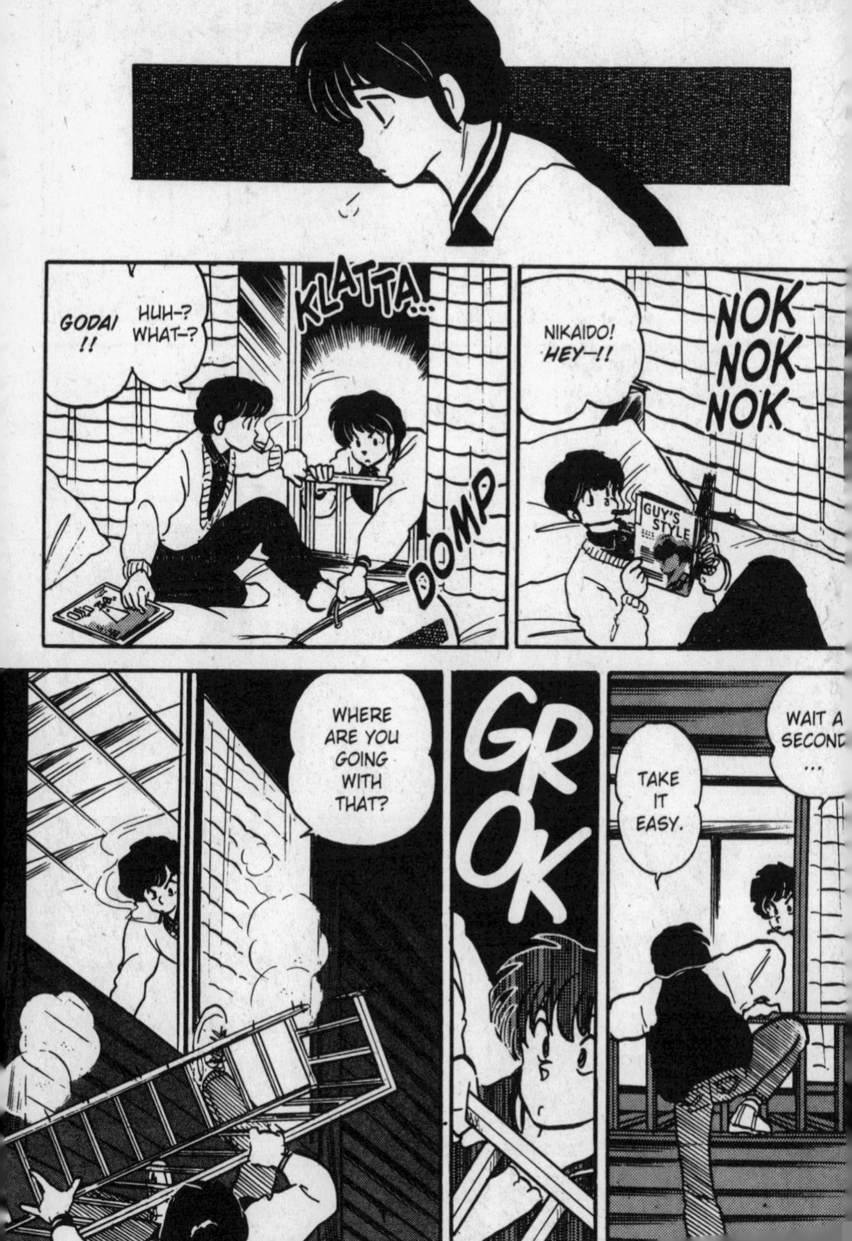
NIKAIDO! HEY—!!
NOK NOK NOK
KLATTA...
GODAI !!
HUH—? WHAT—?
DOMP
WAIT A SECOND ...
TAKE IT EASY.
GROK
WHERE ARE YOU GOING WITH THAT?
GUY'S STYLE

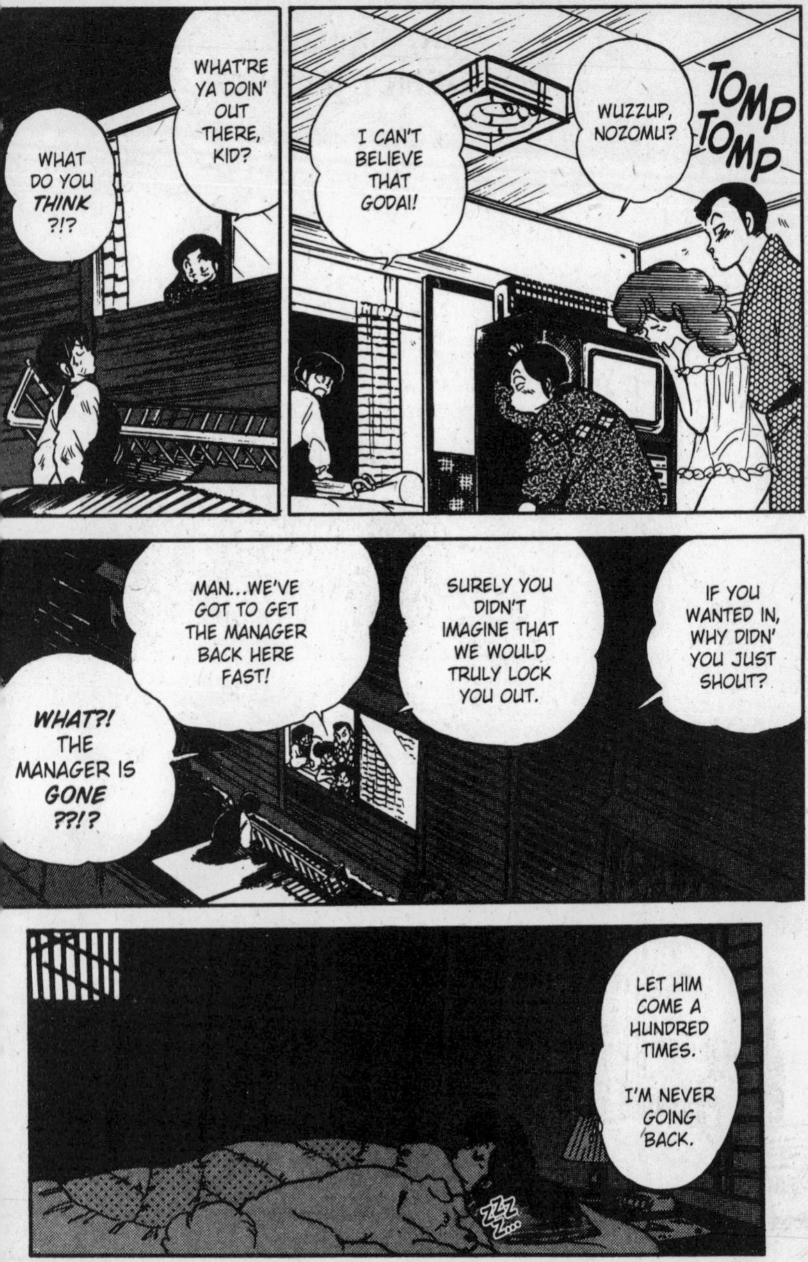
WHAT'RE YA DOIN' OUT THERE, KID?
WHAT DO YOU *THINK* ?!?
I CAN'T BELIEVE THAT GODAI!
WUZZUP, NOZOMU?
TOMP TOMP
IF YOU WANTED IN, WHY DIDN' YOU JUST SHOUT?
SURELY YOU DIDN'T IMAGINE THAT WE WOULD TRULY LOCK YOU OUT.
MAN...WE'VE GOT TO GET THE MANAGER BACK HERE FAST!
WHAT?! THE MANAGER IS *GONE* ??!?
LET HIM COME A HUNDRED TIMES.
I'M NEVER GOING BACK.
ZZZ Z...

PART SEVEN
SUDDENLY KYOKO

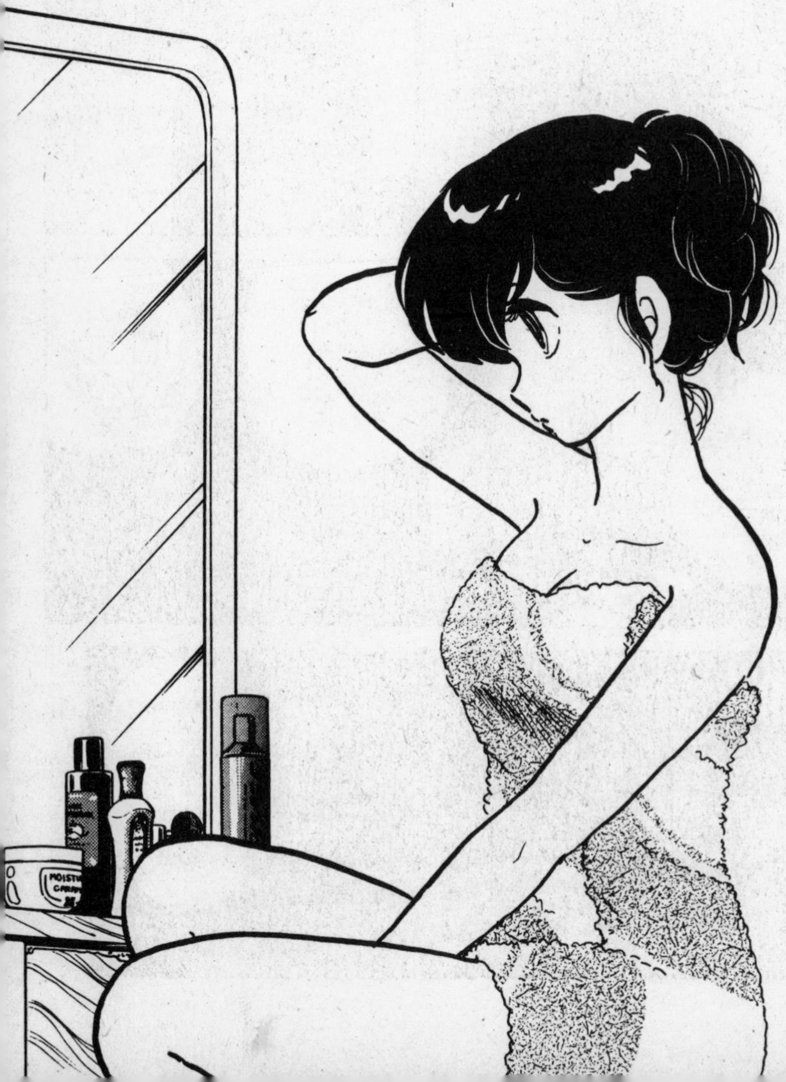

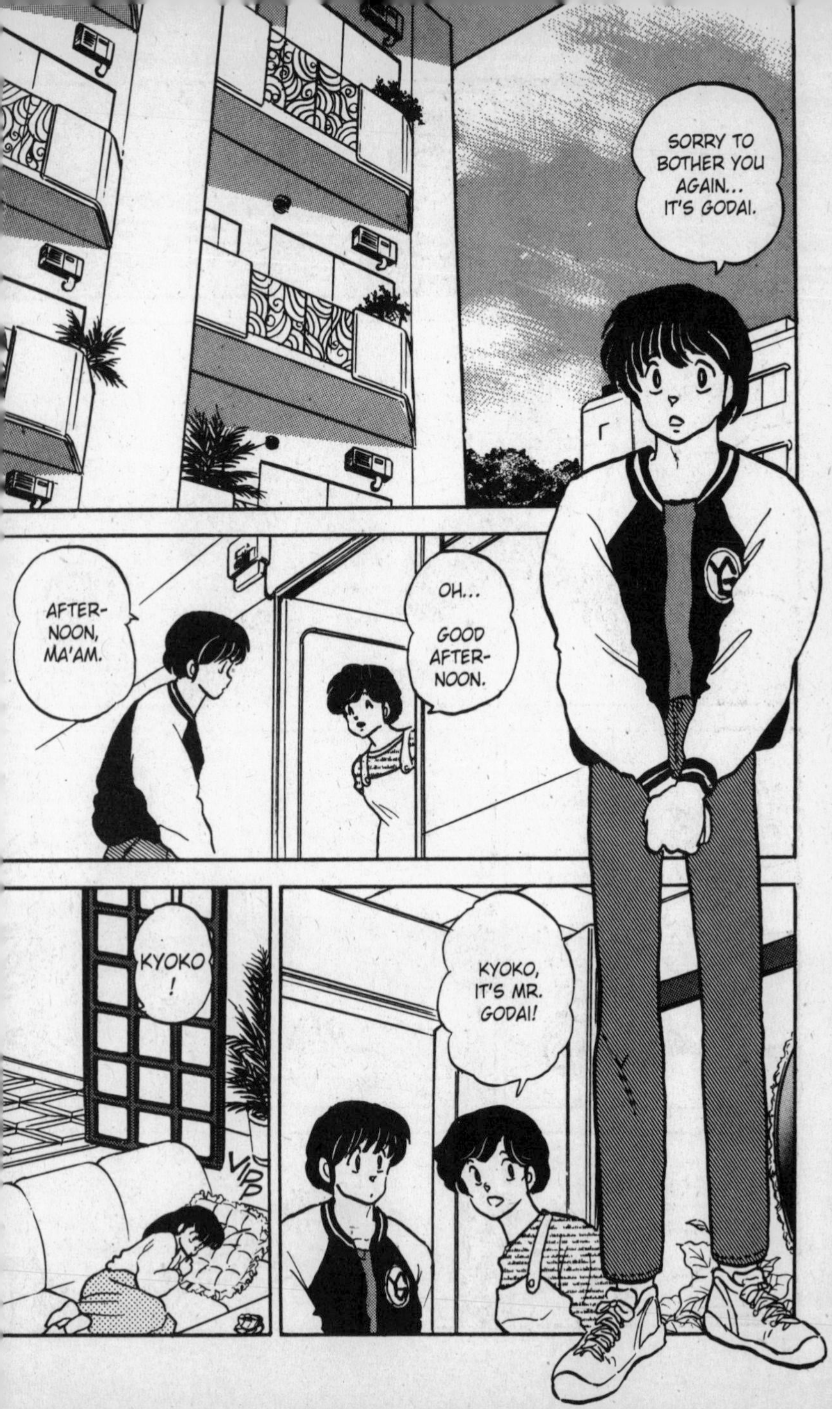
SORRY TO BOTHER YOU AGAIN... IT'S GODAI.
AFTER-NOON, MA'AM.
OH... GOOD AFTER-NOON.
KYOKO!
VIP
KYOKO, IT'S MR. GODAI!

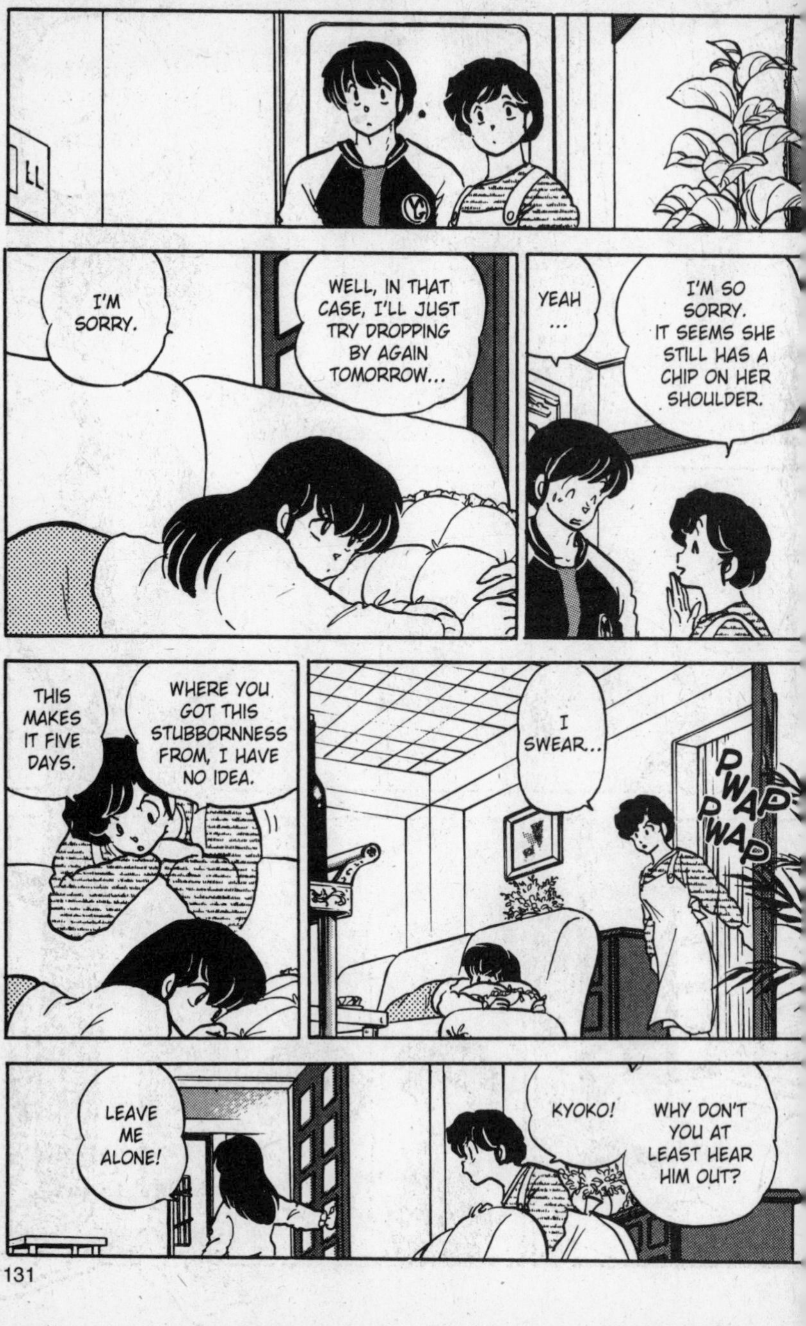
I'M SORRY.
WELL, IN THAT CASE, I'LL JUST TRY DROPPING BY AGAIN TOMORROW...
YEAH ...
I'M SO SORRY. IT SEEMS SHE STILL HAS A CHIP ON HER SHOULDER.
THIS MAKES IT FIVE DAYS.
WHERE YOU GOT THIS STUBBORNNESS FROM, I HAVE NO IDEA.
I SWEAR...
PWAP PWAP
LEAVE ME ALONE!
KYOKO!
WHY DON'T YOU AT LEAST HEAR HIM OUT?

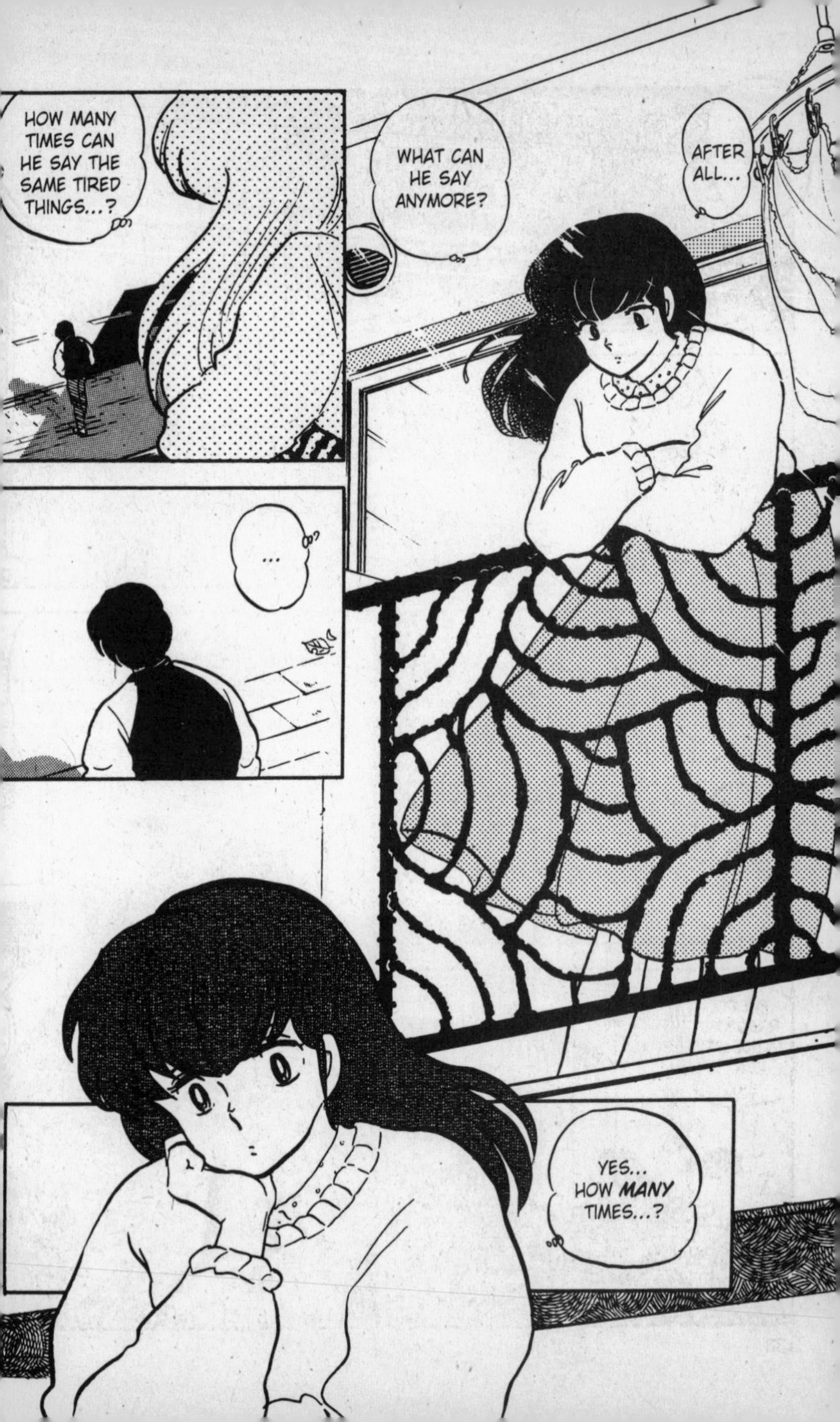
AFTER ALL...
WHAT CAN HE SAY ANYMORE?
HOW MANY TIMES CAN HE SAY THE SAME TIRED THINGS...?
...
YES... HOW *MANY* TIMES...?

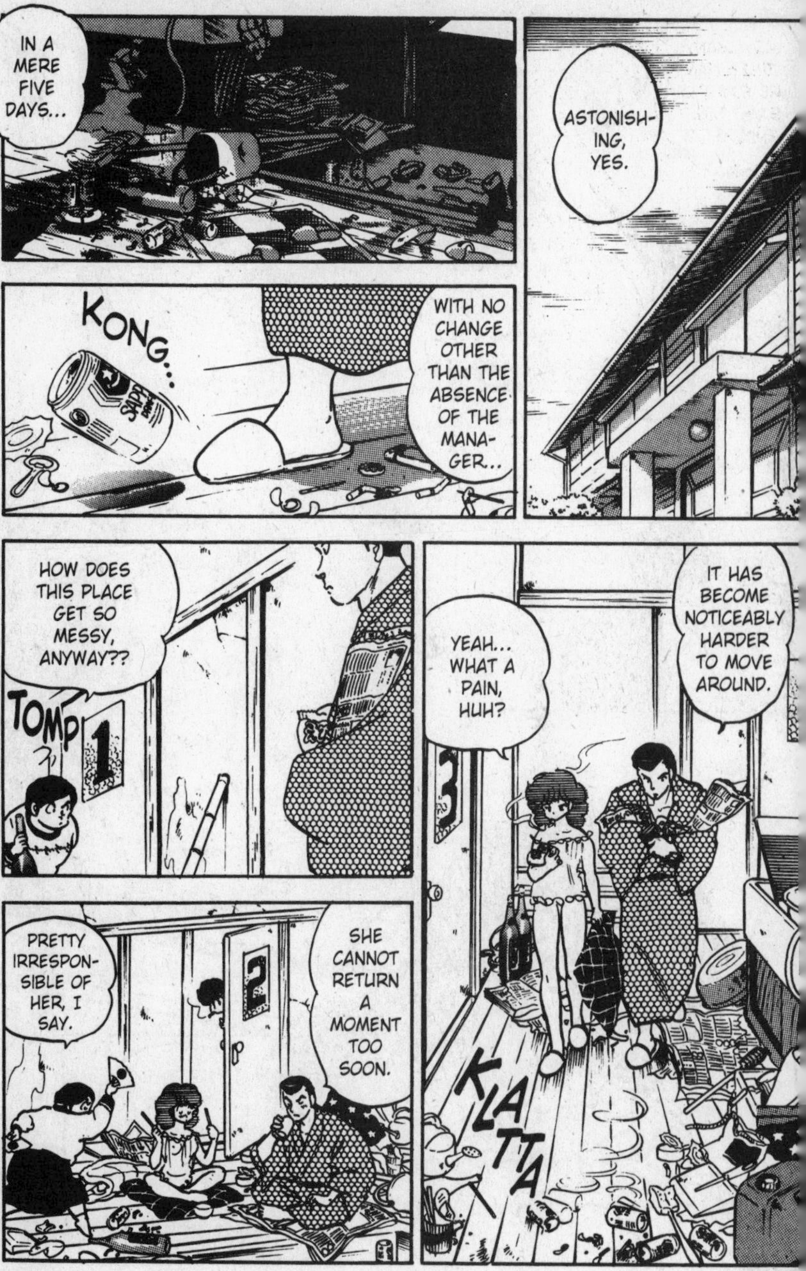
IN A MERE FIVE DAYS...
ASTONISHING, YES.
KONG...
WITH NO CHANGE OTHER THAN THE ABSENCE OF THE MANAGER...
HOW DOES THIS PLACE GET SO MESSY, ANYWAY??
TOMP
PRETTY IRRESPONSIBLE OF HER, I SAY.
SHE CANNOT RETURN A MOMENT TOO SOON.
IT HAS BECOME NOTICEABLY HARDER TO MOVE AROUND.
YEAH... WHAT A PAIN, HUH?
KLATTA

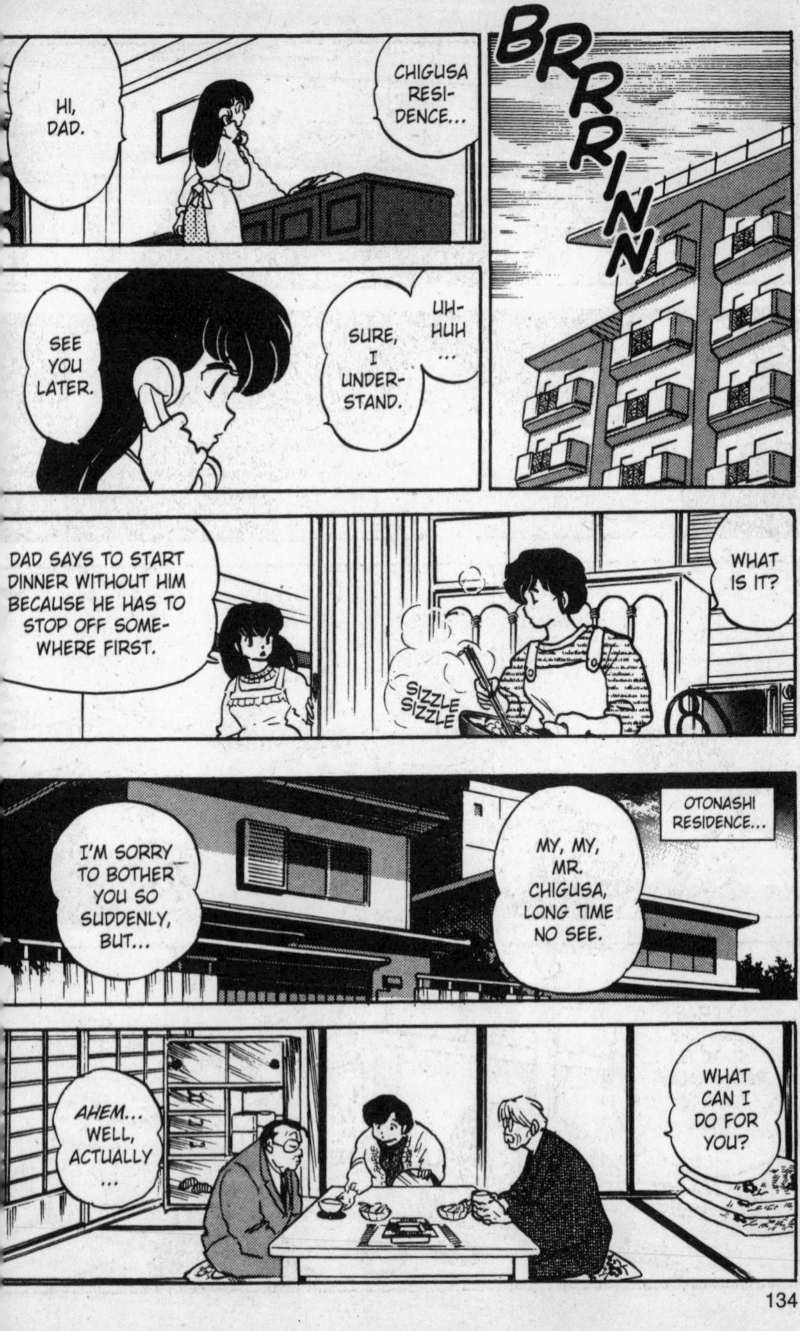
BRRRINN
CHIGUSA RESIDENCE...
HI, DAD.
UH-HUH...
SURE, I UNDERSTAND.
SEE YOU LATER.
WHAT IS IT?
SIZZLE SIZZLE
DAD SAYS TO START DINNER WITHOUT HIM BECAUSE HE HAS TO STOP OFF SOMEWHERE FIRST.
OTONASHI RESIDENCE...
MY, MY, MR. CHIGUSA, LONG TIME NO SEE.
I'M SORRY TO BOTHER YOU SO SUDDENLY, BUT...
WHAT CAN I DO FOR YOU?
AHEM... WELL, ACTUALLY...

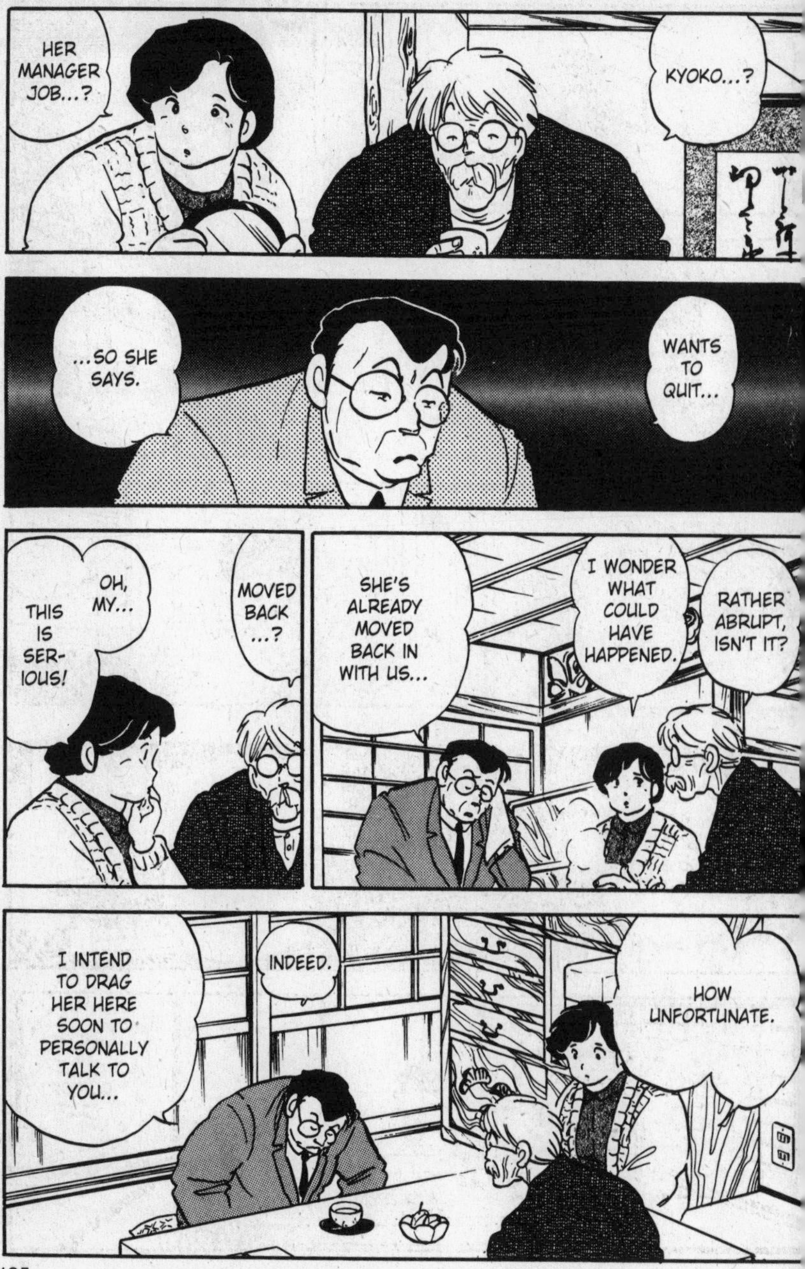
KYOKO...?
HER MANAGER JOB...?
WANTS TO QUIT...
...SO SHE SAYS.
RATHER ABRUPT, ISN'T IT?
I WONDER WHAT COULD HAVE HAPPENED.
SHE'S ALREADY MOVED BACK IN WITH US...
MOVED BACK ...?
OH, MY...
THIS IS SER-IOUS!
HOW UNFORTUNATE.
INDEED.
I INTEND TO DRAG HER HERE SOON TO PERSONALLY TALK TO YOU...

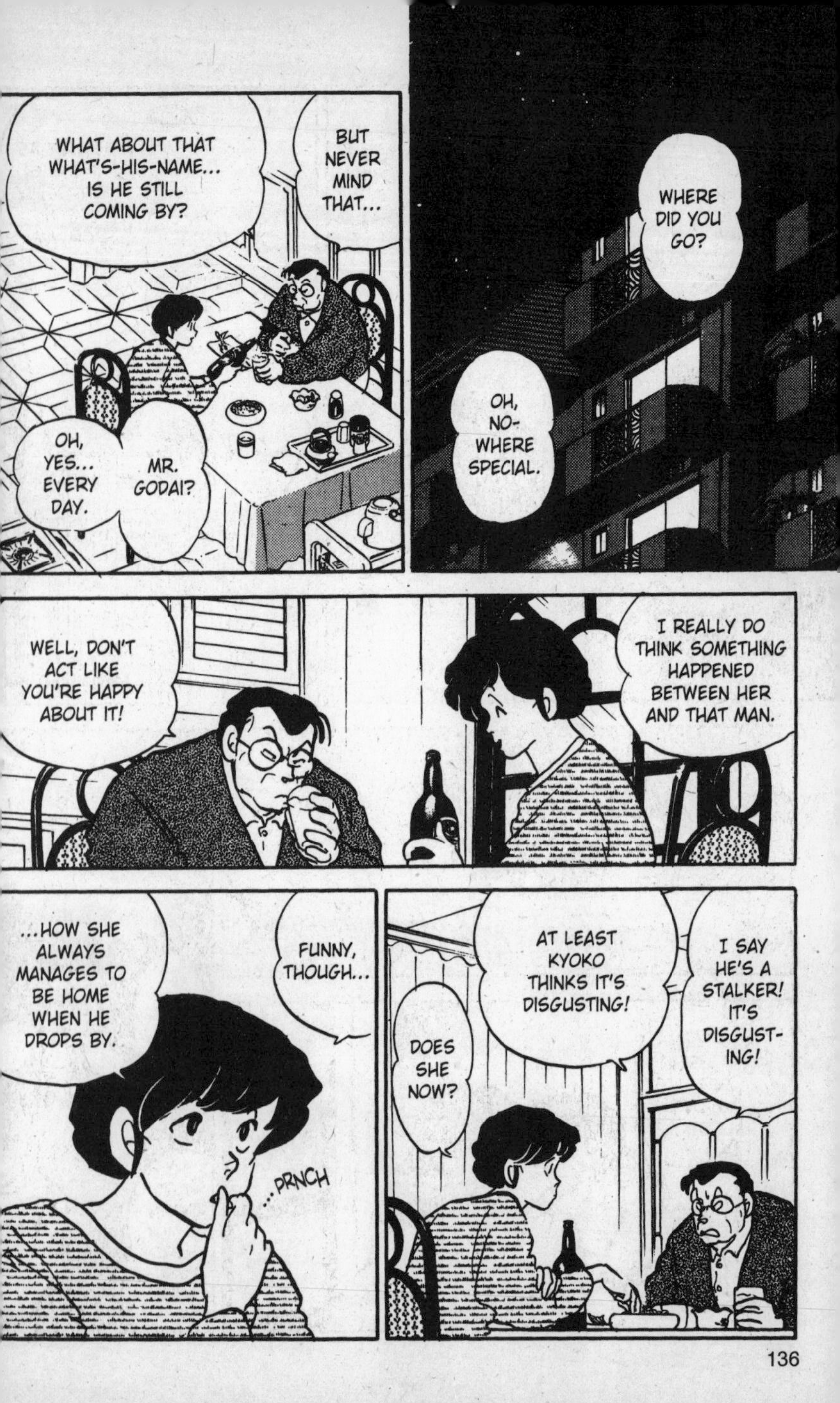

WHERE DID YOU GO?
OH, NO-WHERE SPECIAL.
BUT NEVER MIND THAT...
WHAT ABOUT THAT WHAT'S-HIS-NAME... IS HE STILL COMING BY?
MR. GODAI?
OH, YES... EVERY DAY.
I REALLY DO THINK SOMETHING HAPPENED BETWEEN HER AND THAT MAN.
WELL, DON'T ACT LIKE YOU'RE HAPPY ABOUT IT!
I SAY HE'S A STALKER! IT'S DISGUST-ING!
AT LEAST KYOKO THINKS IT'S DISGUSTING!
DOES SHE NOW?
FUNNY, THOUGH...
...HOW SHE ALWAYS MANAGES TO BE HOME WHEN HE DROPS BY.
...PRNCH

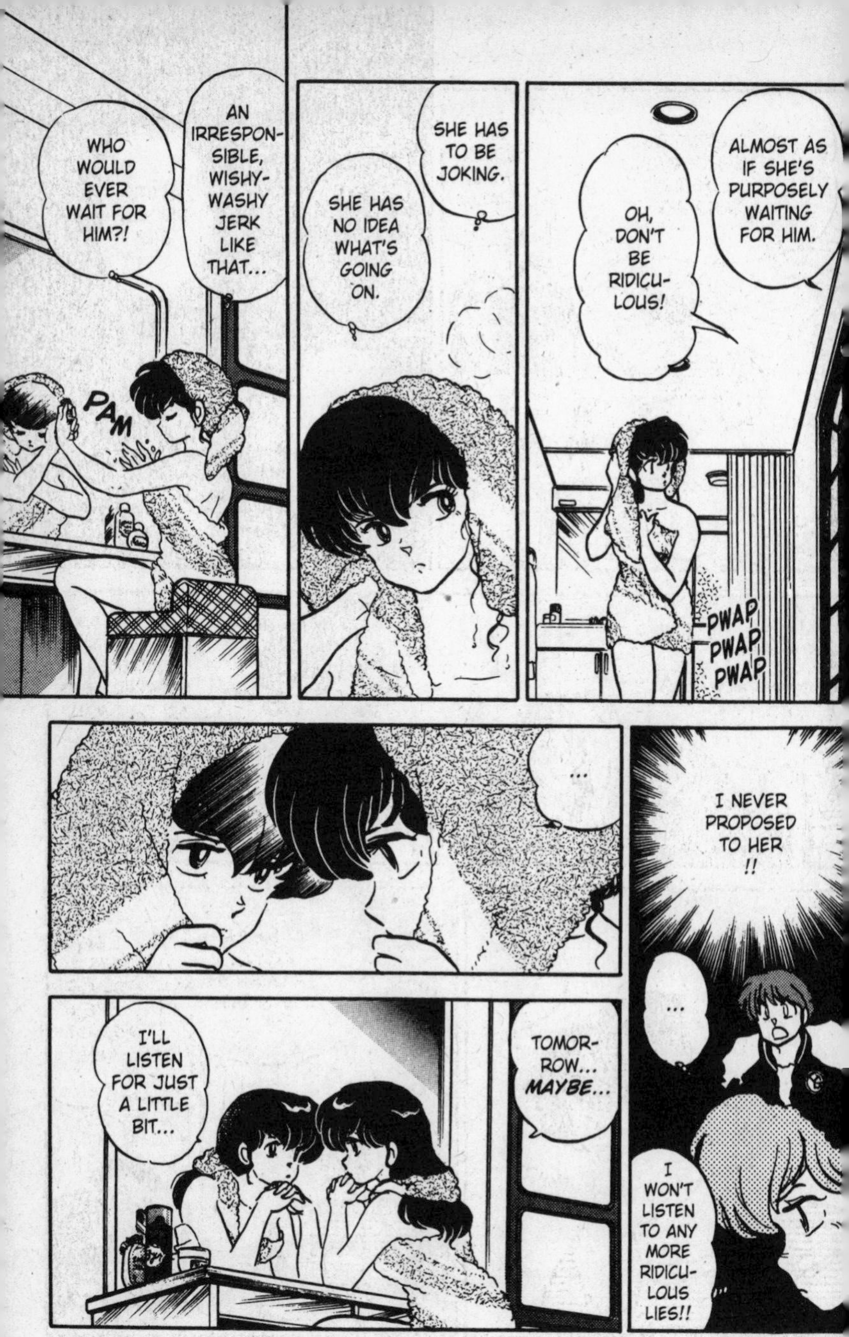
ALMOST AS IF SHE'S PURPOSELY WAITING FOR HIM.
OH, DON'T BE RIDICULOUS!
PWAP PWAP PWAP
SHE HAS TO BE JOKING.
SHE HAS NO IDEA WHAT'S GOING ON.
AN IRRESPONSIBLE, WISHY-WASHY JERK LIKE THAT...
WHO WOULD EVER WAIT FOR HIM?!
PAM
I NEVER PROPOSED TO HER!!
...
I WON'T LISTEN TO ANY MORE RIDICULOUS LIES!!
...
TOMORROW... *MAYBE*...
I'LL LISTEN FOR JUST A LITTLE BIT...

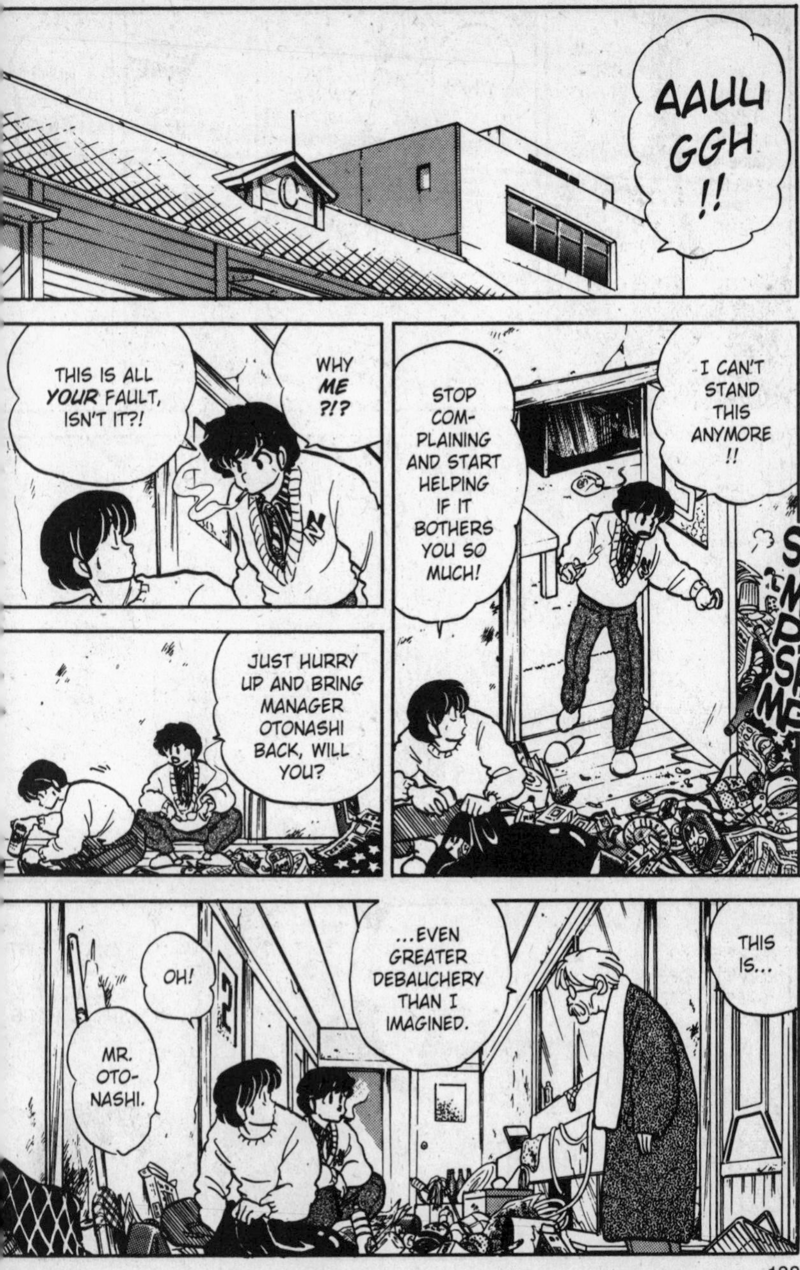
AAUGH GGH !!
WHY ME ?!?
THIS IS ALL YOUR FAULT, ISN'T IT?!
I CAN'T STAND THIS ANYMORE !!
SHMPSHMP
STOP COMPLAINING AND START HELPING IF IT BOTHERS YOU SO MUCH!
JUST HURRY UP AND BRING MANAGER OTONASHI BACK, WILL YOU?
THIS IS...
...EVEN GREATER DEBAUCHERY THAN I IMAGINED.
OH!
MR. OTONASHI.

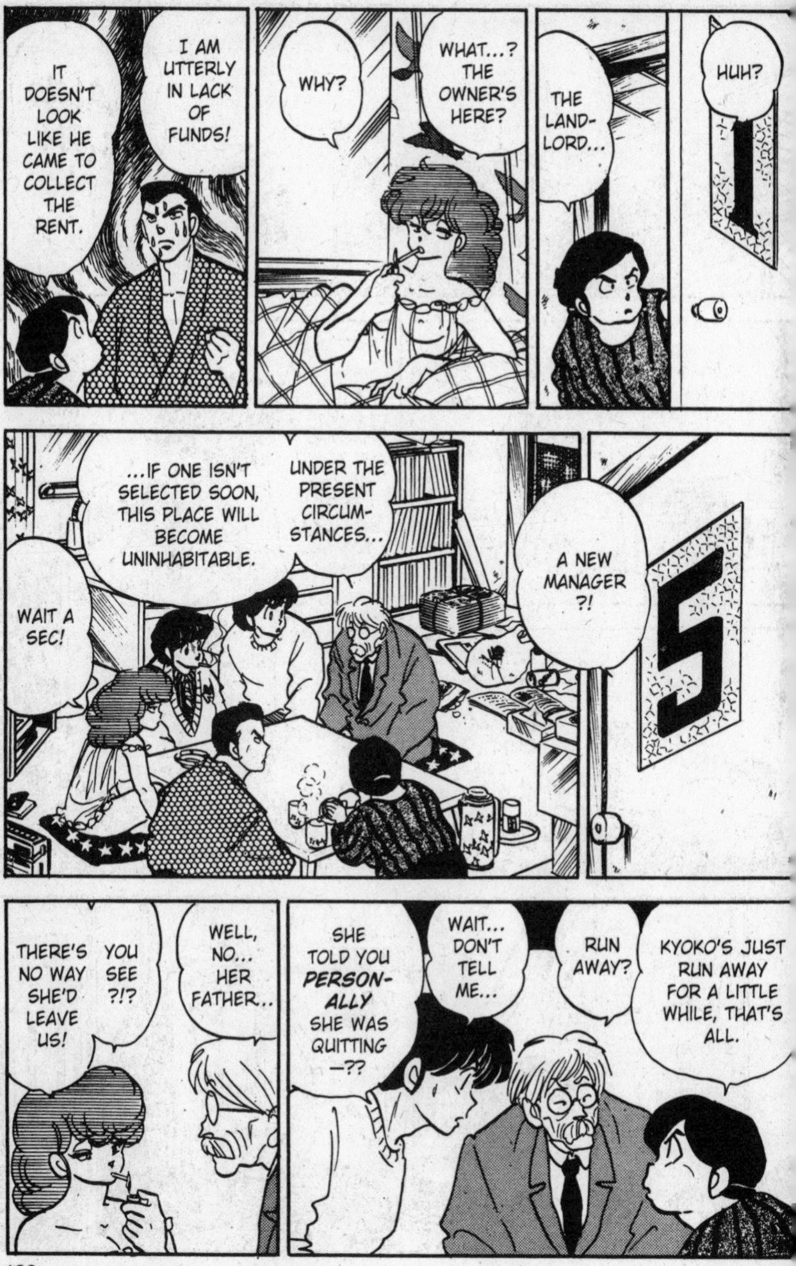
HUH?
THE LANDLORD...
WHAT...? THE OWNER'S HERE?
WHY?
I AM UTTERLY IN LACK OF FUNDS!
IT DOESN'T LOOK LIKE HE CAME TO COLLECT THE RENT.
A NEW MANAGER ?!
UNDER THE PRESENT CIRCUMSTANCES...
...IF ONE ISN'T SELECTED SOON, THIS PLACE WILL BECOME UNINHABITABLE.
WAIT A SEC!
KYOKO'S JUST RUN AWAY FOR A LITTLE WHILE, THAT'S ALL.
RUN AWAY?
WAIT... DON'T TELL ME...
SHE TOLD YOU *PERSONALLY* SHE WAS QUITTING —??
WELL, NO... HER FATHER...
YOU SEE ?!?
THERE'S NO WAY SHE'D LEAVE US!

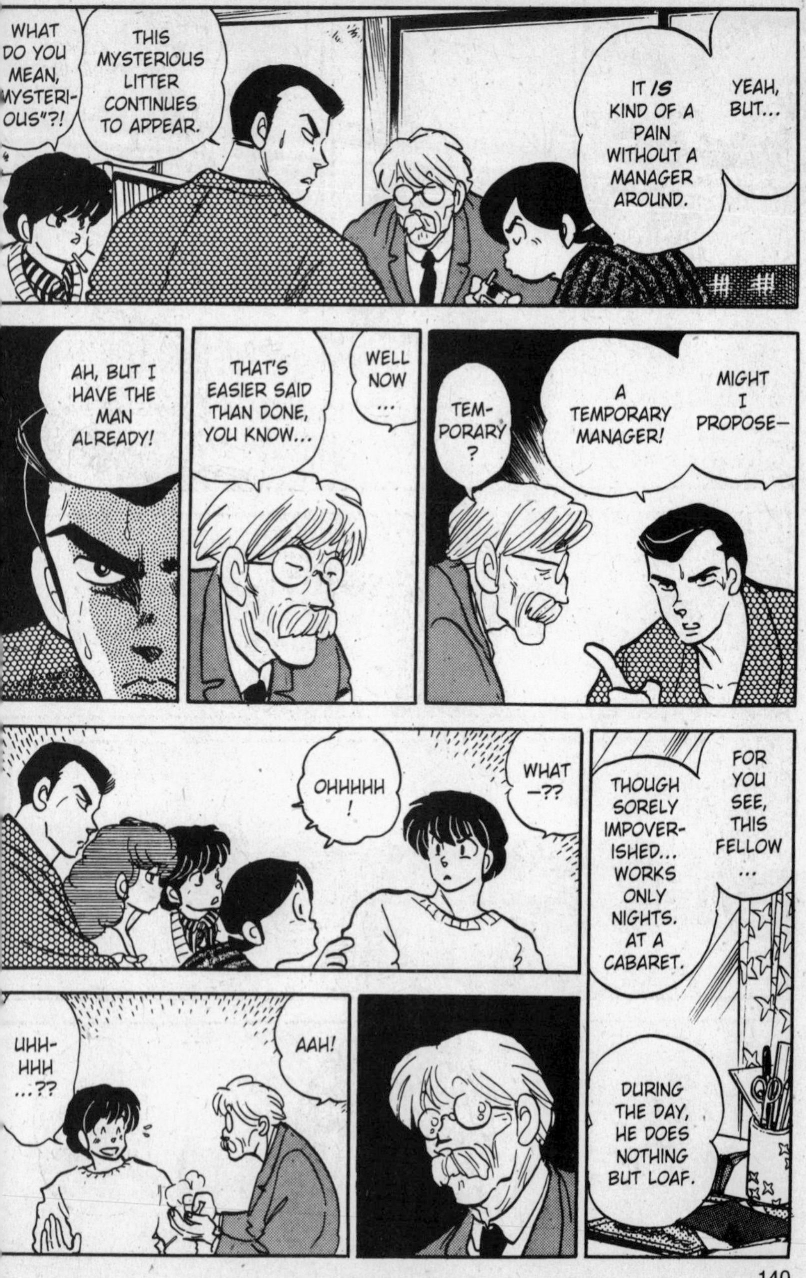
YEAH, BUT...
IT *IS* KIND OF A PAIN WITHOUT A MANAGER AROUND.
THIS MYSTERIOUS LITTER CONTINUES TO APPEAR.
WHAT DO YOU MEAN, "MYSTERIOUS"?!
MIGHT I PROPOSE—
A TEMPORARY MANAGER!
TEMPORARY?
WELL NOW...
THAT'S EASIER SAID THAN DONE, YOU KNOW...
AH, BUT I HAVE THE MAN ALREADY!
FOR YOU SEE, THIS FELLOW...
THOUGH SORELY IMPOVERISHED... WORKS ONLY NIGHTS. AT A CABARET.
DURING THE DAY, HE DOES NOTHING BUT LOAF.
WHAT—??
OHHHHH!
AAH!
UHHHHH...??

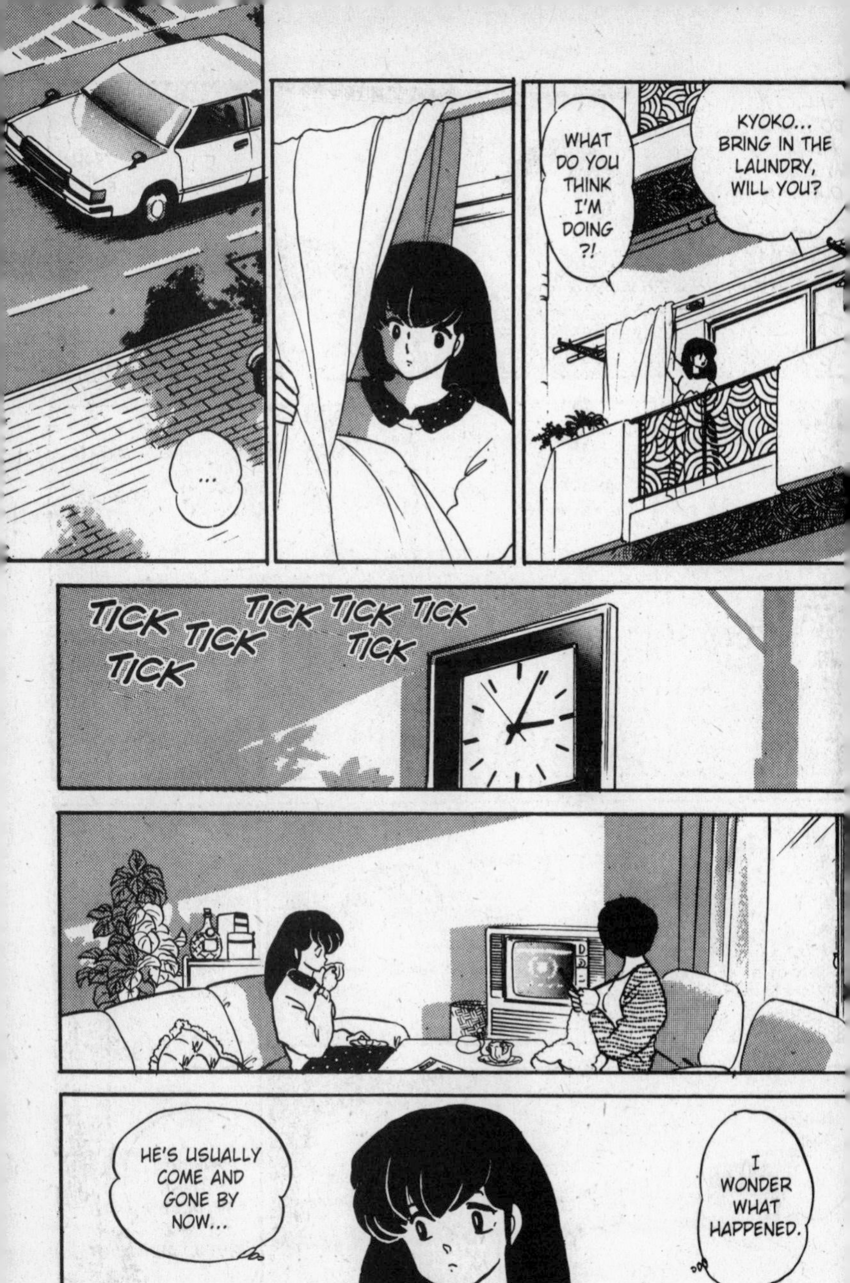
KYOKO... BRING IN THE LAUNDRY, WILL YOU?
WHAT DO YOU THINK I'M DOING ?!
...
TICK TICK TICK TICK TICK TICK TICK
I WONDER WHAT HAPPENED.
HE'S USUALLY COME AND GONE BY NOW...

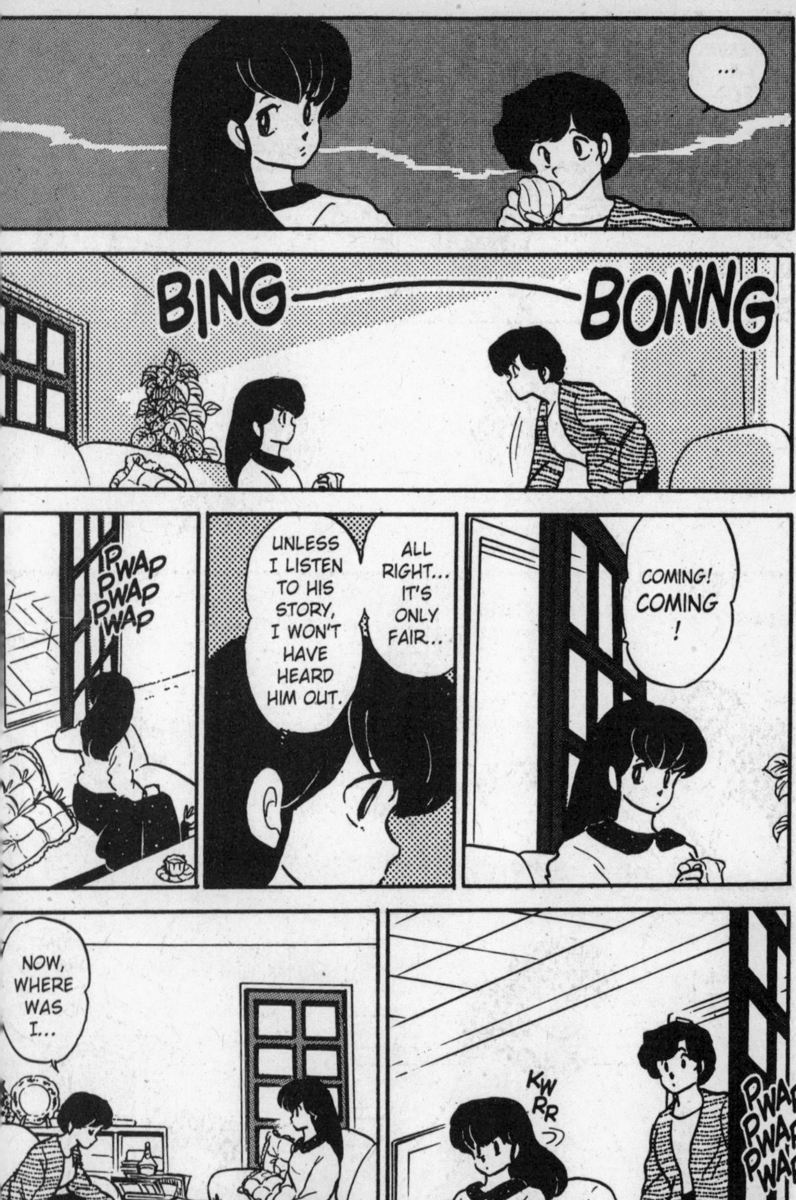
...
BING—BONNG
PWAP PWAP PWAP
UNLESS I LISTEN TO HIS STORY, I WON'T HAVE HEARD HIM OUT.
ALL RIGHT... IT'S ONLY FAIR..
COMING! COMING!
NOW, WHERE WAS I...
KWRR
PWAP PWAP PWAP

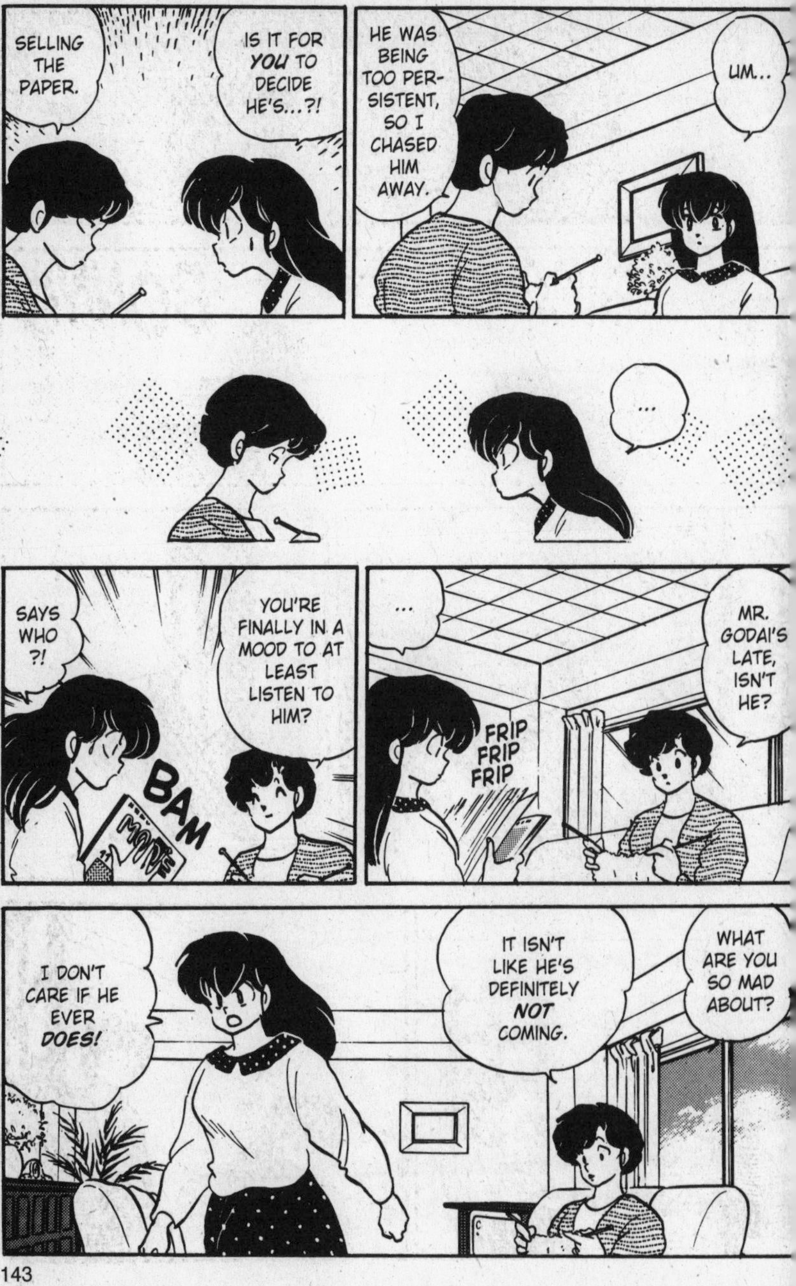
SELLING THE PAPER.
IS IT FOR *YOU* TO DECIDE HE'S...?!
HE WAS BEING TOO PER-SISTENT, SO I CHASED HIM AWAY.
UM...
...
SAYS WHO ?!
YOU'RE FINALLY IN A MOOD TO AT LEAST LISTEN TO HIM?
BAM
MODE
...
MR. GODAI'S LATE, ISN'T HE?
FRIP FRIP FRIP
I DON'T CARE IF HE EVER *DOES!*
IT ISN'T LIKE HE'S DEFINITELY *NOT* COMING.
WHAT ARE YOU SO MAD ABOUT?

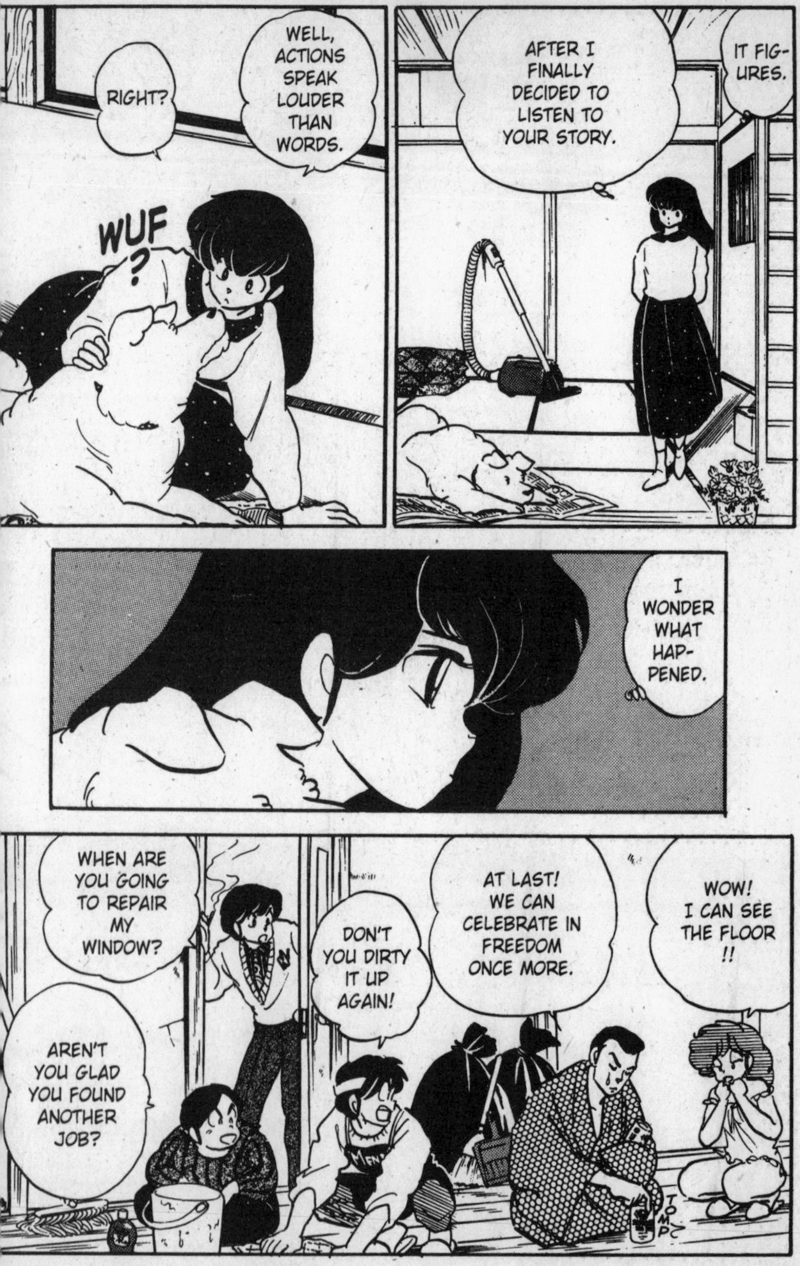
WELL, ACTIONS SPEAK LOUDER THAN WORDS.
RIGHT?
WUF ?
IT FIG-URES.
AFTER I FINALLY DECIDED TO LISTEN TO YOUR STORY.
I WONDER WHAT HAP-PENED.
WHEN ARE YOU GOING TO REPAIR MY WINDOW?
AREN'T YOU GLAD YOU FOUND ANOTHER JOB?
DON'T YOU DIRTY IT UP AGAIN!
AT LAST! WE CAN CELEBRATE IN FREEDOM ONCE MORE.
WOW! I CAN SEE THE FLOOR !!
TOMP

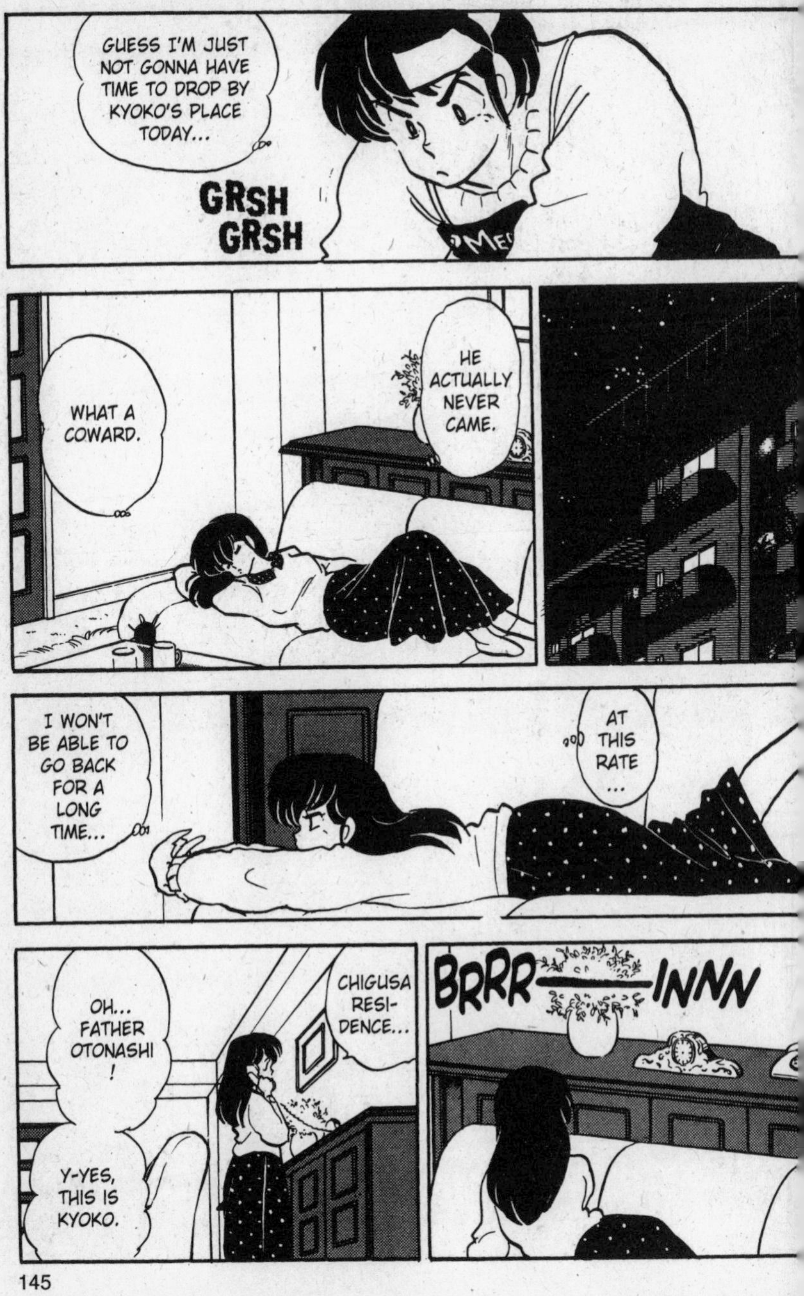
GUESS I'M JUST NOT GONNA HAVE TIME TO DROP BY KYOKO'S PLACE TODAY...
GRSH GRSH
HE ACTUALLY NEVER CAME.
WHAT A COWARD.
AT THIS RATE ...
I WON'T BE ABLE TO GO BACK FOR A LONG TIME...
BRRR——INNN
CHIGUSA RESI- DENCE...
OH... FATHER OTONASHI !
Y-YES, THIS IS KYOKO.

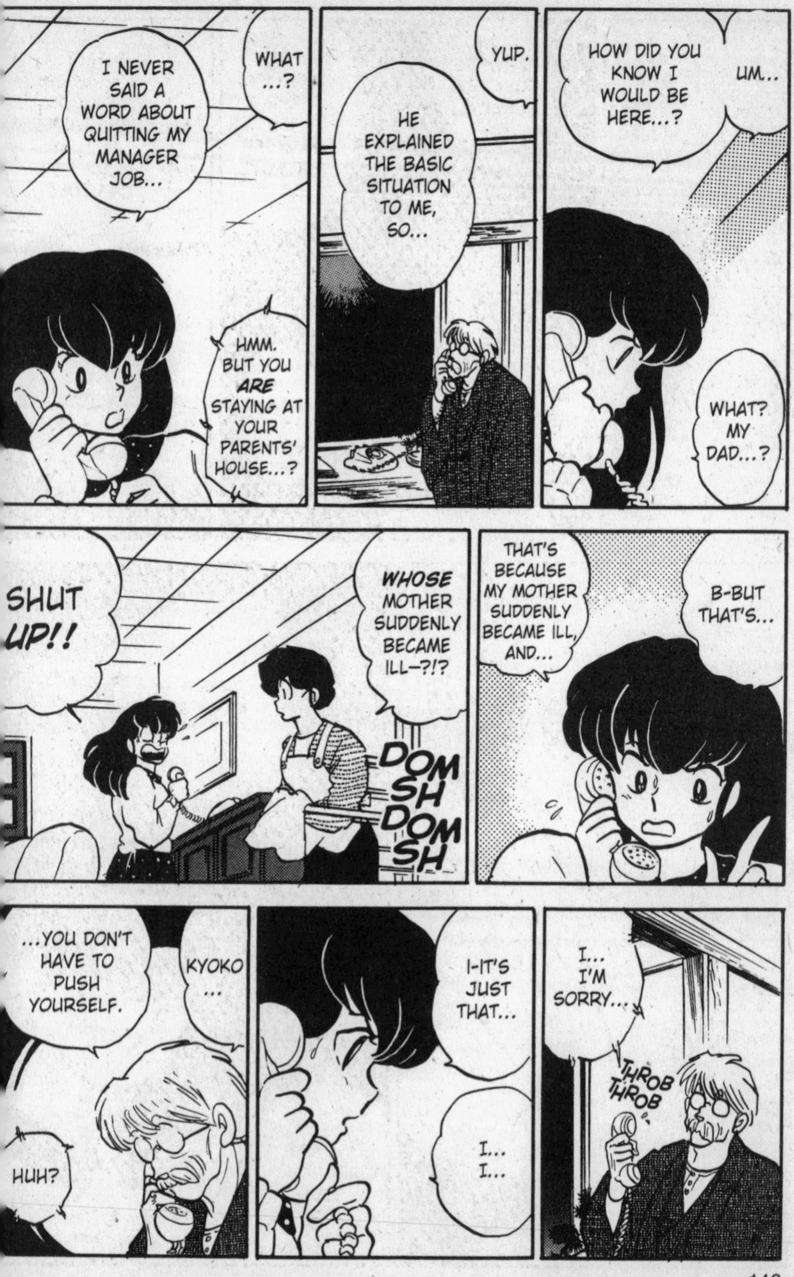
WHAT ...?
I NEVER SAID A WORD ABOUT QUITTING MY MANAGER JOB...
HMM. BUT YOU *ARE* STAYING AT YOUR PARENTS' HOUSE...?
YUP.
HE EXPLAINED THE BASIC SITUATION TO ME, SO...
UM...
HOW DID YOU KNOW I WOULD BE HERE...?
WHAT? MY DAD...?
B-BUT THAT'S...
THAT'S BECAUSE MY MOTHER SUDDENLY BECAME ILL, AND...
WHOSE MOTHER SUDDENLY BECAME ILL—?!?
SHUT UP!!
DOMSH DOMSH
KYOKO ...
...YOU DON'T HAVE TO PUSH YOURSELF.
HUH?
I-IT'S JUST THAT...
I... I...
I... I'M SORRY...
THROB THROB

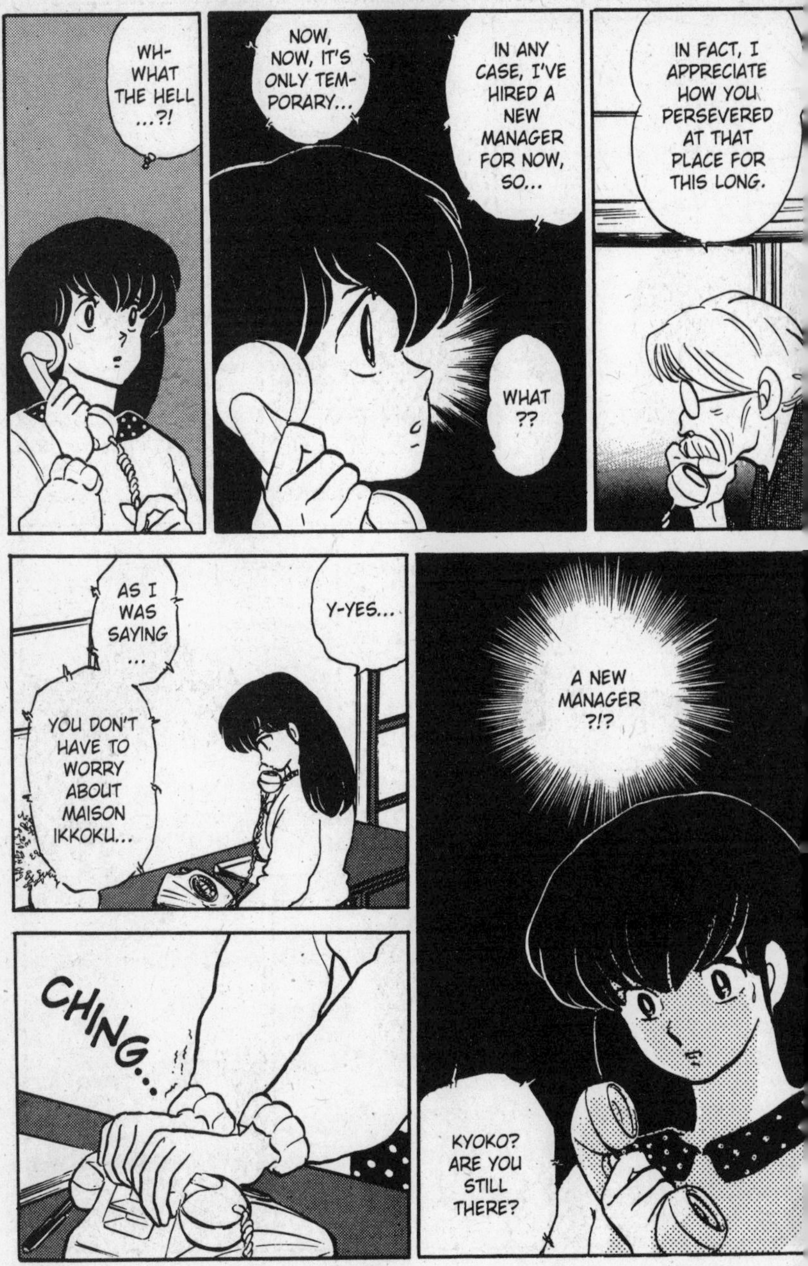
WH- WHAT THE HELL ...?!
NOW, NOW, IT'S ONLY TEMPORARY...
IN ANY CASE, I'VE HIRED A NEW MANAGER FOR NOW, SO...
WHAT ??
IN FACT, I APPRECIATE HOW YOU PERSEVERED AT THAT PLACE FOR THIS LONG.
AS I WAS SAYING ...
YOU DON'T HAVE TO WORRY ABOUT MAISON IKKOKU...
Y-YES...
A NEW MANAGER ?!?
KYOKO? ARE YOU STILL THERE?
CHING...

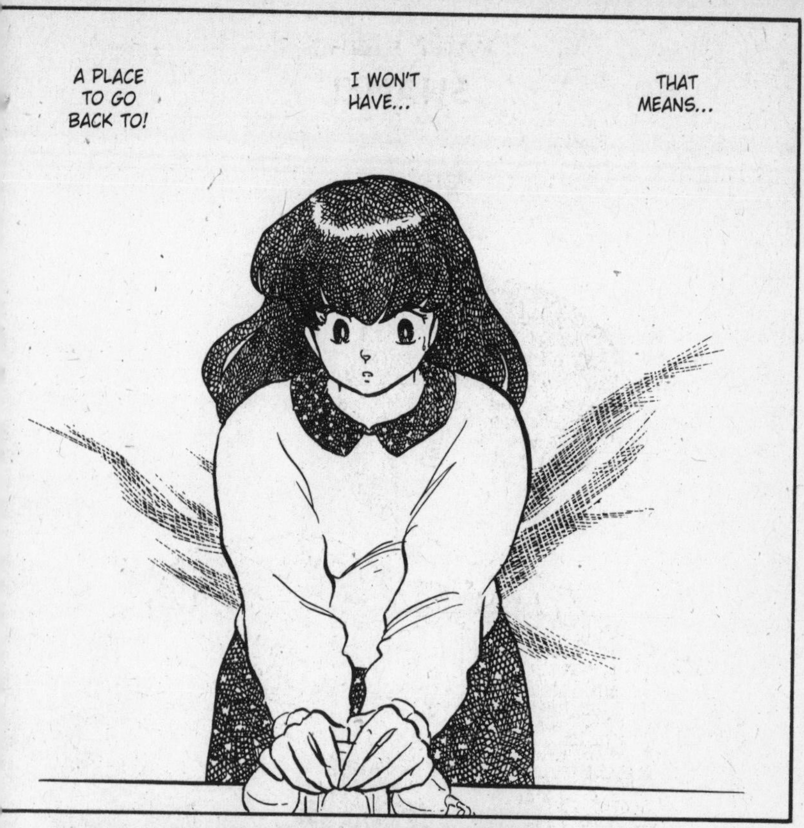
THAT MEANS...
I WON'T HAVE...
A PLACE TO GO BACK TO!

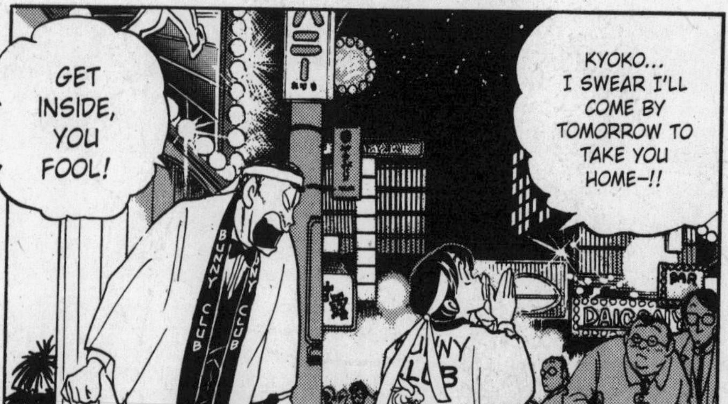
KYOKO... I SWEAR I'LL COME BY TOMORROW TO TAKE YOU HOME–!!
GET INSIDE, YOU FOOL!
BUNNY CLUB
BUNNY CLUB
BAR

PART EIGHT
SHAME!

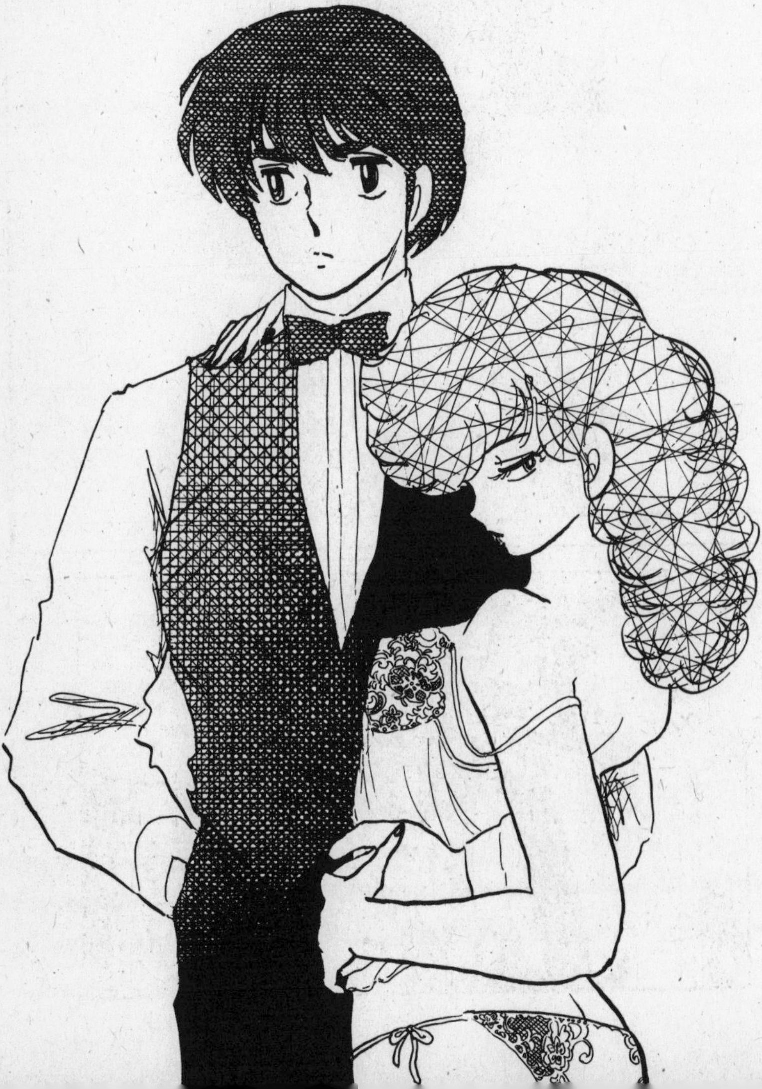

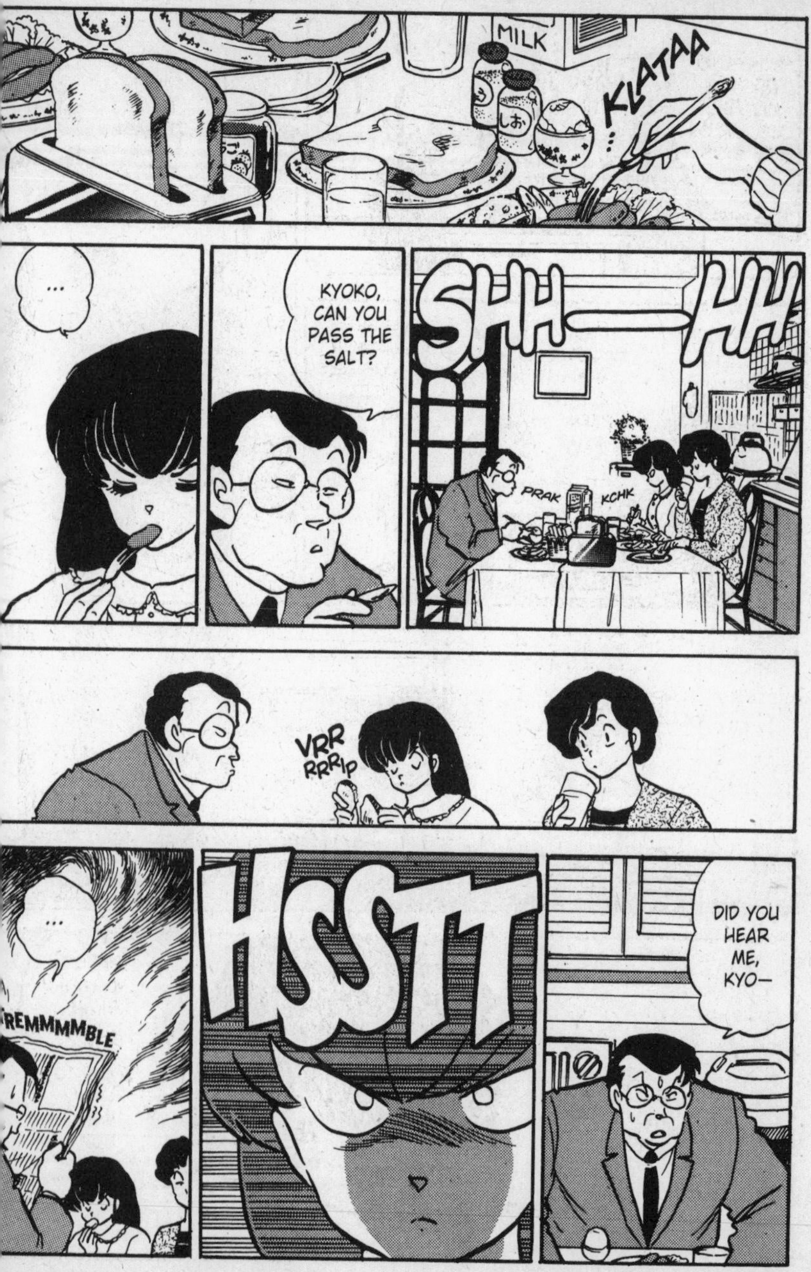

MILK
KLATAA
SHH—HH
PRAK
KCHK
KYOKO, CAN YOU PASS THE SALT?
...
VRR RRRIP
DID YOU HEAR ME, KYO—
HSSTT
...
REMMMMMBLE

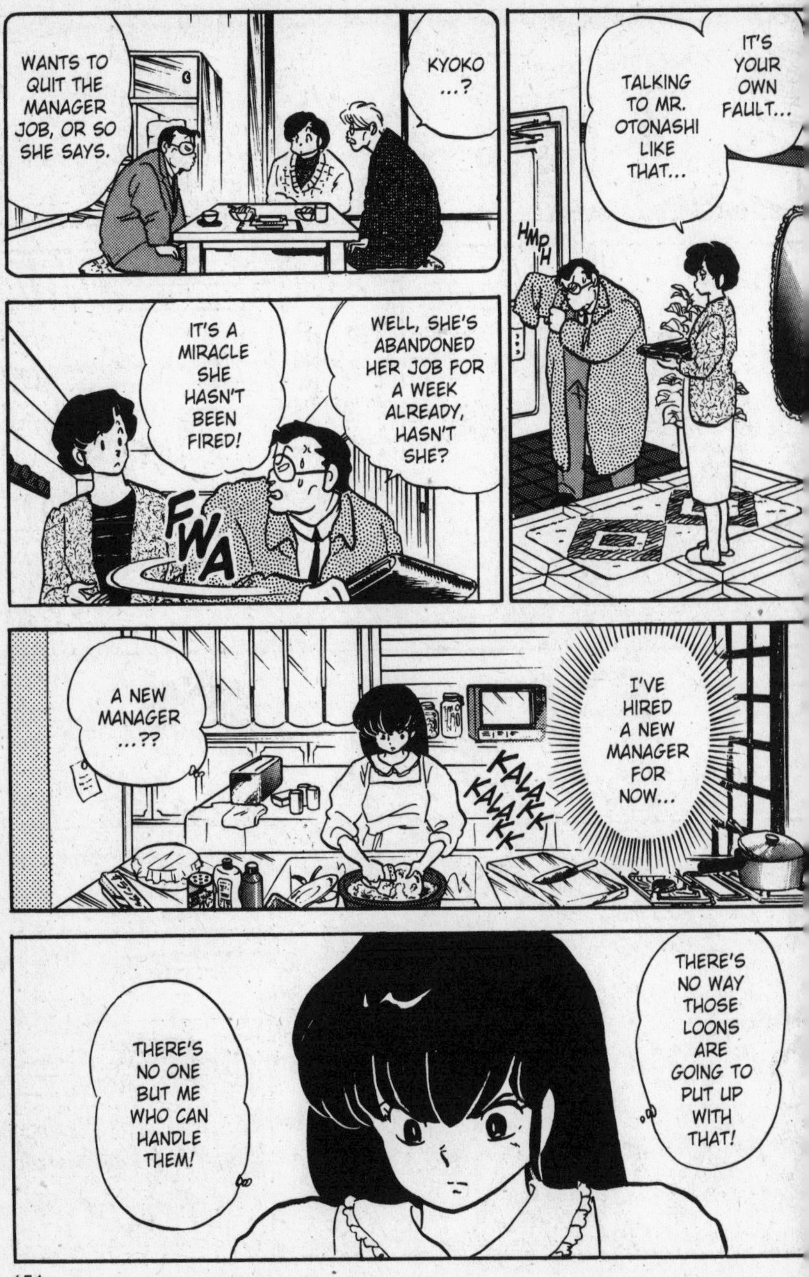
WANTS TO QUIT THE MANAGER JOB, OR SO SHE SAYS.
KYOKO ...?
IT'S A MIRACLE SHE HASN'T BEEN FIRED!
WELL, SHE'S ABANDONED HER JOB FOR A WEEK ALREADY, HASN'T SHE?
FWA
TALKING TO MR. OTONASHI LIKE THAT...
IT'S YOUR OWN FAULT...
HMPH
I'VE HIRED A NEW MANAGER FOR NOW...
A NEW MANAGER ...??
KALAKK KALAKK
THERE'S NO WAY THOSE LOONS ARE GOING TO PUT UP WITH THAT!
THERE'S NO ONE BUT ME WHO CAN HANDLE THEM!

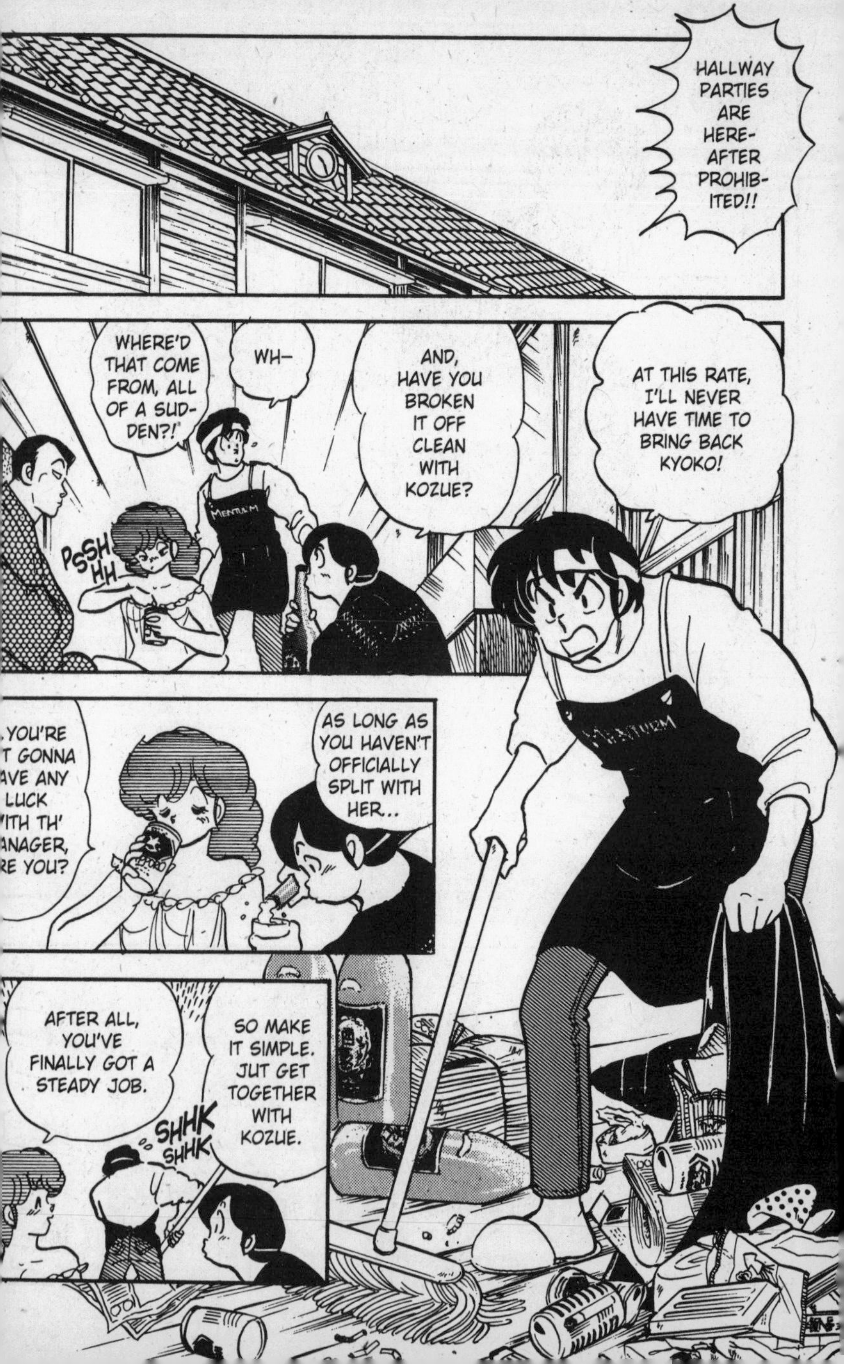
HALLWAY PARTIES ARE HERE-AFTER PROHIB-ITED!!
AT THIS RATE, I'LL NEVER HAVE TIME TO BRING BACK KYOKO!
AND, HAVE YOU BROKEN IT OFF CLEAN WITH KOZUE?
WH—
WHERE'D THAT COME FROM, ALL OF A SUD-DEN?!
PSSHHH
AS LONG AS YOU HAVEN'T OFFICIALLY SPLIT WITH HER...
. YOU'RE T GONNA AVE ANY LUCK ITH TH' ANAGER, RE YOU?
SO MAKE IT SIMPLE. JUT GET TOGETHER WITH KOZUE.
AFTER ALL, YOU'VE FINALLY GOT A STEADY JOB.
SHHK SHHK

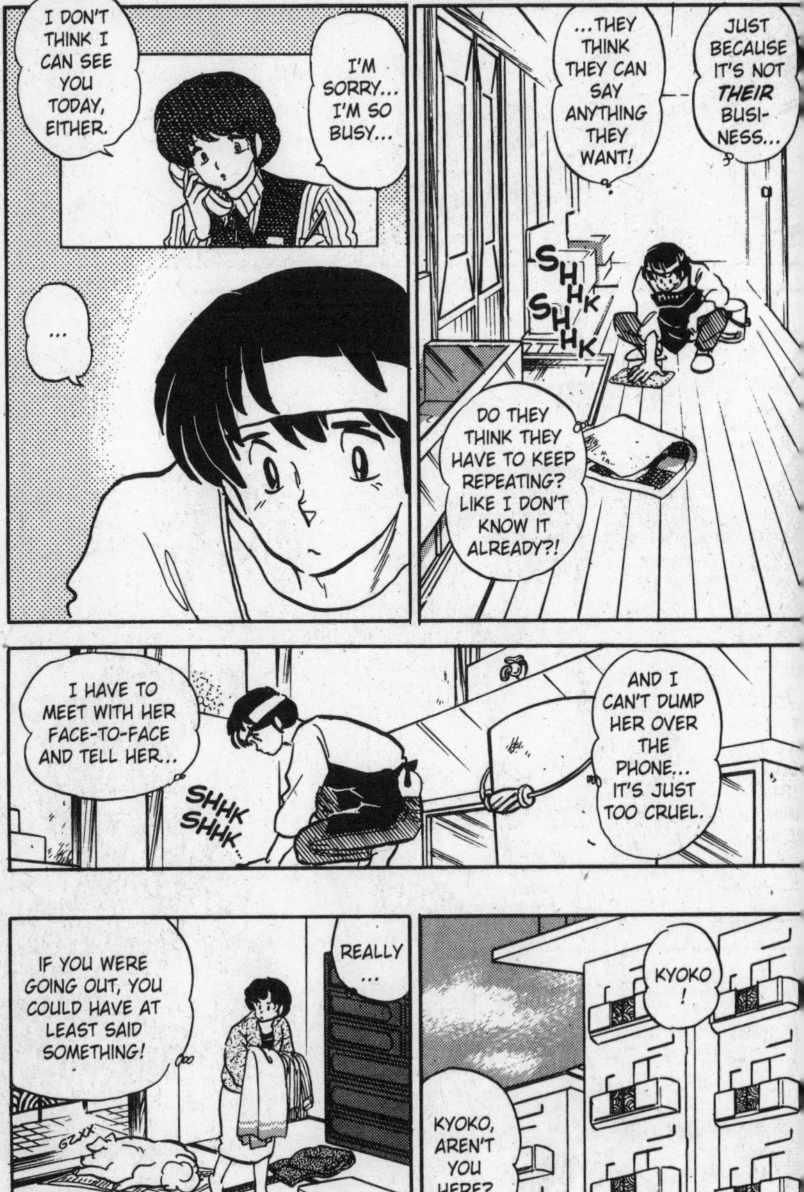
I DON'T THINK I CAN SEE YOU TODAY, EITHER.
I'M SORRY... I'M SO BUSY...
...
JUST BECAUSE IT'S NOT *THEIR* BUSI-NESS...
...THEY THINK THEY CAN SAY ANYTHING THEY WANT!
SHHK SHHK
DO THEY THINK THEY HAVE TO KEEP REPEATING? LIKE I DON'T KNOW IT ALREADY?!
I HAVE TO MEET WITH HER FACE-TO-FACE AND TELL HER...
SHHK SHHK...
AND I CAN'T DUMP HER OVER THE PHONE... IT'S JUST TOO CRUEL.
IF YOU WERE GOING OUT, YOU COULD HAVE AT LEAST SAID SOMETHING!
REALLY...
GZXX
KYOKO!
KYOKO, AREN'T YOU HERE?

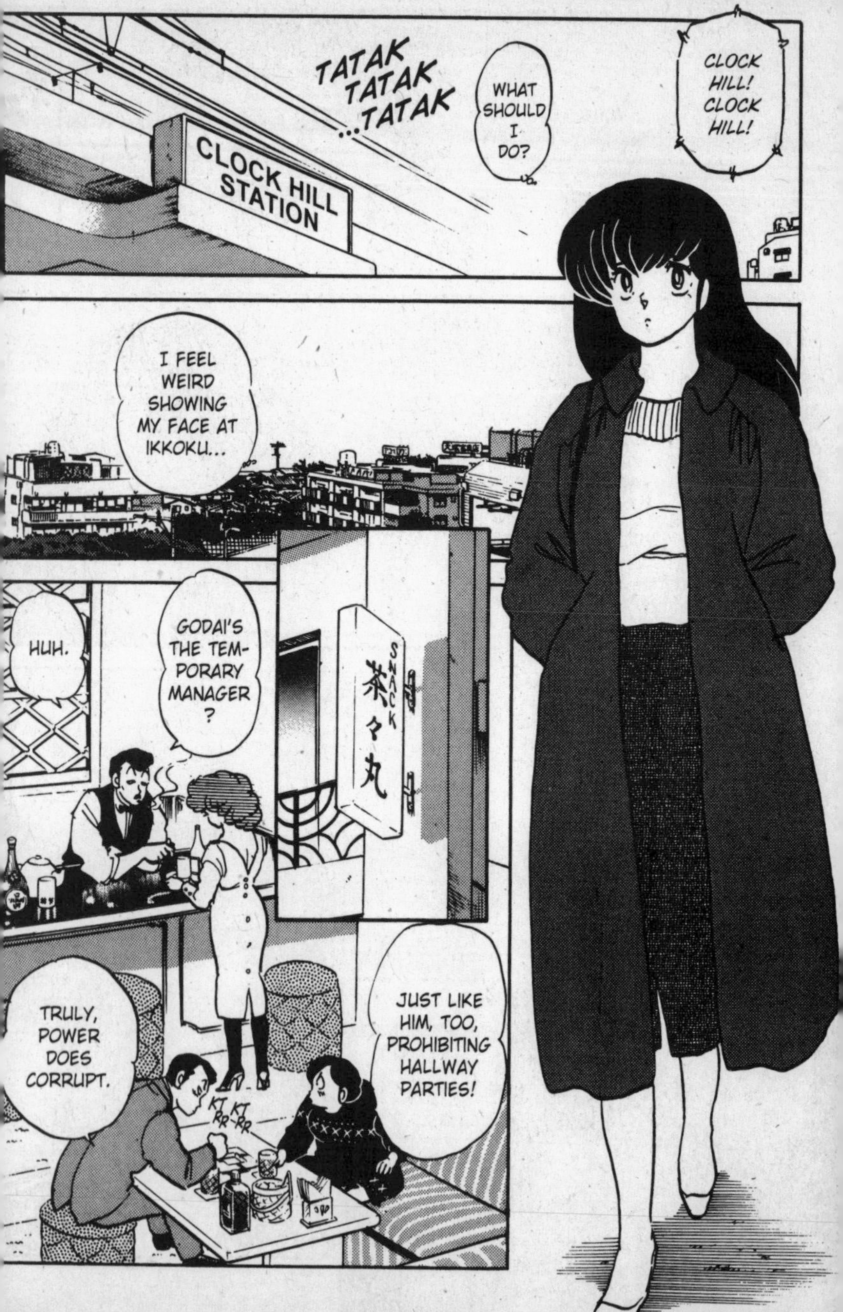
CLOCK HILL! CLOCK HILL!
WHAT SHOULD I DO?
TATAK TATAK ...TATAK
CLOCK HILL STATION
I FEEL WEIRD SHOWING MY FACE AT IKKOKU...
SNACK 茶々丸
GODAI'S THE TEMPORARY MANAGER?
HUH.
JUST LIKE HIM, TOO, PROHIBITING HALLWAY PARTIES!
KT KT RR-RR
TRULY, POWER DOES CORRUPT.

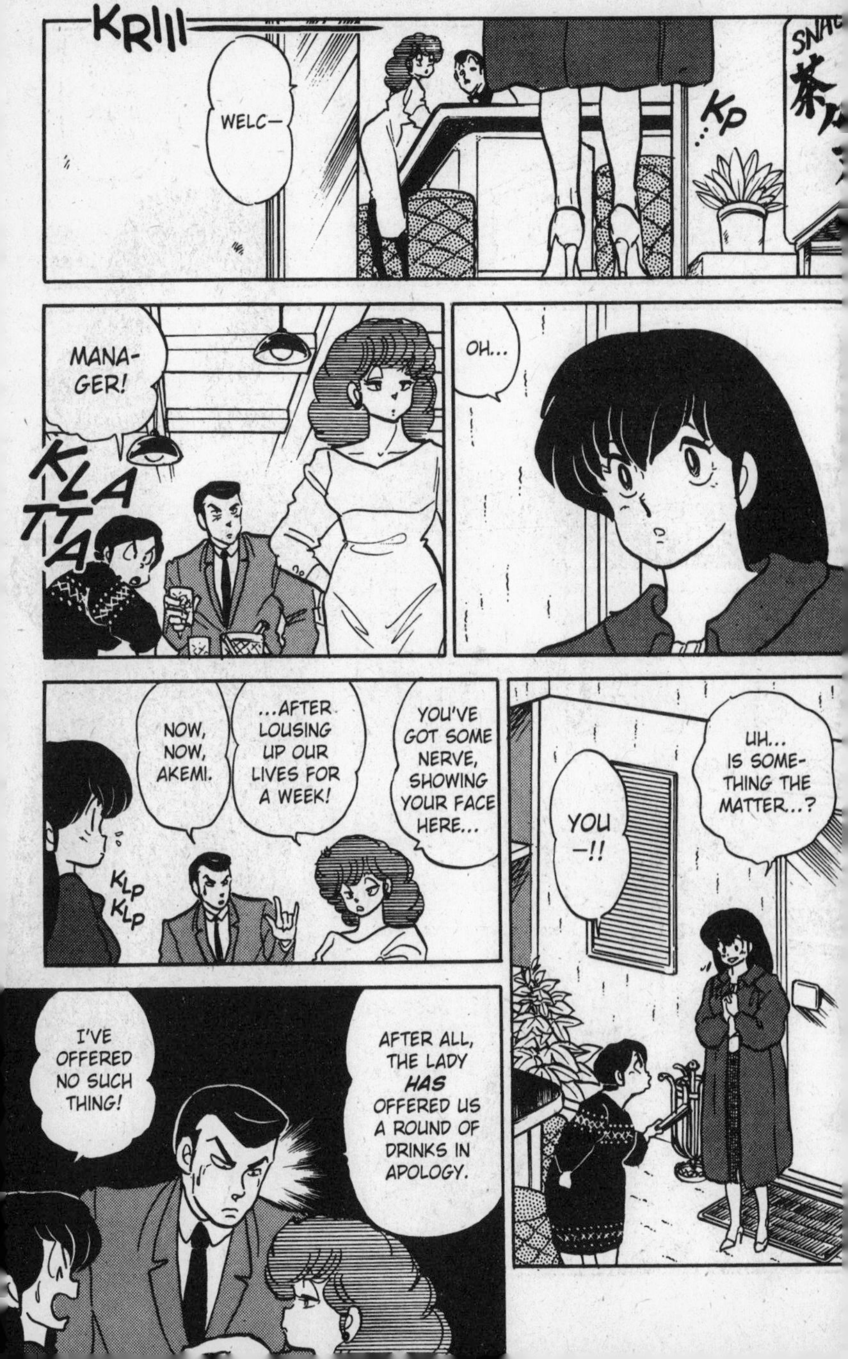

KRIII
WELC—
KP
OH...
MANA-GER!
KLATTA
UH... IS SOME-THING THE MATTER...?
YOU—!!
YOU'VE GOT SOME NERVE, SHOWING YOUR FACE HERE...
...AFTER LOUSING UP OUR LIVES FOR A WEEK!
NOW, NOW, AKEMI.
KLP KLP
AFTER ALL, THE LADY *HAS* OFFERED US A ROUND OF DRINKS IN APOLOGY.
I'VE OFFERED NO SUCH THING!

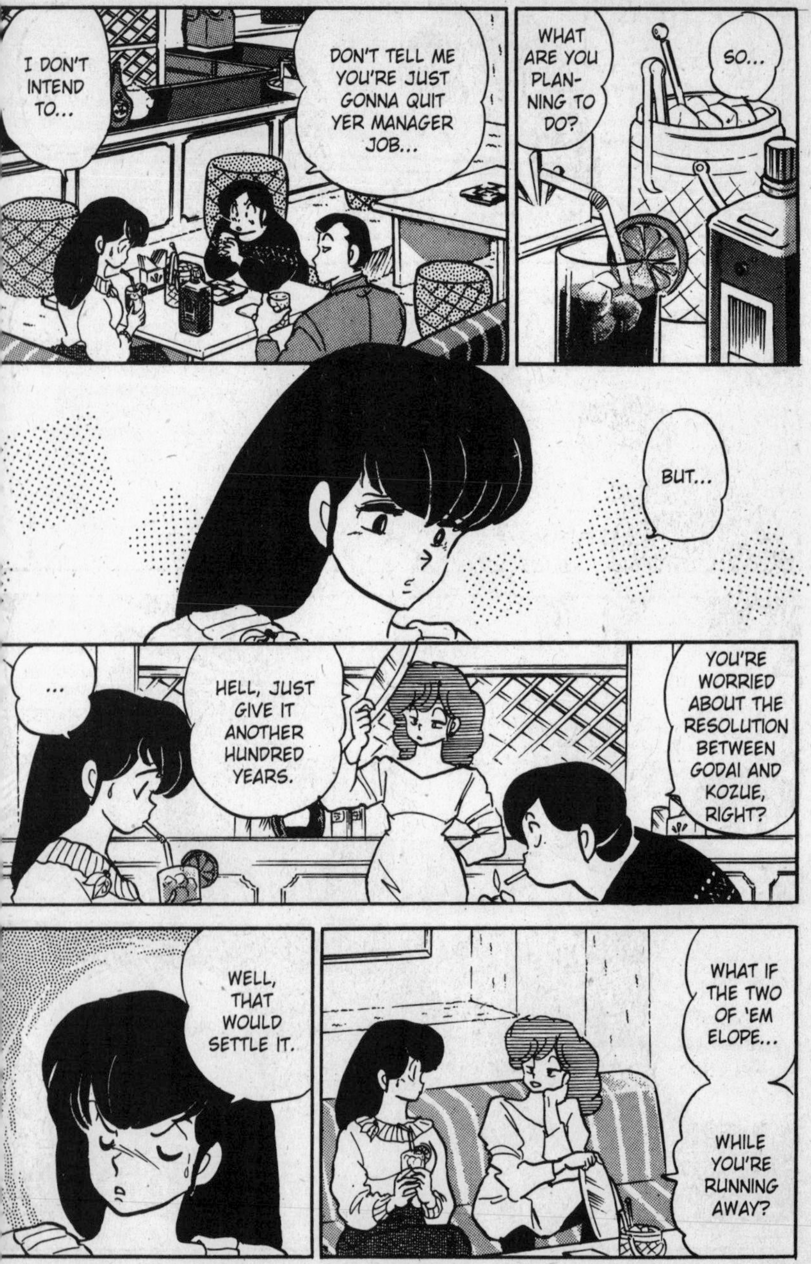

SO...
WHAT ARE YOU PLAN-NING TO DO?
DON'T TELL ME YOU'RE JUST GONNA QUIT YER MANAGER JOB...
I DON'T INTEND TO...
BUT...
YOU'RE WORRIED ABOUT THE RESOLUTION BETWEEN GODAI AND KOZUE, RIGHT?
HELL, JUST GIVE IT ANOTHER HUNDRED YEARS.
...
WHAT IF THE TWO OF 'EM ELOPE...
WHILE YOU'RE RUNNING AWAY?
WELL, THAT WOULD SETTLE IT.

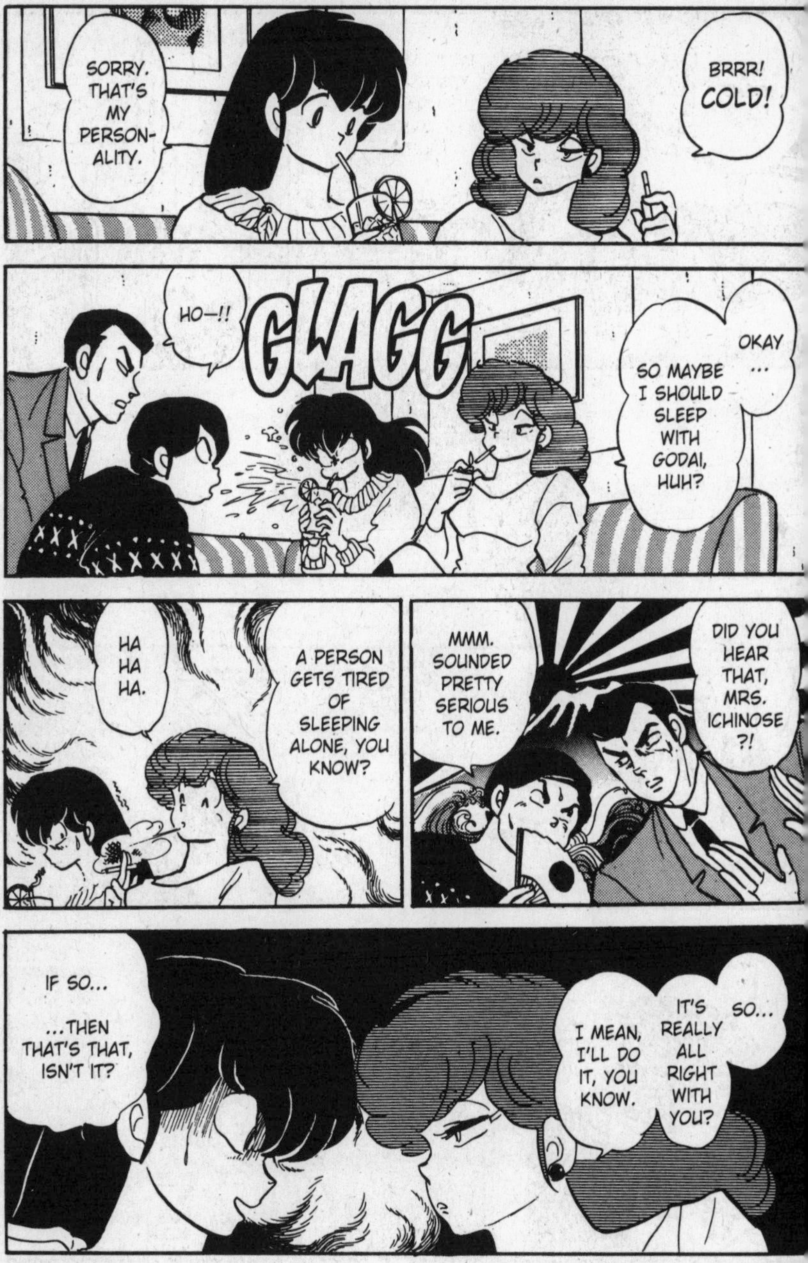
SORRY. THAT'S MY PERSONALITY.
BRRR! COLD!
OKAY ...
SO MAYBE I SHOULD SLEEP WITH GODAI, HUH?
GLAGG
HO—!!
HA HA HA.
A PERSON GETS TIRED OF SLEEPING ALONE, YOU KNOW?
MMM. SOUNDED PRETTY SERIOUS TO ME.
DID YOU HEAR THAT, MRS. ICHINOSE?!
SO...
IT'S REALLY ALL RIGHT WITH YOU?
I MEAN, I'LL DO IT, YOU KNOW.
IF SO...
...THEN THAT'S THAT, ISN'T IT?

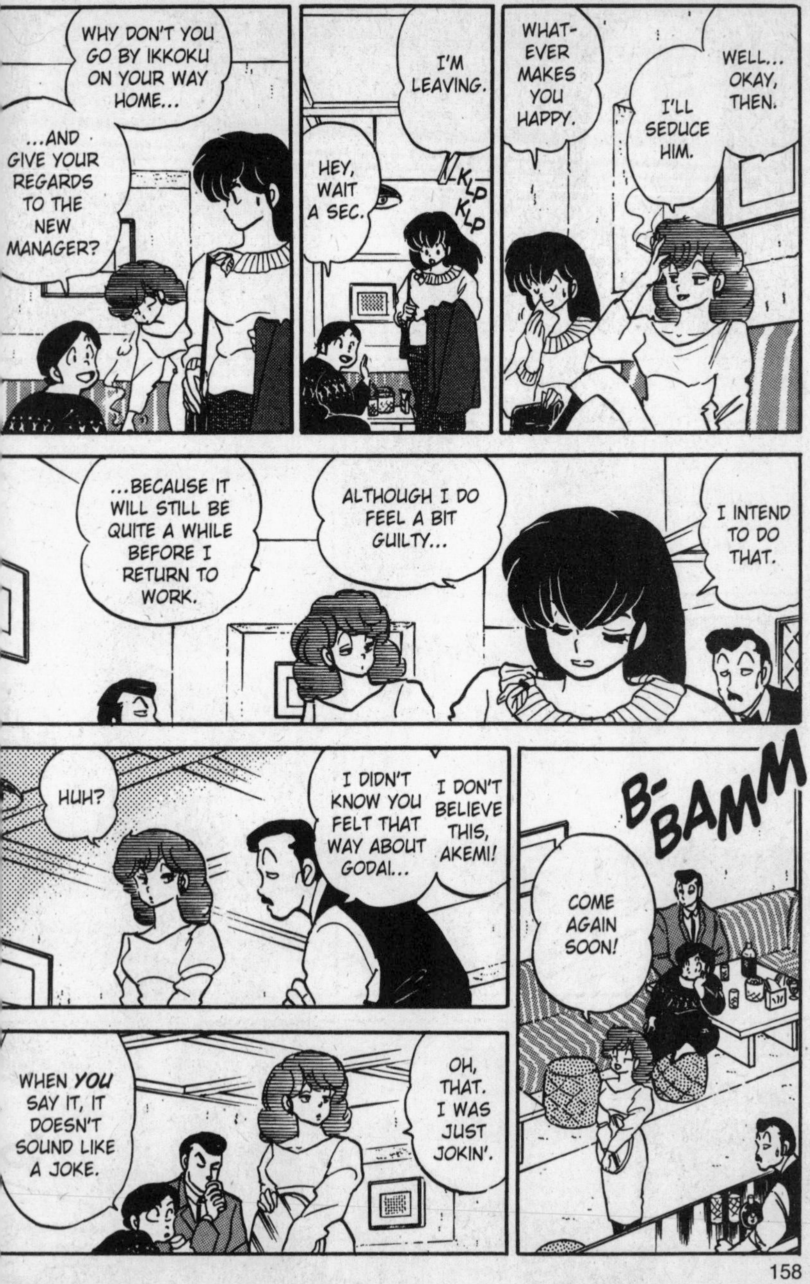
WELL... OKAY, THEN.
I'LL SEDUCE HIM.
WHAT-EVER MAKES YOU HAPPY.
I'M LEAVING.
KLP KLP
HEY, WAIT A SEC.
WHY DON'T YOU GO BY IKKOKU ON YOUR WAY HOME...
...AND GIVE YOUR REGARDS TO THE NEW MANAGER?
I INTEND TO DO THAT.
ALTHOUGH I DO FEEL A BIT GUILTY...
...BECAUSE IT WILL STILL BE QUITE A WHILE BEFORE I RETURN TO WORK.
B-BAMM
COME AGAIN SOON!
I DON'T BELIEVE THIS, AKEMI!
I DIDN'T KNOW YOU FELT THAT WAY ABOUT GODAI...
HUH?
OH, THAT. I WAS JUST JOKIN'.
WHEN *YOU* SAY IT, IT DOESN'T SOUND LIKE A JOKE.

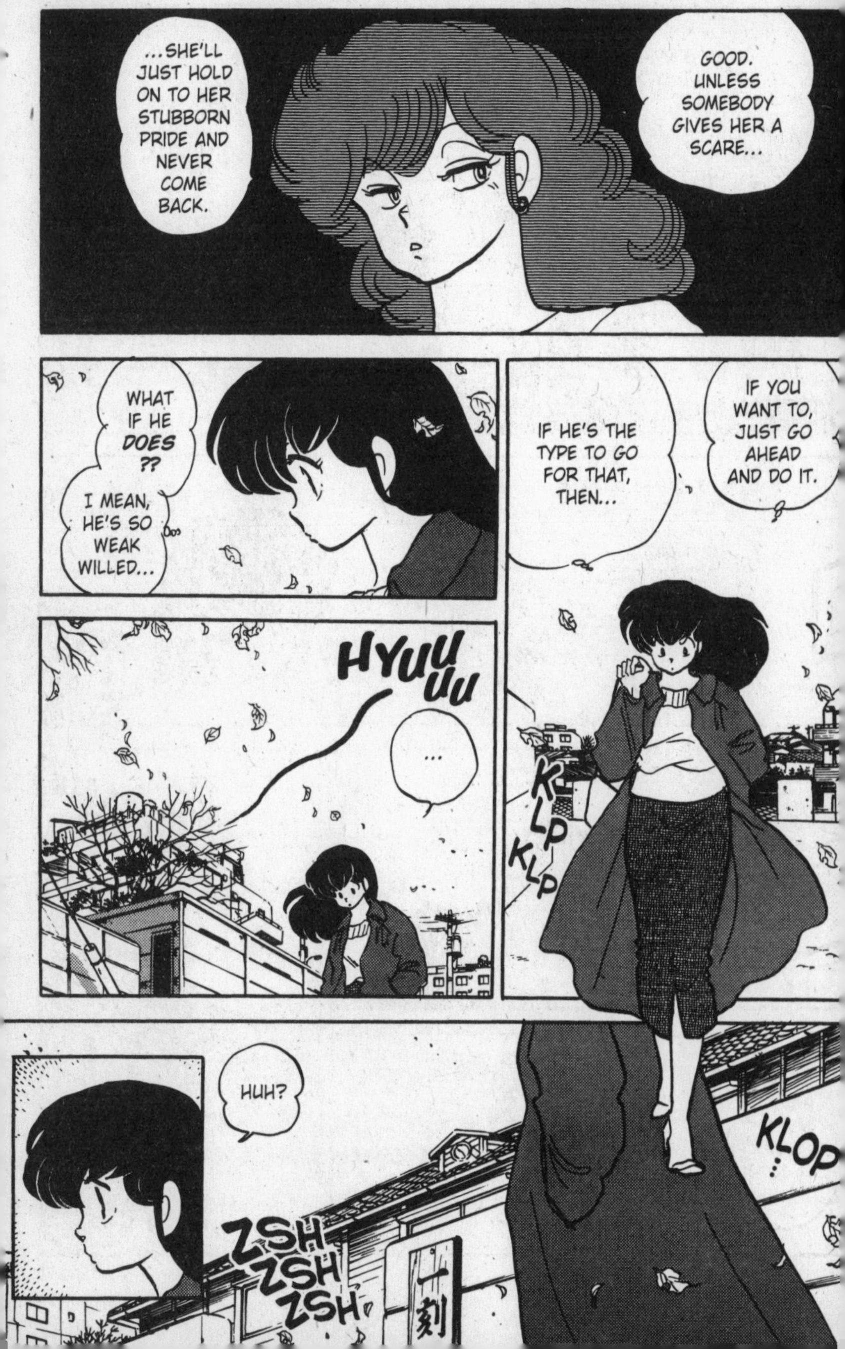
GOOD. UNLESS SOMEBODY GIVES HER A SCARE...
...SHE'LL JUST HOLD ON TO HER STUBBORN PRIDE AND NEVER COME BACK.
IF YOU WANT TO, JUST GO AHEAD AND DO IT.
IF HE'S THE TYPE TO GO FOR THAT, THEN...
WHAT IF HE DOES??
I MEAN, HE'S SO WEAK WILLED...
KLP KLP
HYUUUU
...
HUH?
KLOP
ZSH ZSH ZSH
一刻

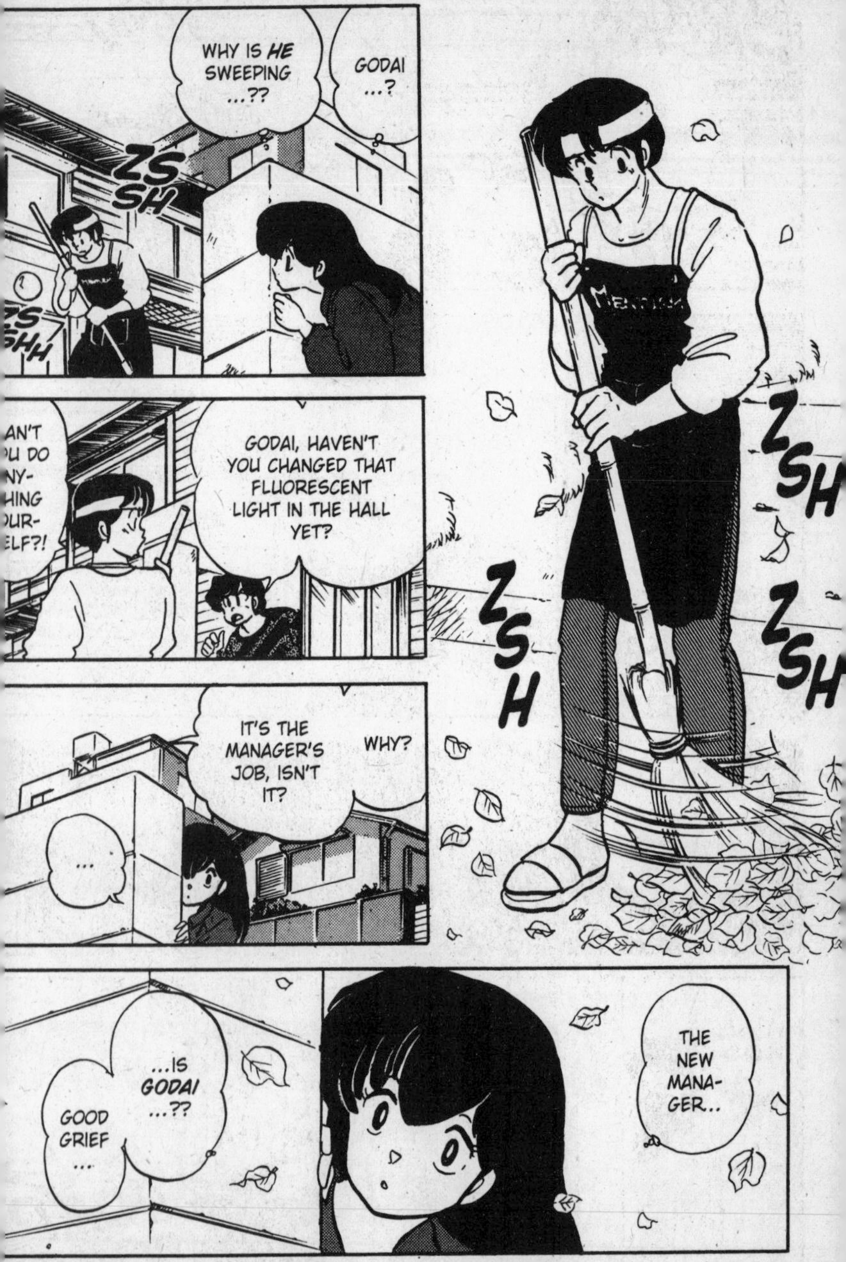
ZSH
ZSH
ZSH
GODAI ...?
WHY IS HE SWEEPING ...??
ZSSH
ZSSHH
GODAI, HAVEN'T YOU CHANGED THAT FLUORESCENT LIGHT IN THE HALL YET?
AN'T U DO NY- HING OUR- ELF?!
WHY?
IT'S THE MANAGER'S JOB, ISN'T IT?
...
THE NEW MANA- GER..
...IS GODAI ...??
GOOD GRIEF ...

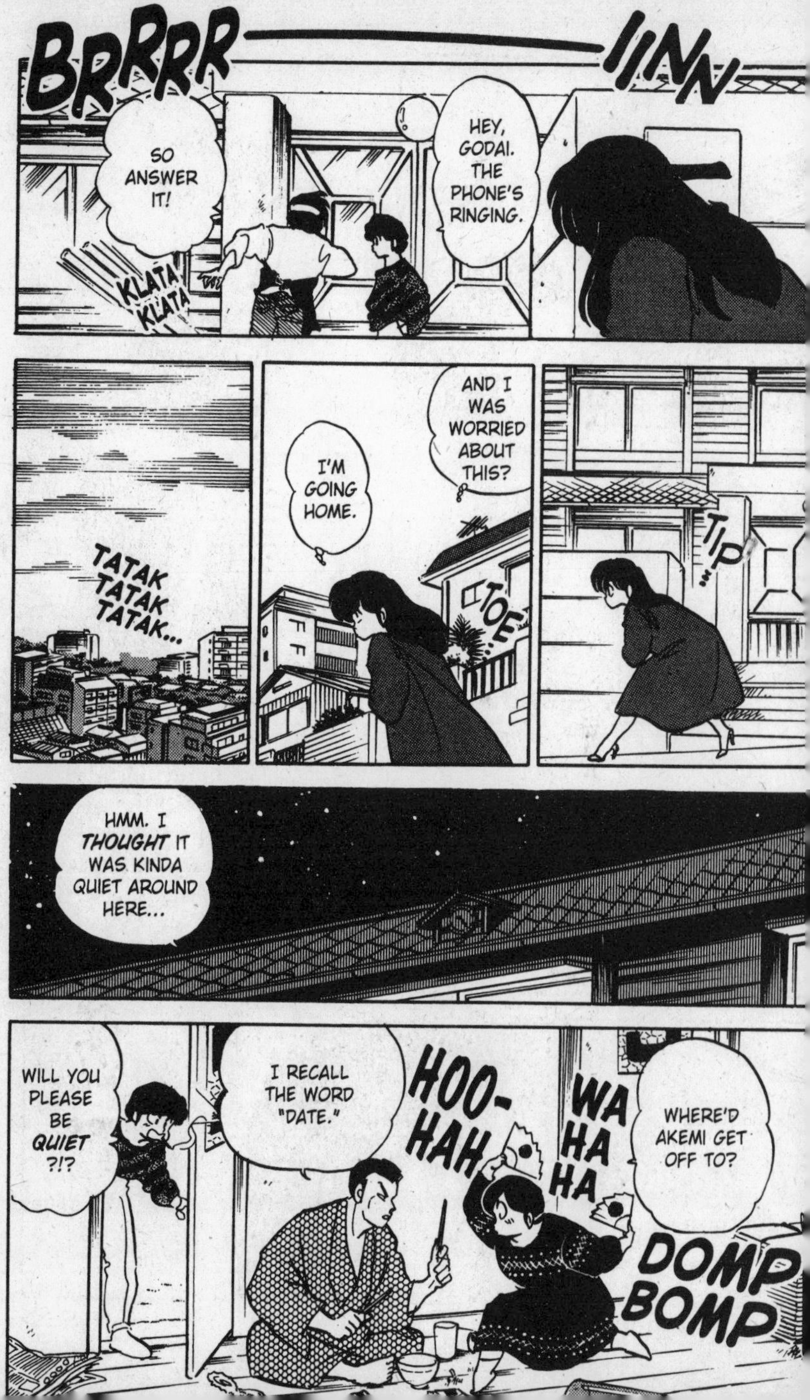
BRRRR——IINN
SO ANSWER IT!
KLATA KLATA
HEY, GODAI. THE PHONE'S RINGING.
TATAK TATAK TATAK...
I'M GOING HOME.
AND I WAS WORRIED ABOUT THIS?
TOE...
TIP...
HMM. I *THOUGHT* IT WAS KINDA QUIET AROUND HERE...
WILL YOU PLEASE BE *QUIET* ?!?
I RECALL THE WORD "DATE."
HOO-HAH
WA HA HA
WHERE'D AKEMI GET OFF TO?
DOMP BOMP

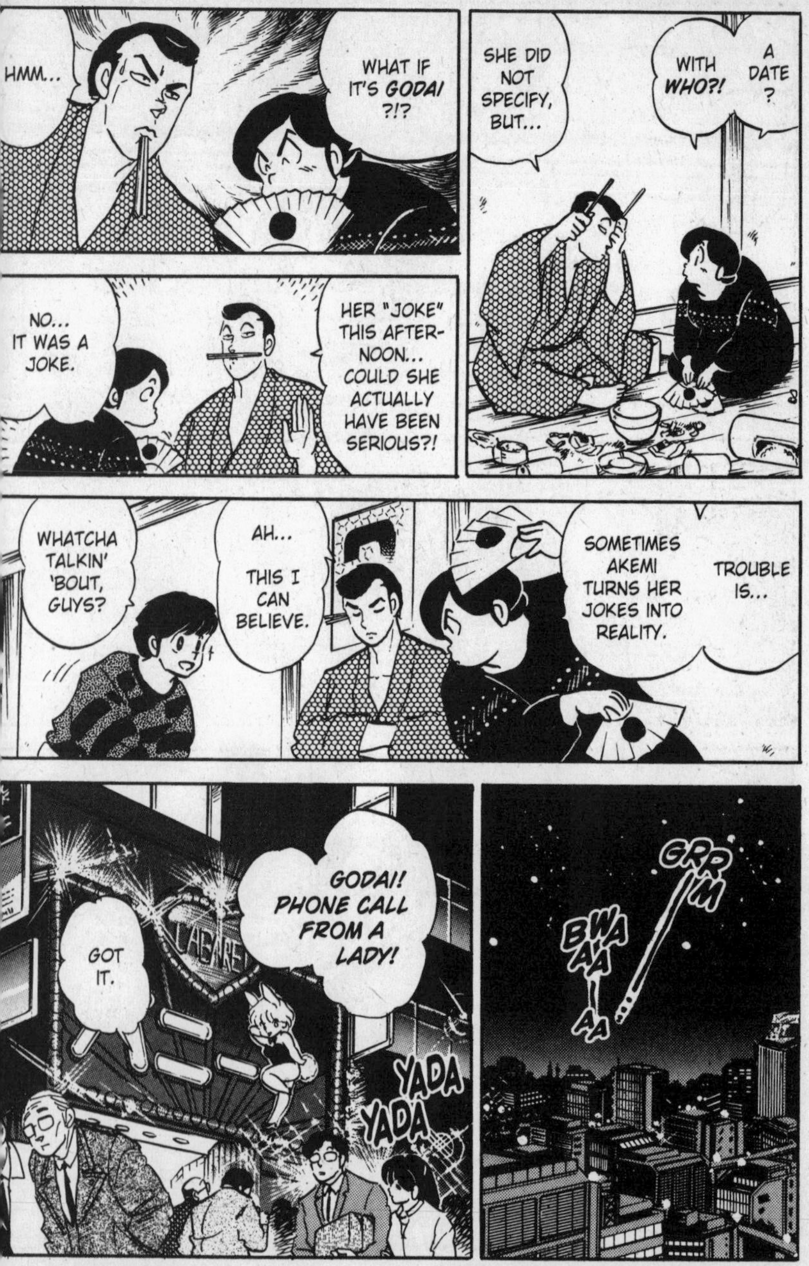

A DATE ?
WITH WHO?!
SHE DID NOT SPECIFY, BUT...
WHAT IF IT'S GODAI ?!?
HMM...
HER "JOKE" THIS AFTERNOON... COULD SHE ACTUALLY HAVE BEEN SERIOUS?!
NO... IT WAS A JOKE.
TROUBLE IS...
SOMETIMES AKEMI TURNS HER JOKES INTO REALITY.
AH... THIS I CAN BELIEVE.
WHATCHA TALKIN' 'BOUT, GUYS?
GRRR M
BWAAA IAA
CABARET
YADA YADA
GODAI! PHONE CALL FROM A LADY!
GOT IT.

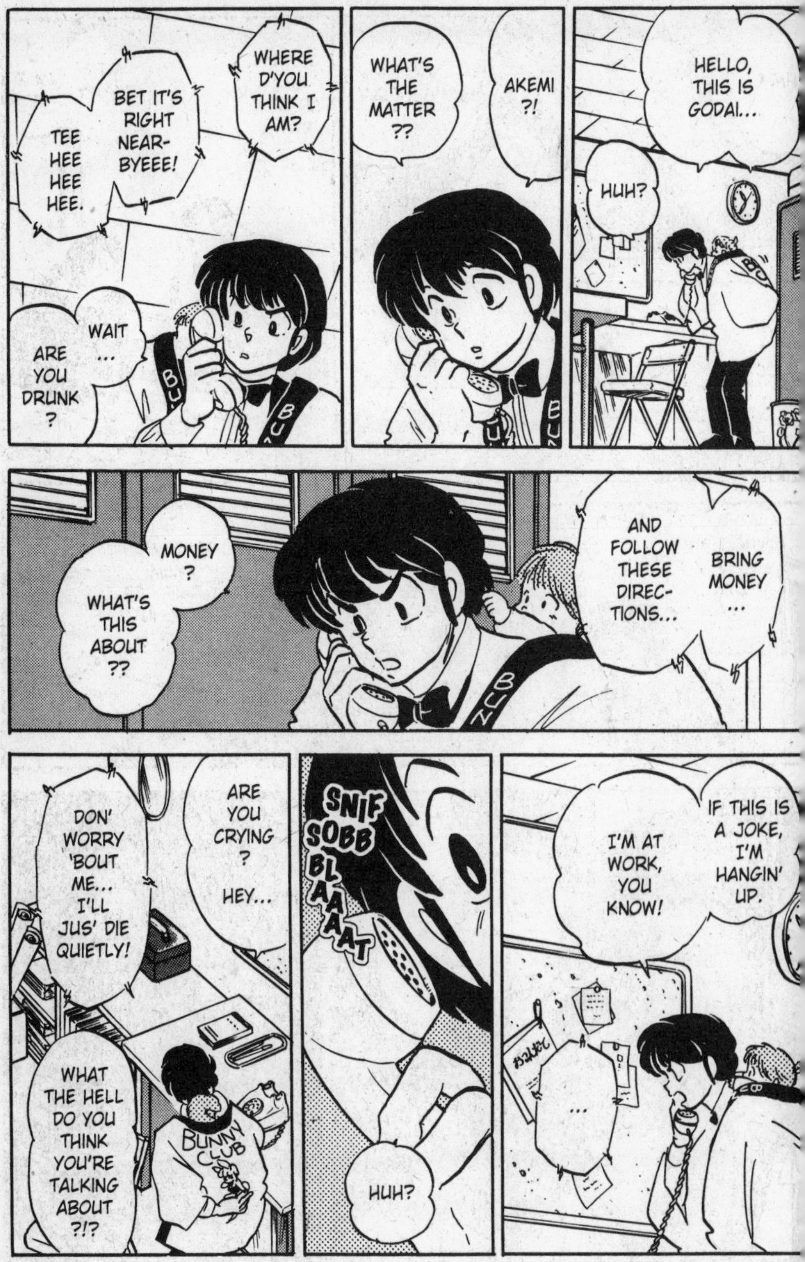
HELLO, THIS IS GODAI...
HUH?
AKEMI ?!
WHAT'S THE MATTER ??
WHERE D'YOU THINK I AM?
BET IT'S RIGHT NEAR-BYEEE!
TEE HEE HEE HEE.
WAIT ... ARE YOU DRUNK ?
BRING MONEY ...
AND FOLLOW THESE DIREC-TIONS...
MONEY ?
WHAT'S THIS ABOUT ??
IF THIS IS A JOKE, I'M HANGIN' UP.
I'M AT WORK, YOU KNOW!
...
SNIF SOBB BLAAAAT
HUH?
HEY... ARE YOU CRYING ?
DON' WORRY 'BOUT ME... I'LL JUS' DIE QUIETLY!
WHAT THE HELL DO YOU THINK YOU'RE TALKING ABOUT ?!?
BUNNY CLUB

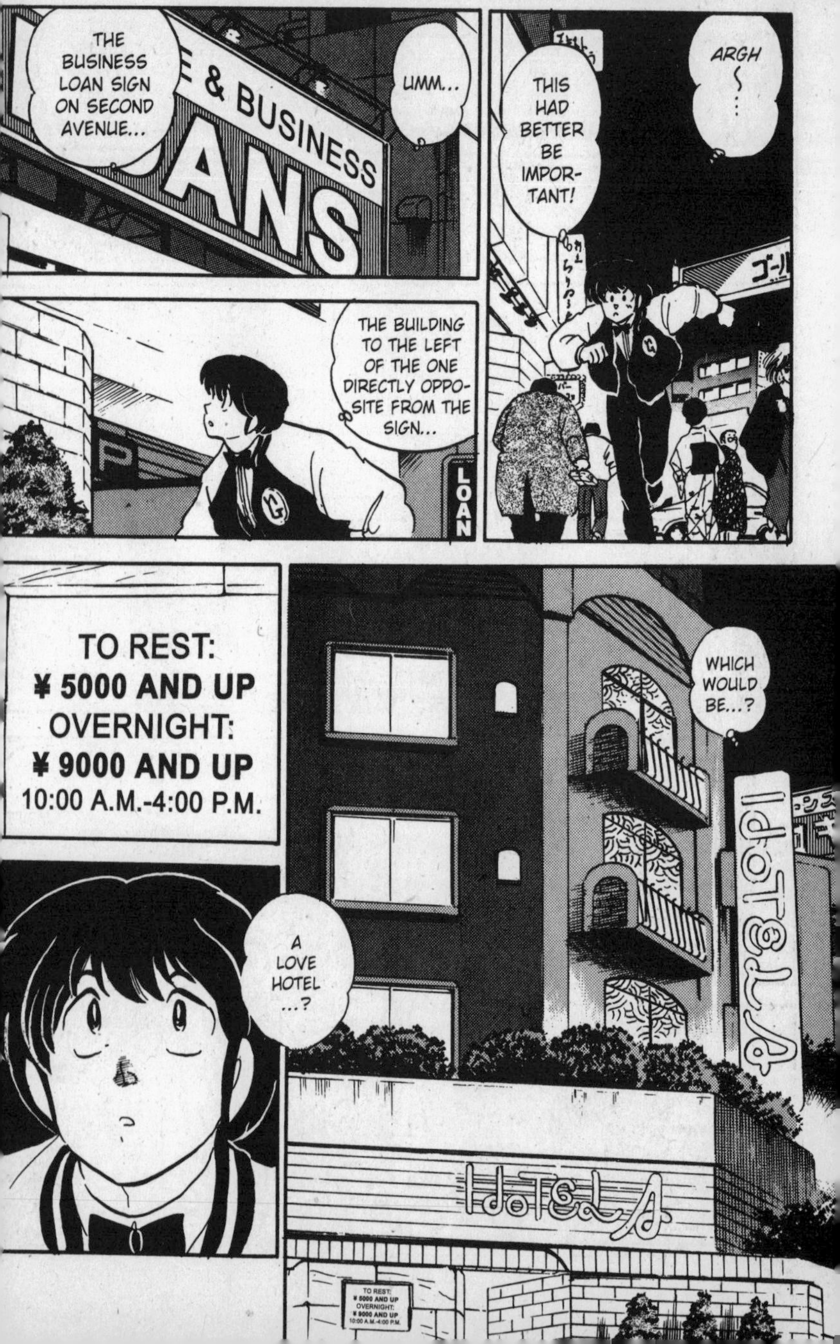
ARGH ~...
THIS HAD BETTER BE IMPOR-TANT!
UMM...
THE BUSINESS LOAN SIGN ON SECOND AVENUE...
& BUSINESS
ANS
THE BUILDING TO THE LEFT OF THE ONE DIRECTLY OPPO-SITE FROM THE SIGN...
LOAN
WHICH WOULD BE...?
TO REST:
¥ 5000 AND UP
OVERNIGHT:
¥ 9000 AND UP
10:00 A.M.-4:00 P.M.
A LOVE HOTEL ...?

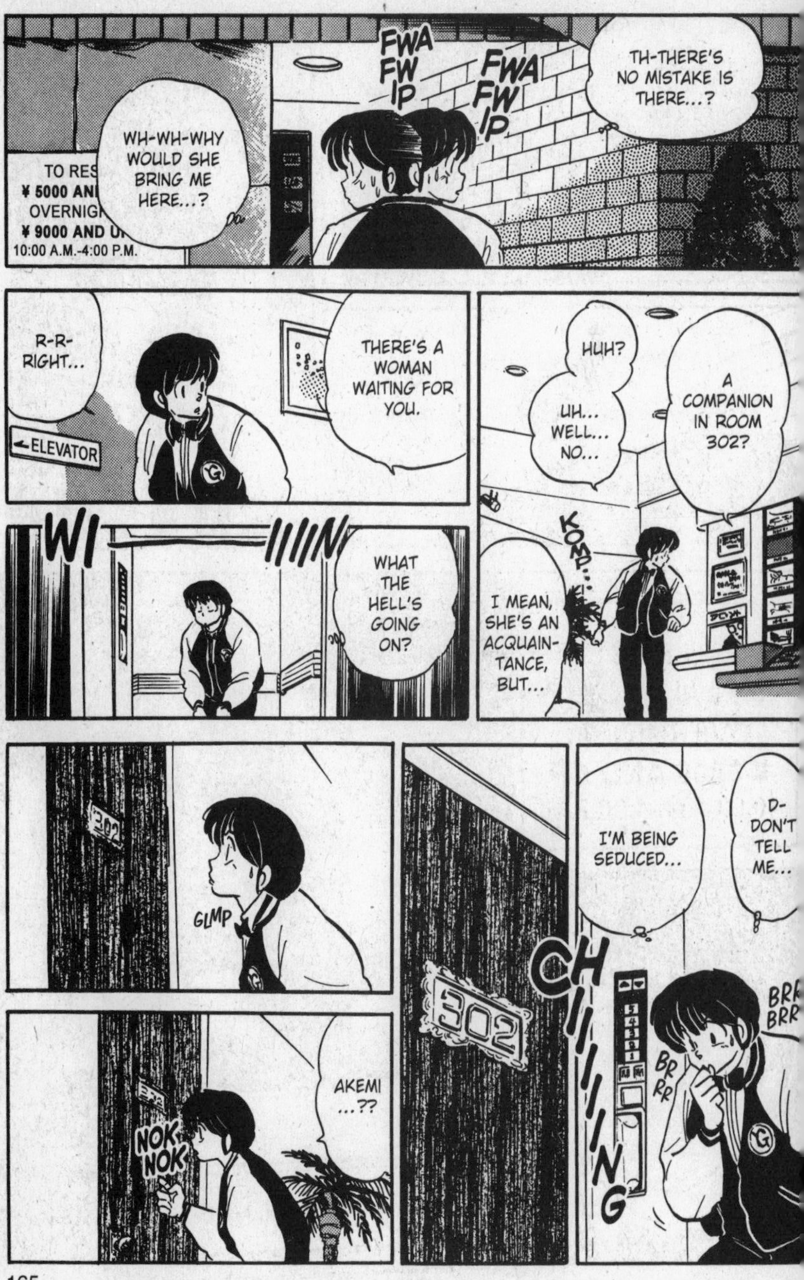
TO RES
¥ 5000 AN
OVERNIG
¥ 9000 AND U
10:00 A.M.-4:00 P.M.
WH-WH-WHY WOULD SHE BRING ME HERE...?
FWA FWIP
FWA FWIP
TH-THERE'S NO MISTAKE IS THERE...?
ELEVATOR
R-R-RIGHT...
THERE'S A WOMAN WAITING FOR YOU.
A COMPANION IN ROOM 302?
HUH?
UH... WELL... NO...
KOMP...
I MEAN, SHE'S AN ACQUAINTANCE, BUT...
WI IIIIN
WHAT THE HELL'S GOING ON?
302
GLMP
NOK NOK
AKEMI ...??
302
CHIIIIING
D-DON'T TELL ME...
I'M BEING SEDUCED...
BRR BRR
BRRR

THE DOOR'S OPEN...

HUH ...

CHK

AKEMI !!

HEY!

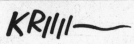

NOK NOK

SHH–HH

KRIIII—

AKEM—

!!

FYUUUUU—

KK KK

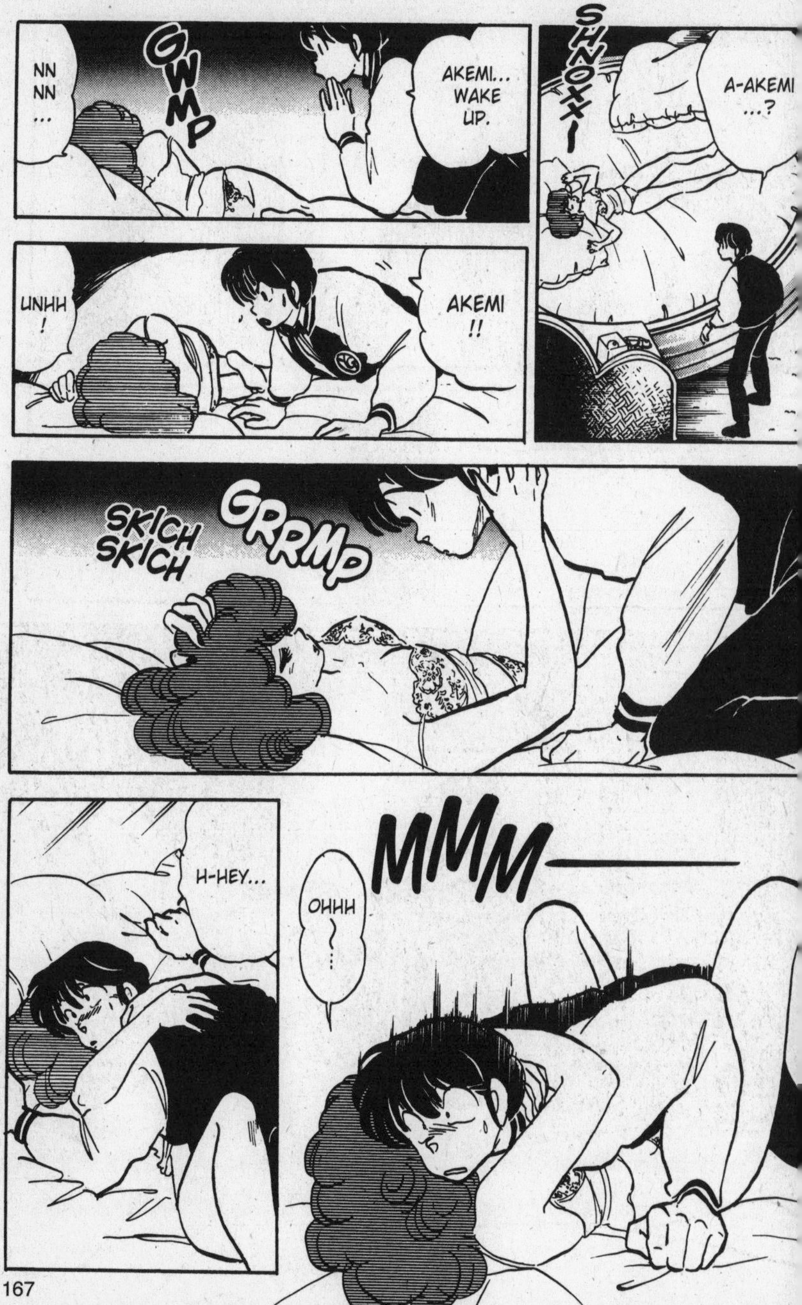
SHNOXXI
A-AKEMI ...?
AKEMI... WAKE UP.
GWMP
NN NN ...
AKEMI !!
UNHH !
GRRMP
SKICH SKICH
MMM
OHHH ~ ...
H-HEY...

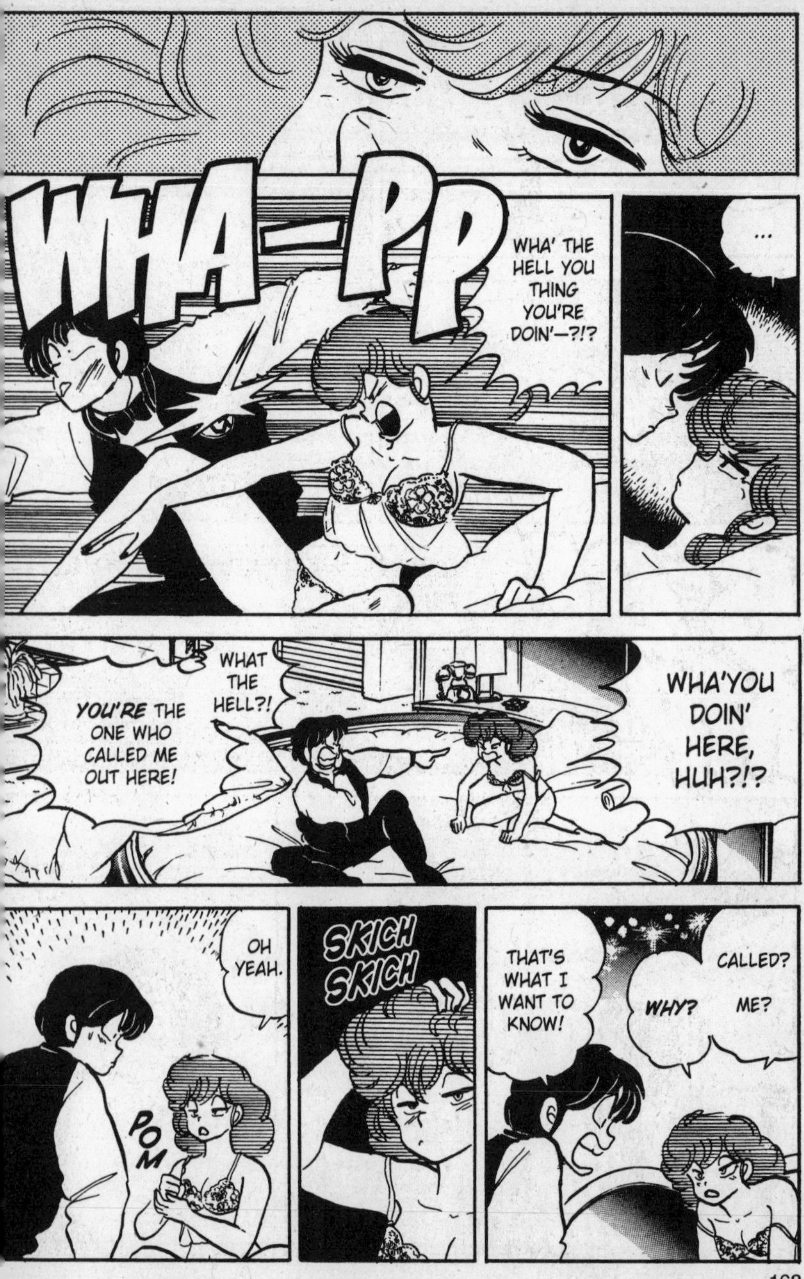
WHA-PP
WHA' THE HELL YOU THING YOU'RE DOIN'—?!?
...
WHA'YOU DOIN' HERE, HUH?!?
WHAT THE HELL?!
YOU'RE THE ONE WHO CALLED ME OUT HERE!
OH YEAH.
POM
SKICH SKICH
CALLED? ME?
WHY?
THAT'S WHAT I WANT TO KNOW!

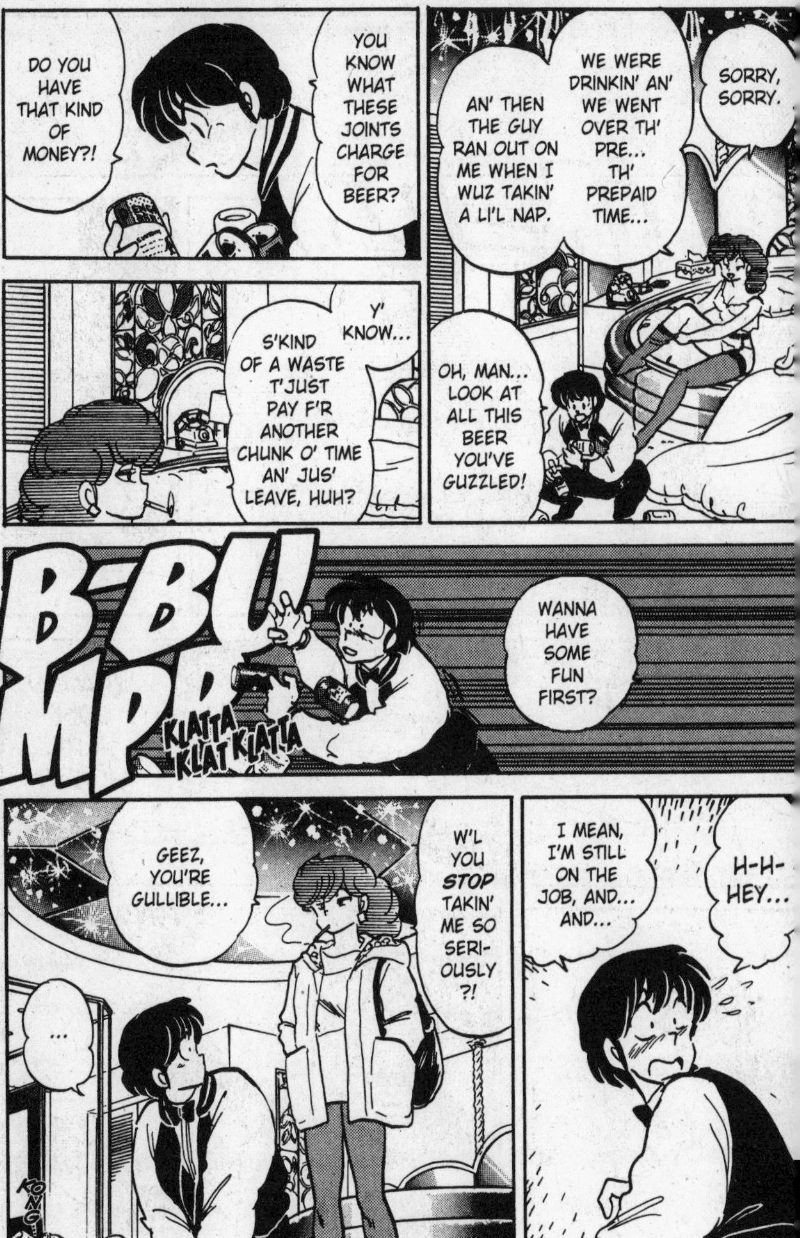

SORRY, SORRY.
WE WERE DRINKIN' AN' WE WENT OVER TH' PRE... TH' PREPAID TIME...
AN' THEN THE GUY RAN OUT ON ME WHEN I WUZ TAKIN' A LI'L NAP.
OH, MAN... LOOK AT ALL THIS BEER YOU'VE GUZZLED!
YOU KNOW WHAT THESE JOINTS CHARGE FOR BEER?
DO YOU HAVE THAT KIND OF MONEY?!
Y' KNOW...
S'KIND OF A WASTE T'JUST PAY F'R ANOTHER CHUNK O' TIME AN' JUS' LEAVE, HUH?
WANNA HAVE SOME FUN FIRST?
B-BUMP
KLATTA KLAT KLATTA
H-H-HEY...
I MEAN, I'M STILL ON THE JOB, AND... AND...
W'L YOU STOP TAKIN' ME SO SERIOUSLY?!
GEEZ, YOU'RE GULLIBLE...
...
KONG

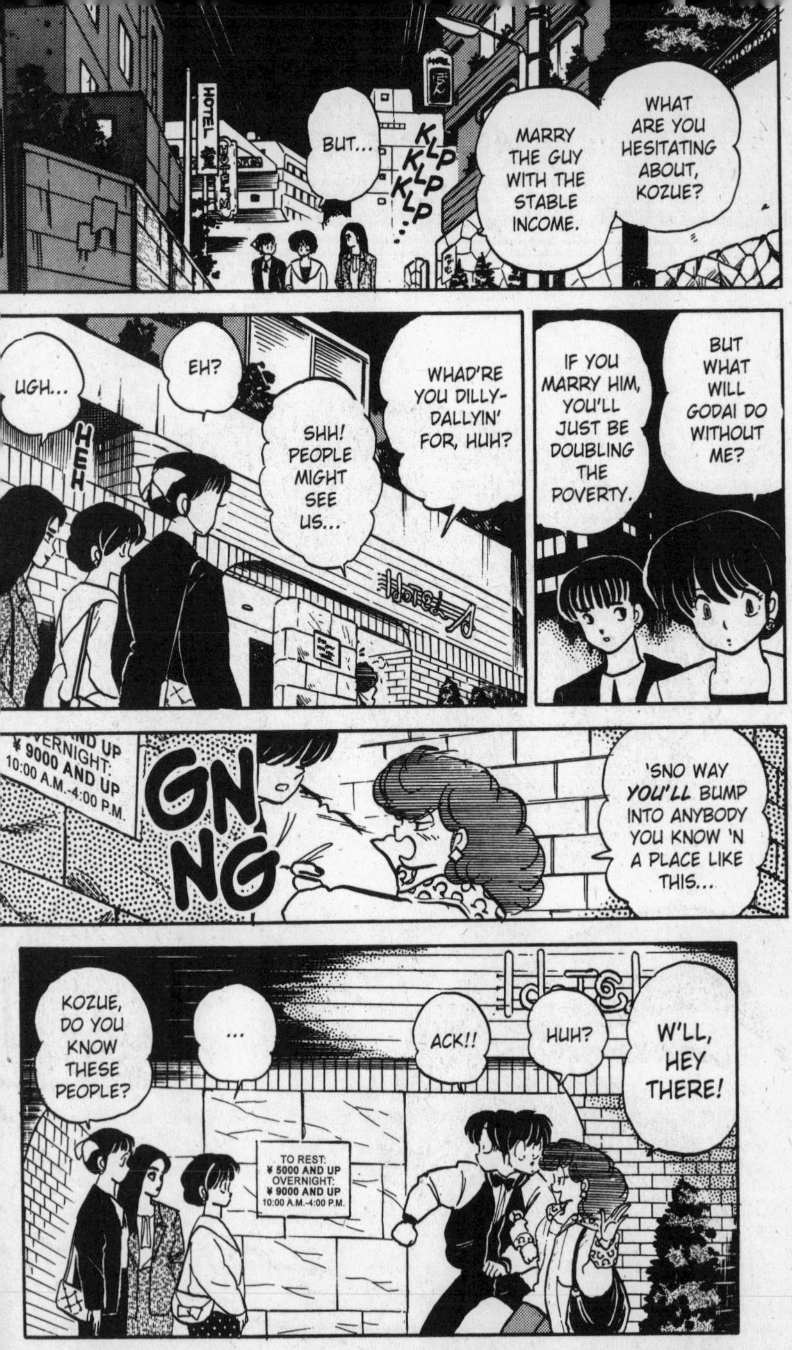
HOTEL
WHAT ARE YOU HESITATING ABOUT, KOZUE?
MARRY THE GUY WITH THE STABLE INCOME.
KLP KLP KLP KLP
BUT...
BUT WHAT WILL GODAI DO WITHOUT ME?
IF YOU MARRY HIM, YOU'LL JUST BE DOUBLING THE POVERTY.
WHAD'RE YOU DILLY-DALLYIN' FOR, HUH?
SHH! PEOPLE MIGHT SEE US...
EH?
HEH
UGH...
'SNO WAY *YOU'LL* BUMP INTO ANYBODY YOU KNOW 'N A PLACE LIKE THIS...
GN NG
ND UP OVERNIGHT: ¥ 9000 AND UP 10:00 A.M.-4:00 P.M.
W'LL, HEY THERE!
HUH?
ACK!!
...
KOZUE, DO YOU KNOW THESE PEOPLE?
TO REST: ¥ 5000 AND UP OVERNIGHT: ¥ 9000 AND UP 10:00 A.M.-4:00 P.M.

PART NINE
THE LOVE HOTEL INCIDENT

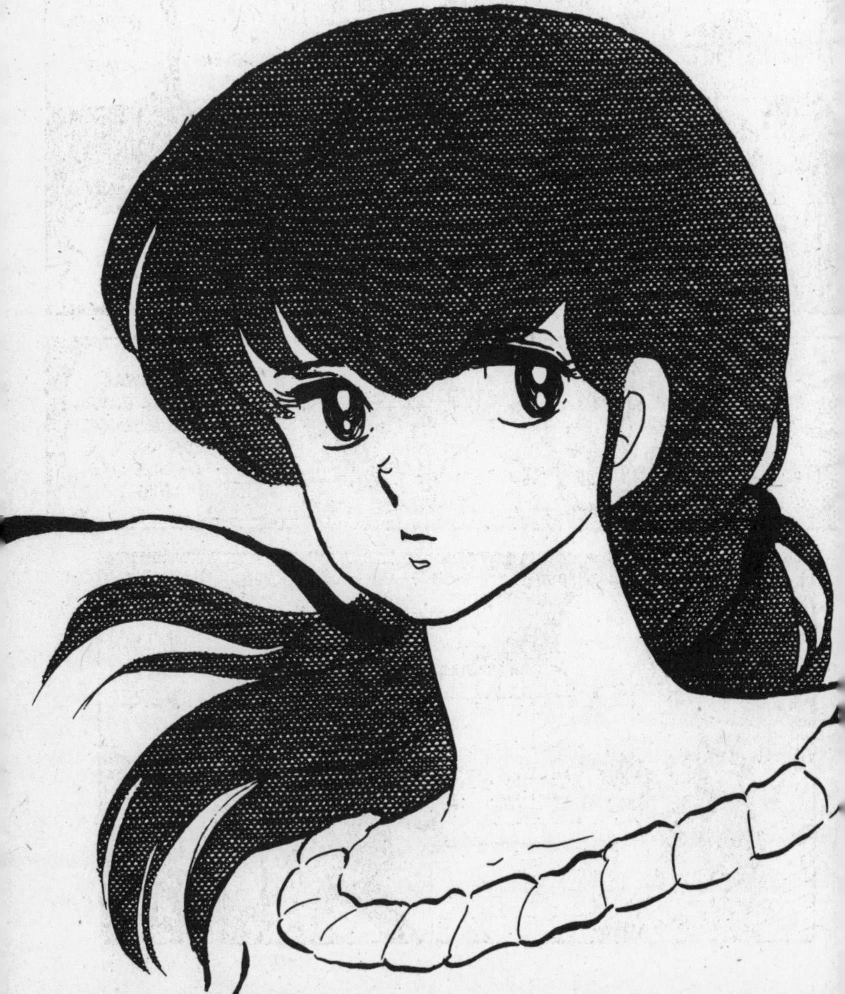

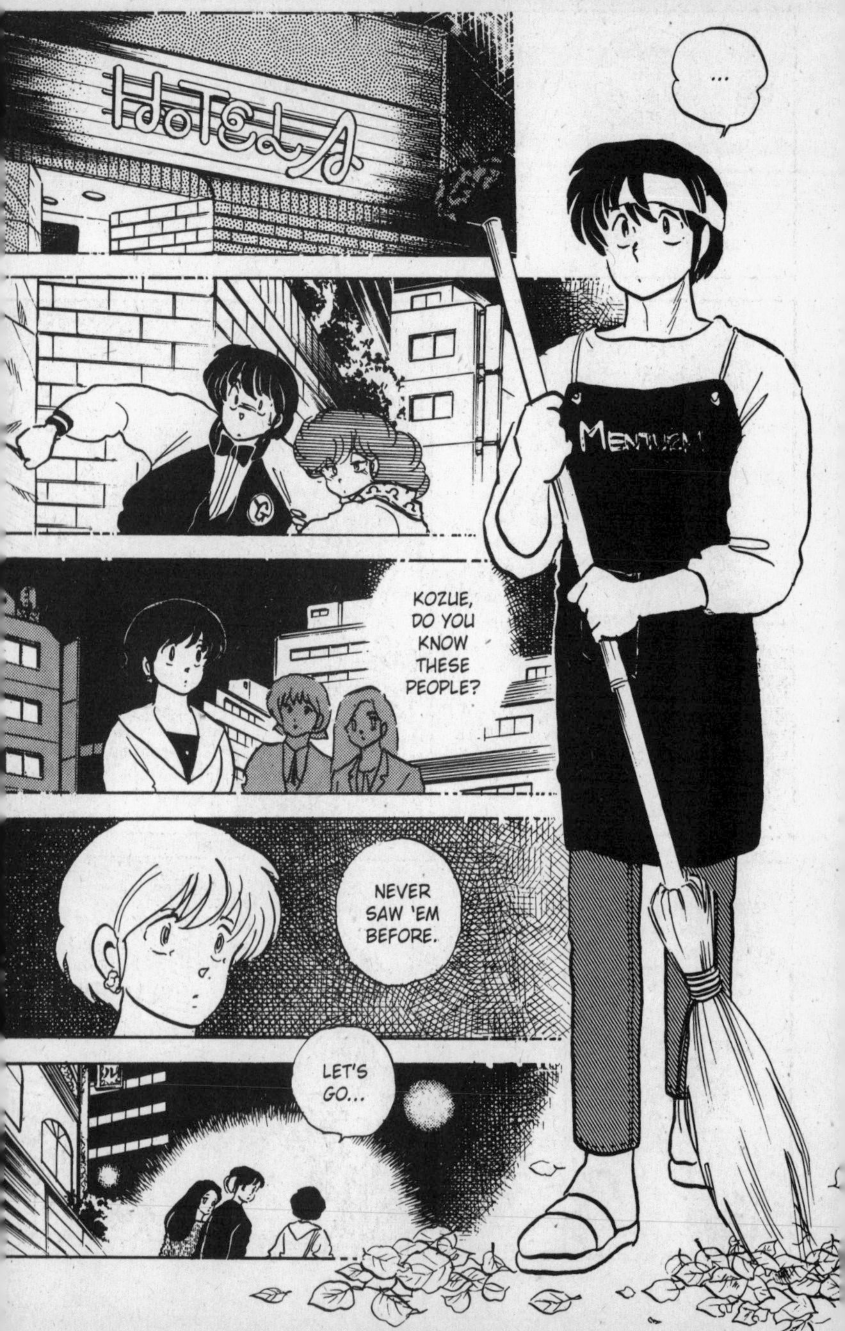
HOTEL A
...
MENTUZM
KOZUE, DO YOU KNOW THESE PEOPLE?
NEVER SAW 'EM BEFORE.
LET'S GO...

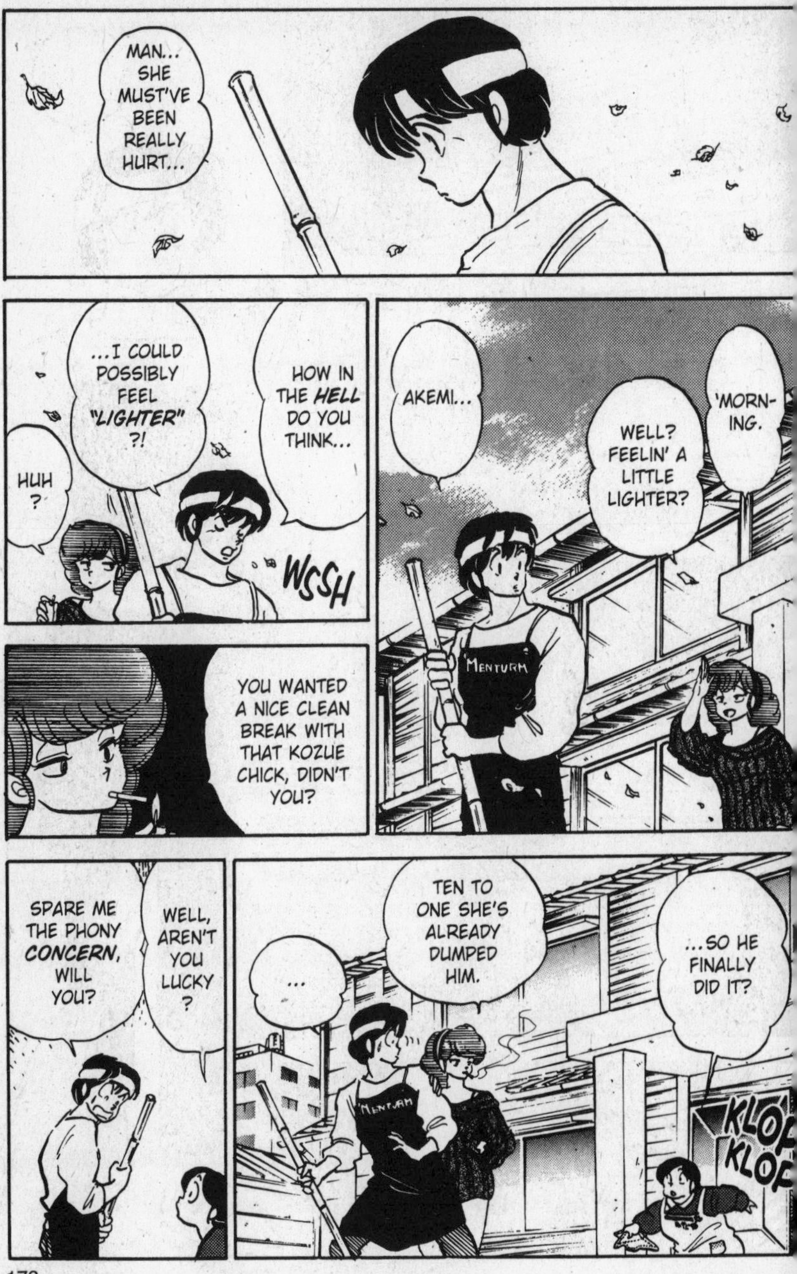
MAN... SHE MUST'VE BEEN REALLY HURT...
'MORNING.
WELL? FEELIN' A LITTLE LIGHTER?
AKEMI...
HOW IN THE *HELL* DO YOU THINK...
...I COULD POSSIBLY FEEL *"LIGHTER"* ?!
WSSH
HUH?
YOU WANTED A NICE CLEAN BREAK WITH THAT KOZUE CHICK, DIDN'T YOU?
KLOP KLOP
...SO HE FINALLY DID IT?
TEN TO ONE SHE'S ALREADY DUMPED HIM.
...
WELL, AREN'T YOU LUCKY?
SPARE ME THE PHONY *CONCERN*, WILL YOU?

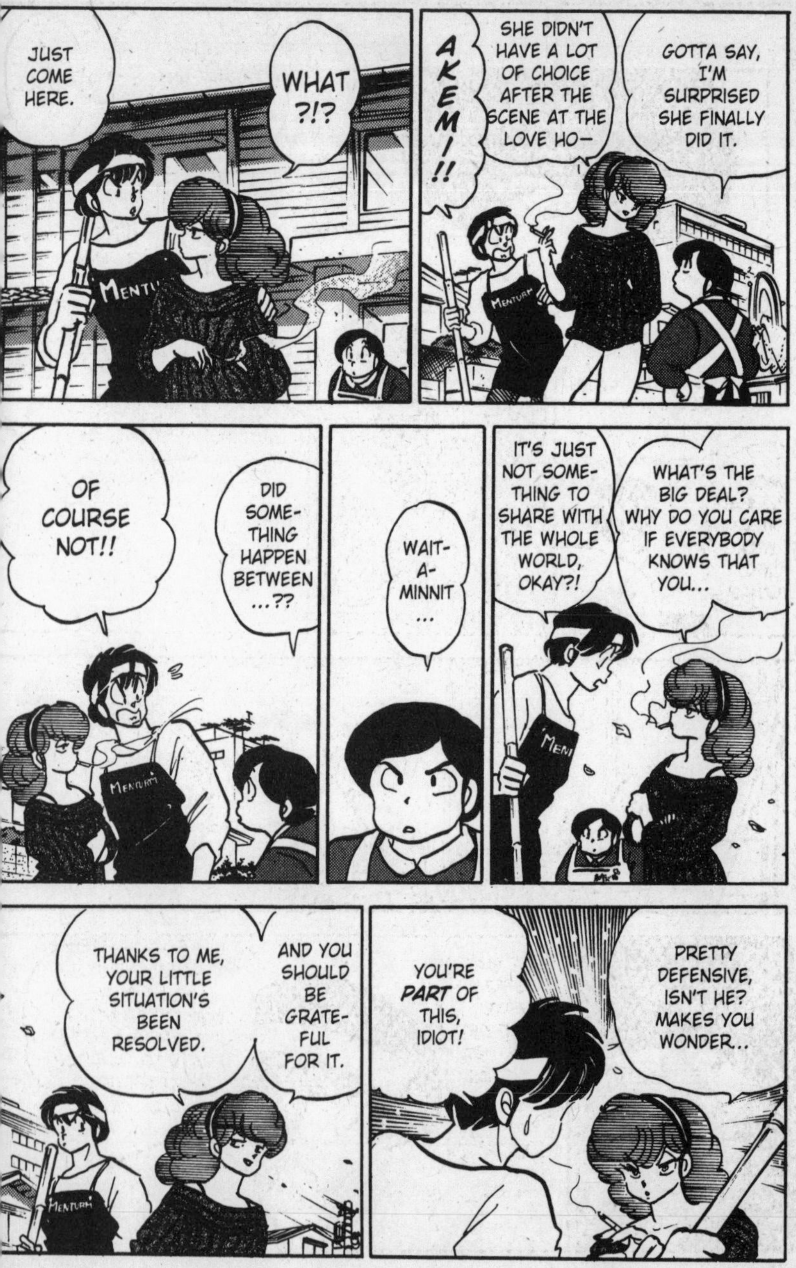
GOTTA SAY, I'M SURPRISED SHE FINALLY DID IT.
SHE DIDN'T HAVE A LOT OF CHOICE AFTER THE SCENE AT THE LOVE HO—
AKEMI!!
JUST COME HERE.
WHAT?!?
WHAT'S THE BIG DEAL? WHY DO YOU CARE IF EVERYBODY KNOWS THAT YOU...
IT'S JUST NOT SOMETHING TO SHARE WITH THE WHOLE WORLD, OKAY?!
WAIT-A-MINNIT...
DID SOMETHING HAPPEN BETWEEN...??
OF COURSE NOT!!
PRETTY DEFENSIVE, ISN'T HE? MAKES YOU WONDER...
YOU'RE *PART* OF THIS, IDIOT!
THANKS TO ME, YOUR LITTLE SITUATION'S BEEN RESOLVED.
AND YOU SHOULD BE GRATEFUL FOR IT.

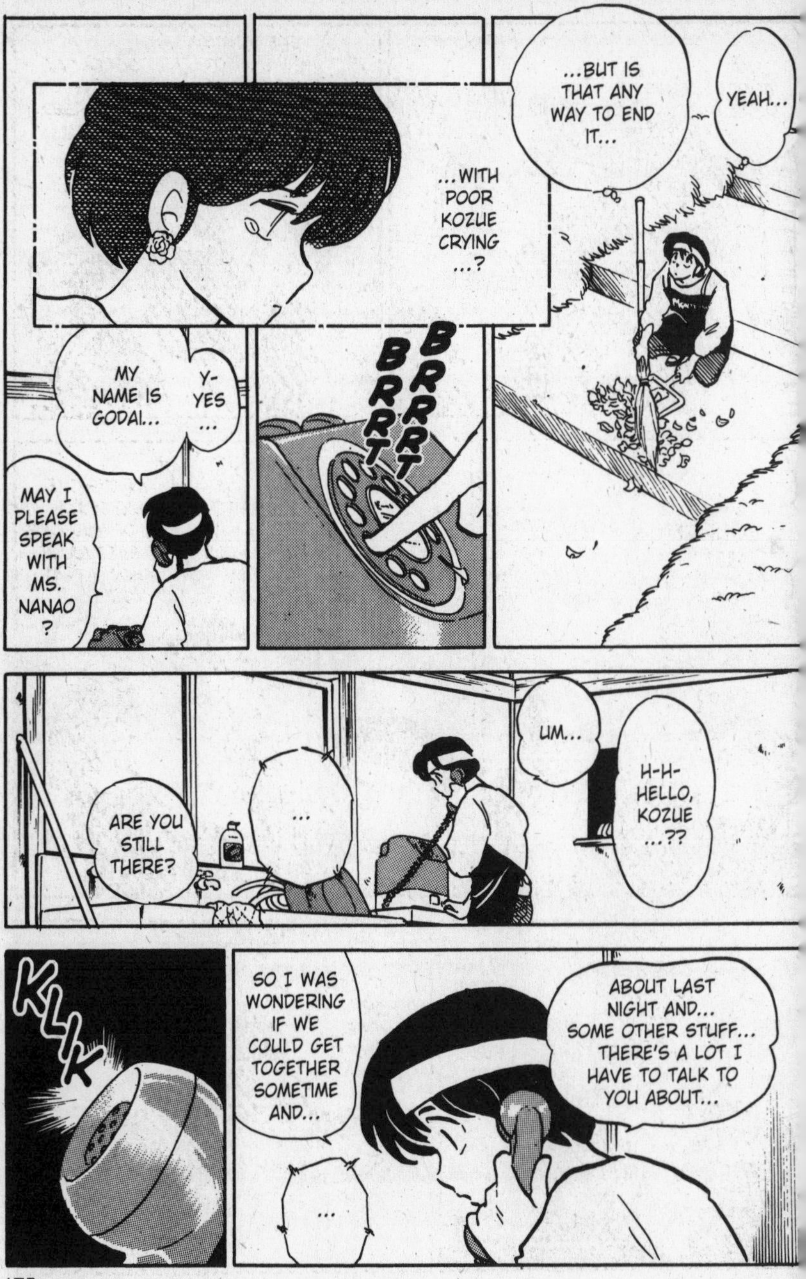
YEAH...
...BUT IS THAT ANY WAY TO END IT...
...WITH POOR KOZUE CRYING ...?
BRRRT
BRRRT
Y-YES...
MY NAME IS GODAI...
MAY I PLEASE SPEAK WITH MS. NANAO?
H-H-HELLO, KOZUE ...??
UM...
...
ARE YOU STILL THERE?
ABOUT LAST NIGHT AND... SOME OTHER STUFF... THERE'S A LOT I HAVE TO TALK TO YOU ABOUT...
SO I WAS WONDERING IF WE COULD GET TOGETHER SOMETIME AND...
...
KLIK

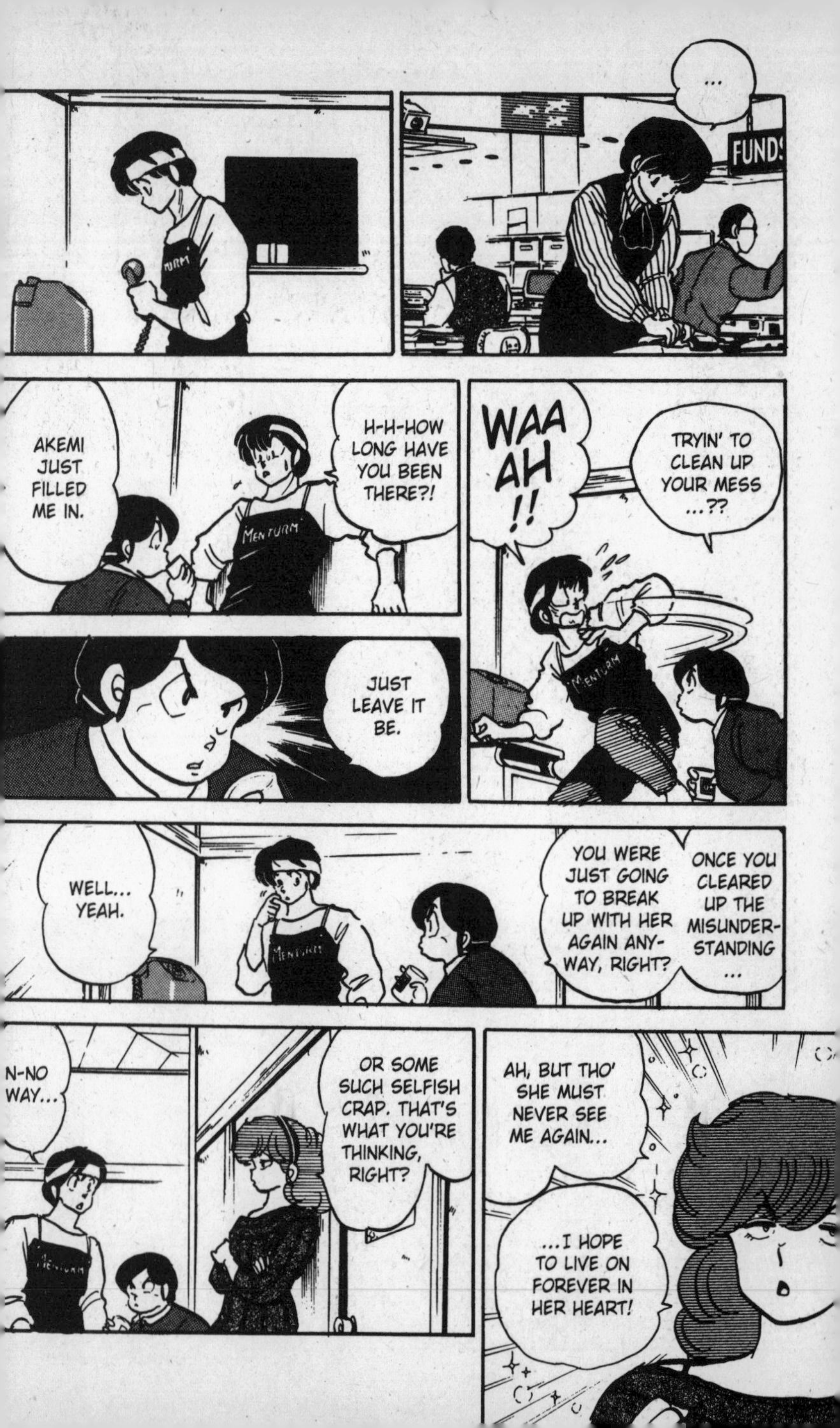
...
FUNDS
AKEMI JUST FILLED ME IN.
H-H-HOW LONG HAVE YOU BEEN THERE?!
WAA AH !!
TRYIN' TO CLEAN UP YOUR MESS ...??
JUST LEAVE IT BE.
WELL... YEAH.
YOU WERE JUST GOING TO BREAK UP WITH HER AGAIN ANY-WAY, RIGHT?
ONCE YOU CLEARED UP THE MISUNDER-STANDING ...
N-NO WAY...
OR SOME SUCH SELFISH CRAP. THAT'S WHAT YOU'RE THINKING, RIGHT?
AH, BUT THO' SHE MUST NEVER SEE ME AGAIN...
...I HOPE TO LIVE ON FOREVER IN HER HEART!

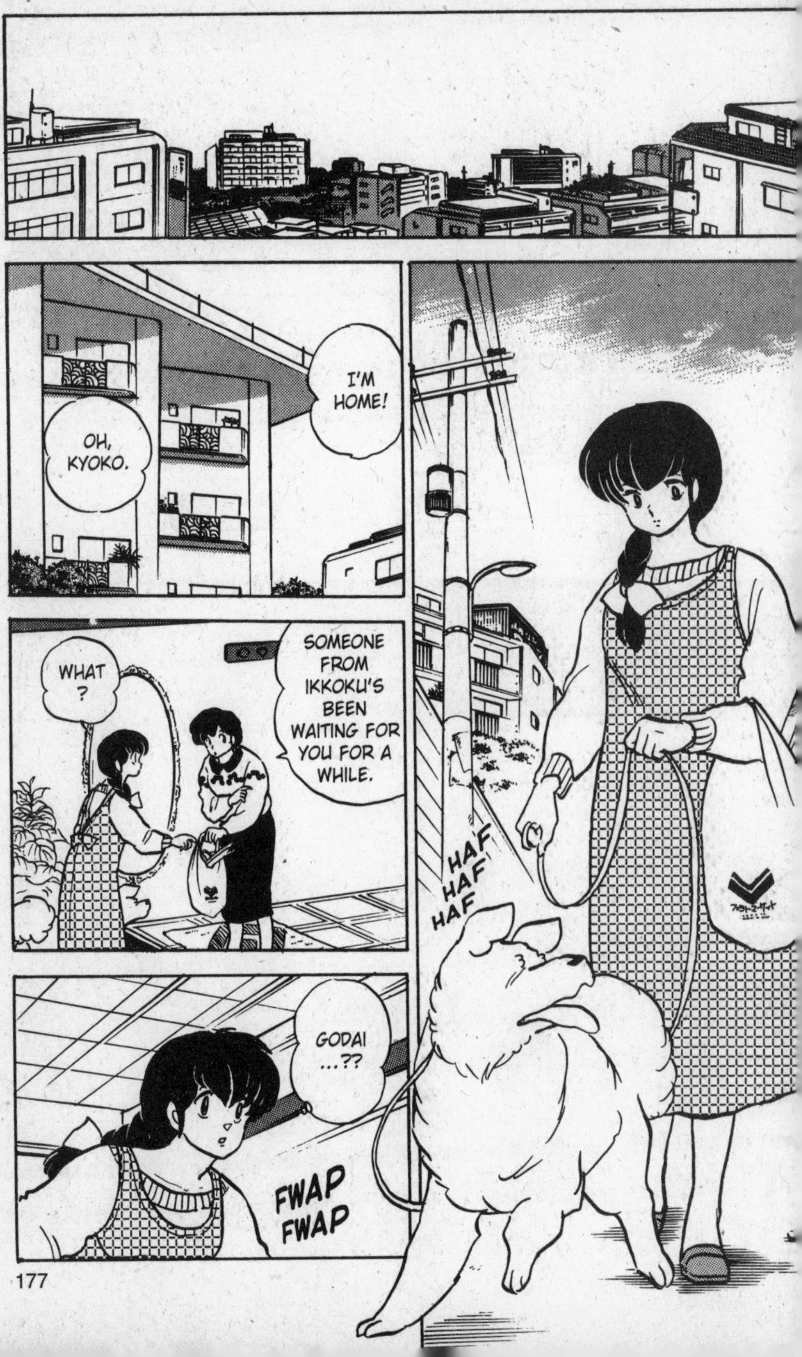
HAF
HAF
HAF
I'M HOME!
OH, KYOKO.
SOMEONE FROM IKKOKU'S BEEN WAITING FOR YOU FOR A WHILE.
WHAT ?
GODAI ...??
FWAP
FWAP

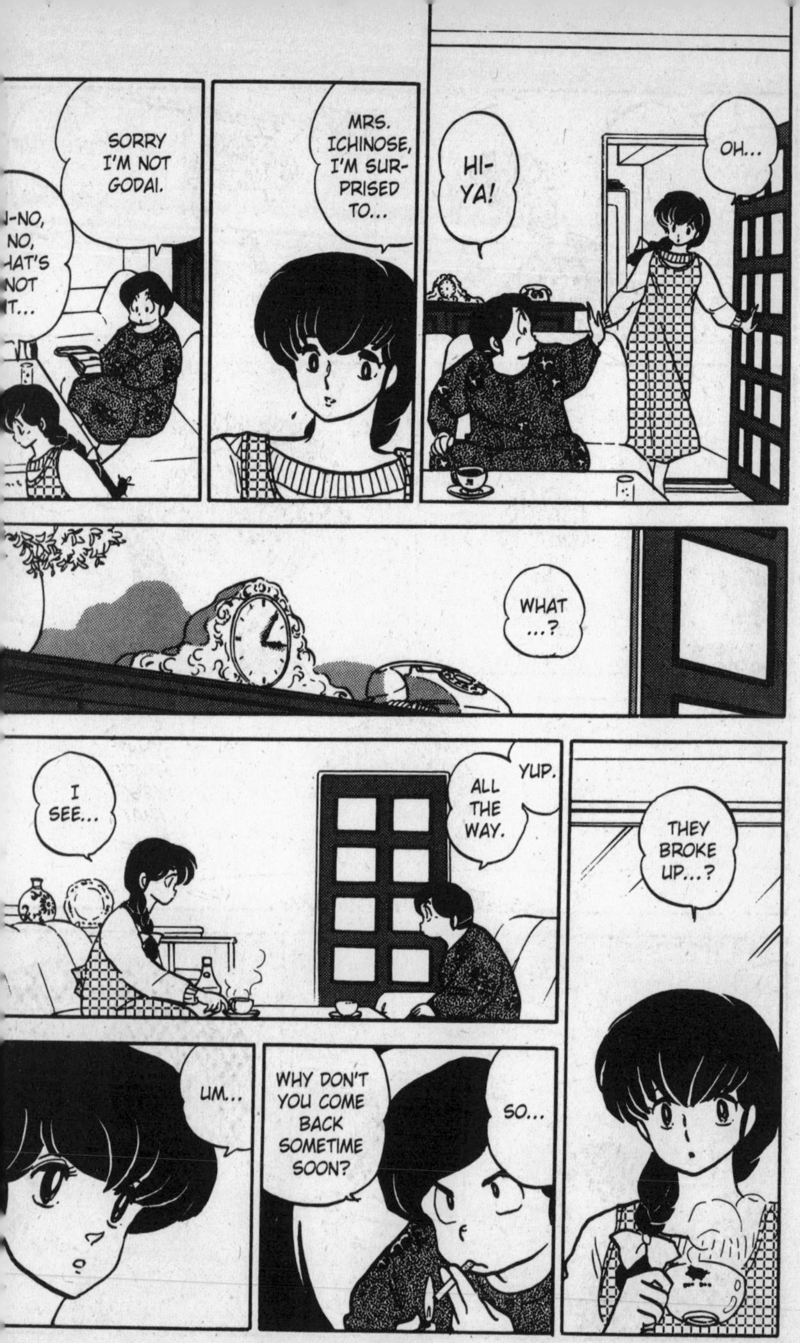
OH...
HI-YA!
MRS. ICHINOSE, I'M SURPRISED TO...
SORRY I'M NOT GODAI.
-NO, NO, HAT'S NOT T...
WHAT ...?
THEY BROKE UP...?
YUP.
ALL THE WAY.
I SEE...
SO...
WHY DON'T YOU COME BACK SOMETIME SOON?
UM...

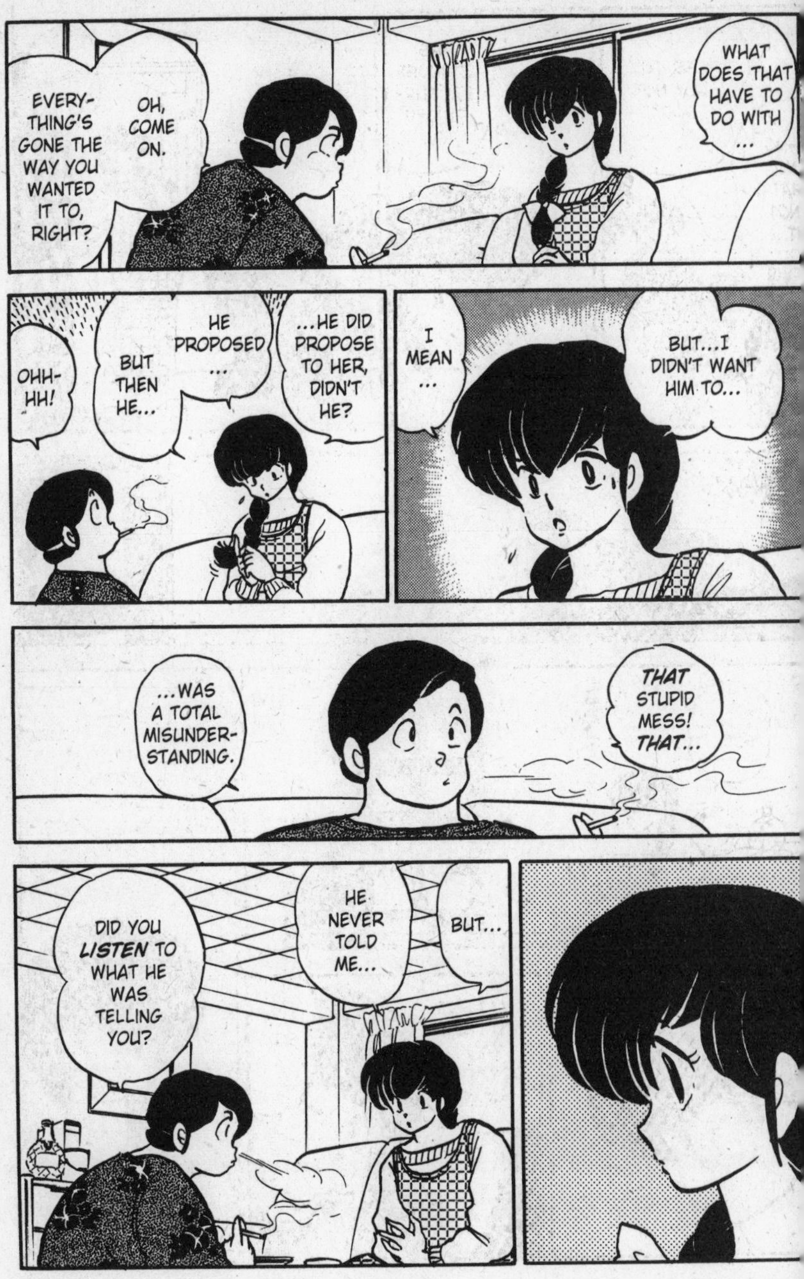
WHAT DOES THAT HAVE TO DO WITH ...
OH, COME ON.
EVERY-THING'S GONE THE WAY YOU WANTED IT TO, RIGHT?
BUT...I DIDN'T WANT HIM TO...
I MEAN ...
...HE DID PROPOSE TO HER, DIDN'T HE?
HE PROPOSED ...
BUT THEN HE...
OHH-HH!
THAT STUPID MESS! *THAT*...
...WAS A TOTAL MISUNDER-STANDING.
BUT...
HE NEVER TOLD ME...
DID YOU *LISTEN* TO WHAT HE WAS TELLING YOU?

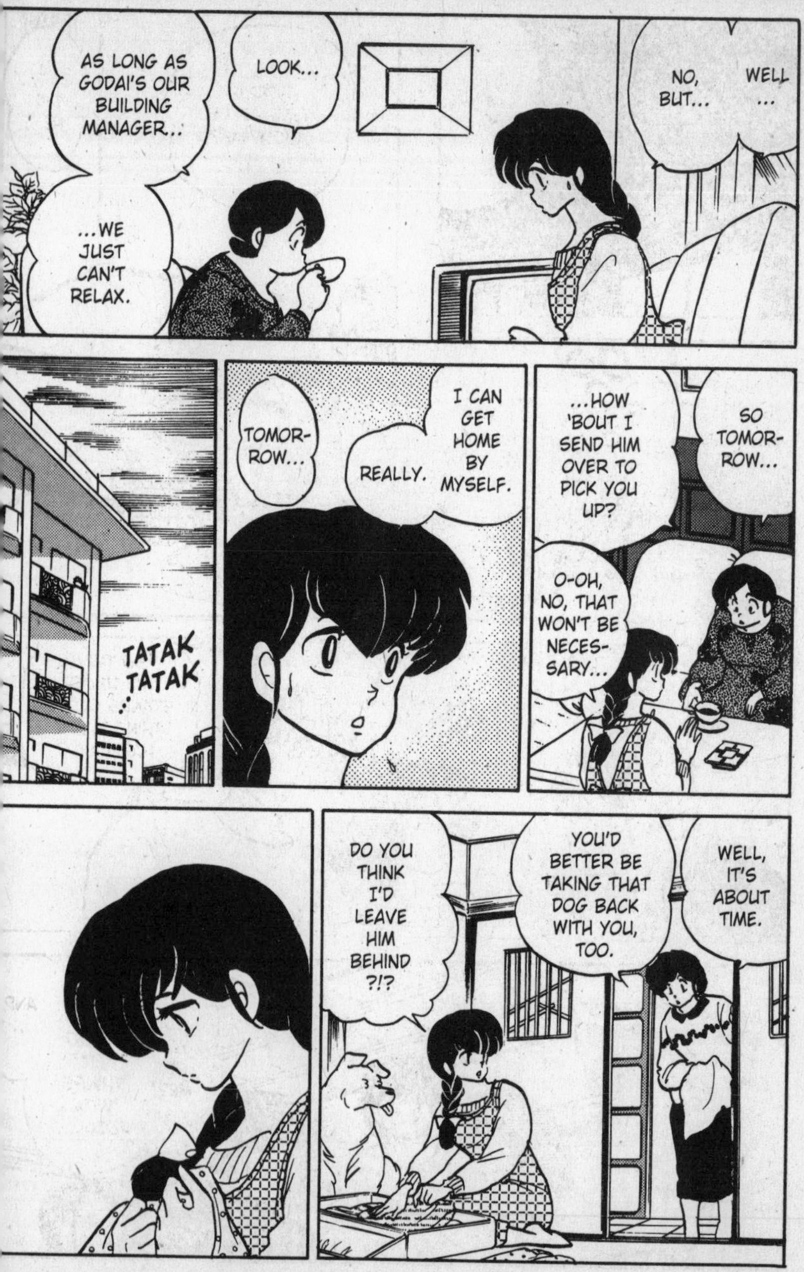
AS LONG AS GODAI'S OUR BUILDING MANAGER..
...WE JUST CAN'T RELAX.
LOOK...
NO, BUT... WELL ...
TATAK TATAK...
SO TOMORROW...
...HOW 'BOUT I SEND HIM OVER TO PICK YOU UP?
O-OH, NO, THAT WON'T BE NECESSARY...
I CAN GET HOME BY MYSELF.
REALLY.
TOMORROW...
WELL, IT'S ABOUT TIME.
YOU'D BETTER BE TAKING THAT DOG BACK WITH YOU, TOO.
DO YOU THINK I'D LEAVE HIM BEHIND ?!?

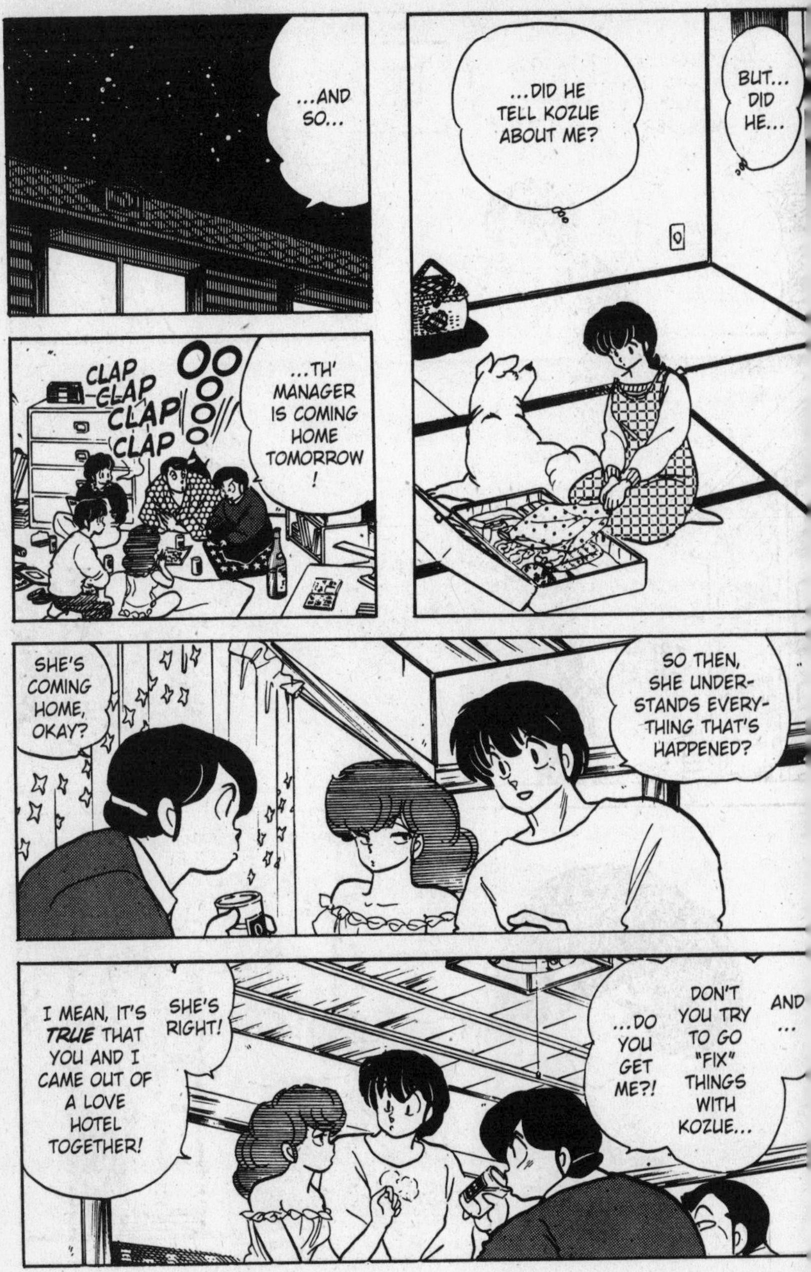

BUT... DID HE...
...DID HE TELL KOZUE ABOUT ME?
...AND SO...
...TH' MANAGER IS COMING HOME TOMORROW!
OOOOOO
CLAP CLAP CLAP CLAP
SO THEN, SHE UNDERSTANDS EVERYTHING THAT'S HAPPENED?
SHE'S COMING HOME, OKAY?
AND...
DON'T YOU TRY TO GO "FIX" THINGS WITH KOZUE...
...DO YOU GET ME?!
SHE'S RIGHT!
I MEAN, IT'S TRUE THAT YOU AND I CAME OUT OF A LOVE HOTEL TOGETHER!

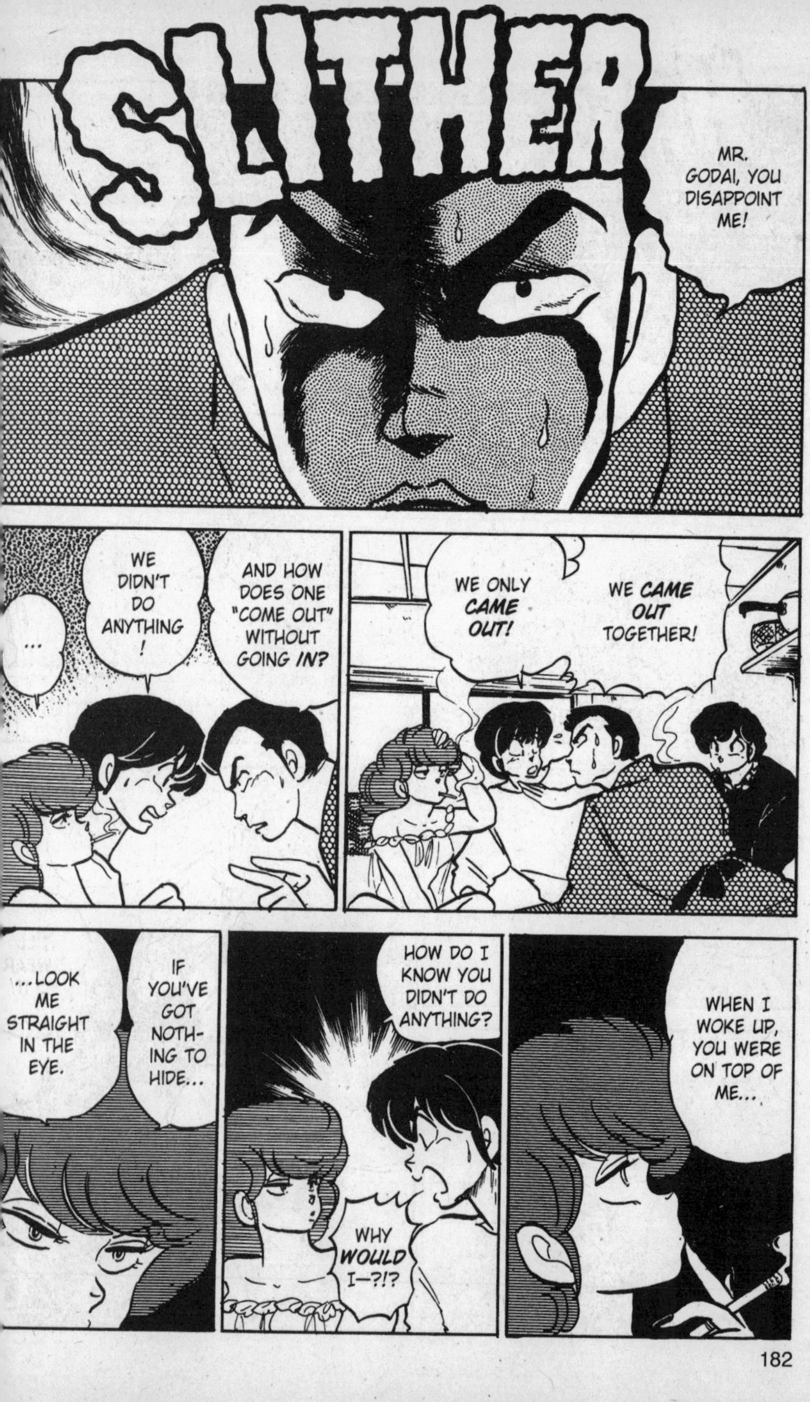
SLITHER
MR. GODAI, YOU DISAPPOINT ME!
...
WE DIDN'T DO ANYTHING!
AND HOW DOES ONE "COME OUT" WITHOUT GOING *IN?*
WE ONLY *CAME OUT!*
WE *CAME OUT* TOGETHER!
IF YOU'VE GOT NOTH-ING TO HIDE...
...LOOK ME STRAIGHT IN THE EYE.
HOW DO I KNOW YOU DIDN'T DO ANYTHING?
WHY *WOULD* I—?!?
WHEN I WOKE UP, YOU WERE ON TOP OF ME...

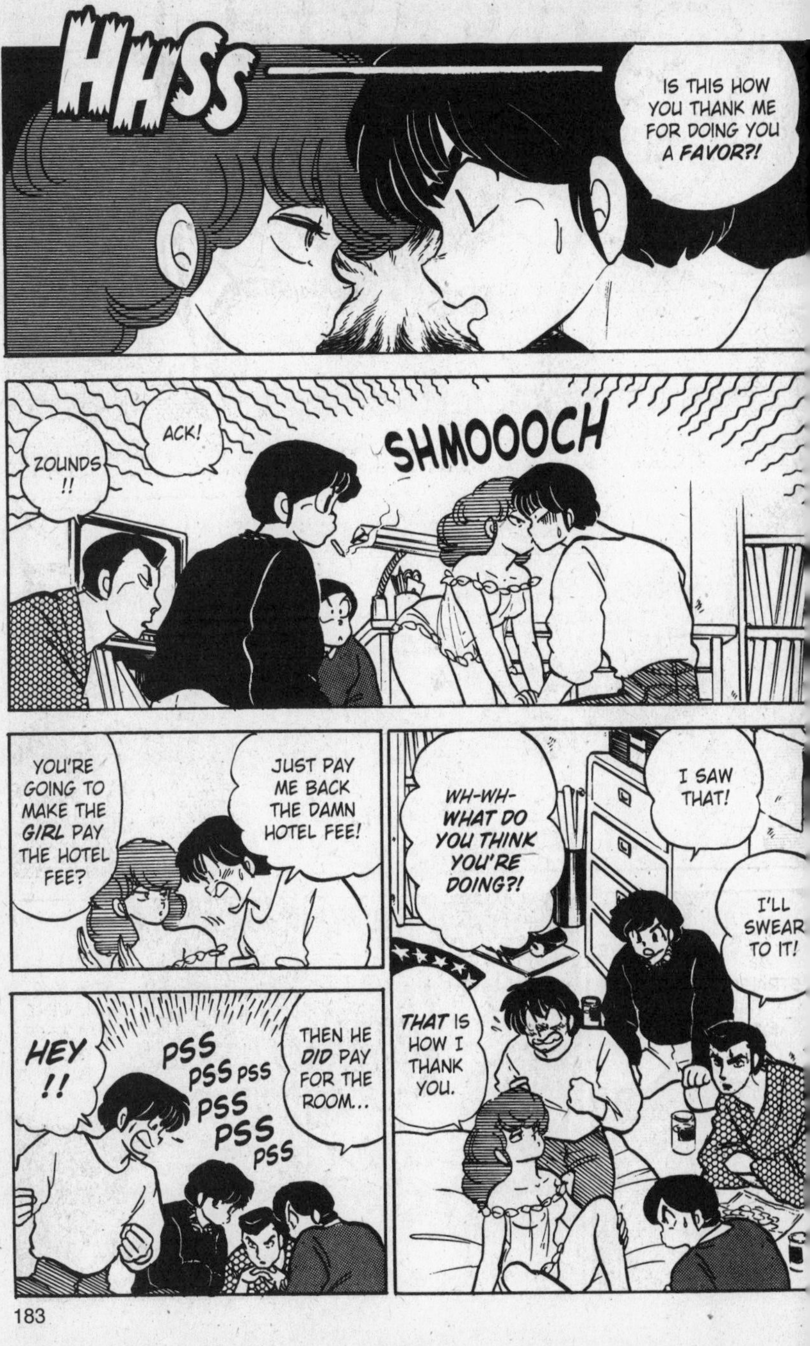
HHSS
IS THIS HOW YOU THANK ME FOR DOING YOU A *FAVOR?!*
ZOUNDS !!
ACK!
SHMOOOCH
YOU'RE GOING TO MAKE THE *GIRL* PAY THE HOTEL FEE?
JUST PAY ME BACK THE DAMN HOTEL FEE!
THEN HE *DID* PAY FOR THE ROOM...
PSS PSS PSS PSS PSS PSS
HEY !!
WH-WH-WHAT DO YOU THINK YOU'RE DOING?!
I SAW THAT!
I'LL SWEAR TO IT!
THAT IS HOW I THANK YOU.

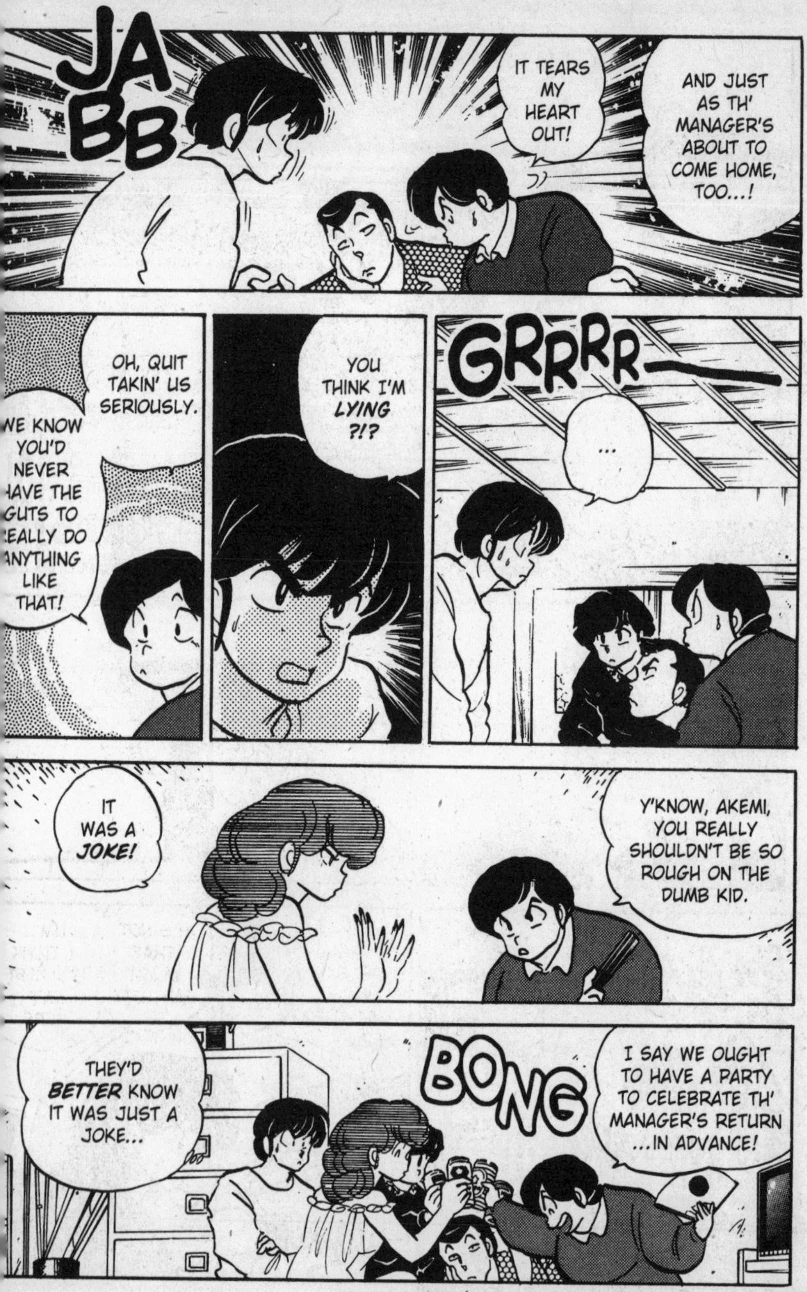
JABB
IT TEARS MY HEART OUT!
AND JUST AS TH' MANAGER'S ABOUT TO COME HOME, TOO...!
OH, QUIT TAKIN' US SERIOUSLY.
E KNOW YOU'D NEVER AVE THE GUTS TO EALLY DO NYTHING LIKE THAT!
YOU THINK I'M *LYING* ?!?
GRRRR—
...
IT WAS A *JOKE!*
Y'KNOW, AKEMI, YOU REALLY SHOULDN'T BE SO ROUGH ON THE DUMB KID.
THEY'D *BETTER* KNOW IT WAS JUST A JOKE...
BONG
I SAY WE OUGHT TO HAVE A PARTY TO CELEBRATE TH' MANAGER'S RETURN ...IN ADVANCE!

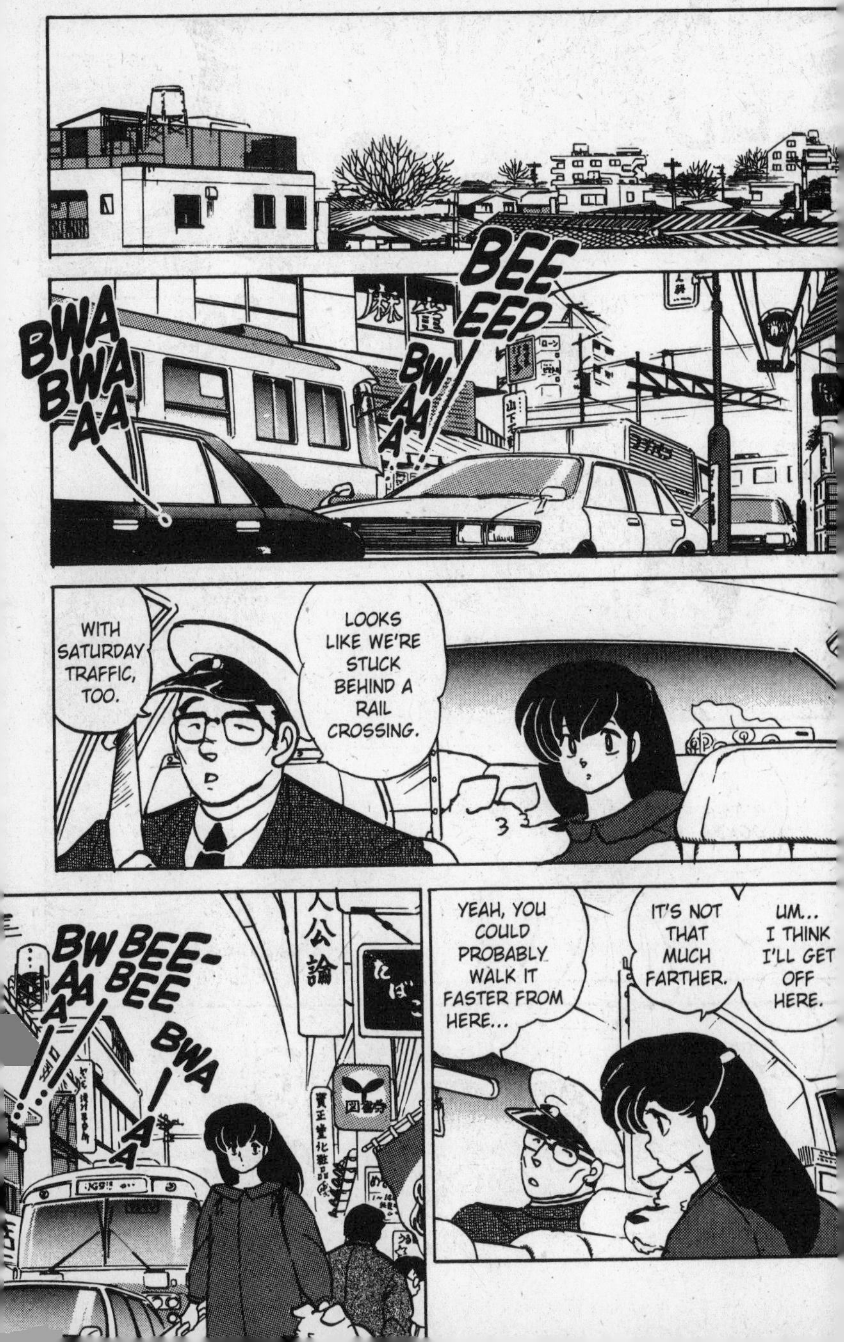
BEEEEP
BWAAA
BWA BWA BWAAA
LOOKS LIKE WE'RE STUCK BEHIND A RAIL CROSSING.
WITH SATURDAY TRAFFIC, TOO.
UM... I THINK I'LL GET OFF HERE.
IT'S NOT THAT MUCH FARTHER.
YEAH, YOU COULD PROBABLY WALK IT FASTER FROM HERE...
BEE-BEE
BWAAA
BWA AA

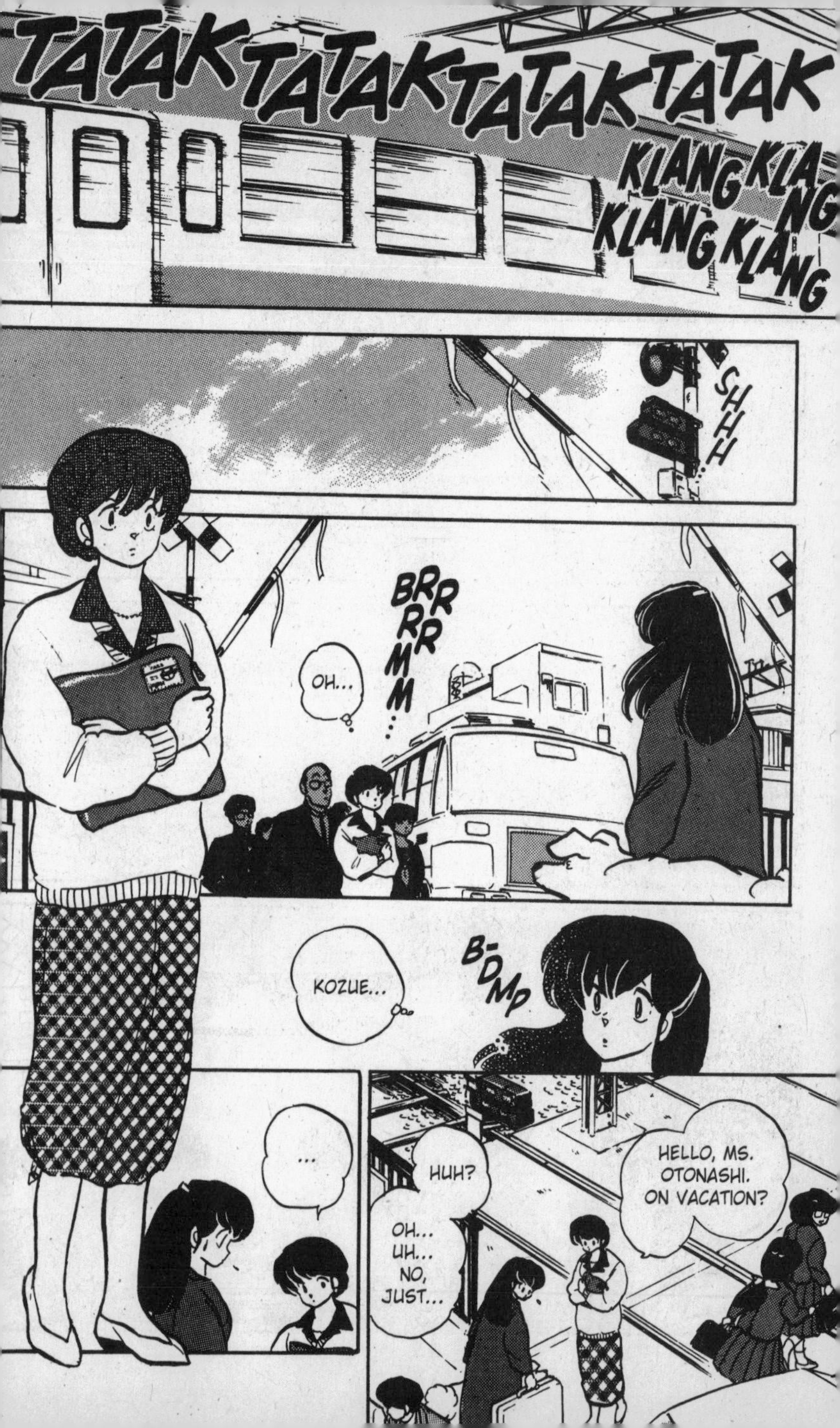
TATAK TATAK TATAK TATAK
KLANG KLANG KLANG KLANG KLANG KLANG
SHHH...
BRRRRRMM...
OH...
KOZUE...
B-DMP
HELLO, MS. OTONASHI. ON VACATION?
HUH?
OH... UH... NO, JUST...
...

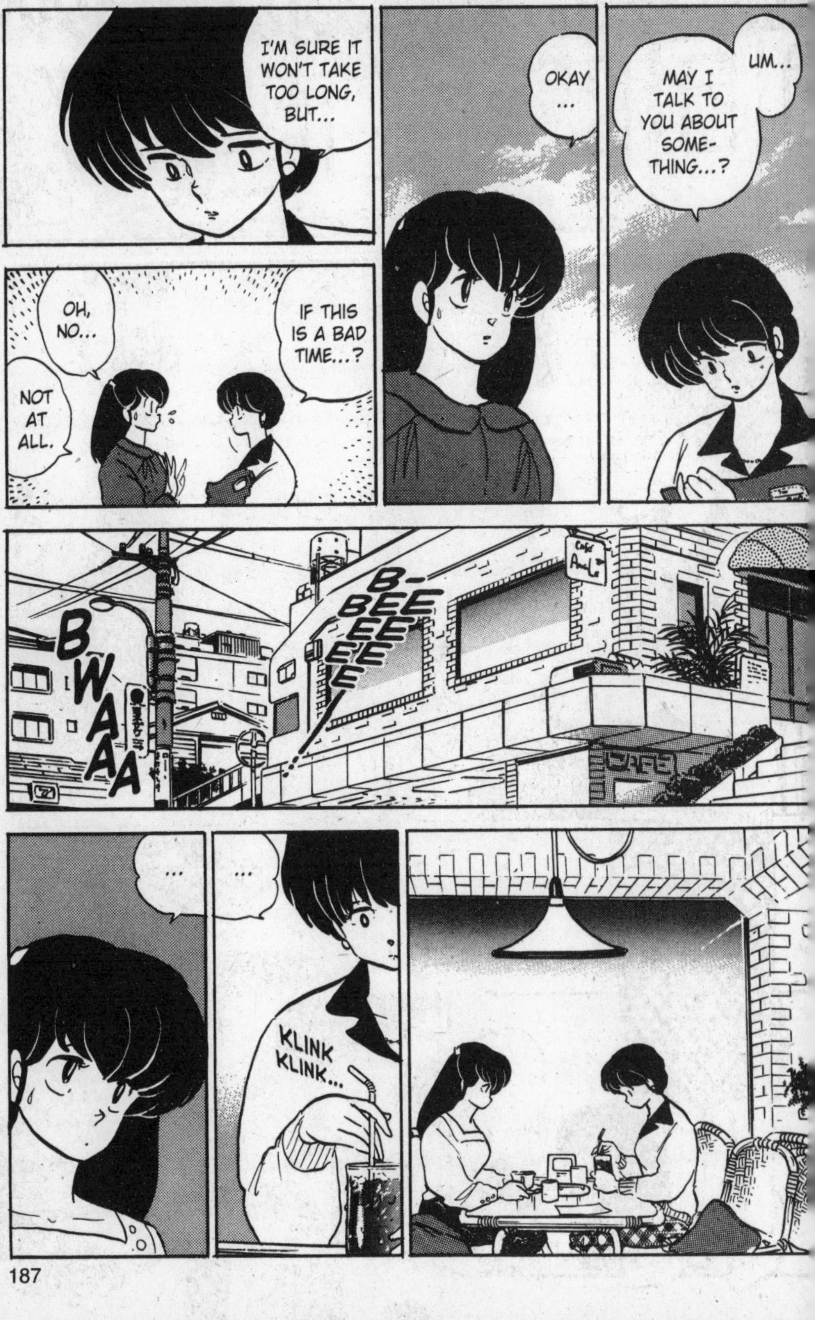
UM...
MAY I TALK TO YOU ABOUT SOME-THING...?
OKAY ...
I'M SURE IT WON'T TAKE TOO LONG, BUT...
IF THIS IS A BAD TIME...?
OH, NO...
NOT AT ALL.
B-BEEEEEEE...!
BWAAA
KLINK KLINK...
...
...

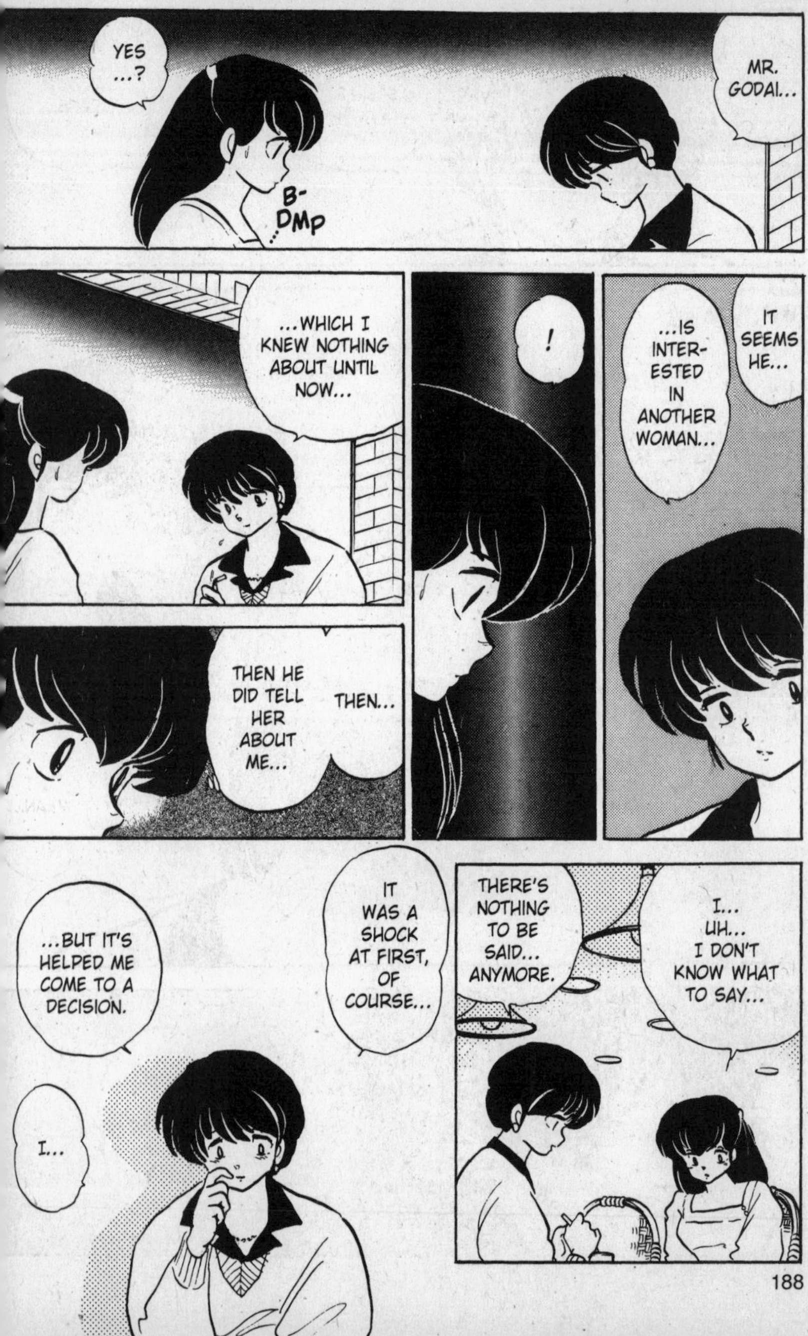
MR. GODAI...
YES ...?
B-DMP
IT SEEMS HE...
...IS INTERESTED IN ANOTHER WOMAN...
!
...WHICH I KNEW NOTHING ABOUT UNTIL NOW...
THEN...
THEN HE DID TELL HER ABOUT ME...
I... UH... I DON'T KNOW WHAT TO SAY...
THERE'S NOTHING TO BE SAID... ANYMORE.
IT WAS A SHOCK AT FIRST, OF COURSE...
...BUT IT'S HELPED ME COME TO A DECISION.
I...

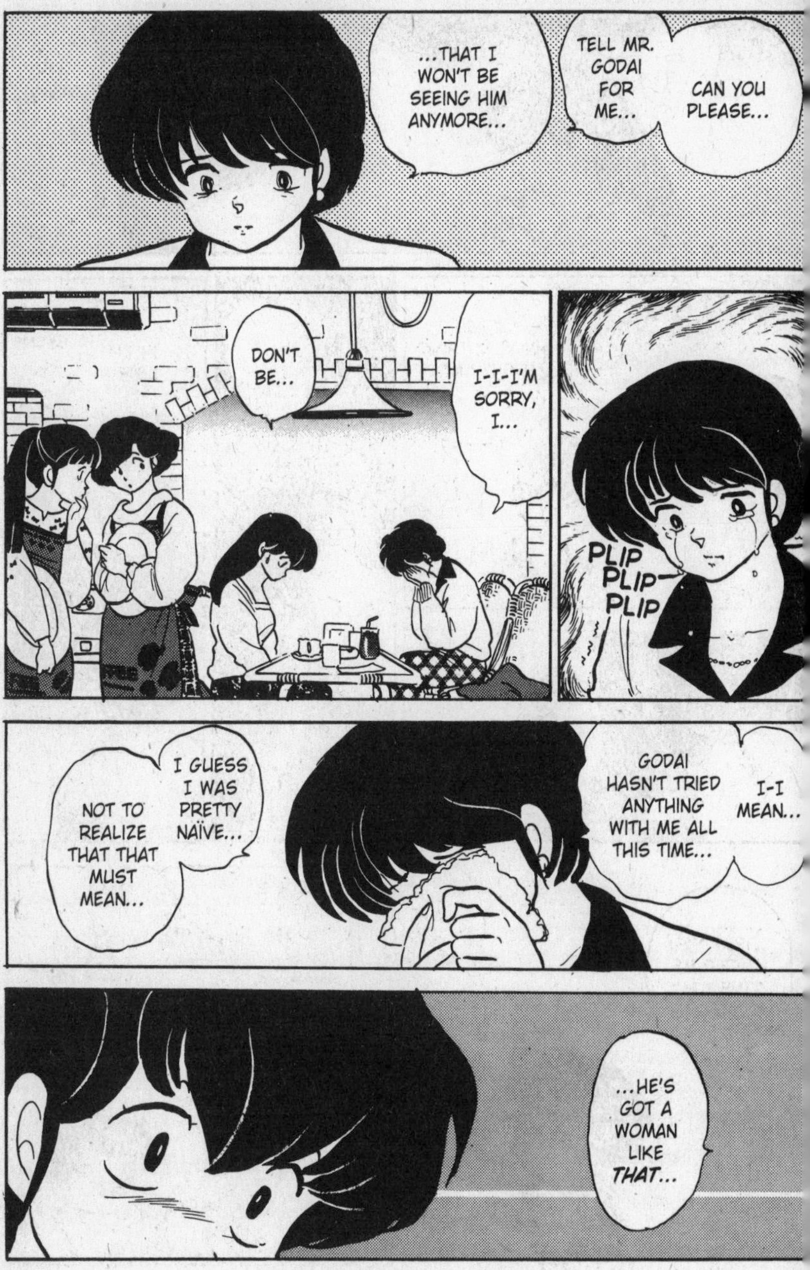
CAN YOU PLEASE...
TELL MR. GODAI FOR ME...
...THAT I WON'T BE SEEING HIM ANYMORE...
PLIP PLIP PLIP
I-I-I'M SORRY, I...
DON'T BE...
I-I MEAN...
GODAI HASN'T TRIED ANYTHING WITH ME ALL THIS TIME...
I GUESS I WAS PRETTY NAÏVE...
NOT TO REALIZE THAT THAT MUST MEAN...
...HE'S GOT A WOMAN LIKE *THAT*...

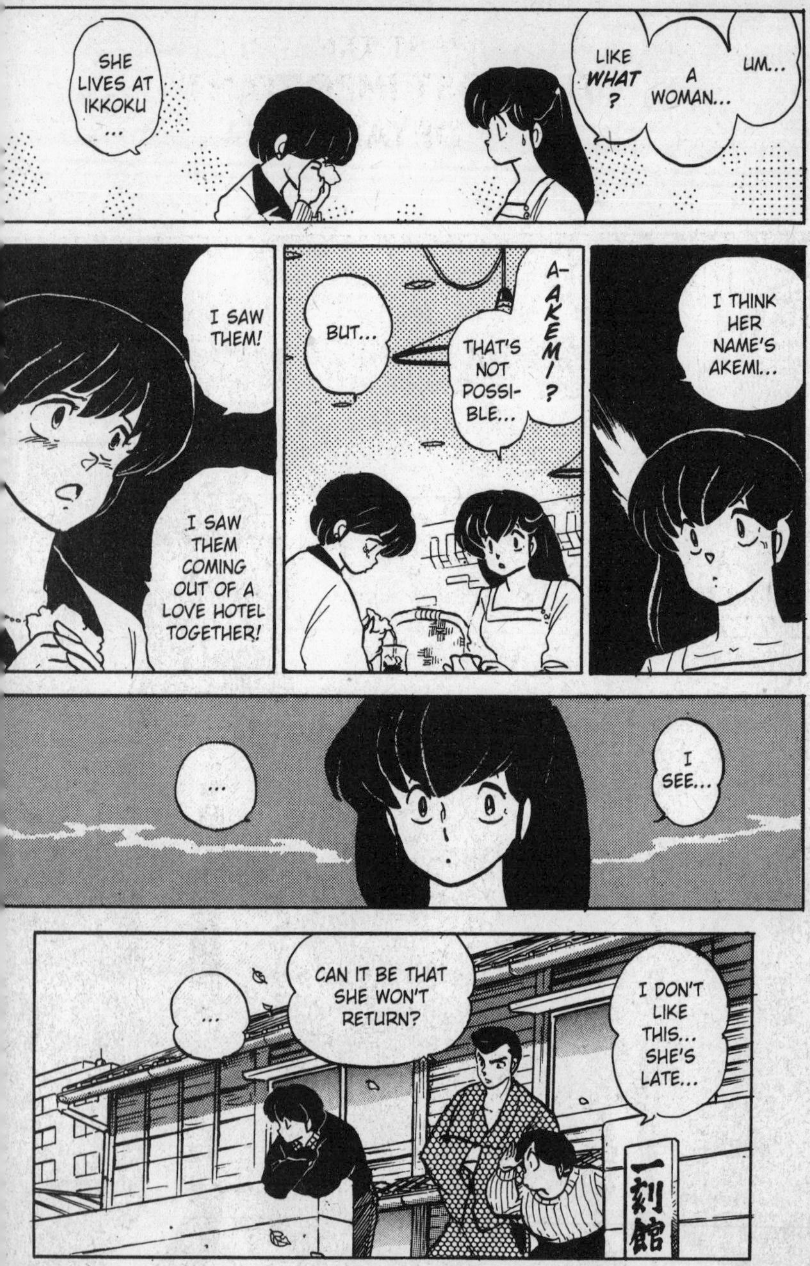
UM... A WOMAN...
LIKE WHAT?
SHE LIVES AT IKKOKU...
I THINK HER NAME'S AKEMI...
A-AKEMI?
THAT'S NOT POSSIBLE...
BUT...
I SAW THEM!
I SAW THEM COMING OUT OF A LOVE HOTEL TOGETHER!
I SEE...
...
I DON'T LIKE THIS... SHE'S LATE...
CAN IT BE THAT SHE WON'T RETURN?
...
一刻館

PART TEN

THE MOST IMPORTANT DETAIL

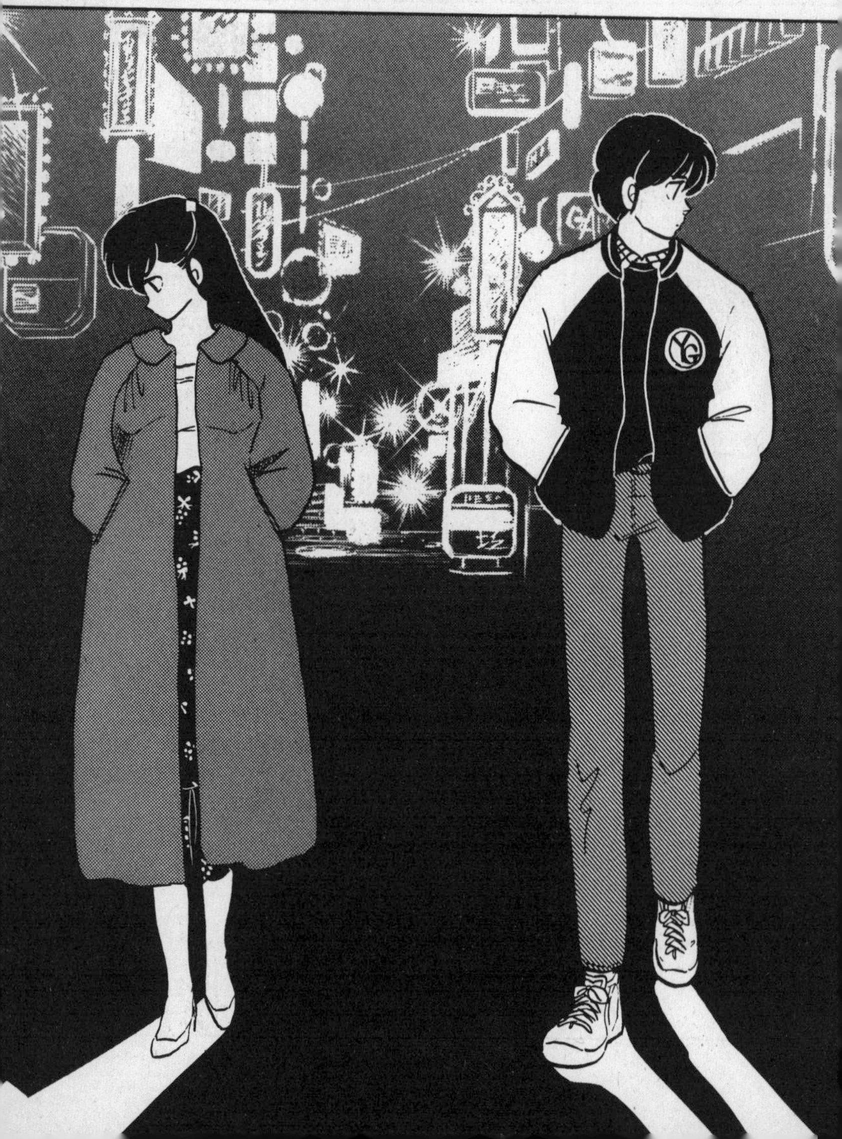

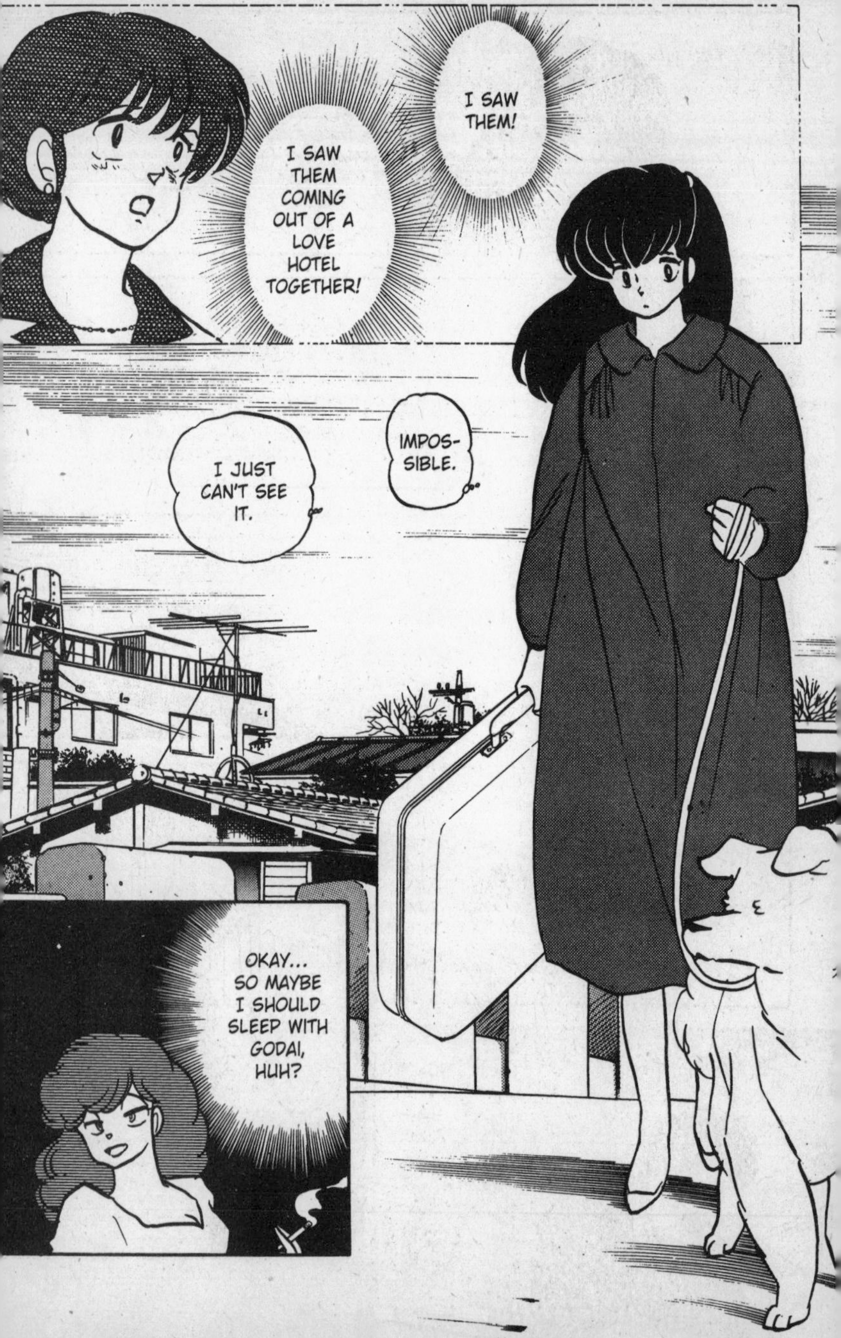
I SAW THEM!
I SAW THEM COMING OUT OF A LOVE HOTEL TOGETHER!
IMPOS-SIBLE.
I JUST CAN'T SEE IT.
OKAY... SO MAYBE I SHOULD SLEEP WITH GODAI, HUH?

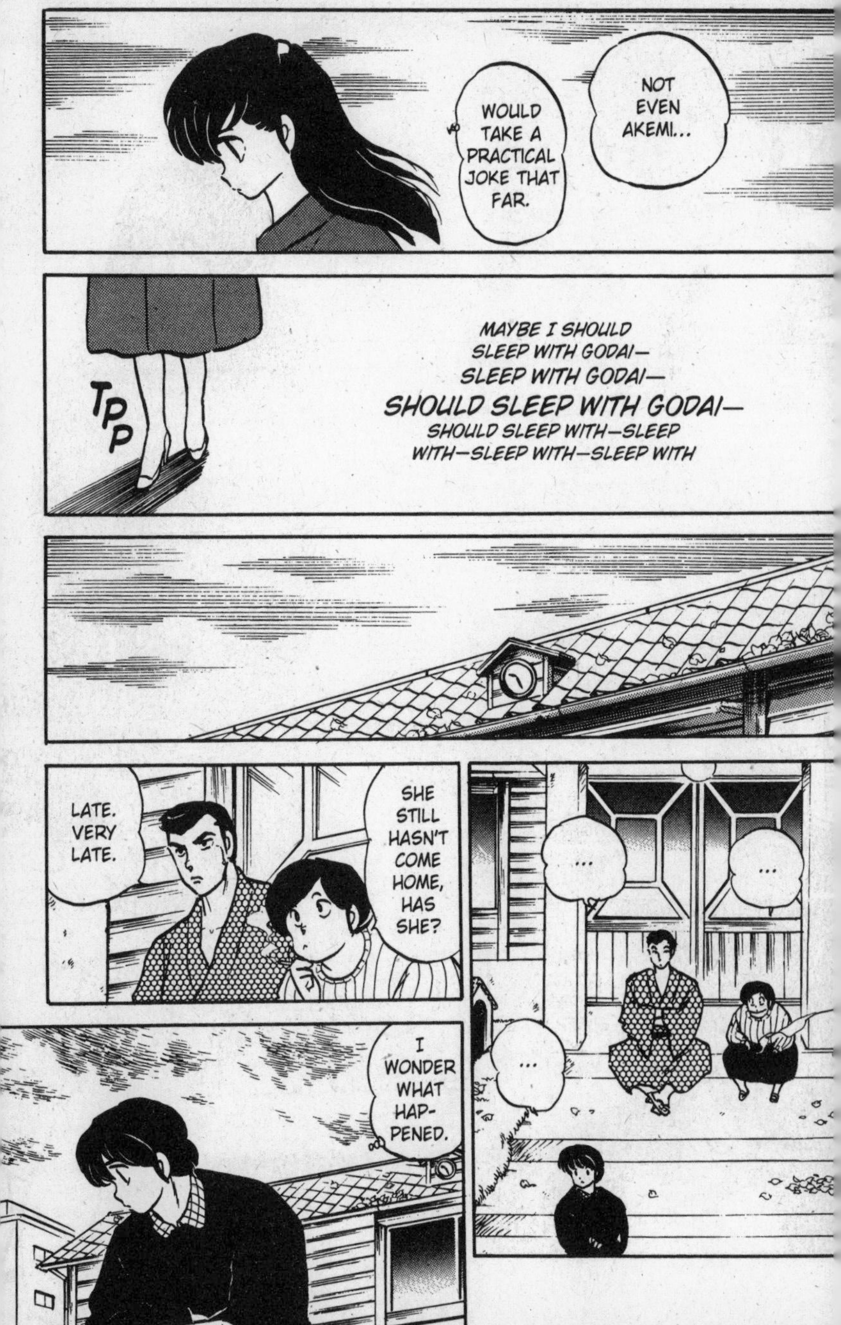
NOT EVEN AKEMI...
WOULD TAKE A PRACTICAL JOKE THAT FAR.
TPP
MAYBE I SHOULD SLEEP WITH GODAI—
SLEEP WITH GODAI—
SHOULD SLEEP WITH GODAI—
SHOULD SLEEP WITH—SLEEP WITH—SLEEP WITH—SLEEP WITH
LATE. VERY LATE.
SHE STILL HASN'T COME HOME, HAS SHE?
...
...
...
I WONDER WHAT HAP-PENED.

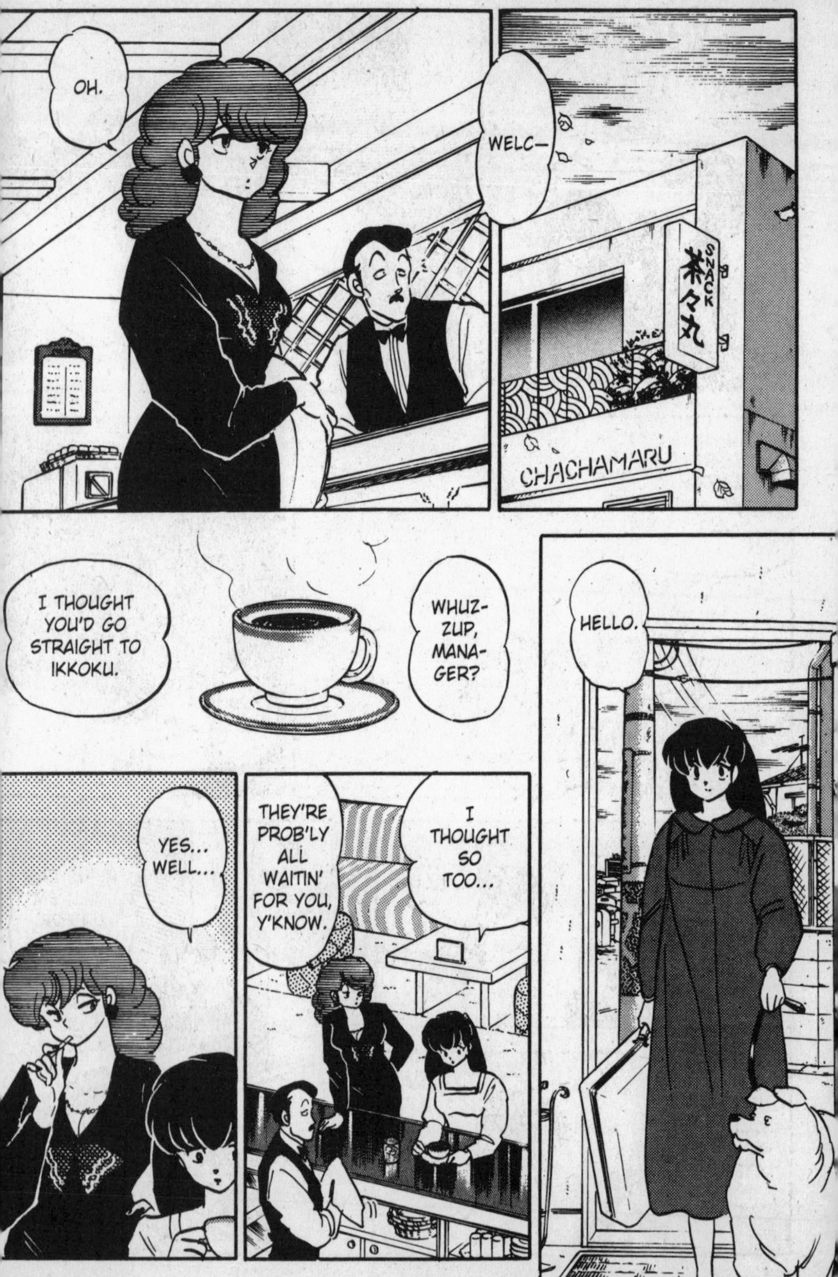
WELC—
SNACK
茶々丸
CHACHAMARU
OH.
HELLO.
WHUZ-ZUP, MANA-GER?
I THOUGHT YOU'D GO STRAIGHT TO IKKOKU.
I THOUGHT SO TOO...
THEY'RE PROB'LY ALL WAITIN' FOR YOU, Y'KNOW.
YES... WELL...

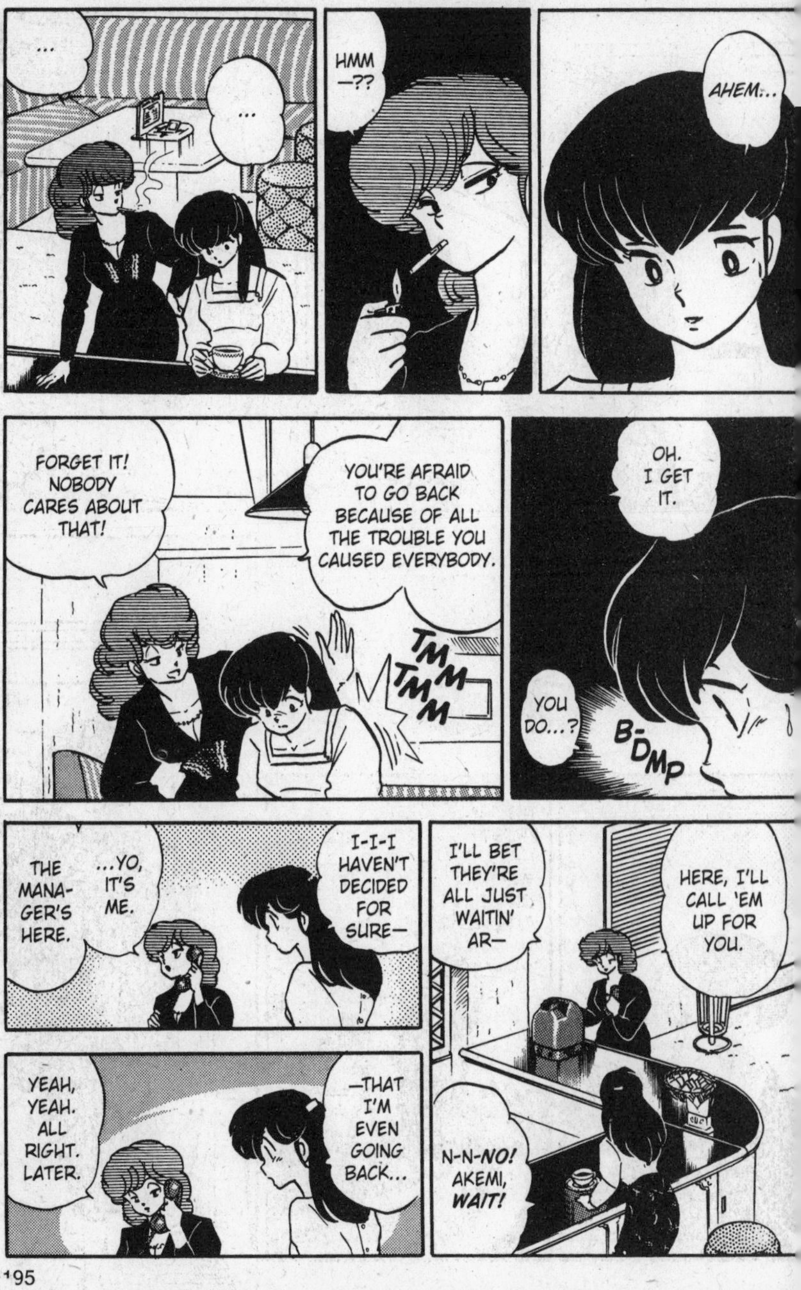
...
...
HMM —??
AHEM...
OH. I GET IT.
YOU DO...?
B-DMP
YOU'RE AFRAID TO GO BACK BECAUSE OF ALL THE TROUBLE YOU CAUSED EVERYBODY.
TMM TMM
FORGET IT! NOBODY CARES ABOUT THAT!
I'LL BET THEY'RE ALL JUST WAITIN' AR—
HERE, I'LL CALL 'EM UP FOR YOU.
N-N-NO! AKEMI, WAIT!
...YO, IT'S ME.
THE MANA-GER'S HERE.
I-I-I HAVEN'T DECIDED FOR SURE—
YEAH, YEAH. ALL RIGHT. LATER.
—THAT I'M EVEN GOING BACK...

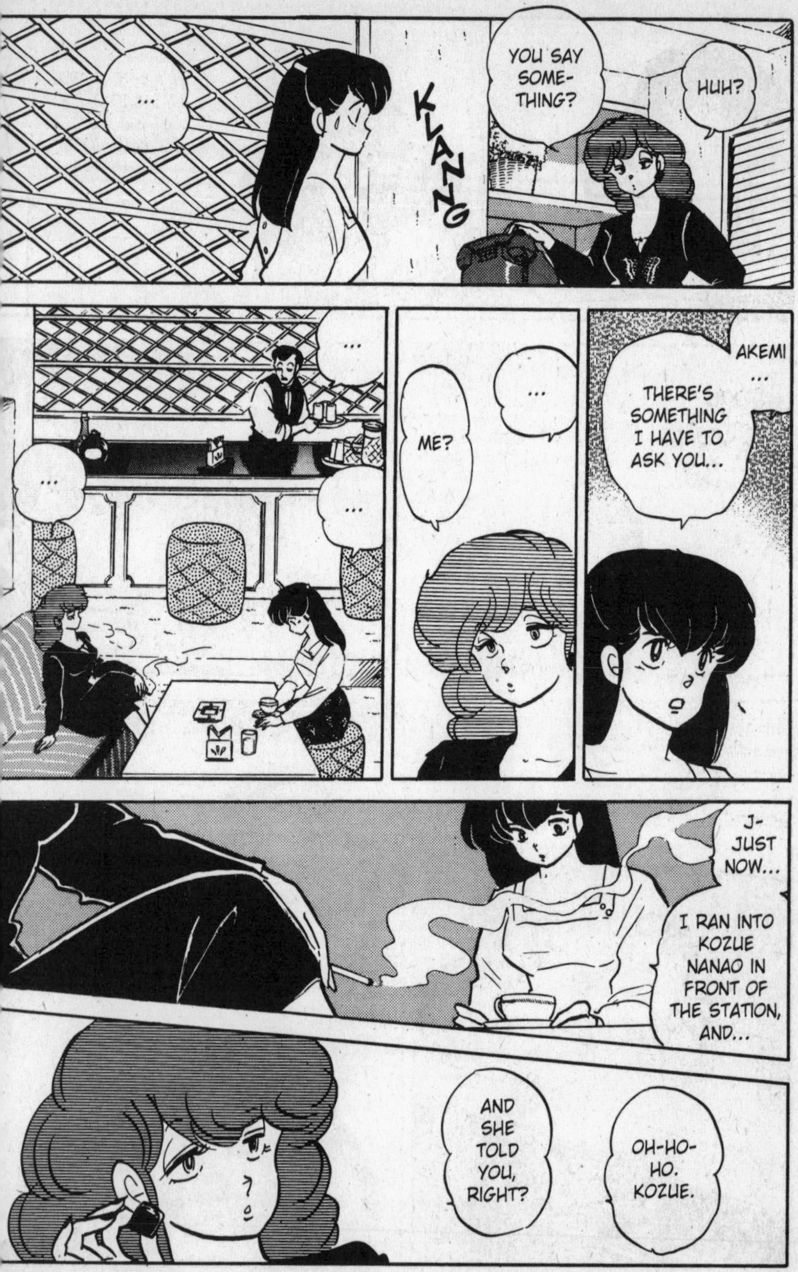
HUH?
YOU SAY SOME-THING?
KLANG
...
AKEMI ...
THERE'S SOMETHING I HAVE TO ASK YOU...
...
ME?
...
...
...
J-JUST NOW...
I RAN INTO KOZUE NANAO IN FRONT OF THE STATION, AND...
OH-HO-HO. KOZUE.
AND SHE TOLD YOU, RIGHT?

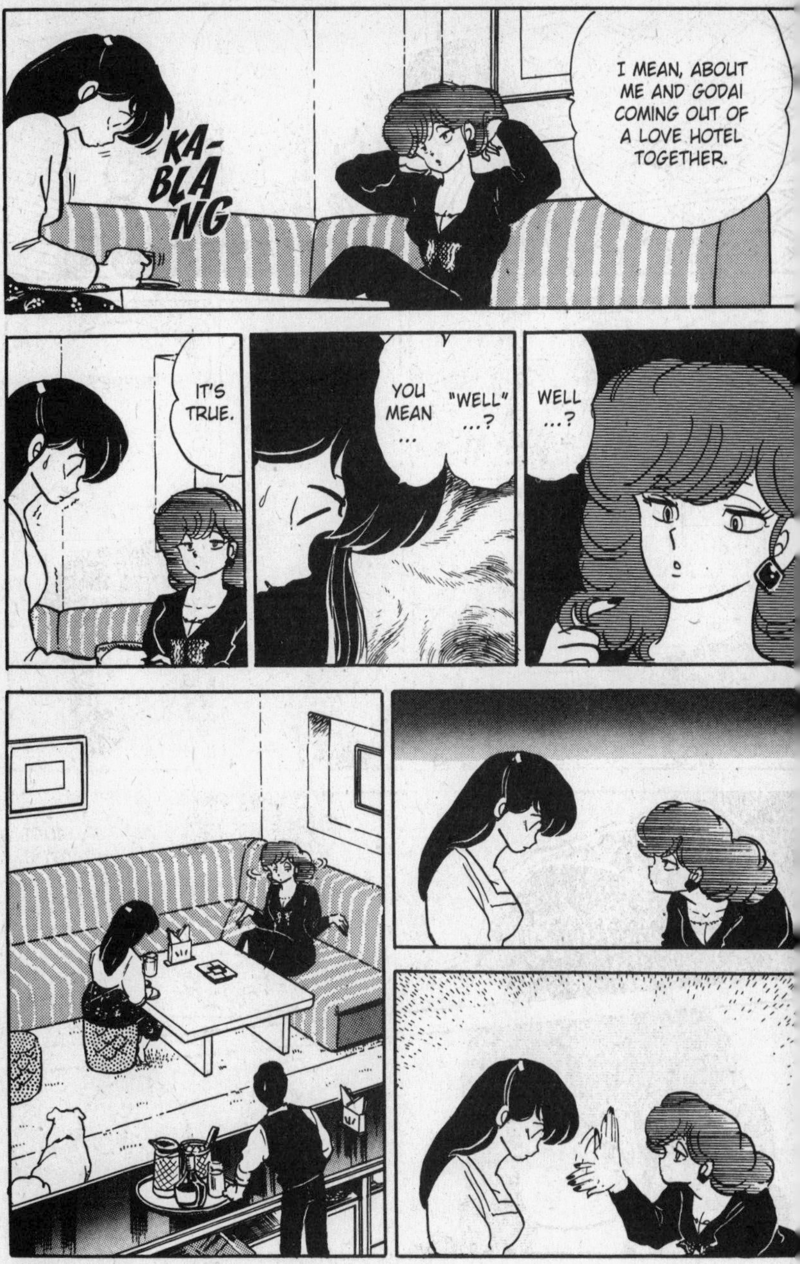
KA-BLANG
I MEAN, ABOUT ME AND GODAI COMING OUT OF A LOVE HOTEL TOGETHER.
IT'S TRUE.
YOU MEAN ...
"WELL" ...?
WELL ...?

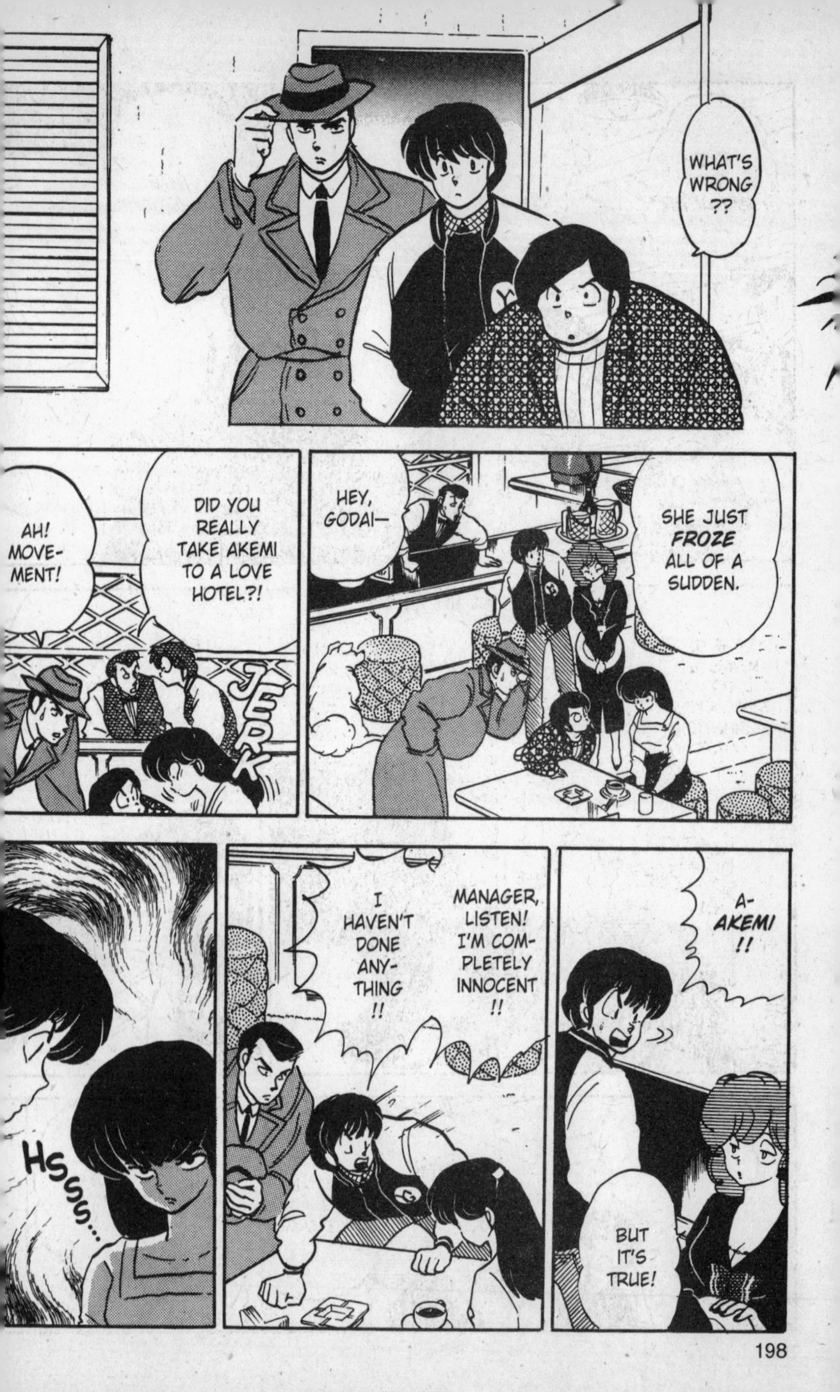
WHAT'S WRONG ??
AH! MOVEMENT!
DID YOU REALLY TAKE AKEMI TO A LOVE HOTEL?!
JERK
HEY, GODAI—
SHE JUST FROZE ALL OF A SUDDEN.
HSSS...
I HAVEN'T DONE ANYTHING !!
MANAGER, LISTEN! I'M COMPLETELY INNOCENT !!
A-AKEMI !!
BUT IT'S TRUE!

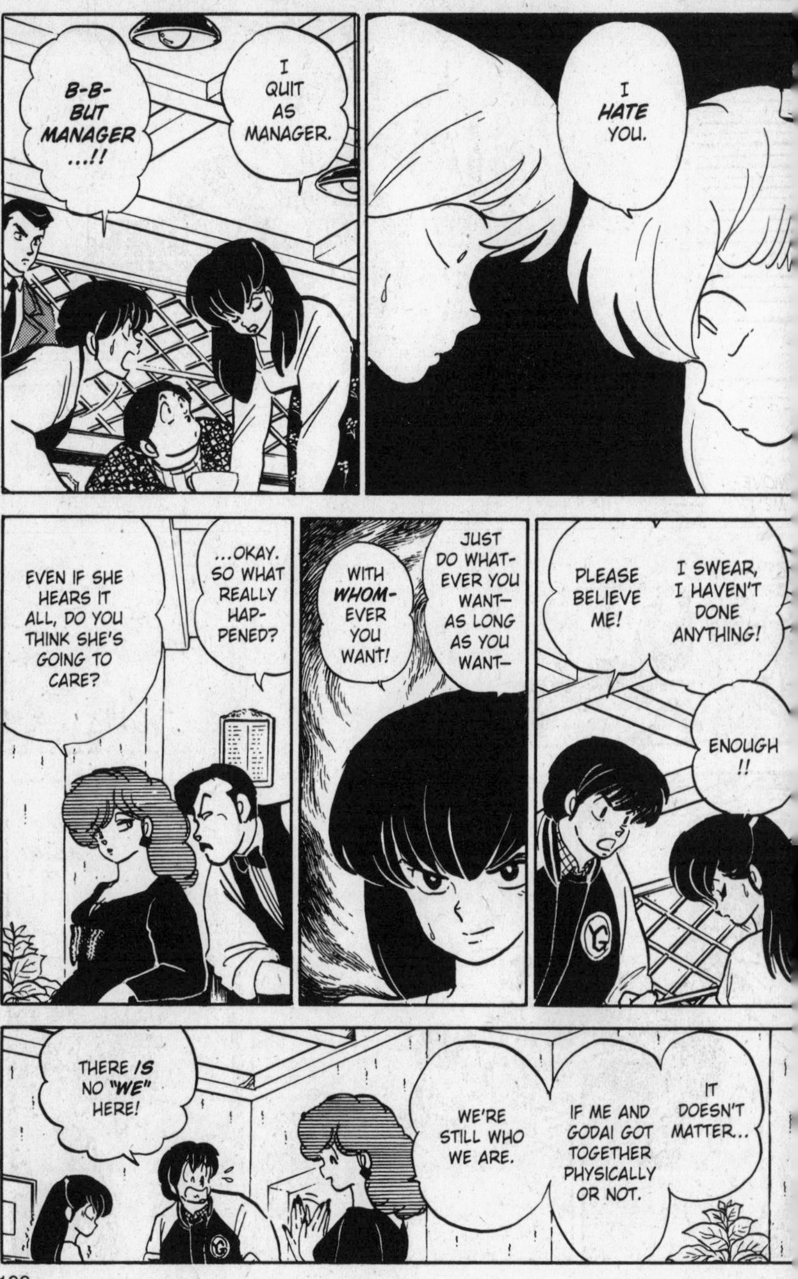
I *HATE* YOU.
I QUIT AS MANAGER.
B-B-BUT MANAGER ...!!
I SWEAR, I HAVEN'T DONE ANYTHING!
PLEASE BELIEVE ME!
ENOUGH !!
JUST DO WHAT-EVER YOU WANT— AS LONG AS YOU WANT—
WITH *WHOM*-EVER YOU WANT!
...OKAY. SO WHAT REALLY HAP-PENED?
EVEN IF SHE HEARS IT ALL, DO YOU THINK SHE'S GOING TO CARE?
IT DOESN'T MATTER...
IF ME AND GODAI GOT TOGETHER PHYSICALLY OR NOT.
WE'RE STILL WHO WE ARE.
THERE *IS* NO *"WE"* HERE!

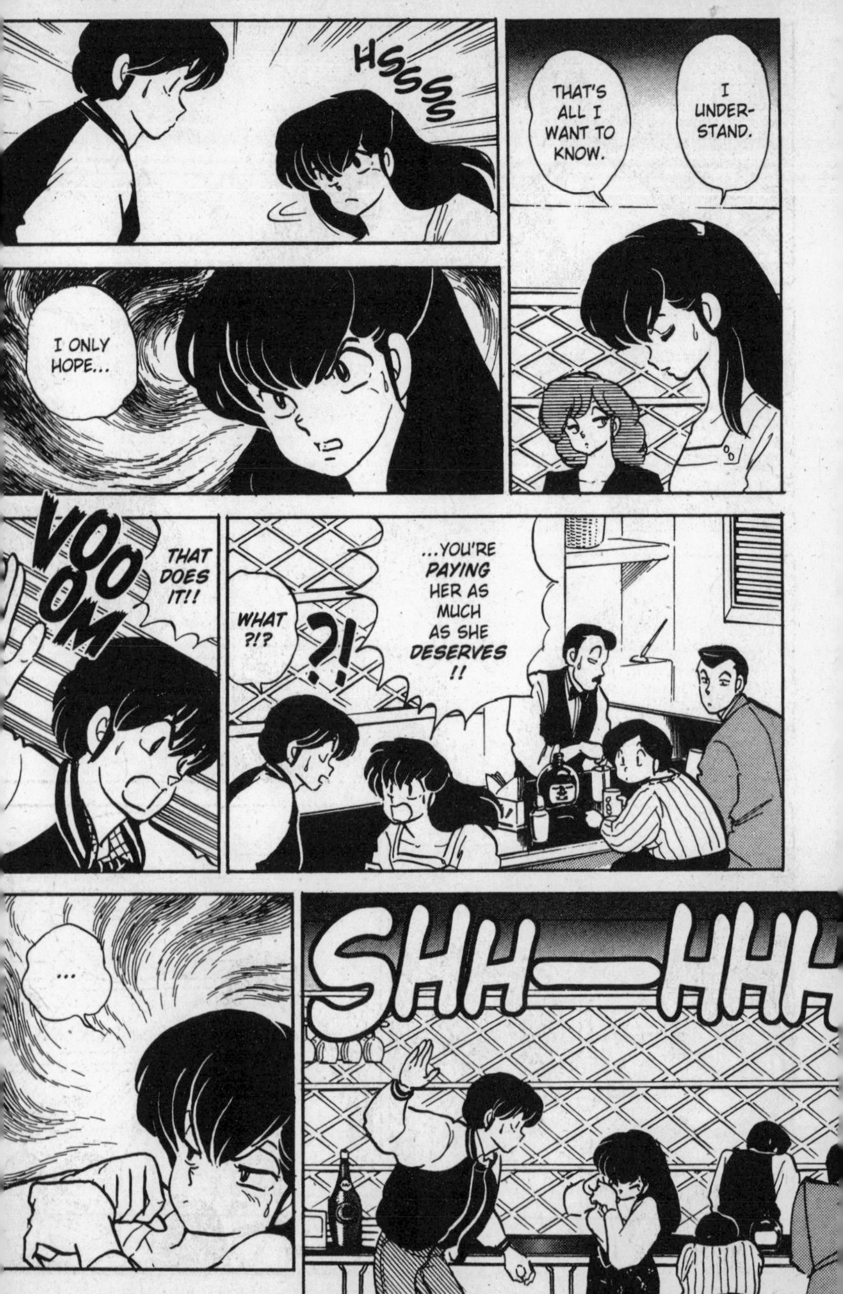
HSSSS
THAT'S ALL I WANT TO KNOW.
I UNDERSTAND.
I ONLY HOPE...
VOOOOM
THAT DOES IT!!
WHAT?!?
?!
...YOU'RE PAYING HER AS MUCH AS SHE DESERVES!!
...
SHH—HHH

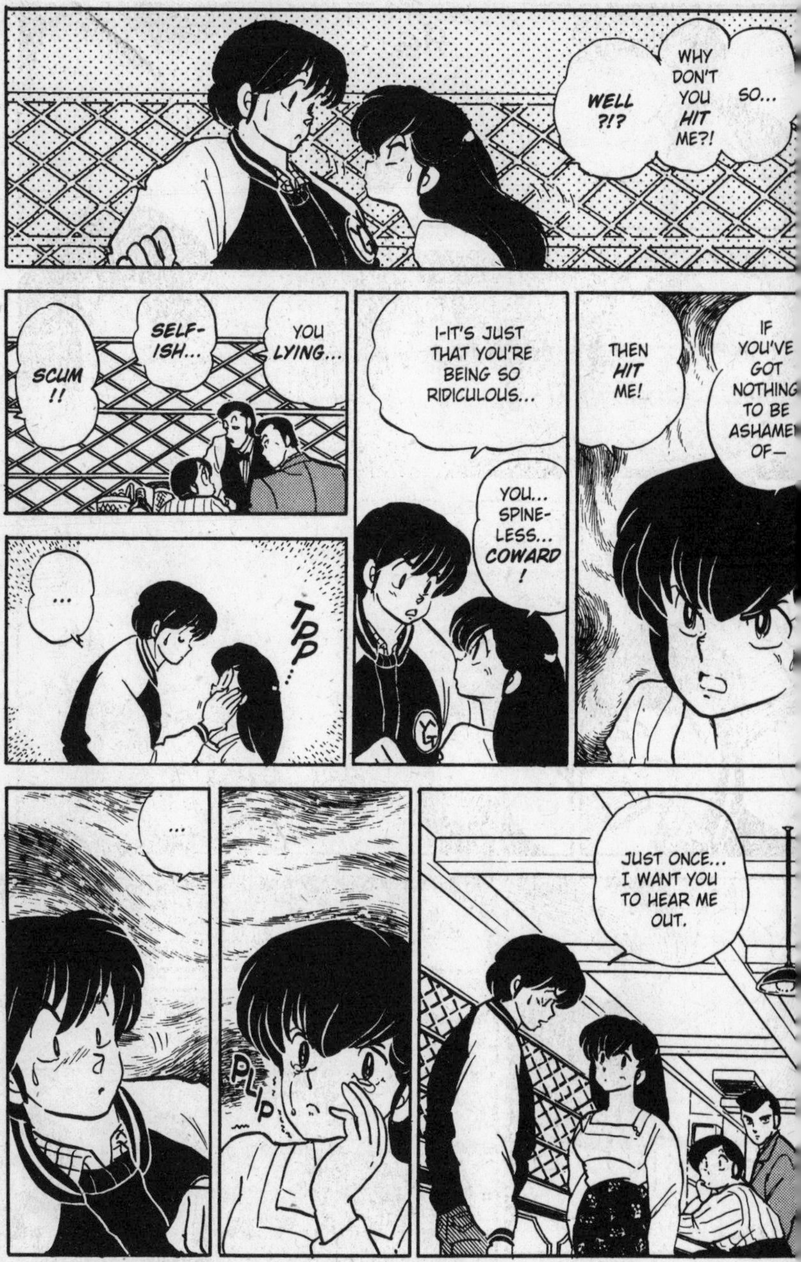
SO...
WHY DON'T YOU HIT ME?!
WELL ?!?
IF YOU'VE GOT NOTHING TO BE ASHAME OF—
THEN HIT ME!
I-IT'S JUST THAT YOU'RE BEING SO RIDICULOUS...
YOU... SPINELESS... COWARD!
YOU LYING...
SELFISH...
SCUM!!
...
TPP...
JUST ONCE... I WANT YOU TO HEAR ME OUT.
PLIP
...

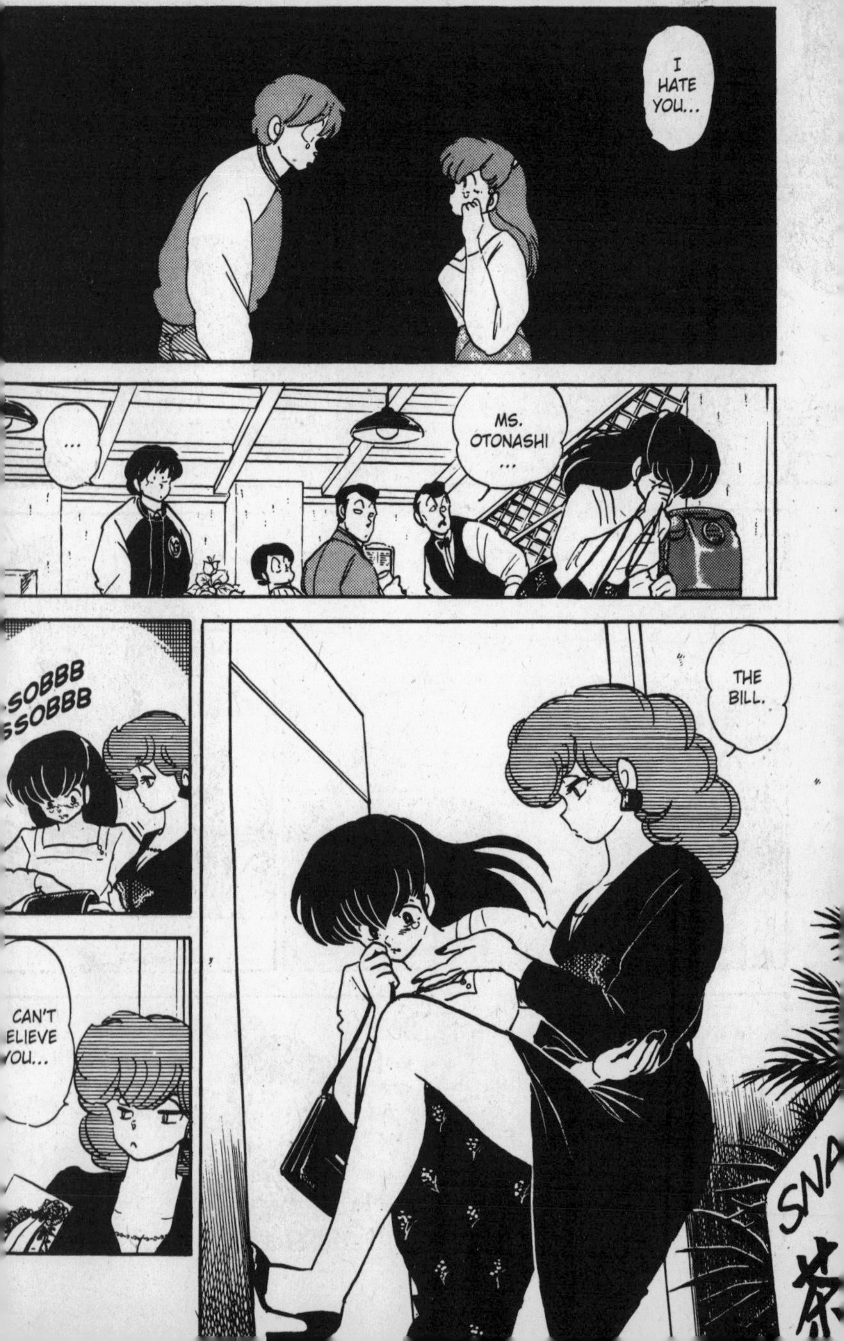
I HATE YOU...
MS. OTONASHI ...
...
THE BILL.
SOBBB SSOBBB
CAN'T ELIEVE YOU...
SNA

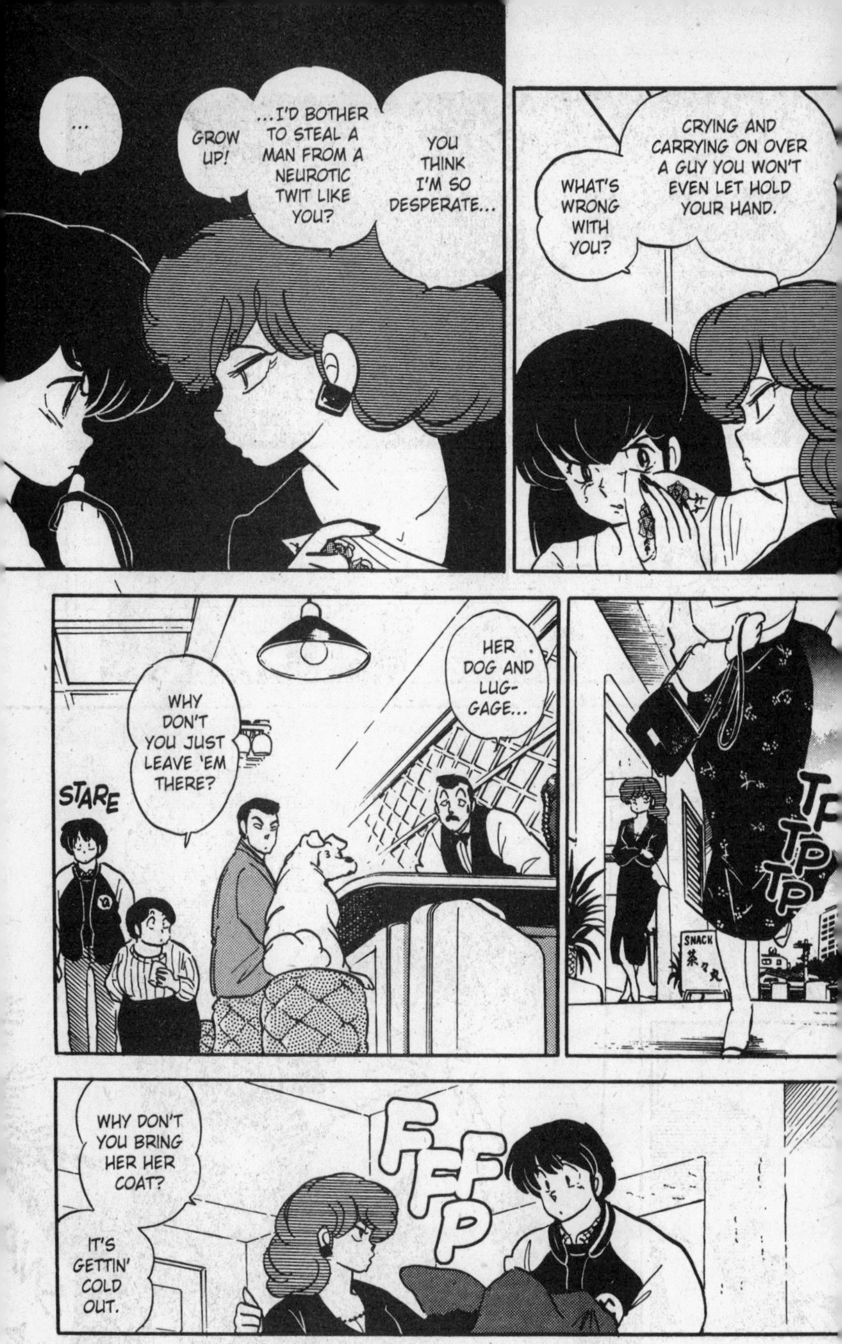
CRYING AND CARRYING ON OVER A GUY YOU WON'T EVEN LET HOLD YOUR HAND.
WHAT'S WRONG WITH YOU?
YOU THINK I'M SO DESPERATE...
...I'D BOTHER TO STEAL A MAN FROM A NEUROTIC TWIT LIKE YOU?
GROW UP!
...
TP TP TP
HER DOG AND LUG-GAGE...
WHY DON'T YOU JUST LEAVE 'EM THERE?
STARE
FFFP
WHY DON'T YOU BRING HER HER COAT?
IT'S GETTIN' COLD OUT.
SNACK

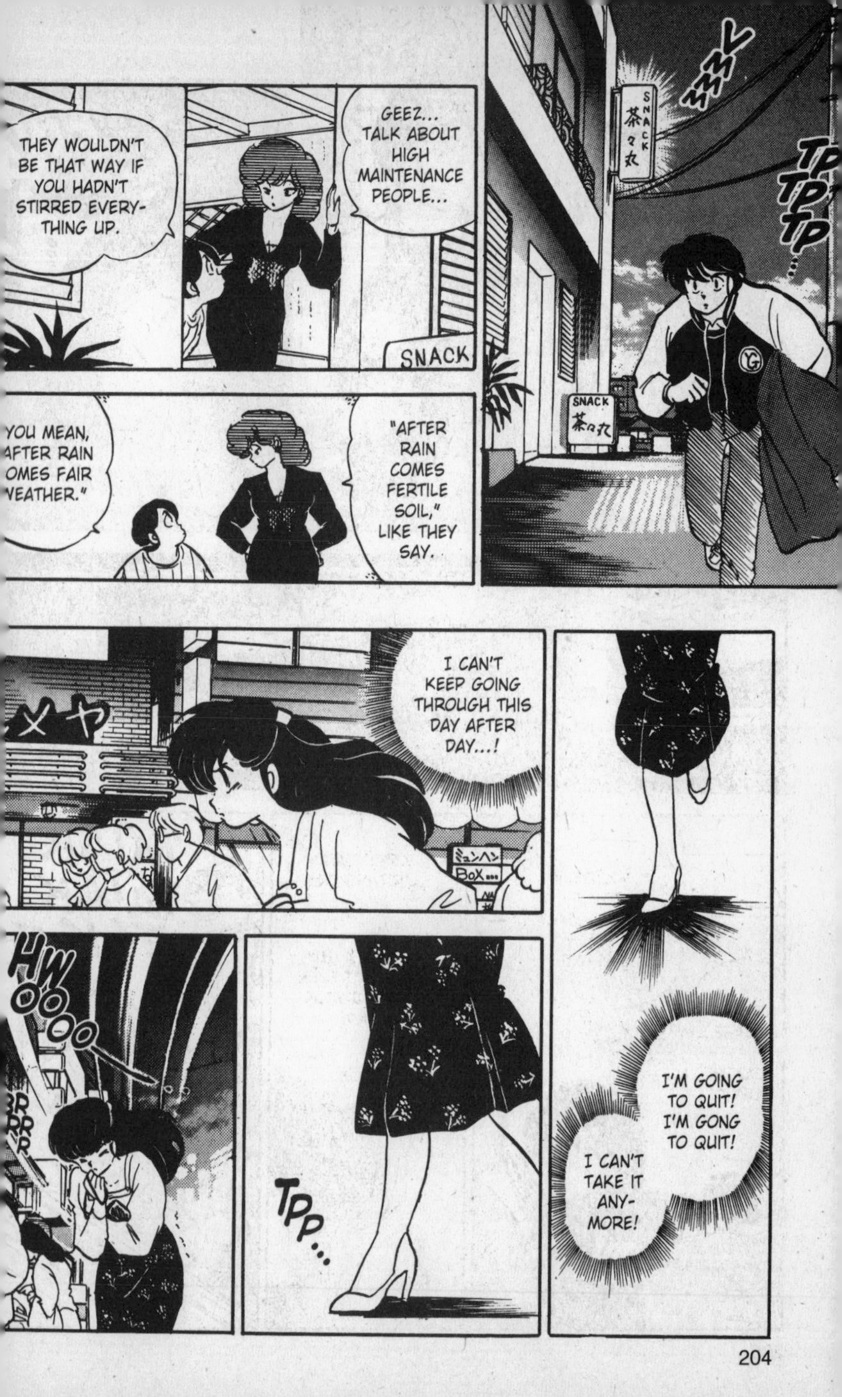
VMMM
SNACK 茶々丸
TP TP TP...
GEEZ... TALK ABOUT HIGH MAINTENANCE PEOPLE...
THEY WOULDN'T BE THAT WAY IF YOU HADN'T STIRRED EVERY-THING UP.
SNACK
SNACK 茶々丸
"AFTER RAIN COMES FERTILE SOIL," LIKE THEY SAY.
YOU MEAN, AFTER RAIN OMES FAIR EATHER."
I CAN'T KEEP GOING THROUGH THIS DAY AFTER DAY...!
HWOOOOO
BRRR
TPP...
I'M GOING TO QUIT! I'M GONG TO QUIT!
I CAN'T TAKE IT ANY-MORE!

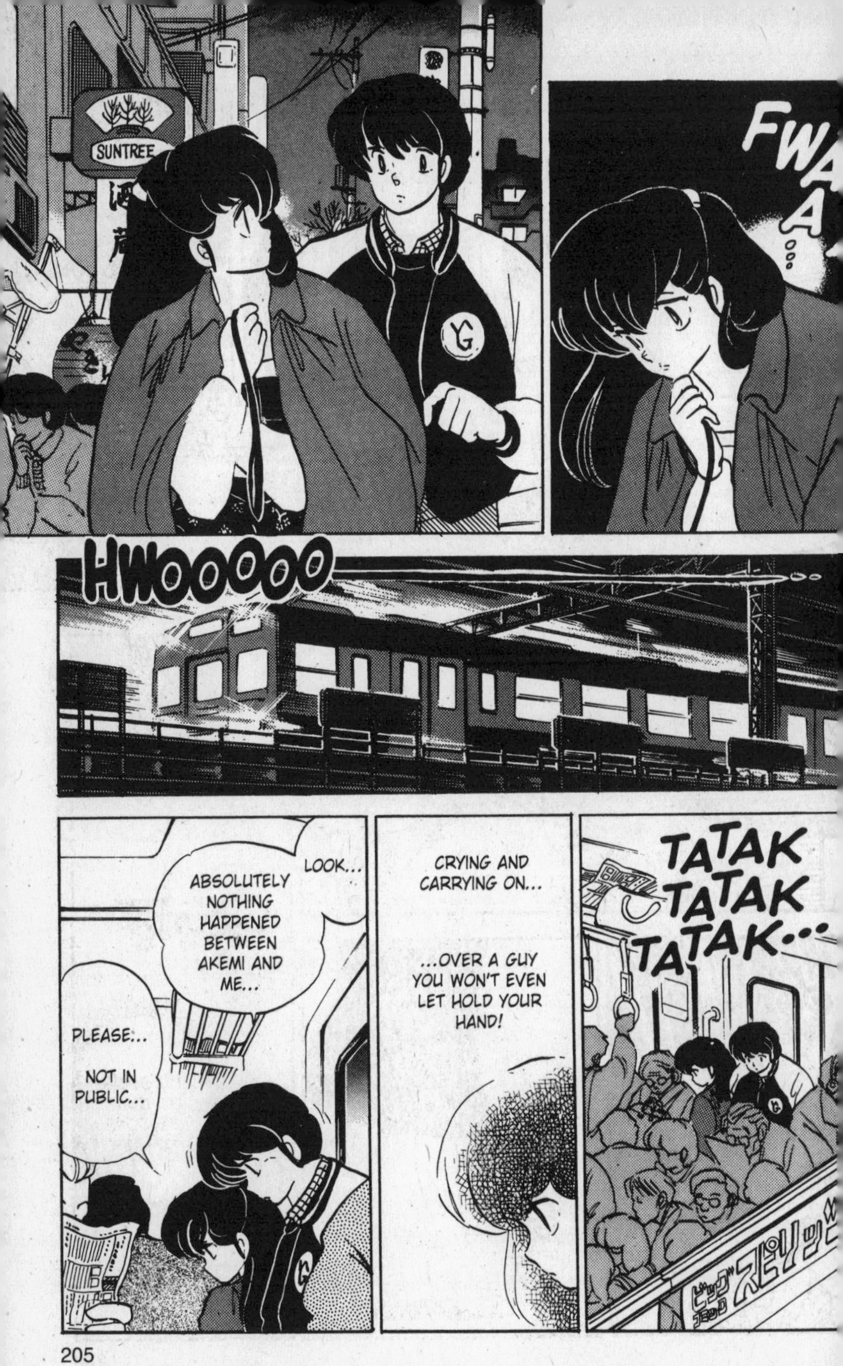
SUNTREE
FWAAA...
HWOOOOO
LOOK...
ABSOLUTELY NOTHING HAPPENED BETWEEN AKEMI AND ME...
PLEASE... NOT IN PUBLIC...
CRYING AND CARRYING ON...
...OVER A GUY YOU WON'T EVEN LET HOLD YOUR HAND!
TATAK TATAK TATAK...

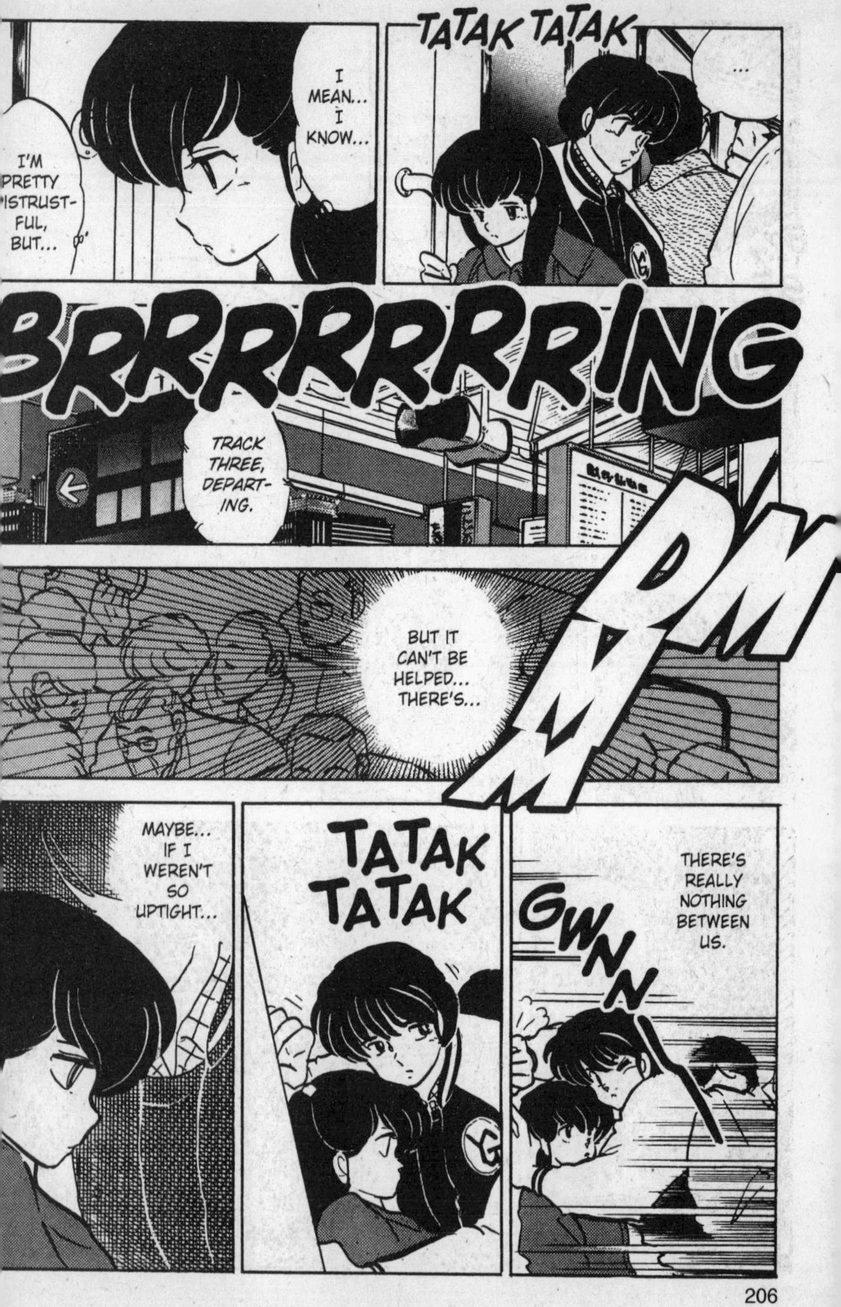
I'M PRETTY 'ISTRUST-FUL, BUT...
I MEAN... I KNOW...
TATAK TATAK
...
BRRRRRRRING
TRACK THREE, DEPART-ING.
BUT IT CAN'T BE HELPED... THERE'S...
MAYBE... IF I WEREN'T SO UPTIGHT...
TATAK TATAK
GWNN
THERE'S REALLY NOTHING BETWEEN US.

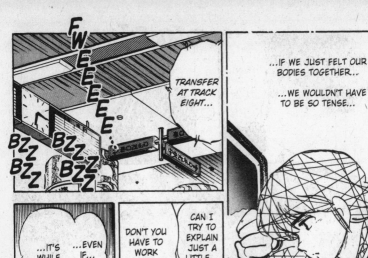

FWEEEEEE...
BZZ BZZ BZZ BZZ
TRANSFER AT TRACK EIGHT...
...IF WE JUST FELT OUR BODIES TOGETHER...
...WE WOULDN'T HAVE TO BE SO TENSE...
CAN I TRY TO EXPLAIN JUST A LITTLE...
DON'T YOU HAVE TO WORK NOW, GODAI?
...EVEN IF...
...IT'S WHILE WE'RE WALKING?
SEE, EVERY-THING THAT'S HAPPENED UP TILL NOW...
2000
GONG
BEEEEP
BWAAA
GONG

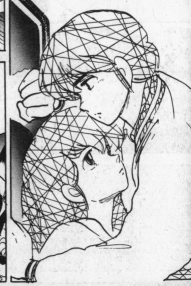

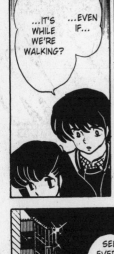

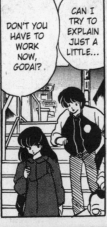

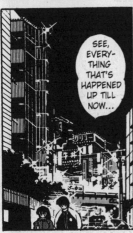

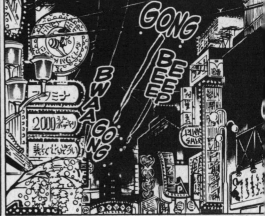

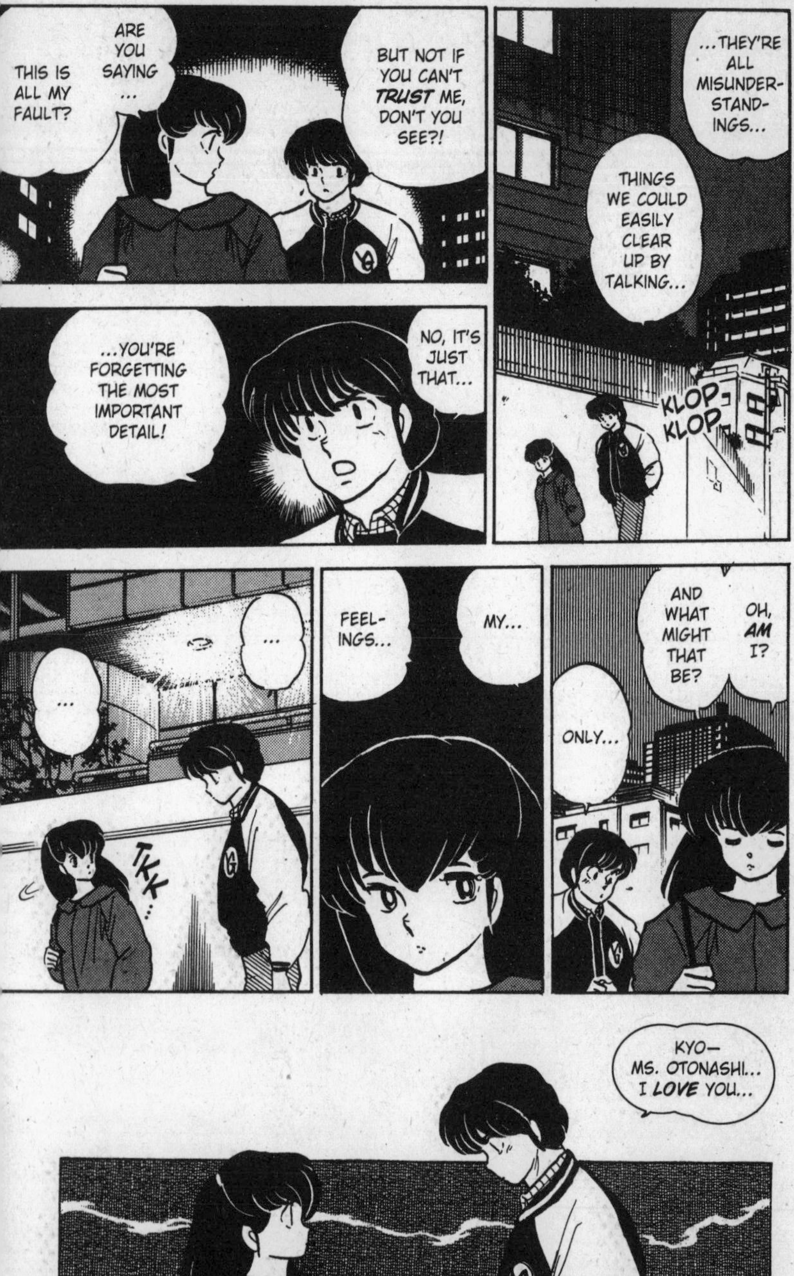
...THEY'RE ALL MISUNDER-STAND-INGS...
THINGS WE COULD EASILY CLEAR UP BY TALKING...
KLOP KLOP
BUT NOT IF YOU CAN'T *TRUST* ME, DON'T YOU SEE?!
ARE YOU SAYING ...
THIS IS ALL MY FAULT?
NO, IT'S JUST THAT...
...YOU'RE FORGETTING THE MOST IMPORTANT DETAIL!
OH, *AM* I?
AND WHAT MIGHT THAT BE?
ONLY...
MY...
FEEL-INGS...
...
...
TKK...
KYO— MS. OTONASHI... I *LOVE* YOU...

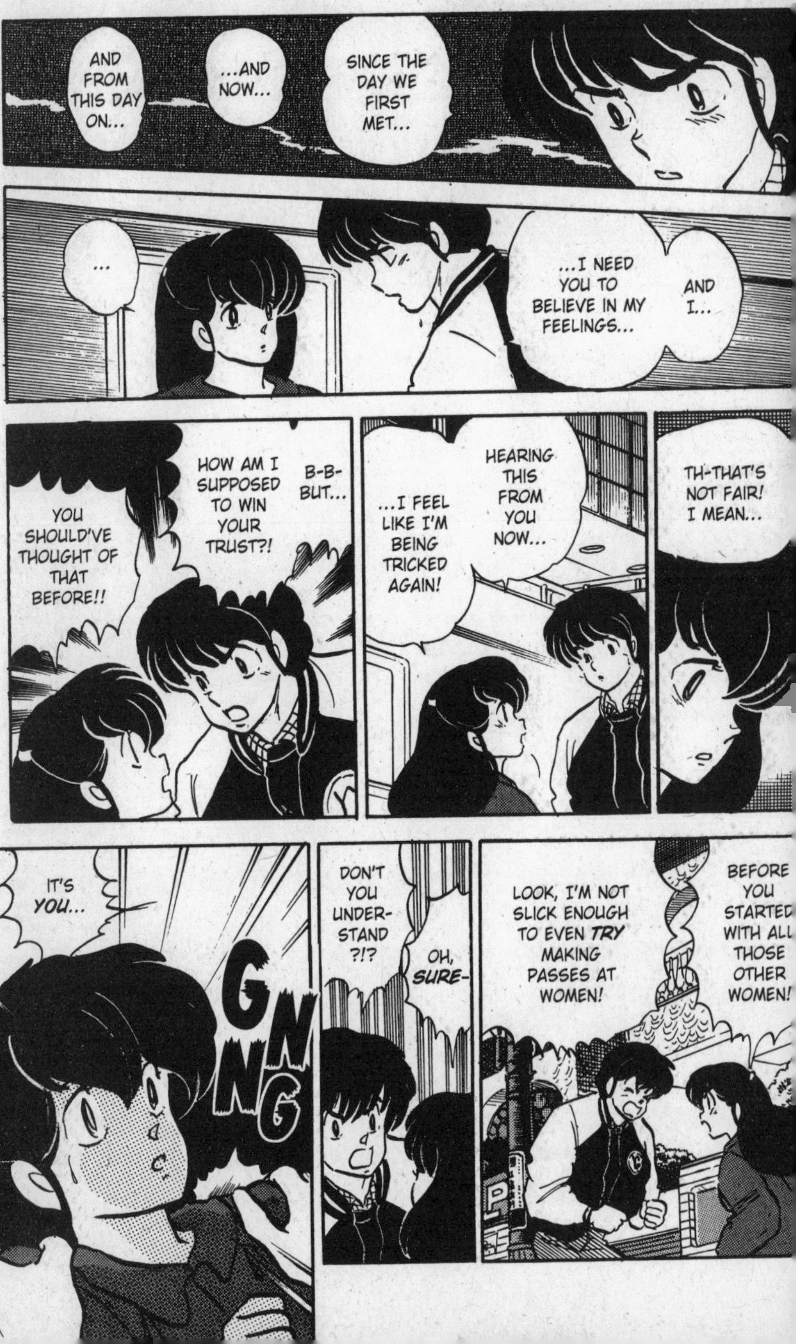
SINCE THE DAY WE FIRST MET...
...AND NOW...
AND FROM THIS DAY ON...
AND I...
...I NEED YOU TO BELIEVE IN MY FEELINGS...
...
TH-THAT'S NOT FAIR! I MEAN...
HEARING THIS FROM YOU NOW...
...I FEEL LIKE I'M BEING TRICKED AGAIN!
B-B-BUT...
HOW AM I SUPPOSED TO WIN YOUR TRUST?!
YOU SHOULD'VE THOUGHT OF THAT BEFORE!!
BEFORE YOU STARTED WITH ALL THOSE OTHER WOMEN!
LOOK, I'M NOT SLICK ENOUGH TO EVEN *TRY* MAKING PASSES AT WOMEN!
OH, *SURE*-
DON'T YOU UNDER-STAND ?!?
IT'S *YOU*...
GNNG

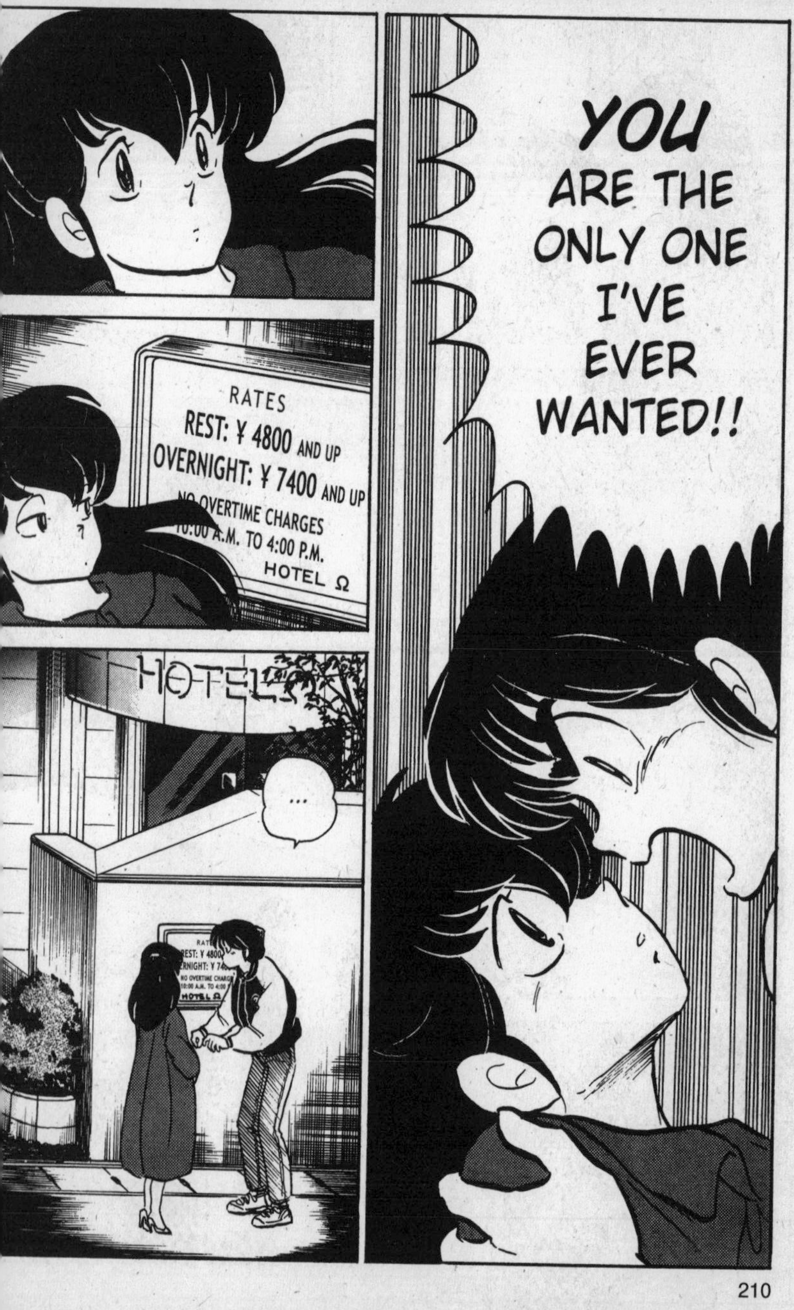
YOU ARE THE ONLY ONE I'VE EVER WANTED!!
RATES
REST: ¥ 4800 AND UP
OVERNIGHT: ¥ 7400 AND UP
NO OVERTIME CHARGES
10:00 A.M. TO 4:00 P.M.
HOTEL Ω
HOTEL
...

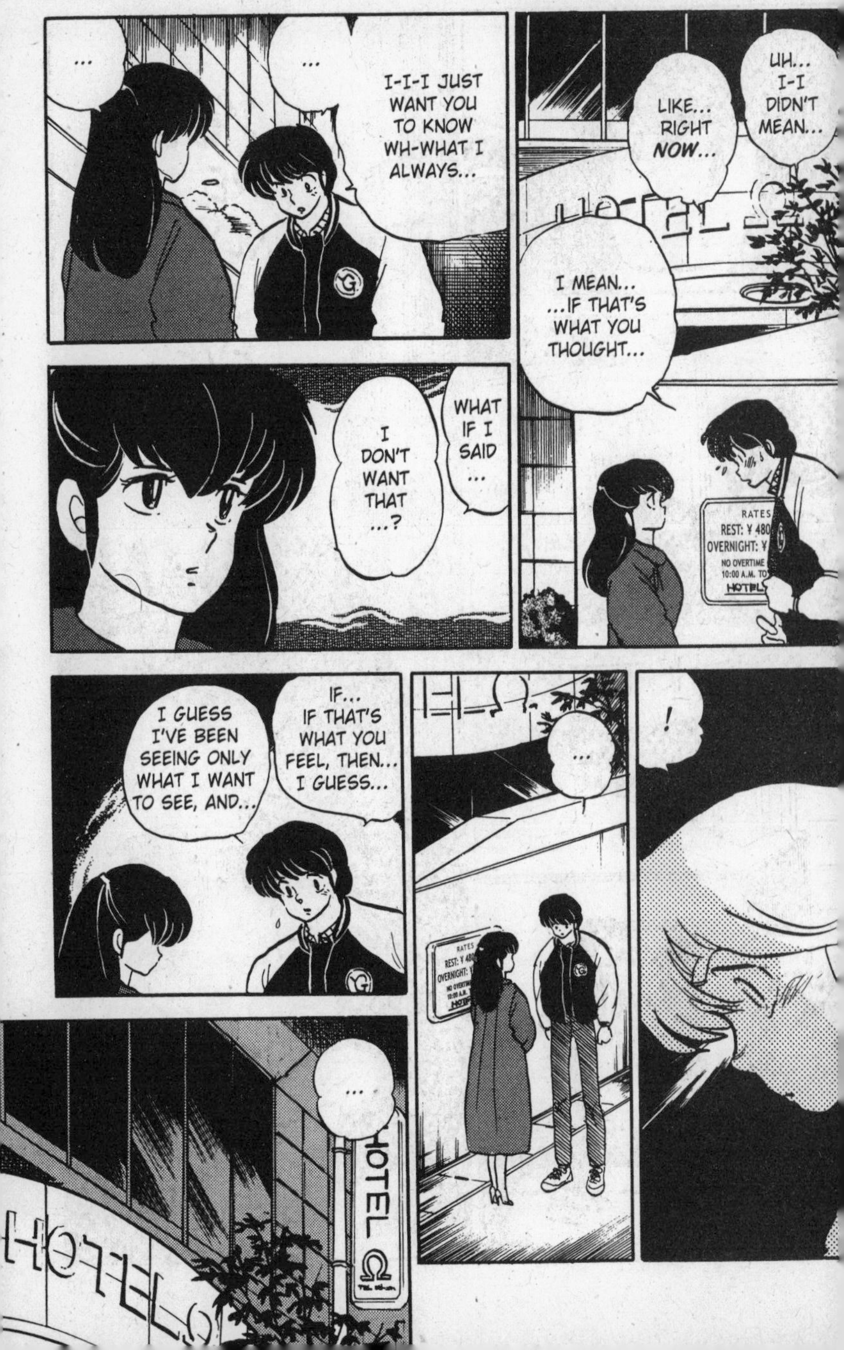

UH... I-I DIDN'T MEAN...
LIKE... RIGHT *NOW*...
I MEAN... ...IF THAT'S WHAT YOU THOUGHT...
RATES
REST: ¥ 480
OVERNIGHT: ¥
NO OVERTIME
10:00 A.M. TO
HOTEL
...
...
I-I-I JUST WANT YOU TO KNOW WH-WHAT I ALWAYS...
WHAT IF I SAID ...
I DON'T WANT THAT ...?
!
...
IF... IF THAT'S WHAT YOU FEEL, THEN... I GUESS...
I GUESS I'VE BEEN SEEING ONLY WHAT I WANT TO SEE, AND...
...
HOTEL Ω
HOTEL Ω

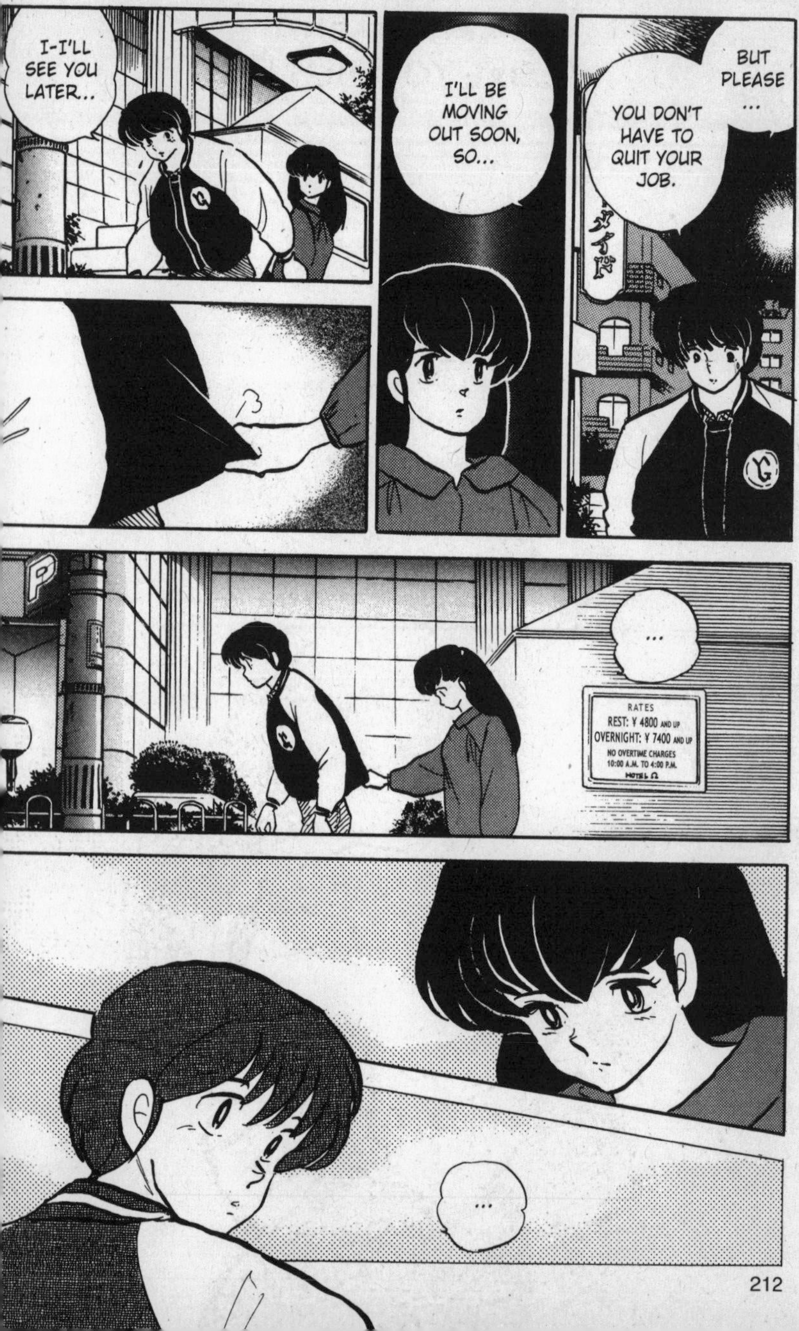
I-I'LL SEE YOU LATER...
I'LL BE MOVING OUT SOON, SO...
YOU DON'T HAVE TO QUIT YOUR JOB.
BUT PLEASE ...
...
RATES
REST: ¥ 4800 AND UP
OVERNIGHT: ¥ 7400 AND UP
NO OVERTIME CHARGES
10:00 A.M. TO 4:00 P.M.
HOTEL Ω
...

PART ELEVEN

I LOVE YOU, BUT...

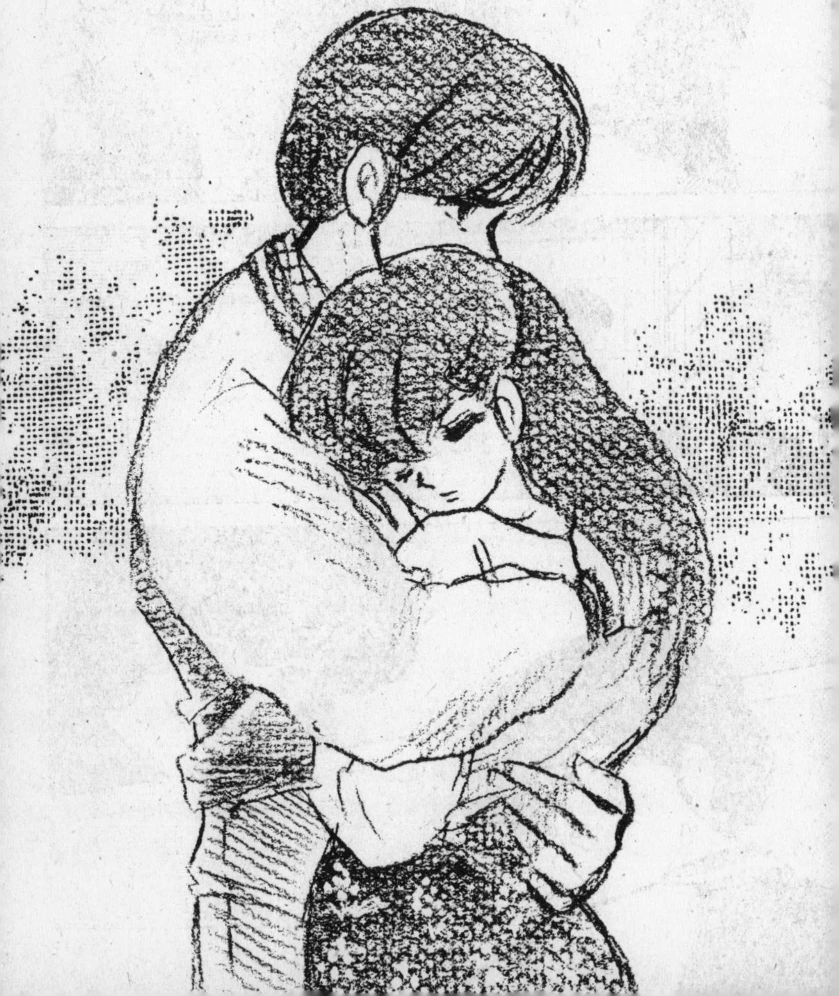

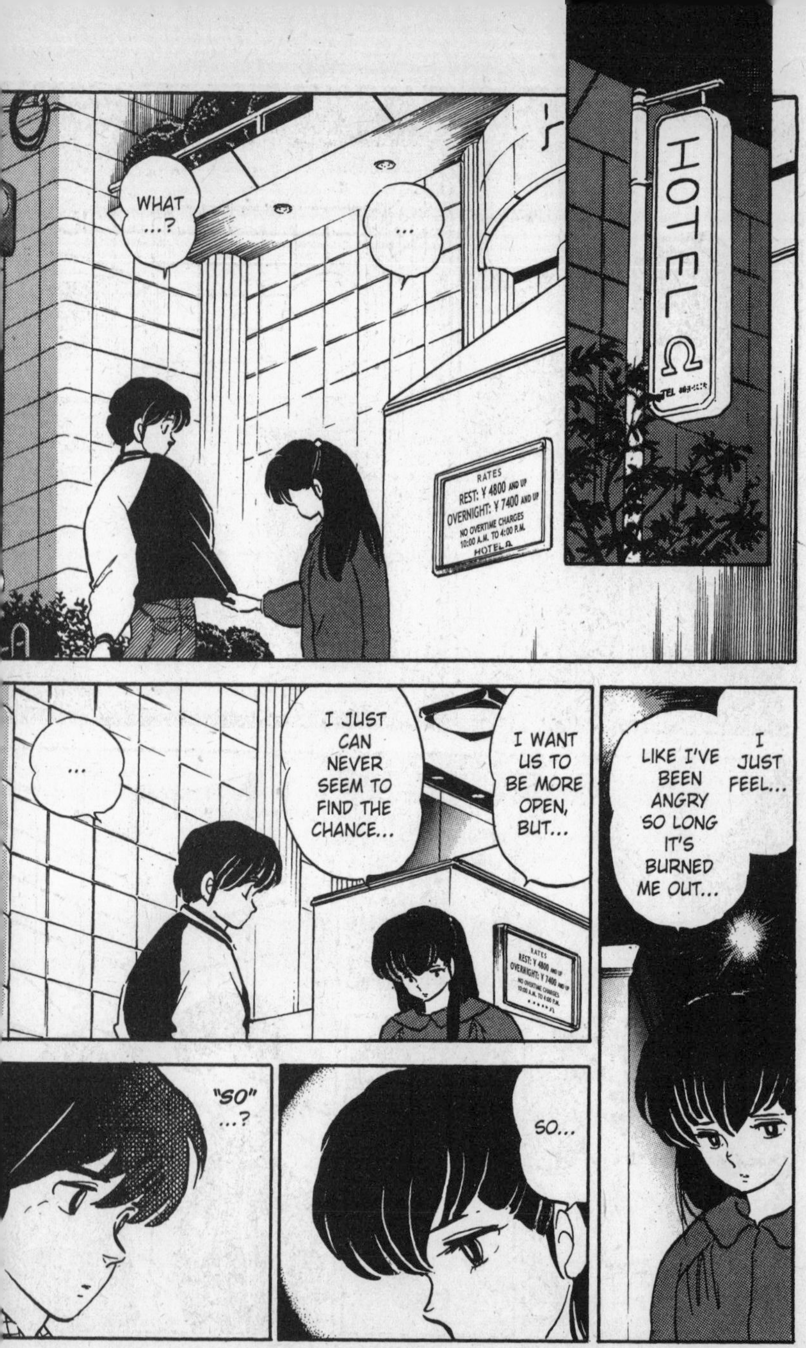
HOTEL Ω
RATES
REST: ¥ 4800 AND UP
OVERNIGHT: ¥ 7400 AND UP
NO OVERTIME CHARGES
10:00 A.M. TO 4:00 P.M.
...
WHAT ...?
I JUST FEEL...
LIKE I'VE BEEN ANGRY SO LONG IT'S BURNED ME OUT...
I WANT US TO BE MORE OPEN, BUT...
I JUST CAN NEVER SEEM TO FIND THE CHANCE...
...
SO...
"SO" ...?

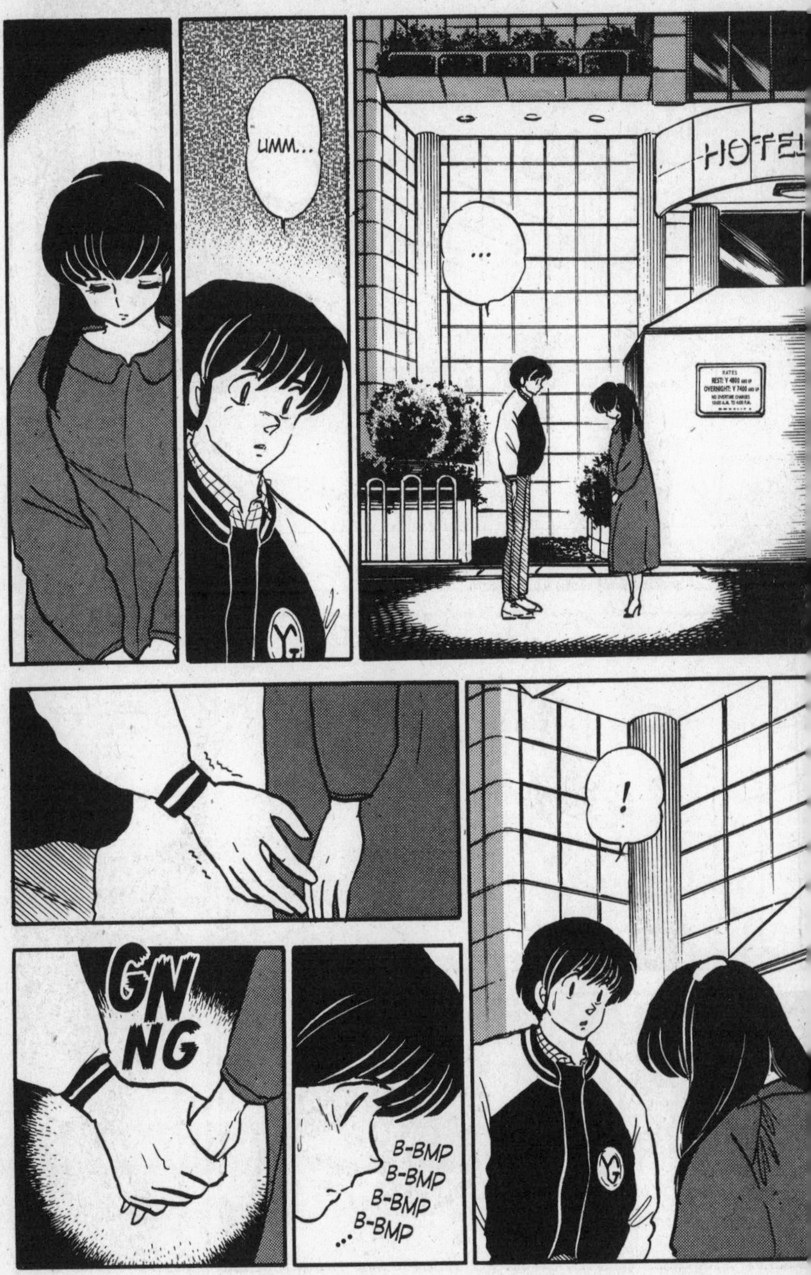
HOTEL
...
RATES
REST: Y 4800 AND UP
OVERNIGHT: Y 7400 AND UP
NO OVERTIME CHARGES
10:00 A.M. TO 4:00 P.M.
UMM...
!
B-BMP
B-BMP
B-BMP
...B-BMP
GN
NG

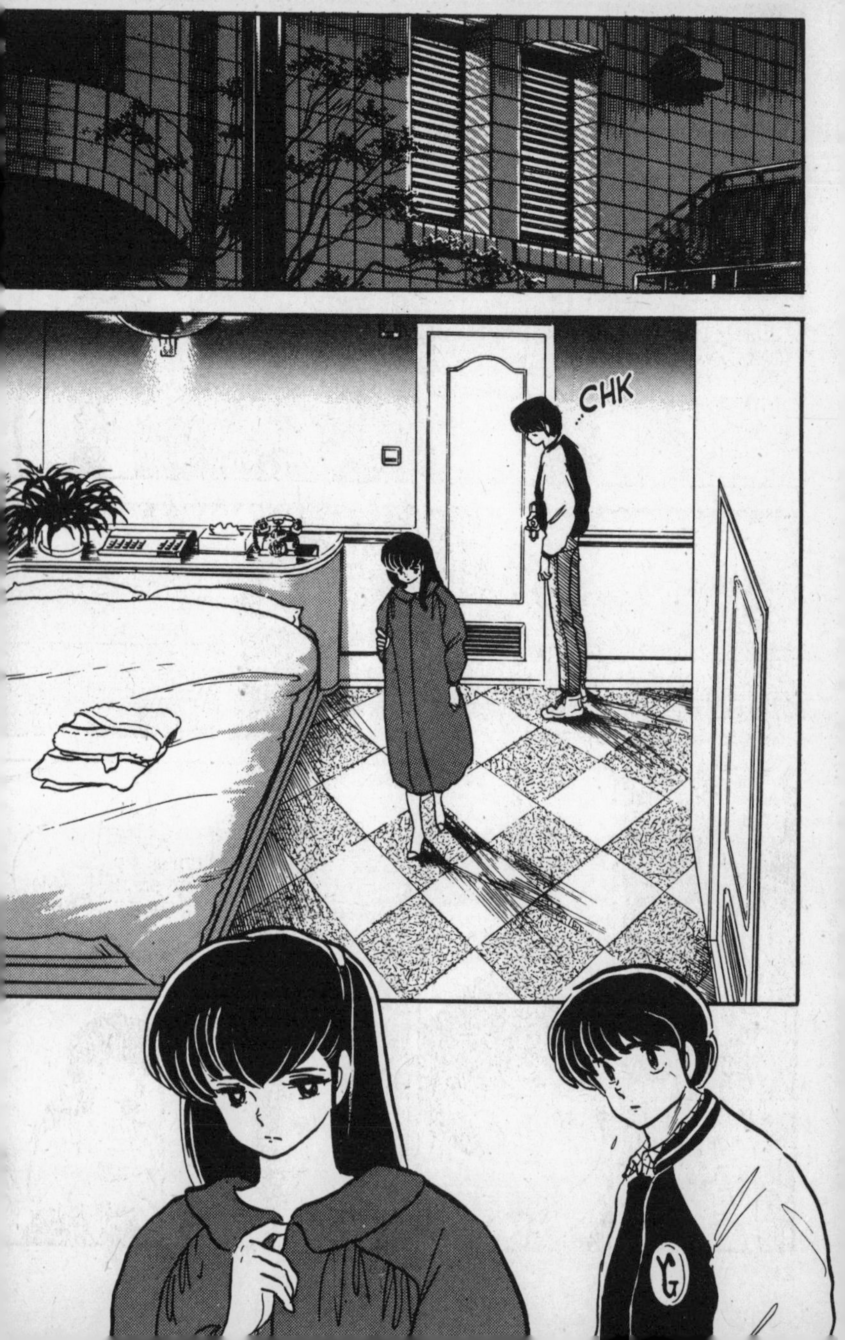
...CHK

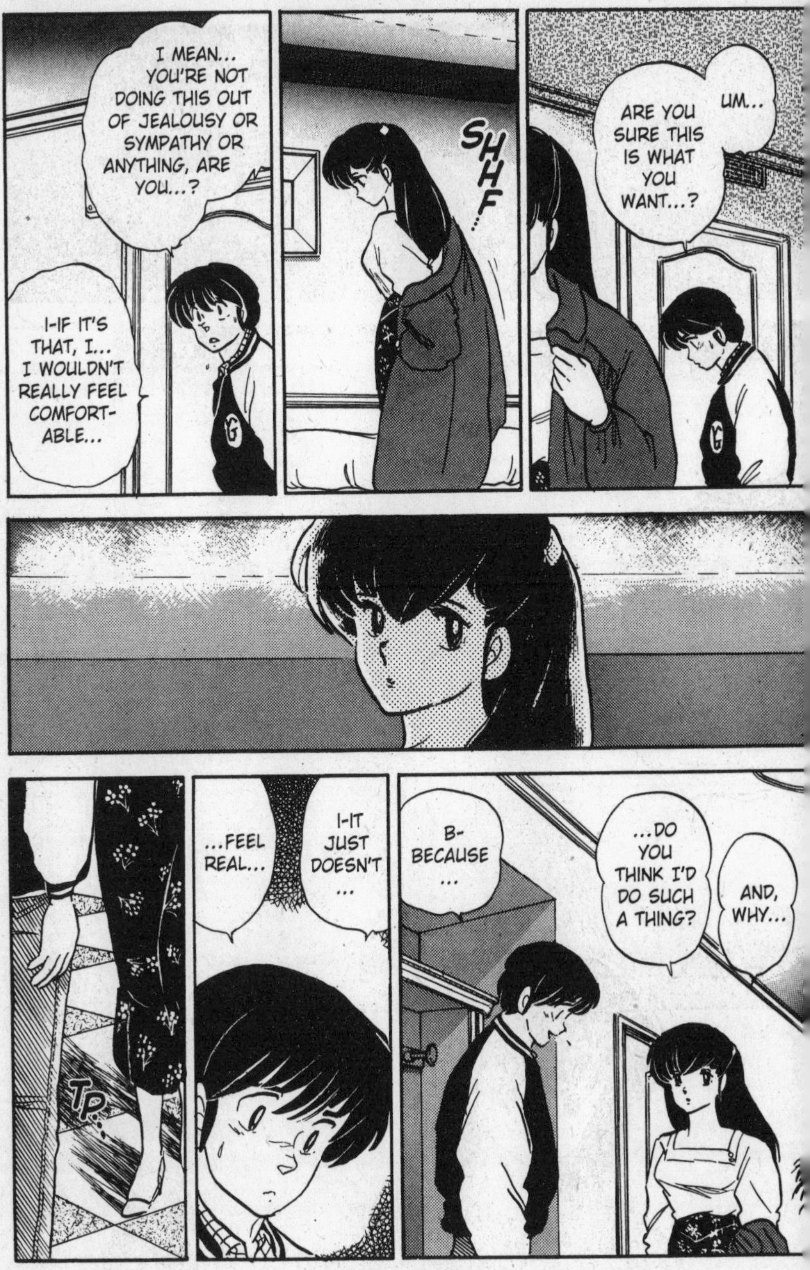
UM...
ARE YOU SURE THIS IS WHAT YOU WANT...?
SHHF...
I MEAN... YOU'RE NOT DOING THIS OUT OF JEALOUSY OR SYMPATHY OR ANYTHING, ARE YOU...?
I-IF IT'S THAT, I... I WOULDN'T REALLY FEEL COMFORT-ABLE...
AND, WHY...
...DO YOU THINK I'D DO SUCH A THING?
B-BECAUSE ...
I-IT JUST DOESN'T ...
...FEEL REAL...
TP.

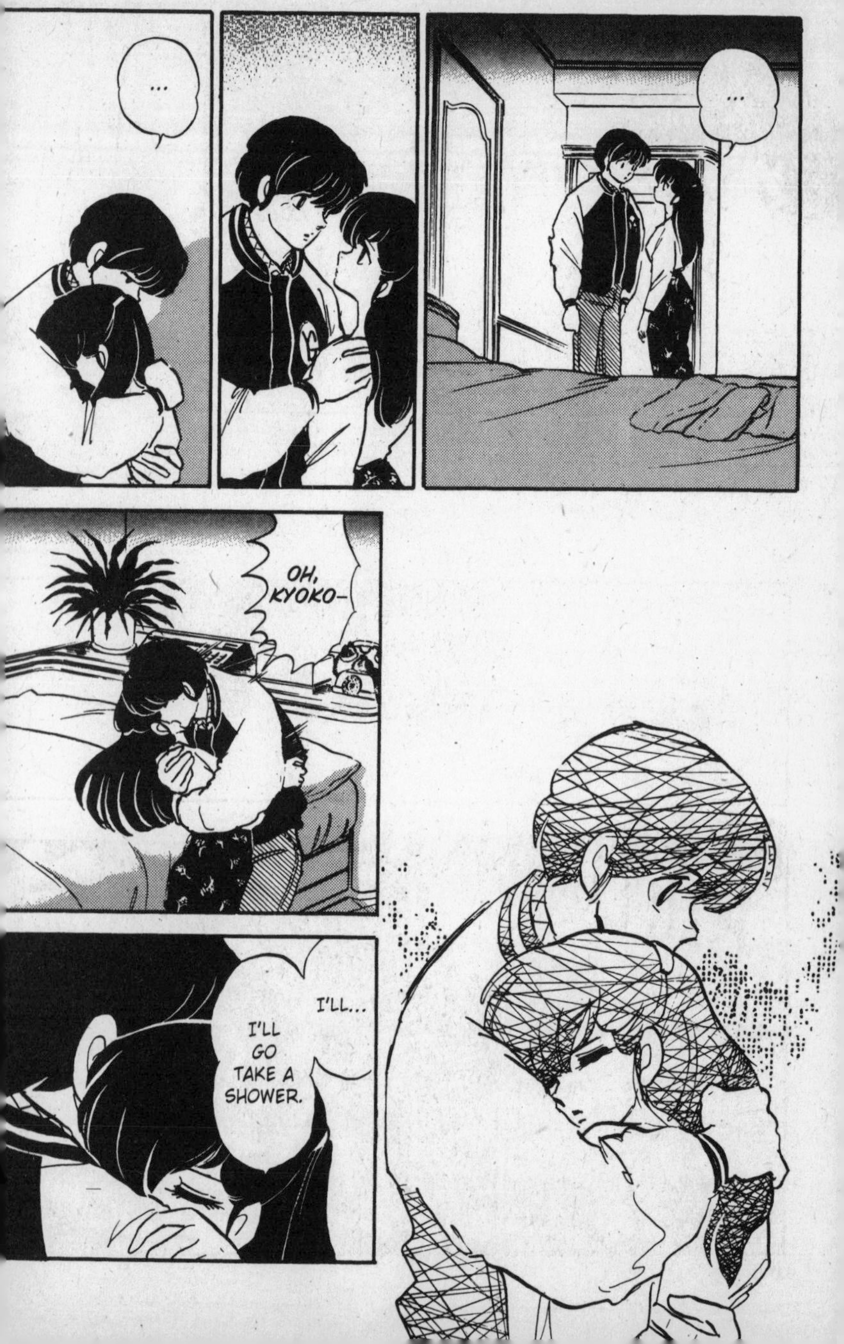
...
...
OH, KYOKO-
I'LL...
I'LL GO TAKE A SHOWER.

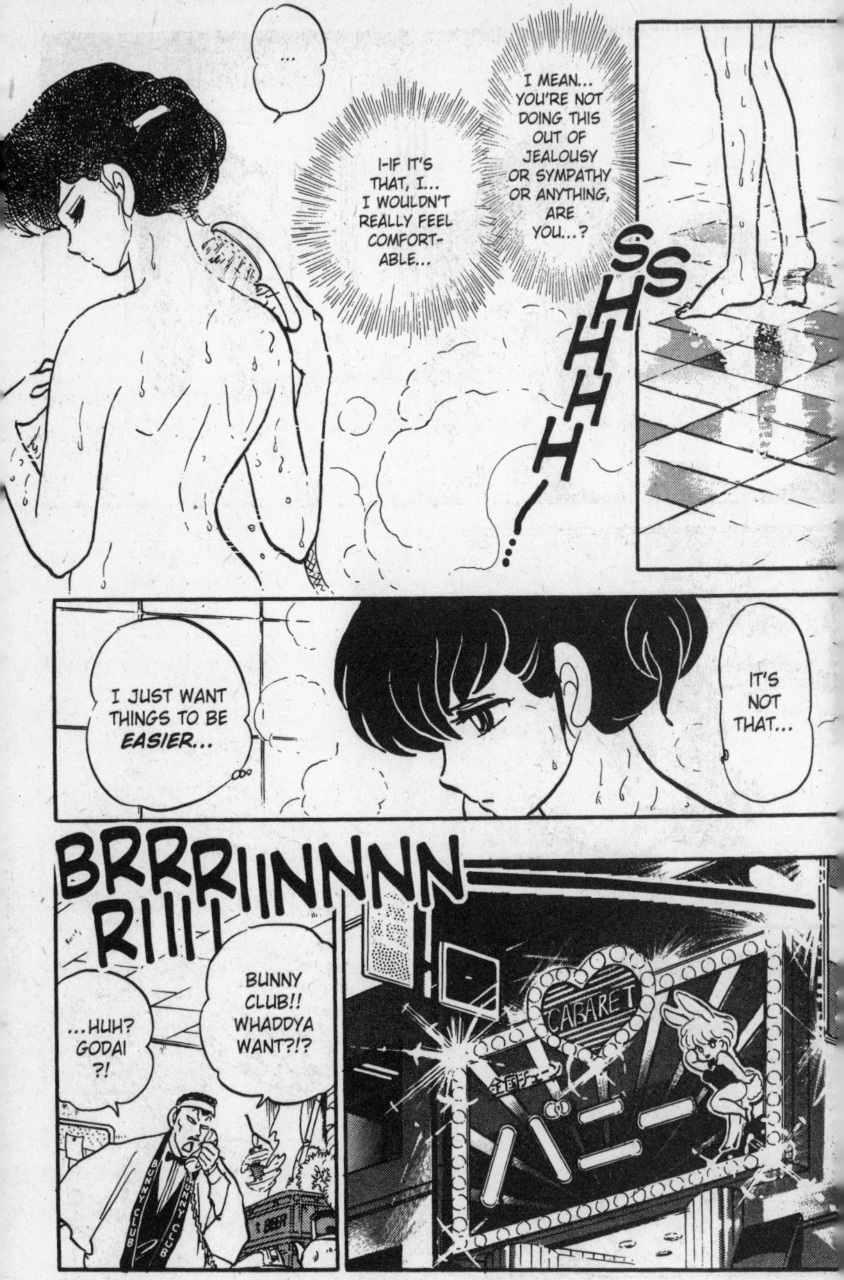
...
I MEAN... YOU'RE NOT DOING THIS OUT OF JEALOUSY OR SYMPATHY OR ANYTHING, ARE YOU...?
I-IF IT'S THAT, I... I WOULDN'T REALLY FEEL COMFORT-ABLE...
SSHHHHH...
IT'S NOT THAT...
I JUST WANT THINGS TO BE *EASIER...*
BRRRIINNNN RIII
BUNNY CLUB!! WHADDYA WANT?!?
...HUH? GODAI ?!
CABARET
バニー
BUNNY CLUB

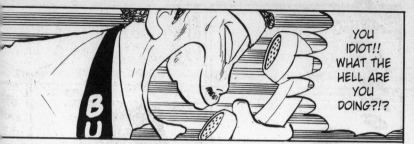

YOU IDIOT!! WHAT THE HELL ARE YOU DOING?!?

WHERE'S DIREKKER?

THE BRATS ARE ALL CRYING!!

WHERE IN HELL *ARE* YOU?!!

I'M... SORRY.

B-BMP B-BMP

I-I KNOW, BUT...

TWO HOURS.

THAT'S ALL.

PLEASE.

I'M SORRY, I PROMISE I'LL BE THERE.

TWIK

...YOU'RE STAGIN' A *QUICKIE* ON *MY* TIME!?

DON'T TELL ME...

HEY.

TWO HOURS ...??

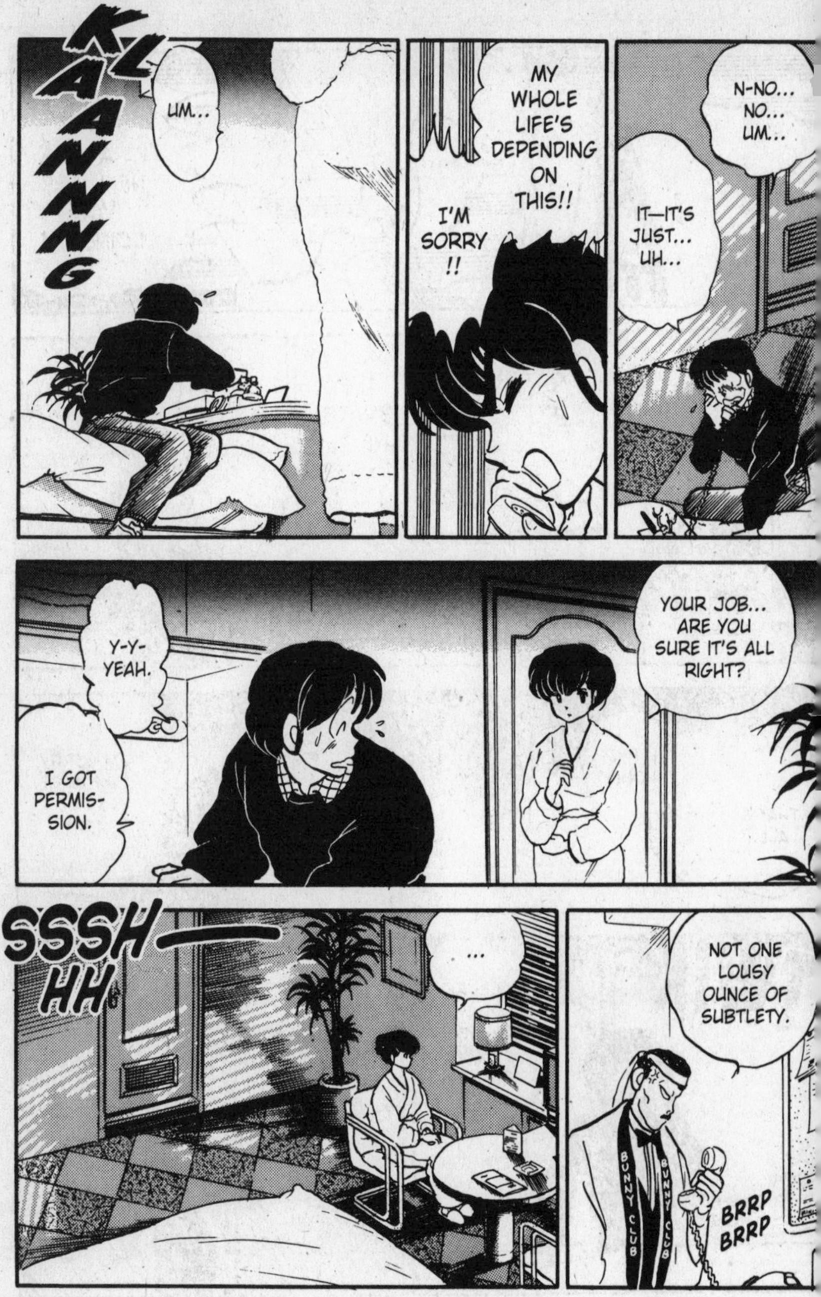
KLAANNNG
UM...
MY WHOLE LIFE'S DEPENDING ON THIS!!
I'M SORRY !!
N-NO... NO... UM...
IT—IT'S JUST... UH...
Y-Y-YEAH.
I GOT PERMIS-SION.
YOUR JOB... ARE YOU SURE IT'S ALL RIGHT?
SSSH—HH
...
NOT ONE LOUSY OUNCE OF SUBTLETY.
BUNNY CLUB
BUNNY CLUB
BRRP BRRP

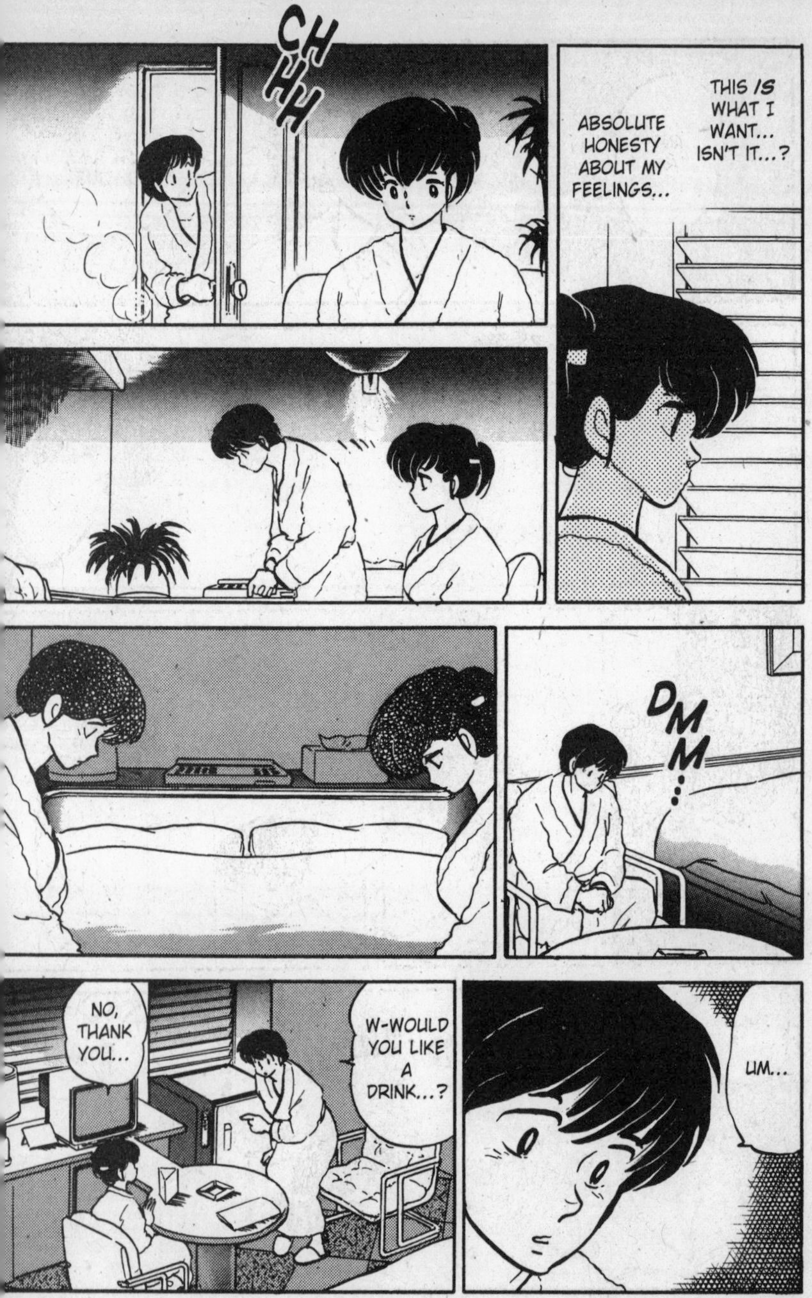
CHHH
ABSOLUTE HONESTY ABOUT MY FEELINGS...
THIS *IS* WHAT I WANT... ISN'T IT...?
DMM...
W-WOULD YOU LIKE A DRINK...?
NO, THANK YOU...
UM...

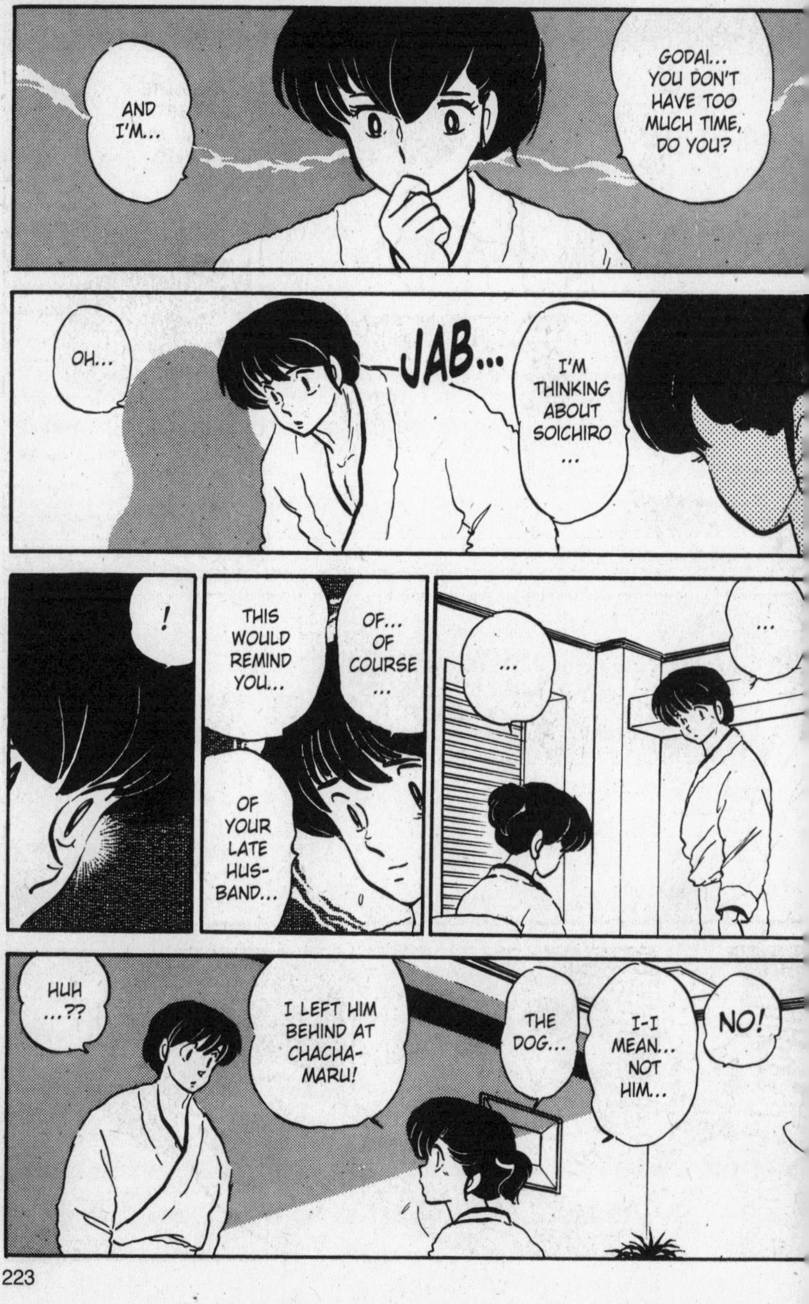
GODAI... YOU DON'T HAVE TOO MUCH TIME, DO YOU?
AND I'M...
I'M THINKING ABOUT SOICHIRO ...
JAB...
OH...
...
...
OF... OF COURSE ...
THIS WOULD REMIND YOU...
OF YOUR LATE HUS-BAND...
!
NO!
I-I MEAN... NOT HIM...
THE DOG...
I LEFT HIM BEHIND AT CHACHA-MARU!
HUH ...??

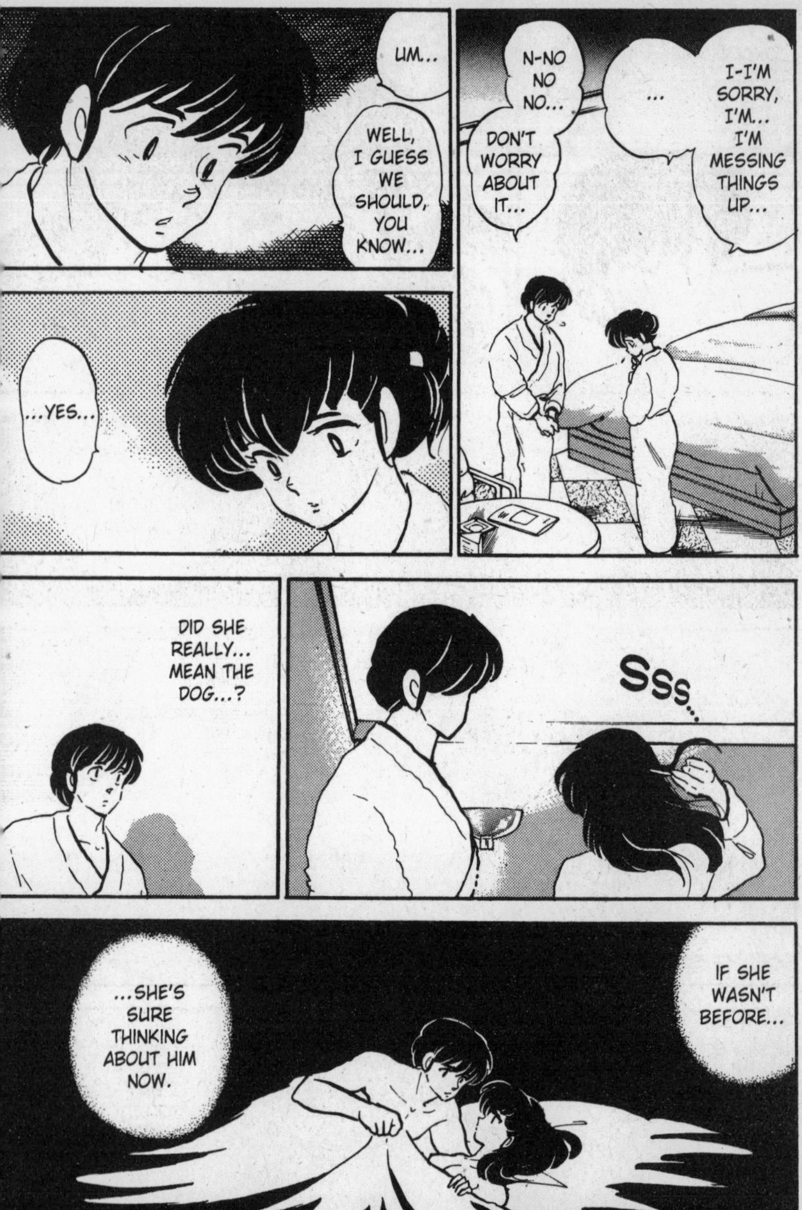
UM...
WELL, I GUESS WE SHOULD, YOU KNOW...
...YES...
N-NO NO NO...
DON'T WORRY ABOUT IT...
...
I-I'M SORRY, I'M... I'M MESSING THINGS UP...
DID SHE REALLY... MEAN THE DOG...?
Sss...
...SHE'S SURE THINKING ABOUT HIM NOW.
IF SHE WASN'T BEFORE...

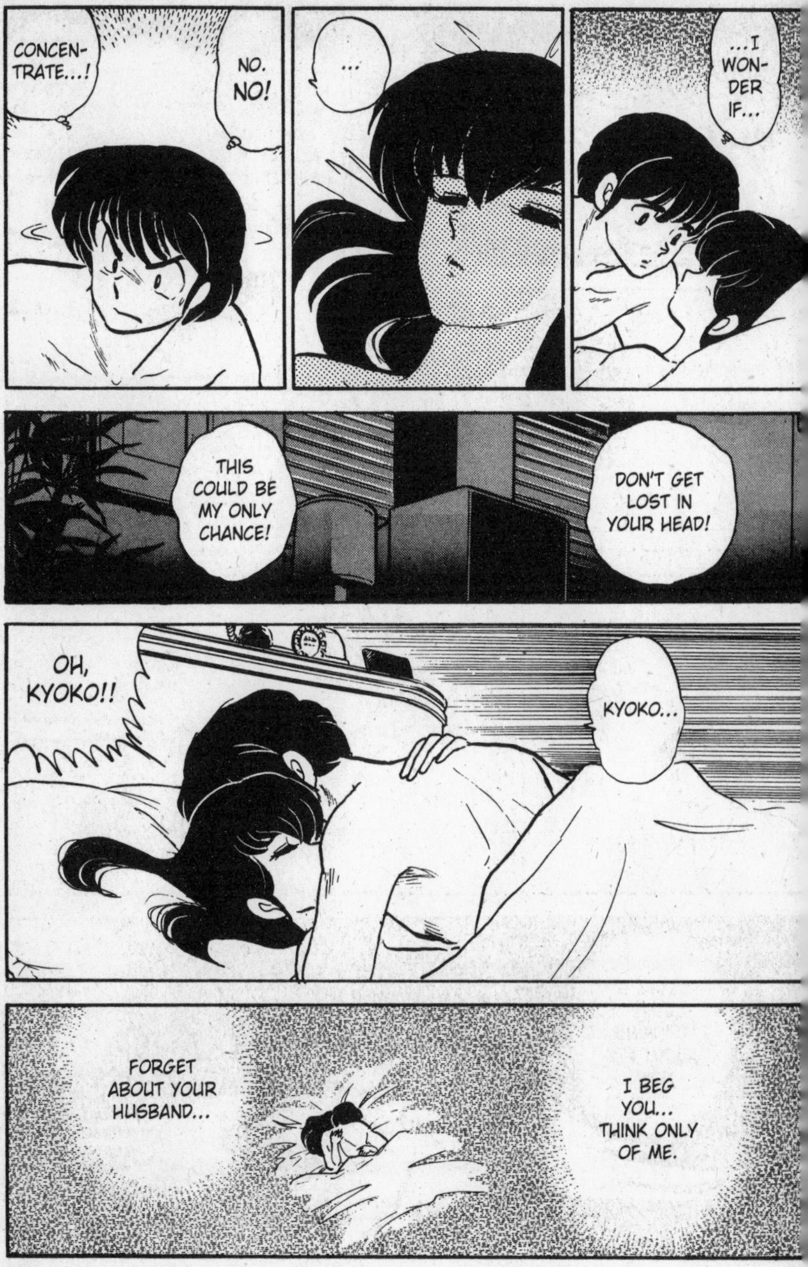
CONCEN-
TRATE...!
NO.
NO!
...
...I
WON-
DER
IF...
THIS COULD BE MY ONLY CHANCE!
DON'T GET LOST IN YOUR HEAD!
OH, KYOKO!!
KYOKO...
FORGET ABOUT YOUR HUSBAND...
I BEG YOU... THINK ONLY OF ME.

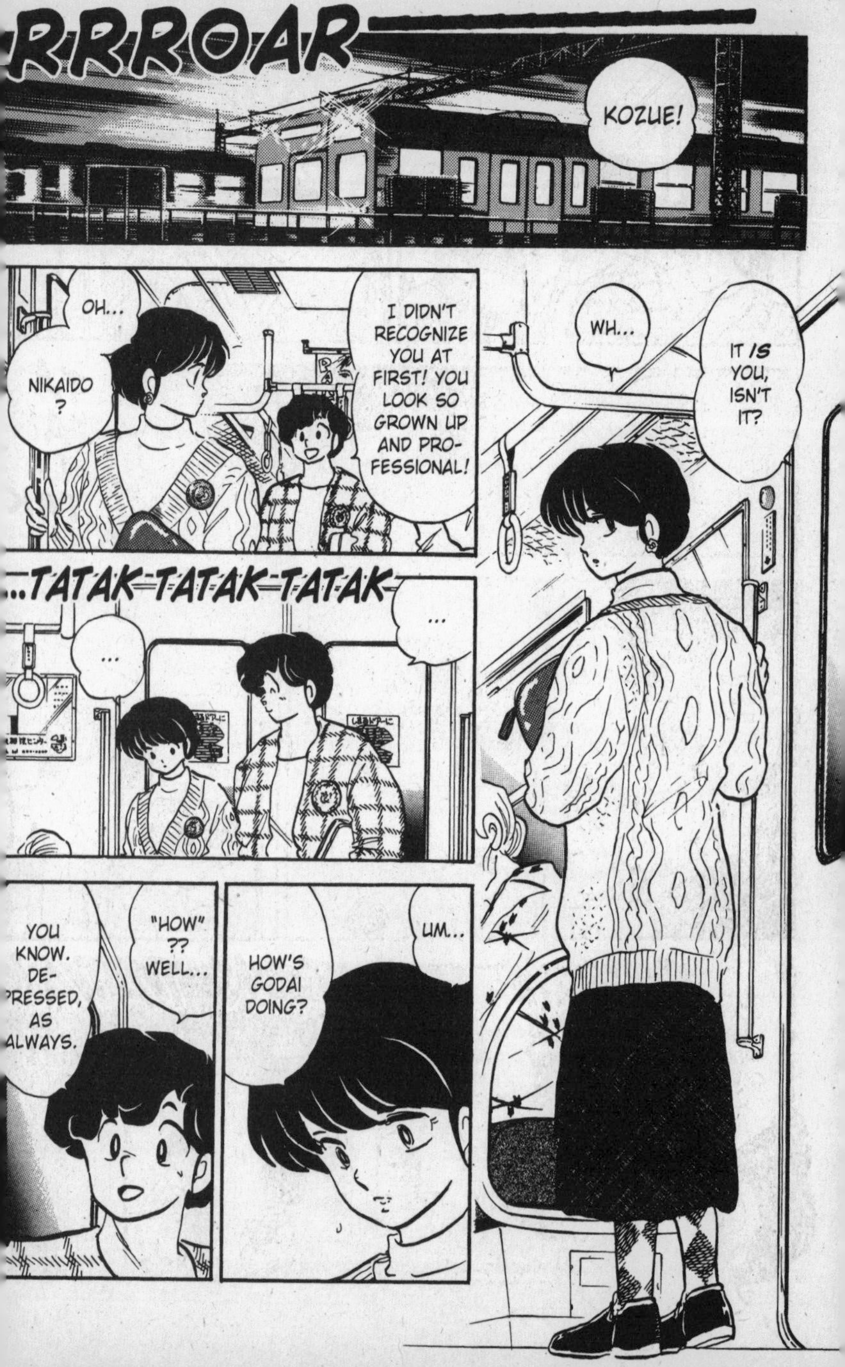
RRROAR
KOZUE!
WH...
IT IS YOU, ISN'T IT?
OH...
NIKAIDO ?
I DIDN'T RECOGNIZE YOU AT FIRST! YOU LOOK SO GROWN UP AND PRO-FESSIONAL!
...TATAK TATAK TATAK
...
...
UM...
HOW'S GODAI DOING?
"HOW" ?? WELL...
YOU KNOW. DE-PRESSED, AS ALWAYS.

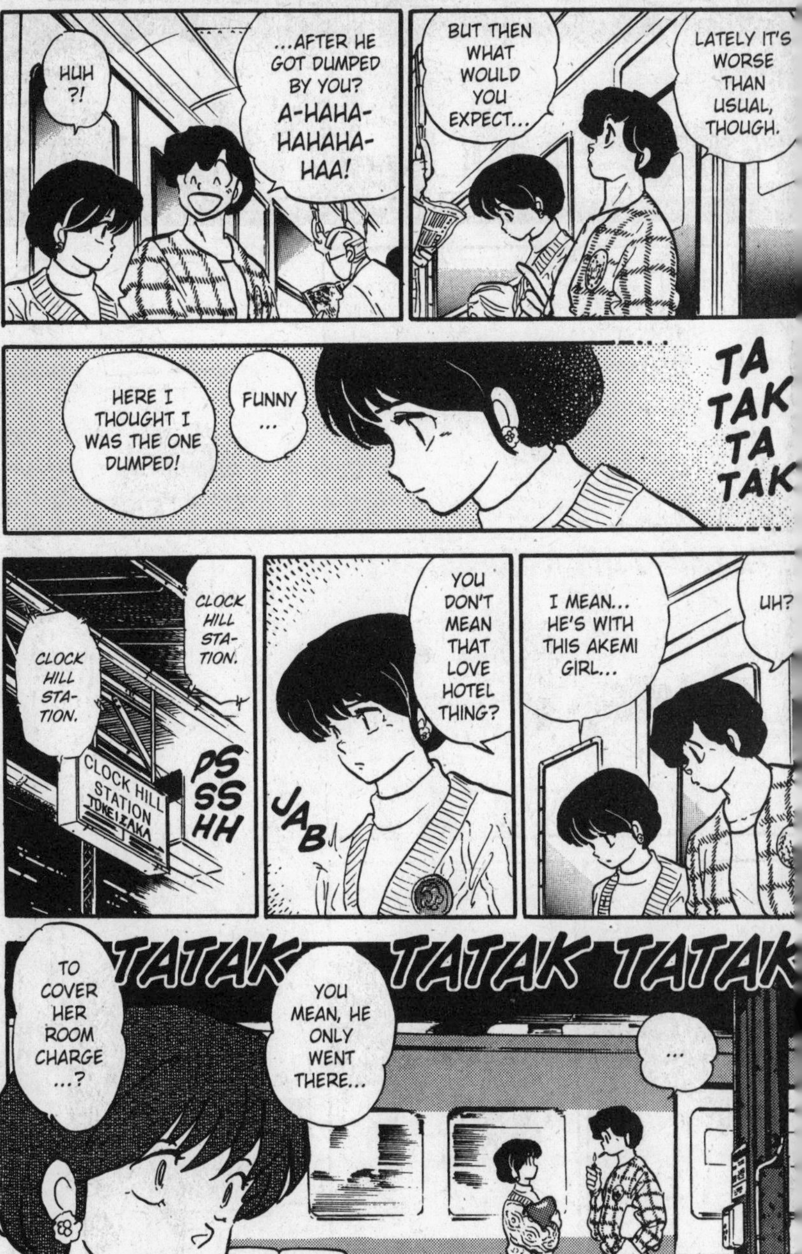
LATELY IT'S WORSE THAN USUAL, THOUGH.
BUT THEN WHAT WOULD YOU EXPECT...
...AFTER HE GOT DUMPED BY YOU? A-HAHA-HAHAHA-HAA!
HUH ?!
TA TAK TA TAK
FUNNY ...
HERE I THOUGHT I WAS THE ONE DUMPED!
UH?
I MEAN... HE'S WITH THIS AKEMI GIRL...
YOU DON'T MEAN THAT LOVE HOTEL THING?
JAB
CLOCK HILL STA-TION.
CLOCK HILL STA-TION.
PS SS HH
CLOCK HILL STATION TOKEIZAKA
TATAK TATAK TATAK
...
YOU MEAN, HE ONLY WENT THERE...
TO COVER HER ROOM CHARGE ...?

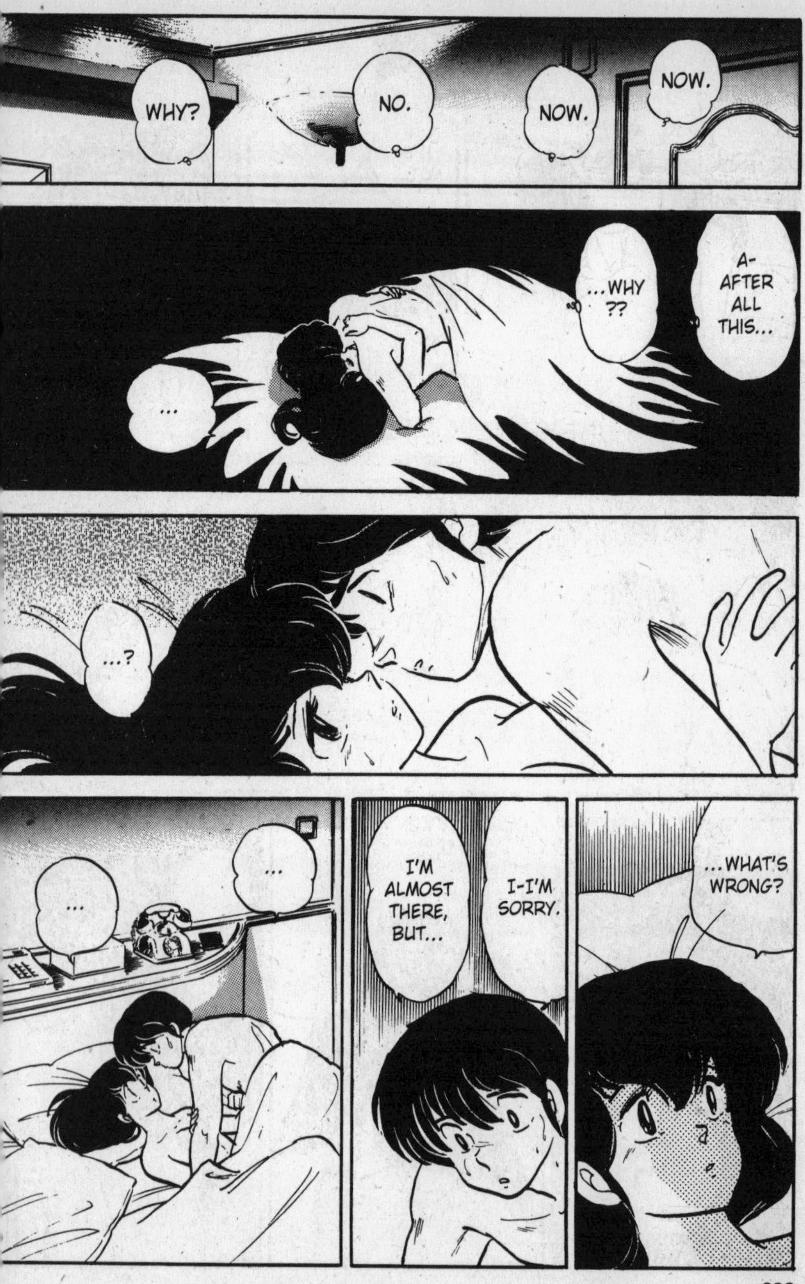
NOW.
NOW.
NO.
WHY?
A- AFTER ALL THIS...
...WHY ??
...
...?
...WHAT'S WRONG?
I-I'M SORRY.
I'M ALMOST THERE, BUT...
...
...

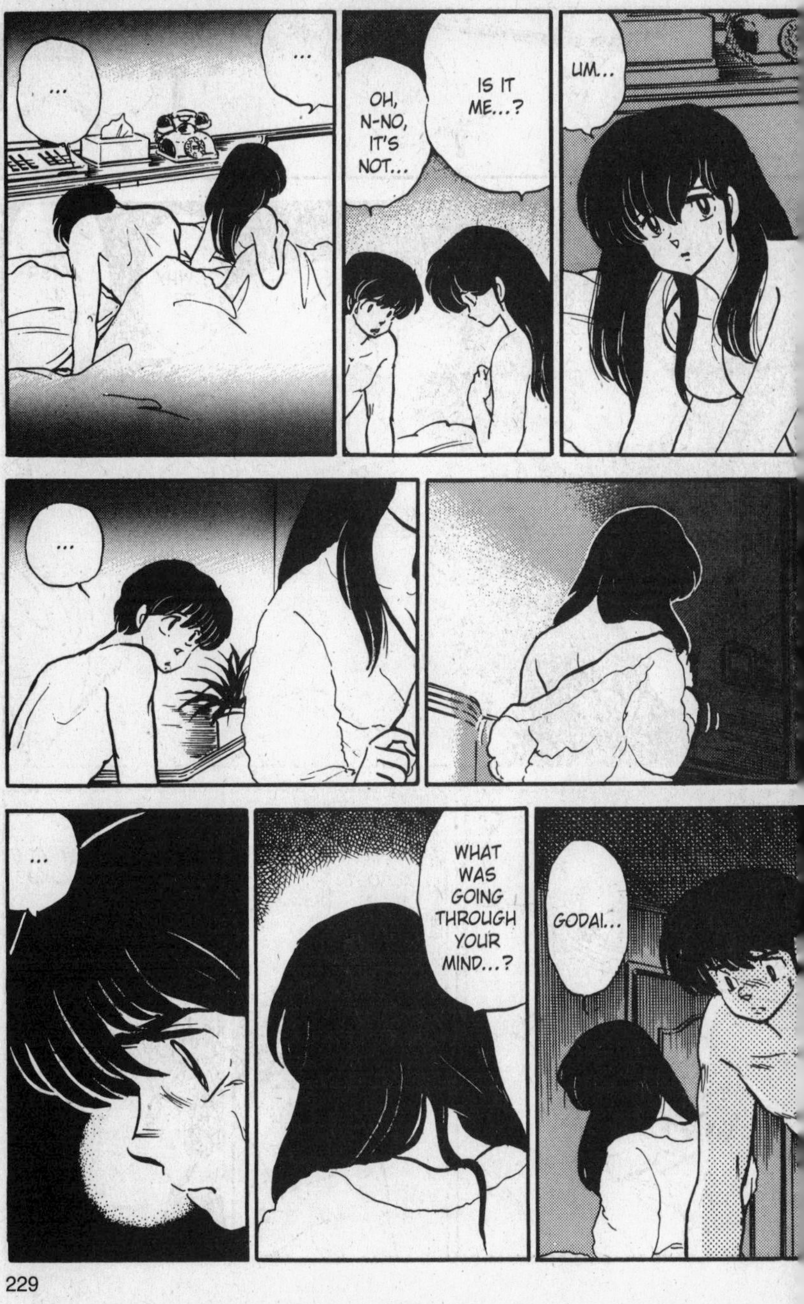
UM...
IS IT ME...?
OH, N-NO, IT'S NOT...
...
...
...
GODAI...
WHAT WAS GOING THROUGH YOUR MIND...?
...

TPP...

YEAH...

PLEASE... GO TO YOUR JOB.

HOTEL Ω

...

...

YES, I LOVE YOU!

...I LOVE YOU, BUT...

TP
TP
TP
...

HUH ...??

GODAI... YOU DO...

LOVE ME, DON'T YOU...?

HOTEL Ω

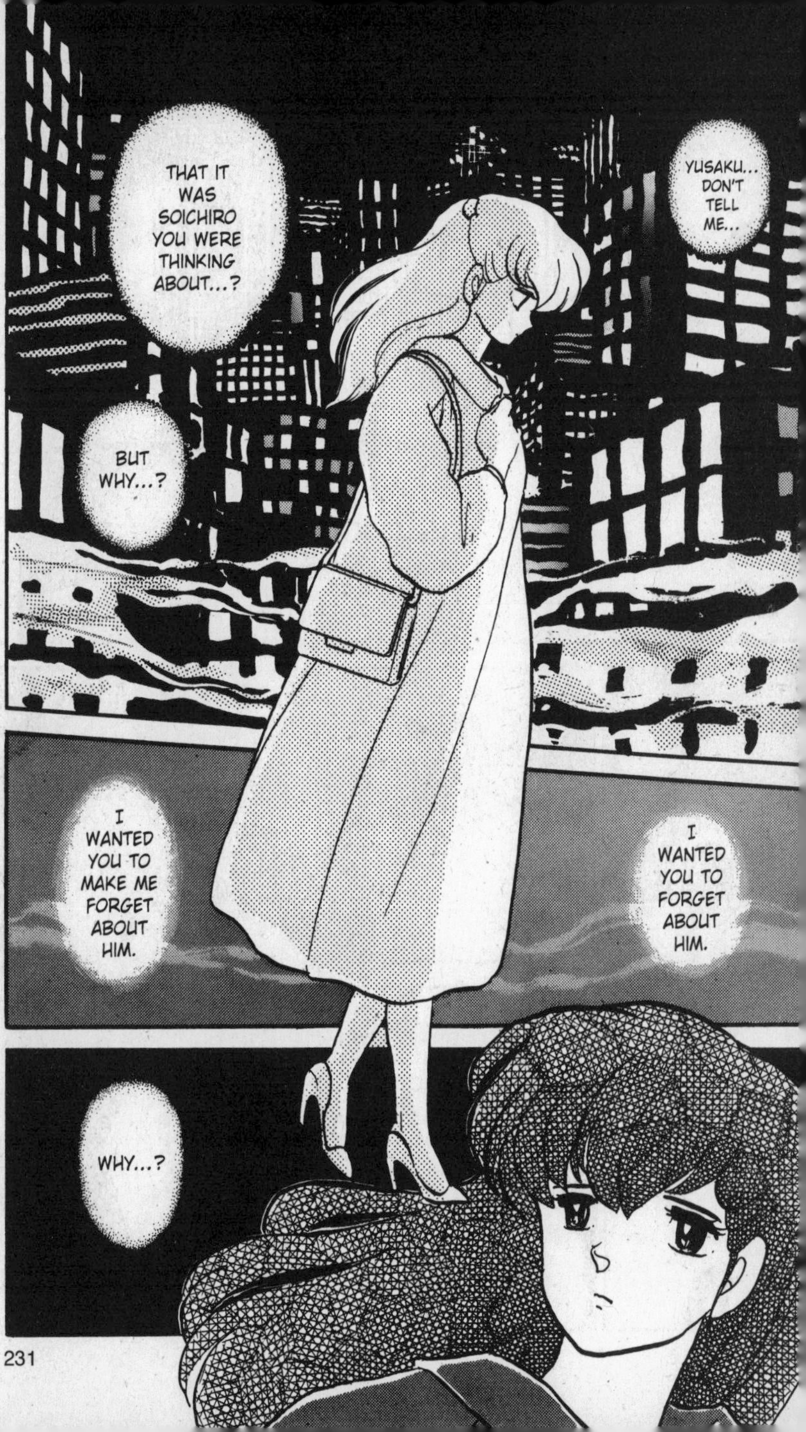
YUSAKU... DON'T TELL ME...
THAT IT WAS SOICHIRO YOU WERE THINKING ABOUT...?
BUT WHY...?
I WANTED YOU TO FORGET ABOUT HIM.
I WANTED YOU TO MAKE ME FORGET ABOUT HIM.
WHY...?

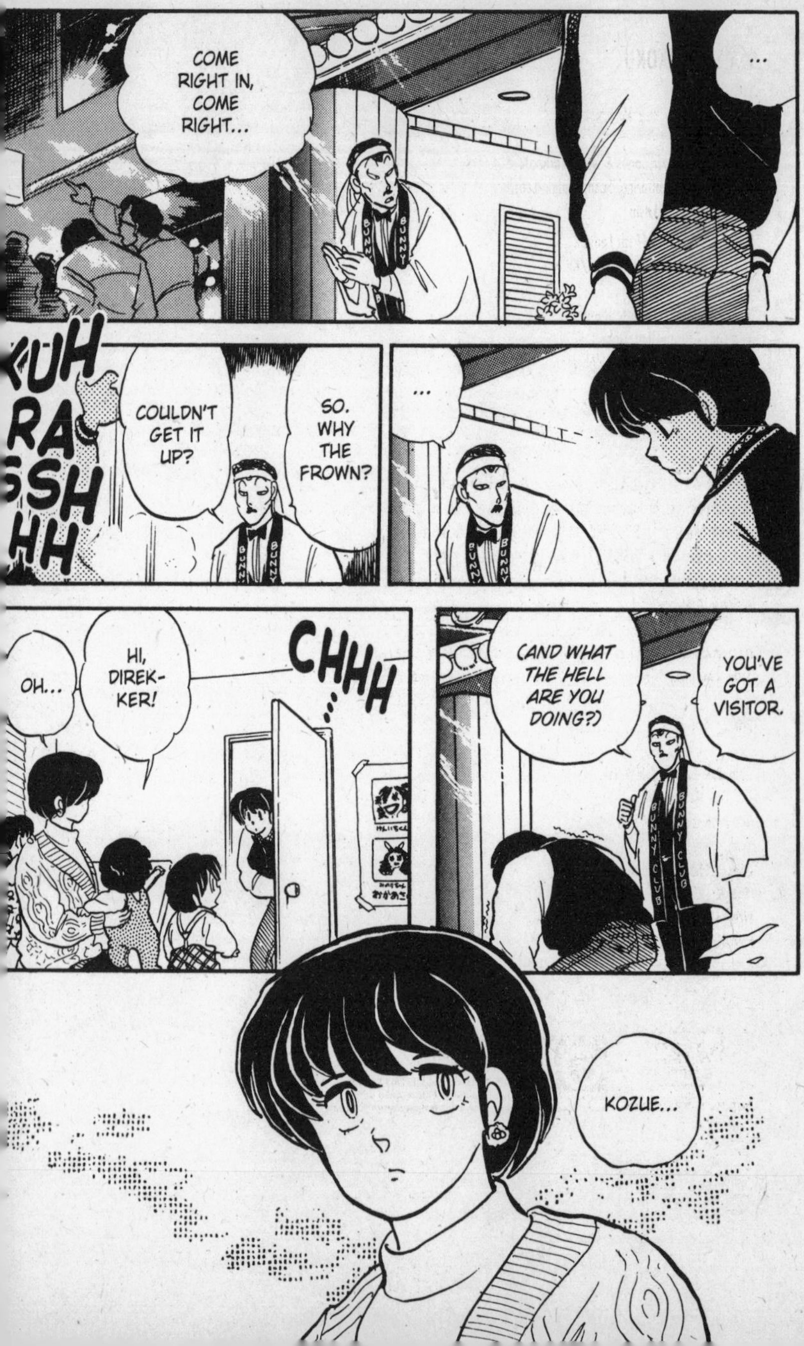
COME RIGHT IN, COME RIGHT...
...
KUH
RA
SSH
HH
COULDN'T GET IT UP?
SO. WHY THE FROWN?
...
OH...
HI, DIREK-KER!
CHHH
(AND WHAT THE HELL ARE YOU DOING?)
YOU'VE GOT A VISITOR.
KOZUE...

MAISON IKKOKU

VOLUME 14

Story and Art by Rumiko Takahashi

Translation/Gerard Jones & Mari Morimoto
Touch-Up Art & Lettering/Susan Daigle-Leach
Design/Nozomi Akashi
Editor – 1st Edition/Trish Ledoux
Editor – Editor's Choice Edition/Kit Fox

Managing Editor/Annette Roman
Director of Production/Noboru Watanabe
Vice President of Publishing/Alvin Lu
Sr. Director of Acquisitions/Rika Inouye
Vice President of Sales & Marketing/Liza Coppola
Publisher/Hyoe Narita

Printed in Canada

Published by VIZ Media, LLC
P.O. Box 77010
San Francisco, CA 94107

Editor's Choice Edition
10 9 8 7 6 5 4 3 2 1
First printing, November 2005
First English edition published 1999

www.viz.com

PARENTAL ADVISORY
MAISON IKKOKU is rated T+ for Older Teen and is recommended for ages 16 and up. This volume contains strong language, alcohol and tobacco use, and sexual themes.

ABOUT THE ARTIST

Rumiko Takahashi, born in 1957 in Niigata, Japan, is the acclaimed creator and artist of *Maison Ikkoku, InuYasha, Ranma 1/2* and *Lum * Urusei Yatsura*.

She lived in a small student apartment in Nakano, Japan, which was the basis for the *Maison Ikkoku* series, while she attended the prestigious Nihon Joseidai (Japan Women's University). At the same time, Takahashi also began studying comics at Gekiga Sonjuku, a famous school for manga artists run by Kazuo Koike, author of *Crying Freeman* and *Lone Wolf and Cub*. In 1978, Takahashi won a prize in Shogakukan's annual New Comic Artist Contest and her boy-meets-alien comedy *Lum * Urusei Yatsura* began appearing in the weekly manga magazine *Shonen Sunday*.

Takahashi's success and critical acclaim continues to grow, with popular titles including *Ranma 1/2* and *InuYasha*. Many of her graphic novel series have also been animated, and are widely available in several languages.

EDITOR'S RECOMMENDATIONS

More manga!
More manga!

Fans of

maison ikkoku

should also read:

© 1988 Rumiko
TAKAHASHI/Shogakukan Inc.

RANMA 1/2

It's a story as old as time itself. Well, not really. Ranma Saotome, a budding martial artist, goes to China with his father to further his training. What he never expected was that a life-altering curse awaited both himself and his bumbling paterfamilias. Everyone has a secret or two to keep from their fiancé, but what happens when your secret is that you turn into a girl when splashed with water? It'll take more than marriage counseling to iron out this doozy of a domestic situation.

© 1997 Rumiko
TAKAHASHI/Shogakukan Inc.

INUYASHA

Takahashi returned to her fantasy roots with this exciting manga that combines elements of historical action, exciting horror, touching romance, and physical comedy. Modern schoolgirl Kagome is pulled into Japan's mystical past and must join forces with a scabrous half-demon named Inu-Yasha. This series has also spawned an immensely popular TV series as well!

© 1999 Hiroyuki
NISHIMORI/Shogakukan Inc.

CHEEKY ANGEL

Tired of wishy-washy manga heroes? Is Godai's congenital passive-aggressiveness rubbing you the wrong way? Then Megumi Amatsuka, the hero (and heroine) of *CHEEKY ANGEL*, should provide you with some much needed proactive entertainment. Long story short, although Megumi is the most gorgeous girl in school, she's not afraid to throw down on any and every punk that gets in her way. (After all, she was a little boy until a magic genie turned her into a girl. Don't you hate it when that happens?)

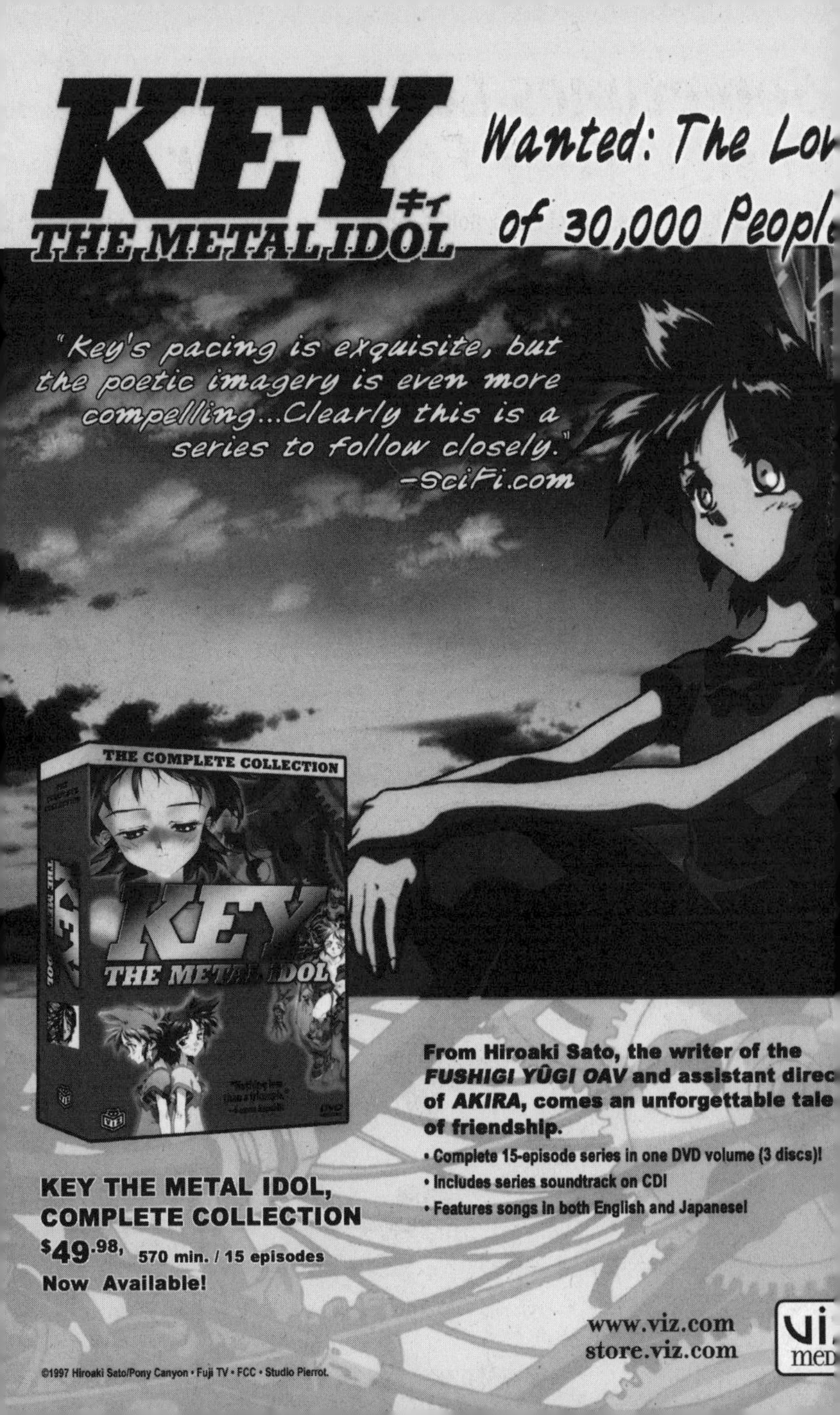
KEY キイ
THE METAL IDOL
Wanted: The Lov
of 30,000 Peopl
"Key's pacing is exquisite, but the poetic imagery is even more compelling...Clearly this is a series to follow closely."
-SciFi.com
THE COMPLETE COLLECTION
KEY THE METAL IDOL
From Hiroaki Sato, the writer of the FUSHIGI YÛGI OAV and assistant direc
of AKIRA, comes an unforgettable tale
of friendship.
• Complete 15-episode series in one DVD volume (3 discs)!
• Includes series soundtrack on CD!
• Features songs in both English and Japanese!
KEY THE METAL IDOL, COMPLETE COLLECTION
$49.98, 570 min. / 15 episodes
Now Available!
www.viz.com
store.viz.com
©1997 Hiroaki Sato/Pony Canyon • Fuji TV • FCC • Studio Pierrot.

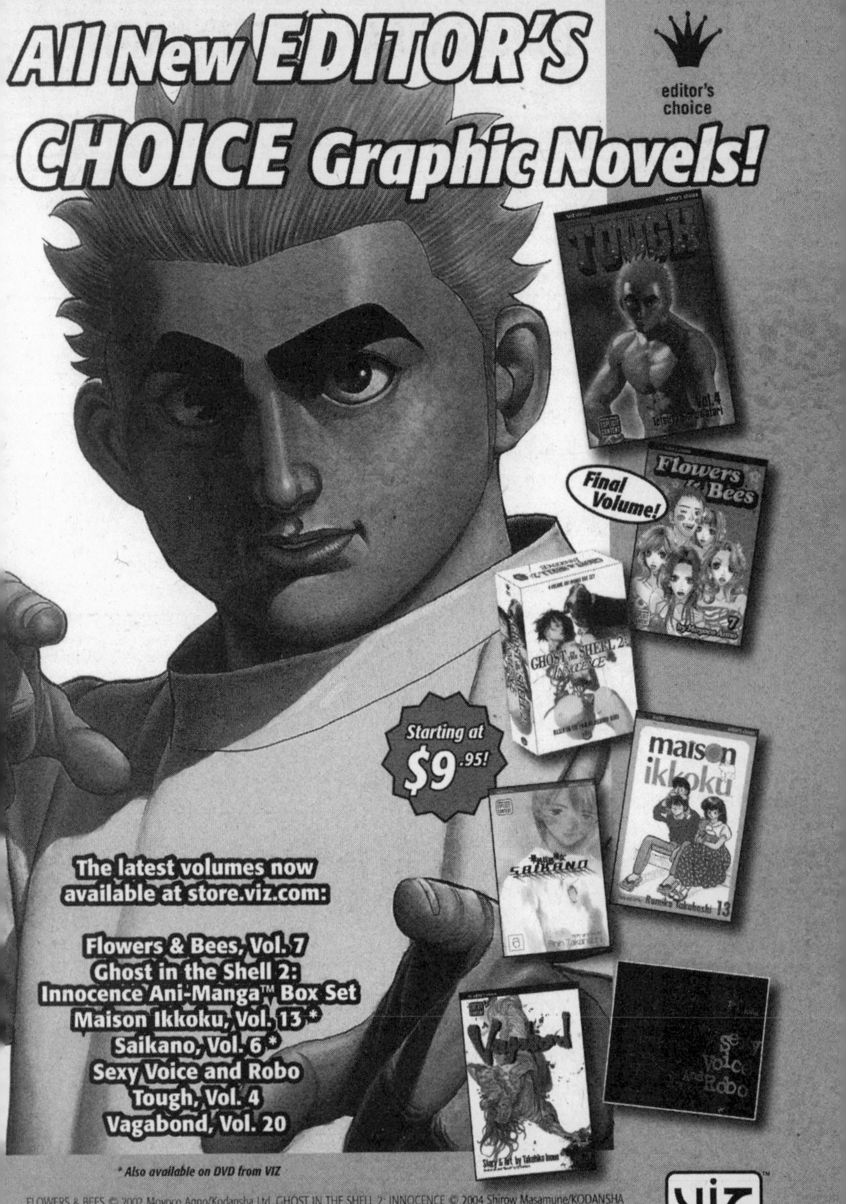

All New EDITOR'S CHOICE Graphic Novels!
editor's choice
Final Volume!
Starting at $9.95!
The latest volumes now available at store.viz.com:
Flowers & Bees, Vol. 7
Ghost in the Shell 2: Innocence Ani-Manga™ Box Set
Maison Ikkoku, Vol. 13 *
Saikano, Vol. 6 *
Sexy Voice and Robo
Tough, Vol. 4
Vagabond, Vol. 20

LOVE MANGA? LET US KNOW!

☐ Please do NOT send me information about VIZ Media products, news and events, special offers, or other information.

☐ Please do NOT send me information from VIZ Media's trusted business partners.

Name: _____

Address: _____

City: _____ State: _____ Zip: _____

E-mail: _____

☐ Male ☐ Female Date of Birth (mm/dd/yyyy): ___/___/_____ (Under 13? Parental consent required)

What race/ethnicity do you consider yourself? (check all that apply)

☐ White/Caucasian   ☐ Black/African American   ☐ Hispanic/Latino

☐ Asian/Pacific Islander ☐ Native American/Alaskan Native ☐ Other: _____

What VIZ Media title(s) did you purchase? (indicate title(s) purchased) _____

_____

What other VIZ Media titles do you own? _____

_____

Reason for purchase: (check all that apply)

☐ Special offer   ☐ Favorite title / author / artist / genre

☐ Gift   ☐ Recommendation   ☐ Collection

☐ Read excerpt in VIZ Media manga sampler ☐ Other _____

Where did you make your purchase? (please check one)

☐ Comic store   ☐ Bookstore   ☐ Grocery Store

☐ Convention   ☐ Newsstand   ☐ Video Game Store

☐ Online (site:_____) ☐ Other _____

How many manga titles have you purchased in the last year? How many were VIZ Media titles?
(please check one from each column)

MANGA	VIZ Media
☐ None	☐ None
☐ 1 – 4	☐ 1 – 4
☐ 5 – 10	☐ 5 – 10
☐ 11+	☐ 11+

How much influence do special promotions and gifts-with-purchase have on the titles you buy?
(please circle, with 5 being great influence and 1 being none)

1 2 3 4 5

Do you purchase every volume of your favorite series?

☐ Yes! Gotta have 'em as my own ☐ No. Please explain: ______________________

What kind of manga storylines do you most enjoy? **(check all that apply)**

☐ Action / Adventure	☐ Science Fiction	☐ Horror
☐ Comedy	☐ Romance (shojo)	☐ Fantasy (shojo)
☐ Fighting	☐ Sports	☐ Historical
☐ Artistic / Alternative	☐ Other ______________________	

If you watch the anime or play a video or TCG game from a series, how likely are you to buy the manga? **(please circle, with 5 being very likely and 1 being unlikely)**

1 2 3 4 5

If unlikely, please explain: ______________________

Who are your favorite authors / artists? ______________________

____

What titles would like you translated and sold in English? ______________________

____

THANK YOU! Please send the completed form to:

NJW Research
42 Catharine Street
Poughkeepsie, NY 12601

Your privacy is very important to us. All information provided will be used for internal purposes only and will not be sold or otherwise divulged.